OOP: BUILDING REUSABLE COMPONENTS
WITH MICROSOFT®
VISUAL BASIC® .NET

Ken Spencer
Tom Eberhard
John Alexander

Microsoft®
.net™

PUBLISHED BY
Microsoft Press
A Division of Microsoft Corporation
One Microsoft Way
Redmond, Washington 98052-6399

Library of Congress Cataloging-in-Publication Data
Spencer, Kenneth L., 1951-
    OOP: Building Reusable Components with Microsoft Visual Basic .NET / Kenneth L.
Spencer, Thomas Eberhard, John Alexander.
       p. cm.
    Includes index.
    ISBN 0-7356-1379-6
    1. Object-oriented programming (Computer science) 2. Computer
software--Reusablility. 3. Microsoft Visual Basic. 4. Microsoft .NET. I. Eberhard,
Thomas. II. Alexander, John. III. Title.

    QA76.64 .S665 2002
    005.1'17--dc21   2002026482

Printed and bound in the United States of America.

1 2 3 4 5 6 7 8 9   QWE   7 6 5 4 3 2

Distributed in Canada by H.B. Fenn and Company Ltd.

A CIP catalogue record for this book is available from the British Library.

Microsoft Press books are available through booksellers and distributors worldwide. For further information about international editions, contact your local Microsoft Corporation office or contact Microsoft Press International directly at fax (425) 936-7329. Visit our Web site at www.microsoft.com/mspress. Send comments to *mspinput@microsoft.com*.

Acquisitions Editor: Anne Hamilton
Project Editor: Sally Stickney
Technical Editor: Jack Beaudry

Body Part No. X08-22426

I am dedicating this book to my lovely wife, Trisha, and my two sons, Jeff and Kenny. I would also like to dedicate this book to my best friend, Ken Miller.

—K.S.

To my wonderful wife and eternal companion, Melody, and to six of the greatest kids ever: my children—Jared, Nicole, Natalie, Jessica, Jacob, and Joshua. You give my work and life purpose and happiness.

—T.E.

To all our loved ones, those whom we hold so dear, and to those departed, whom we miss. This is for you. Life is a measured gift; use it wisely and make it count.

—J.A.

Contents at a Glance

Table of Contents

Acknowledgments

Writing a book about advanced topics in Microsoft Visual Basic .NET wasn't easy. In fact, without the extra hours spent by many more people than the authors, you wouldn't have this book in your hands right now.

First, we want to thank the Microsoft Press team. Special thanks go to Sally Stickney, our project editor, for not giving up on us while trying to keep the book on track. You have been inspiring to us. Jack Beaudry, our technical editor, has been unbelievably supportive and helpful. Many of the samples took an extraordinary effort to run and test. Thanks to Victoria Thulman for further edits and for smoothing out the rough edges. You were a joy to work with during the process of making the chapters presentable. Thanks also to Dan Latimer, the book's desktop publisher, and Michael Kloepfer, the artist. And last but not least, many thanks to Anne Hamilton, who made this whole project possible.

We'd also like to let Rick Culpepper know how much we appreciate him sharing his expertise on exception handling by authoring Chapter 3 for us.

Acknowledgments from the Individual Authors

Ken Spencer

Thanks to Tom and John for working so hard to make this book happen. It wouldn't have been possible without them. Thanks also to my wife for her understanding and support. She has stood beside me during the years in my many endeavors, and I really appreciate her support. Thanks to Ken Miller for understanding why I write books and what I go through to do it. It's also great that he has supported me in this and other efforts. A special thanks to the folks at Microsoft: Sally Stickney, Jack Beaudry, Eileen Crain, Ari Bixhor, Susan Warren, Chris Dias, Rob Brigham, and Jennifer Ritzinger.

Thomas Eberhard

First of all, I would like to thank my wife, Melody, and our six kids (Jared, Nicole, Natalie, Jessica, Jacob, and Joshua) for their sacrifices and for letting me work on this project days and nights and weekends for over a year. They have been a great support. Nothing is more important to me than their love, success, and devotion to our Lord Jesus Christ. I cannot recall how many times I felt his inspiration and help with this work.

Thanks also to InfoLink Screening Services, Inc. Not only will you find samples of their Web site throughout this book, but you'll also see that some of the components presented have been tested with InfoLink's main data-driven Web application, which services thousands of users nationwide. Thanks to Tawnya Gilreath, Calvin Luttrell, and Bruce Krell for reading through the manuscript and testing some of the code samples before I submitted them to Microsoft Press.

John Alexander

Thanks to my family for their patience and graciousness in allowing me the time to write yet another book. Valerie, Nathaniel, and Ian: you are my reason (on earth) for living. Thanks to my Lord and Savior, Jesus Christ, for giving me the strength and patience to get it all done. You truly are my ultimate reason for living. Thanks also to Mike Fraser, Dave Smith, Tom Foster, Don Benage, and Greg Sullivan at G.A. Sullivan for their support and for continually showing what it means to lead a world-class consulting organization—by example.

Lastly, thanks to the following folks at Microsoft for their direct and indirect support: Sally Stickney, Jack Beaudry, Victoria Thulman, Eileen Crain, Ari Bixhorn, Susan Warren, Keith Ballinger, Jennifer Ritzinger, and Steve Loethen.

Introduction

When Microsoft introduced an alpha version of the Microsoft .NET Framework to a small group of developers, the developers were immediately excited. Those of us attending this kickoff meeting understood the vision of .NET right away:

- A common language runtime

- Different languages with the same code base

- Cross-language compatibility

- Full object-oriented programming (OOP) for all languages

- The chance to say goodbye to DLL hell

- The chance to say goodbye to memory leaks

- A truly integrated development environment, or IDE (even though the first alpha version crashed more often than it worked)

Most of us were anxious to get our hands on this new tool and couldn't wait to test its features for developing Web applications, dealing with disconnected data, building more powerful components, and creating applications easier, faster, and more reliably. Almost two years after that initial introduction and after using the public betas for over a year, we finally have the tool in our hands. We had the opportunity to build several large applications with late beta versions and were astounded at these applications' stability and the ease with which we could develop them. Naturally, we used the release version of the .NET Framework with our applications as soon as it was available. Again, we were amazed at the performance gains and even greater stability. One of the components we're going to present in Chapter 4 is a data access component for the data access layer. We created it in early betas, improved it over time, and compiled it in the release version. It has proven to be one of the most powerful and reliable tools we've ever seen. Millions of hits (data accesses to Microsoft SQL Server 7 and Microsoft SQL Server 2000 databases) have been handled by this component without the slightest indications of problems (obviously, after we debugged and performed initial testing). Even better, this component has taken advantage of the performance enhancements Microsoft ADO.NET can offer while decreasing the load on Web servers, middle-tier servers, and SQL servers in a way we never anticipated. This book offers you the full functionality and source code of this component and others for your own applications. In addition to being able to use the components we present in this book, you'll learn the details of how they were created so that you can extend and modify them if necessary.

Many of the early adopters of the technology—authors of Microsoft .NET books and attendees at .NET-centric conferences—share a common feeling: the fun is back in creating applications. Many years ago, we remember having to write applications in various assembler languages; passing individual bytes in and out of processor registers and stacks; packing code for applications into 8 or 16 KB of memory (that's kilobytes, not megabytes or gigabytes, which we're used to today); and creating accounting applications, calculators, games, and so on. That was tough as nails, but it was fun. Around the time when Microsoft Windows and Microsoft Windows 95 entered the scene, we started stepping on each other's toes with conflicting DLLs, quirky windows message calls, and pervasive memory leaks, to name a few issues, and the fun we experienced in the earlier days was slowly but surely dwindling away. We can truly say that it's back again.

How This Book Came to Be

.NET, with its common language runtime, thousands of base classes, fully object-oriented languages such as Microsoft Visual Basic .NET, C#, C++, and the up and coming Visual J# .NET, is a very powerful and robust tool. Whether you need to create a small Windows application serving just a couple of users, or a large enterprise application that needs to serve thousands of simultaneous users with a data-driven Web application, .NET is arguably the best development tool available today. .NET is entirely object oriented. Everything, even variables, are objects. All .NET languages have the richest object-oriented features we've seen anywhere—period. That's why we wanted to write this book—to make sure the word was out. Object-based programming is not new, and neither is object-oriented programming. However, .NET offers the first version of Microsoft Visual Basic that has these features available. It's also the first platform that allows cross-platform inheritance (meaning that you can inherit and build upon classes written in different languages).

Object-oriented programming, when its principles are applied correctly, allows us to build complex and large applications more quickly and easily than ever before, even when we face steep requirements for performance, reliability, and scalability. We're making quite a daring statement, but this book and its concepts will put it to the test. Object-oriented principles call for the creation of reusable objects (components) and framework classes. What's so good about these? Let's take the example of the data access object we already mentioned.

Data access is a common requirement. Why not write a component that's specialized in accessing and handling data? High-performance data methods can be applied to it and most common data access and data handling methods can be implemented. This component can then be used wherever data access is needed. It encapsulates all the features we mentioned earlier. No longer are you required to remember all your tricks and the enhancements you made when writing the component each time you need to access data. Instead, you simply keep using the component's methods. Since much work, testing, and fine-tuning went into the data access component, you inherit its high performance, scalability, and reliability automatically.

What about framework classes? Just like components, they allow you to have a library of functional features that can be used again and again, cutting development time. The .NET Framework has thousands of such classes. There is room for more, and we're going to add some very useful ones in this book as we build components and classes for the sample application named HRnet. HRnet is the beginning of a fully functional HR application that we'll design and create as you read through the 14 chapters of this book.

Who Is This Book For?

We want to point out right away that this book is not for beginning developers who would like to learn about the general principles of object-orientated programming and Visual Basic .NET, ASP.NET, and ADO.NET. Although we're going to build components step by step and add features one at a time, we're not giving basic instructions for creating a project or adding classes, nor do we include tutorials on variables, classes, data connections, and similar concepts. You should have worked with Visual Basic (preferably Visual Basic .NET), know how to create and modify classes and objects, and know how to access data. A basic knowledge of Microsoft Visual Studio .NET, how to add projects and files, and how to create Windows and ASP.NET Web applications is also required.

In this book, we go beyond an introduction of language features and OOP techniques we apply principles and work with code that we use in production applications. We'll use Visual Basic .NET, ASP.NET, and ADO.NET in Visual Studio .NET. All the code samples have been written and tested with the released version of the .NET Framework.

We'll concentrate on how to build large-scale applications based on an n-tier architecture and using .NET Framework classes, custom objects and components, and custom server and user controls. In the final chapters of this book, after you prepare and build these types of components and classes, we'll show you how effortlessly you can wire an application together. In addition, you'll find that many of the components and classes are immediately usable in your applications with few or no modifications.

What Does This Book Cover?

The chapters in this book follow what we consider the natural progression of application development. Each chapter focuses on a specific topic, and the sequence of chapters leads to the building and wiring of the HRnet sample application. To work through a chapter, you need the knowledge of topics covered in the preceding chapter. Therefore, we recommend that you follow the chapters in order. The following sections offer a brief description of each chapter.

Chapter 1: Introduction to Object-Oriented Development by Ken Spencer

This chapter is our *condensed* introduction to Visual Basic .NET and object-oriented programming. You'll find explanations of the features that make Visual Basic .NET and the .NET platform a great choice for your application development platform.

Chapter 2: Architecture and .NET by Tom Eberhard

Architecture and design are topics often avoided among developers. The fun for us is to write great code and make it work. It is, however, very important to understand the architectural options that .NET opens up for us. Gone are many of the headaches and hassles of trying to implement COM/COM+–based techniques in a layered architectural approach. .NET changes how we architect and design applications. Not only do we need to know architectural and design options, but also which .NET features are best used and where. Object-oriented development requires a careful design phase as well as well-planned applications and boundaries. We'll start our quick tour of architectures with one-tier architecture and progress to flexible *n*-tier architectures, and show you where to place specific .NET technologies.

Chapter 3: Exception Handling in the .NET Framework by Rick Culpepper

Exception and error handling, when compared with other programming platforms, has always been Visual Basic's stepchild. This is not the case anymore. Visual Basic .NET has very powerful, easy-to-use, structured exception handling that it inherits from the .NET Framework. We'll show you how to handle exceptions and how to pass them through layers in the *n*-tier architecture.

You'll also learn how to write custom exception handlers using inheritance and other OOP features. We find that event logging has become an important part of reporting exceptions, and you'll learn how to integrate event logging in exception handling.

Chapter 4: Implementing the Data Access Layer by Tom Eberhard

Data access is a requirement for almost any development project. We're going to take a thorough look at the advantages ADO.NET gives us in today's world of high-performance and highly scalable applications. We'll use these advantages to build a data access component that encapsulates major data access functionality into a powerful, fast, and reliable data access tool. The data access component will include methods that allow you to access, modify, add, and delete data with standard SQL or stored procedures. Data can be returned in a multitude of formats, such as in a dataset, as a data stream, with the *Data-reader*, as XML, or as a parameter list. You'll see this component used everywhere in the HRnet sample application, from the security component to the business logic classes to the XML Web services and even directly from Windows Forms and Web Forms pages.

Chapter 5: Implementing the Security Layer by Ken Spencer

Securing applications has always been a challenge. The rise of Web applications has increased the need to protect and secure applications. The .NET Framework has several options that provide security out of the box. It covers both authentication and authorization. We'll cover some of these techniques in this book, but we've found that large-scale enterprise systems might need a security implementation beyond .NET's default options. For this reason, we build a security component that allows us to secure Web and Windows applications for the same groups of users and permission groups.

Chapter 6: Implementing Generic Web Client Handlers by Tom Eberhard

Pre-ASP.NET Web development tools had many limitations that made creating good user interfaces difficult and tedious. ASP.NET is dramatically changing this. We're going to show you how to create your own custom controls, both as custom user controls and custom server controls. You'll also learn when to use each technique. You'll be able to quickly create your own controls that either build upon one or more existing ASP.NET sever controls or are created totally on their own. One of these controls is a TextBox control with functionality that is similar to or even better than that of TextBox controls in Visual Basic.

Chapter 7: Implementing the Menu Handlers by Tom Eberhard

Creating easy-to-use menu and navigation structures has always been a challenge. After sharing some menu strategies with you, we'll build flexible menu and navigation controls that can be totally data driven. Understanding the principles of these controls will allow you to use or modify them easily. You'll also see an example of how to use similar techniques to create data-driven menu structures for Windows Forms applications.

Chapter 8: Implementing the Business Layer by John Alexander

Business logic is at the heart of each application. In this chapter, you'll learn how to encapsulate business rules into business objects that form the business layer of the flexible *n*-tier approach. The same business rules can be accessed by ASP.NET or Windows Forms applications. Business objects are good candidates for the inheritance capability of object-oriented programming. For this reason, we'll cover more details of OOP and the inheritance features in Visual Basic .NET.

Chapter 9: Implementing Facade Layers by Ken Spencer

Facade layers have been important for buffering user interfaces from business logic components. The need for this buffer has decreased in .NET. There are still good reasons to use a facade layer—for example, to increase security.

Chapter 10: Creating the User Interface Template by Tom Eberhard

One of the best ways to create consistency in applications is to work with user interface templates. After summarizing the design specifications for the HRnet sample application, we'll show you how a Web template is created and used. You'll see how the menu handlers from Chapter 7 work in conjunction with a Web template. You'll also discover another option for creating Web templates through a custom Web template that intercepts ASP.NET's standard Web page class. We'll take a closer look at visual inheritance in Windows Forms applications and create inherited templates for them.

Chapter 11: Building Information Pages by Tom Eberhard

Information pages, especially data entry pages, are essential for the types of applications we are asked to provide. After spending a little time with user interface strategies, we'll develop several types of data presentation forms. The two major examples we'll create will allow data access with the list/detail approach. One example shows the DataGrid and detail information on one form; the other example shows the DataGrid and detail information on separate forms. You'll learn how to integrate security in both examples. Forms that include the DataGrid and detail information will automatically handle different states such as view only, view and edit, add, save, cancel, and delete. At the end of the chapter, we'll discuss scalability and performance when DataSets are used and persisted in session state. You'll also learn how you can persist session state and DataSets with local XML files.

Chapter 12: Implementing the Business Layer: XML Web Services by John Alexander

"XML Web Services" is the buzzword—or buzz phrase—you hear everywhere the Web is discussed. In this chapter, we'll show you how to consume existing XML Web services and expose the functionality through the business layer for the HRnet sample application. You'll be surprised at how easily you can build a custom Web control that utilizes the XML Web service's information. We'll also create an XML Web service that exposes the benefits of an employee by using the employee ID. We'll spend the balance of the chapter on an advanced example and learn to create and consume SOAP headers, creating the business object portion of the business layer.

Chapter 13: Using Remoting for Communication by Ken Spencer

Many of today's applications require applications on different computers to be able to communicate with each other. .NET remoting makes this possible. We're going to introduce .NET remoting technology with fairly simple examples of a remoting server and client. After we cover the basics, you'll know how to create remoting for the business objects we created in Chapter 8.

Chapter 14: Wiring the Application Together by Tom Eberhard

With all the components, templates, security features, and business objects in place, we can wire the application together. You'll be astonished at how fast that can happen. We're not talking about rapid application development, or RAD, which mostly fails to create working applications. We're talking about rapid application building, which creates a solid application with all the features we talk about in this book. We'll show you each important step of wiring HRnet into a functioning application. In addition to showing you the ASP.NET Web Forms application for HRnet, we'll show you a Windows Forms example.

System Requirements

You'll need the following hardware and software to compile and run the samples and HRnet demo application:

- Microsoft Visual Studio .NET.

- Microsoft Windows 2000 or Microsoft Windows XP on a computer capable of running Microsoft Visual Studio .NET. See the recommended hardware configuration for Visual Studio .NET at *http://msdn.microsoft.com/vstudio/productinfo/sysreq.asp*

- Microsoft Internet Information Services (IIS) 5 or later.

- Microsoft SQL Server 2000.

Installing and Using the Samples and Demo Files

You can download the sample files from the book's Companion Content page on the Web by connecting to

http://www.microsoft.com/mspress/books/5203.asp

To access the sample files and the links to other resources we've provided, click Companion Content in the More Information menu box on the right side of the page. This will load the Companion Content Web page, which includes a link for downloading the sample files, accessing resource pages for Microsoft Visual Studio .NET, and connecting to Microsoft Press Support.

The download link opens a Web Package executable file containing a license agreement. To copy the sample files onto your hard disk, click the link to run the executable and then accept the license agreement that is presented. By default, the sample files will be copied to the C:\BuildOOP folder. During the installation process, you'll be given the option of changing that destination folder.

Support Information

Every effort has been made to ensure the accuracy of this book and the companion content. Microsoft Press provides corrections for books through the World Wide Web at

http://www.microsoft.com/mspress/support/

To connect directly to the Microsoft Press Knowledge Base and enter a query regarding a question or issue that you may have, go to

http://www.microsoft.com/mspress/support/search.asp

If you have comments, questions, or ideas regarding the book or companion content, or questions that are not answered by querying the Knowledge Base, please send them to Microsoft Press via e-mail to

mspinput@microsoft.com

or via postal mail to

Microsoft Press
Attn: OOP: Building Reusable Components with Microsoft Visual Basic .NET Editor
One Microsoft Way
Redmond, WA 98052-6399

Please note that product support is not offered via the preceding addresses.

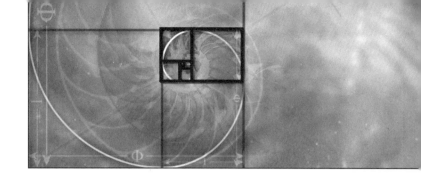

Introduction to Object-Oriented Development

Welcome to the world of object-oriented development with Microsoft Visual Basic .NET and the Microsoft .NET Framework. Visual Basic .NET and the .NET Framework team up to provide developers with a powerful set of tools. If you're a Visual Basic 6 or Microsoft Active Server Pages (ASP) developer, don't be put off by Visual Basic .NET and the .NET Framework. You already have a successful set of skills that you can leverage as you move into the .NET Framework world. If you know Visual Basic or ASP and Microsoft Visual Basic Scripting Edition (VBScript), you're a long way down the road toward building powerful object-oriented solutions, and we intend to show you how to use and extend your skills in the rest of this book.

In this first chapter, we'll talk about key features in Visual Basic .NET that are related to developing component-based, or object-oriented, applications. Component-based programming is really about placing your code into assemblies (called COM components or ActiveX components in the past), which allows the code to be reused. Object-oriented programming (OOP) is similar to component programming but offers you the added capability to build object hierarchies and frameworks. It provides this largely through a feature called *inheritance*, which we'll cover later in this chapter. Thus, using OOP, you can do everything you can with component-based development and more. And OOP makes it easier to develop and maintain code, as you'll see later.

This chapter serves as a primer for the rest of the book. In this chapter, we're not going to cover topics in detail unless they relate closely to object development. For instance, we're not going to dive into developing Windows Forms, even though using them is a powerful way to build applications. Instead we're going to discuss subjects that pertain to OOP, such as class features, inheritance, and language differences between Visual Basic 6 and Visual Basic .NET that directly affect components.

We'd like to mention one other point before we continue. This book is not about theory as much as it is about what you can do in the real world. We offer an approach you can use for your development process so that you can build reliable components that you can easily reuse. For example, Chapter 4 presents a good database component for applications. This component has been used in multiple real-world applications for some time. At Infolink Screening Services, this component is part of an external Web application that, at the time we were writing this book, had run more than 3,500 hours nonstop. In other words, the server and the application were up that entire time, accommodating increasing numbers of users throughout the period.

In this book, component-based development implies building an application that is constructed based on one or more sets of components. Thus component-based development is very similar to the way electronics and other everyday products are made. For example, if you looked inside a modern radio, you would find a small set of electronic components that provided the radio's functionality. Many different styles of radios can be made from those components by simply changing the way the components are hooked up, adding or removing components, and adding other features that are not components.

Your applications can now easily use a similar component-based architecture. The .NET Framework and Visual Basic .NET provide complete OOP features to allow you to build applications on a framework in the same way a radio is built using a framework of components. Building applications on a framework will allow you to program faster and with fewer errors than you could with previous versions of Visual Basic, languages that don't support OOP, or languages that do support OOP but are harder to learn and use than Visual Basic. You'll also be able to maintain those applications more easily because you have a solid component architecture on which they are based. In Chapter 2, we'll cover concepts that apply to designing applications using components.

The .NET Framework

The .NET Framework provides a rich architecture for application development. First, the common language runtime (CLR) provides the run-time environment for all .NET applications. When you create a Visual Basic .NET application, you compile it with either Visual Studio .NET or Visual Basic's command-line compiler (vbc.exe). This compilation process results in an assembly that contains Microsoft intermediate language (MSIL) code and other information. The CLR is responsible for compiling an application's MSIL code into native code for the particular processor of the system running the code. The CLR also handles code access security and a number of other run-time-specific tasks.

The CLR also provides a standard runtime for all .NET applications. Now you can easily write part of an application in Visual Basic .NET and part of it in C#, and have the various parts work together seamlessly. For instance, during the .NET Developer Training Tour, Microsoft demonstrated an application that has a class written in Visual Basic .NET, another class that inherits the Visual Basic .NET class that is written in Fujitsu COBOL, and finally the main part of the application that uses the other two classes and is written in C#. This simple application demonstrates the power of the CLR and the .NET Framework.

Assemblies are the foundation of a .NET application. When you compile a Visual Basic .NET application, the application is compiled into MSIL code, and the MSIL along with other information is placed into an assembly. An assembly file typically has either a .dll or an .exe extension, just as a traditional application does.

With a .NET application, you no longer use a type library because the information normally stored in a type library is now part of the assembly. When the CLR executes an assembly, it can obtain almost any information it needs to run the assembly by looking in the assembly and other places (such as a .config file).

The .NET Framework also provides the foundation for applications by providing not only the run-time environment but also a very rich set of classes (literally thousands of classes). Many features that we use in our applications come directly from the .NET Framework classes. You can use these classes in your applications, and in some cases your applications might use particular classes under the covers to provide certain features. For instance, when you build an ASP.NET application, the application is based on the underlying .NET Framework classes. When you create a Web Forms application, it inherits its base functionality from *System.Web.UI.Page*, as shown in the second line of the following code:

```
Public Class WebForm1
    Inherits System.Web.UI.Page

#Region " Web Form Designer Generated Code "

'This call is required by the Web Form Designer.
<System.Diagnostics.DebuggerStepThrough()> _
Private Sub InitializeComponent()

End Sub
```

(continued)

```
Private Sub Page_Init(ByVal sender As System.Object, _
    ByVal e As System.EventArgs) Handles MyBase.Init
        'CODEGEN: This method call is required by
        'the Web Form Designer
        'Do not modify it using the code editor.
        InitializeComponent()
End Sub

#End Region

Private Sub Page_Load(ByVal sender As System.Object, _
    ByVal e As System.EventArgs) Handles MyBase.Load
        'Put user code to initialize the page here
End Sub

End Class
```

You can see that the .NET Framework provides the functionality for the Web Forms page in *System.Web.UI.Page* and that the Web Forms page gets its functionality directly from the .NET Framework by inheriting from one of its base classes—in this case the *System.Web.UI.Page* class.

```
Inherits System.Web.UI.Page
```

You could look at almost any other aspect of applications created using the .NET Framework and find the same features, such as the use of inheritance and design blocks. For instance, a Windows Forms application is also going to inherit from a class in the .NET Framework, as will an XML Web service. You should also notice from this short Web Forms example that Web Forms are built using classes. In fact, everything you create in Visual Basic .NET involves classes in one way or another.

Attributes are a new feature implemented to make it easier for you to add functionality to a class or to provide information about a class or method directly in the class. For instance, the AssemblyInfo.vb file that is created in each Visual Basic .NET project contains information about the assembly in the form of attributes. A default Assembly.vb file is shown here:

```
Imports System.Reflection
Imports System.Runtime.InteropServices

' General information about an assembly is controlled through the
' following set of attributes. Change these attribute values to
' modify the information associated with an assembly.

' Review the values of the assembly attributes.
```

```
<Assembly: AssemblyTitle("")>
<Assembly: AssemblyDescription("")>
<Assembly: AssemblyCompany("")>
<Assembly: AssemblyProduct("")>
<Assembly: AssemblyCopyright("")>
<Assembly: AssemblyTrademark("")>
<Assembly: CLSCompliant(True)>


' The following GUID is for the ID of the typelib
' if this project is exposed to COM
<Assembly: Guid("7F9C4BDB-257E-4FCB-8FD5-6B4211A598E5")>


' Version information for an assembly consists of the
' following four values:
'
'       Major Version
'       Minor Version
'       Build Number
'       Revision
'
' You can specify all the values or you can default the
' Build and Revision Numbers
' by using the '*' as shown below:

<Assembly: AssemblyVersion("1.0.*")>
```

You can change the attributes by editing them in Visual Studio .NET or any other editor and saving the file. When you recompile the assembly, it will contain the values of these attributes. For instance, to assign the assembly a title, you simply open Assembly.vb and change the *AssemblyTitle* tag. There are many different types of attributes for different application types, such as those for XML Web services or COM+.

Other features that were formerly part of a single language, such as Visual Basic, are now part of the .NET Framework and available to any language that supports the .NET Framework. For instance, Microsoft Windows 2000 allows you to create multithreaded applications. C++ implements good support for multithreading, but Visual Basic 6 does not. Thus C++ developers can build multithreaded applications much easier than Visual Basic 6 developers can: that is, it's possible to build a multithreaded application in Visual Basic 6, but it's a lot of work. Now you can create multithreaded applications in any language using the support from the .NET Framework. Thus, all languages supported by the .NET Framework are first-class players and can perform almost all the same tasks at almost the same level of performance.

Visual Studio .NET Support for Components

Visual Studio .NET also comes into play when you're building component-based or object-based solutions. Visual Studio .NET provides a number of features that component developers can use to shorten the time needed to create and test applications.

One of the nicest features you'll find is the new visual support for working with components and applications. These new rapid application development (RAD) features make it easy to create components and wire powerful features into them. For instance, you can quickly create a component and add features to it using the new designers and the Toolbox. This extended functionality makes Visual Studio .NET a very powerful tool for developers. For instance, the component design surface allows you to drag items from the Toolbox onto the design surface, and it provides the plumbing to make them work.

Figure 1-1 shows the overall interface of Visual Studio .NET with this book's main sample application—HRnet—open.

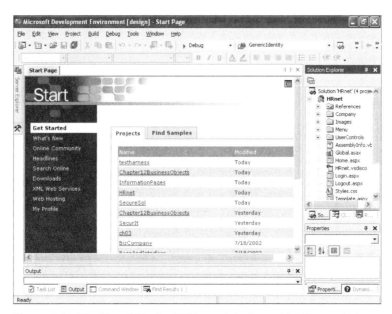

Figure 1-1 The Visual Studio .NET user interface with HRnet solution

Let's take a quick walk through some of the key Visual Studio .NET features. Figure 1-1 shows the Start page as the current page. This discussion is based on the window and menu configuration shown in Figure 1-1 because Visual Studio .NET is very configurable, and you can move the windows around to your liking. On the Start page, you can find a tremendous amount of information, such as previous projects, create and open projects, browse developer sites on the Internet, configure Visual Studio .NET, and more.

The toolbars and menu along the top are self-explanatory. The row of tabs just below the toolbars is the easiest way to access files that are open: you simply click the tab of the file you want to edit. Solution Explorer by default is along the right-hand side of the display and shows the files in your current projects. The Class View window is available by clicking the Class View tab under Solution Explorer. Class View shows you a hierarchical view of the classes in the project. In fact, you can drill down in Class View and see the various members of a class. If you don't see a particular window, you can open most windows from the View menu or by pressing a hot key combination or clicking a toolbar button.

Notice an icon at the far left edge of the interface, next to the Start Page tab. Hidden windows appear nestled along the edge of a window with their icons displayed as shown; in Figure 1-1, it's the Document Outline window. You can hide or show just about any dockable window in Visual Studio .NET by clicking the Auto Hide button, which looks like a pushpin, on the window's toolbar. This button toggles to make the window visible or hidden. To display a hidden window, just hover the mouse over the icon and the window will roll out. We usually keep hidden windows along the right-hand side of the display so that they don't interfere with items open in the editor.

The new Server Explorer provides a view of the servers on your network that you can use as you work with your applications. Server Explorer makes it easy to get at features such as performance counters or Windows Management Instrumentation (WMI) classes. Not only can you see these items as you're developing your application, but you can also interact with them and add them to your application using various tools.

> **Note**   You'll see much more about Visual Studio .NET in this chapter and throughout the rest of the book as we use it to create, work with, and implement components in HRnet, our sample Web-based human resources application.

General Language Changes in Visual Basic .NET

Visual Basic .NET introduces a number of language changes. You need to understand these changes so that you can be aware of how they affect your component-based applications. In this section, we'll discuss some of the Visual Basic .NET changes that pertain to component development.

Data Type Changes

Data types in Visual Basic .NET map to the underlying data types of the .NET Framework. The .NET Framework data types are specified by the common type system (CTS). The CTS defines the data types to provide standardization of types across languages and to enable standard ways of handling them. For instance, since the CTS defines the type, the .NET Framework can provide classes to implement methods for managing various types. The *System.String* class, for example, provides methods for handling strings, offering a standard way of dealing with strings across all languages supported by the .NET Framework. The CLR handles the implementation of the CTS and can verify data types at run time. This allows for interoperation of any .NET application that is written in a language that implements data types based on the CTS—or at least written using only types that map to the CTS.

Table 1-1 shows the Data Type Summary table from the Microsoft Developer Network (MSDN) documentation. This table shows three important things. First, it shows how a data type maps to a CLR type. For instance, you can see that the Boolean data type maps to the *System.Boolean* type. Second, you can see some of the changes from the Visual Basic 6 world. For instance, Visual Basic 6 has a *Currency* data type. Visual Basic .NET uses the *Decimal* data type instead. The table also shows the value range for a particular data type and the data type's size. This is useful to see how Visual Basic 6 data types such as *Integer* map to common data types.

The CTS provides two general categories of data types. A variable defined as a *value type* has its value stored as a representation of the true value. A variable that is a *reference type* contains a reference to the location of an object that contains the value. The concept of types becomes clearer when you consider the handling of data. If your application is working with integers and handling them using standard Visual Basic type methods (such as addition), you're working with a value type. When you refer to a variable by its methods, the variable is boxed and converted to an object. *Boxing* is the conversion of a value type to an object type; boxing takes resources and thus is slower than directly using a value type.

Table 1-1 **Data Type Summary**

Visual Basic Type	CLR Type	Storage Size	Description
Boolean	System.Boolean	2 bytes	*True* or *False*
Byte	*System.Byte*	1 byte	0 through 255 (unsigned)
Char	*System.Char*	2 bytes	0 through 65535 (unsigned)
Date	*System.DateTime*	8 bytes	January 1, 0001 through December 31, 9999
Decimal	*System.Decimal*	16 bytes	0 through +/− 79,228,162,514,264,337,593,543,950,335 with no decimal point; 0 through +/− 7.9228162514264337593543950335 with 28 places to the right of the decimal
Double (double-precision floating-point number)	*System.Double*	8 bytes	−1.79769313486231E+308 through −4.94065645841247E−324 for negative values; 4.94065645841247E−324 through 1.79769313486231E+308 for positive values
Integer	*System.Int32*	4 bytes	−2,147,483,648 through 2,147,483,647
Long (long integer)	*System.Int64*	8 bytes	−9,223,372,036,854,775,808 through 9,223,372,036,854,775,807
Object	*System.Object* (class)	4 bytes	Any type can be stored in a variable of type *Object*.
Short	*System.Int16*	2 bytes	−32,768 through 32,767
Single (single-precision floating-point number)	*System.Single*	4 bytes	−3.402823E+38 through −1.401298E−45 for negative values; 1.401298E−45 through 3.402823E+38 for positive values
String (variable-length)	*System.String* (class)	Depends on implementing platform	0 to approximately 2 billion Unicode characters
User-defined type (structure)	(inherits from *System. ValueType*)	Sum of the sizes of its members	Each member of the structure has a range determined by its data type and independent of the ranges of the other members.

Arrays

There are several important changes to the way arrays are handled in Visual Basic .NET. First, arrays are all zero-based, and this can't be changed. Second, the number you specify when you create an array is the number of elements in the array. Lastly, the *ReDim* statement is used differently than in Visual Basic 6; you must now dimension an array first and then use *ReDim* to change the upper bounds.

ReDim can be used only in a procedure block. You also can't create an array that has fixed bounds because any array can be changed using the *ReDim* statement. To illustrate the first two changes to arrays, consider this statement:

```
Dim CustomerList(30) As String
```

This statement creates an array of 30 elements with bounds of 0 through 29. To access the last element, you would use this:

```
X = CustomerList(29)
```

Like many other changes, the array changes were implemented to make Visual Basic .NET compatible with other languages supported by the .NET Framework. This compatibility is especially important when you're calling a method of a component that is written in another language. It's also interesting to note that arrays are based on the *System.Array* class, thus providing arrays with quite a bit of power. For instance, you can sort a single-dimension array by calling the *Sort* method of the *System.Array* class.

String Handling

Working with strings has always been interesting in any language. String handling was implemented by each language, and some languages were more efficient at it than others. This is another area that changes with Visual Basic .NET, because now the .NET Framework provides the data types and the string handling for those data types.

First, you can create and work with strings just as you always did in Visual Basic. For instance, you can create a variable to hold a string like so:

```
Dim sCustomer As String
Dim sAddress As String
```

Then you can set the variable like this:

```
sCustomer = "My Customer"
sAddress = "2000 First Street, Anytown"
```

And you can concatenate this string with another in this way:

```
Dim sFullAddress As String
sFullAddress = sCustomer & "  " & sAddress
```

There are also lots of new tricks in store for you when working with strings. For instance, you can concatenate the strings using this new syntax:

```
sFullAddress &= "  " & sAddress
```

This syntax results in slightly less code, making the typing easier and the resulting code less cluttered.

You can also use the *System.String* class from the .NET Framework to work with strings. This class has several methods that you can use for various tasks. Table 1-2 provides a list of several of these methods and a short description of their uses.

Table 1-2   Selected Methods of the *System.String* Class

Method	Description
Format	Applies formatting to a string and returns the result
Concat	Concatenates two strings together and returns the resulting string
Join	Creates a string by combing an array of strings
Insert	Inserts a new string into an existing string and returns the new string
CopyTo	Copies characters from a string into a particular position in an array of characters

So how do you use these methods? Let's look at our last example and see how to concatenate the string using the *Concat* method.

```
sFullAddress = String.Concat(sFullAddress, " "c, sAddress)
```

Notice that you have a number of ways to manage string handling in Visual Basic .NET. Do it the way you did in Visual Basic 6, or adapt the new features of Visual Basic .NET and the .NET Framework.

There are, of course, new features that you'll want to use. For instance, Table 1-2 lists the *Format* method, which can be very useful in business objects that work with various types of data. You can also use the *Format* method to format strings. For instance, you can format a number as a decimal by using the following code:

```
Dim dMyNo As Decimal
dMyNo = CDec(txtInput.Text)
txtOutput.Text = Format(dMyNo, "##,##0.00")
```

You can also use the *String.Format* method to perform this task.

> **Tip**   Watch out for type differences in .NET. For instance, if you pass the *Format* method a string and try to format it as number, *Format* returns the format string and not a formatted number. Thus, if you executed the preceding statement with a string, *Format* would return "##,##0.00". That's why the incoming string is converted to a decimal and then formatted.

The *String.Format* method also takes a different approach to formatting. For instance, let's say you want to format the previous number but also place the resulting string in another string. You can accomplish this with the following code:

```
Dim dMyNo As Decimal
dMyNo = CDec(txtInput.Text)
txtOutput.Text = String.Format("Your total is {0:C}.", dMyNo)
```

In this example, the *Format* method takes the incoming object (*dMyNo*) and places it in the string in which it finds the first placeholder (*{0}*). The *:C* is added to the placeholder to format the number as currency.

You can see from this quick example and the example in the preceding tip that formatting strings and other values is easy but also powerful in the .NET Framework world.

The *StringBuilder* class also provides a handy set of methods for working with strings. This class can be used to create new string objects and manipulate their values. The *StringBuilder* class is particularly useful when you're building a high-performance application that does many string manipulations. *StringBuilder* can be used in these cases to handle string operations and dramatically reduce the overhead. Selected string modification methods of the *StringBuilder* class are shown in Table 1-3.

Table 1-3 Selected *StringBuilder* String Manipulation Methods

Method	Description
Append	Appends a new string to the current object
AppendFormat	Appends a new string to the current object with optional formatting
Insert	Inserts a string or an object into a particular location in the string of the current object
Remove	Removes a specified number of characters from the current object's string
Replace	Replaces characters in the current object's string

Structured Exception Handling

Error handling must go into every application. Visual Basic .NET supports structured exception handling as well as the traditional error handling from earlier Visual Basic days. Structured error handling is basically a block form of exception handling that allows you to structure your code to trap errors that generate exceptions. The basic structure of this type of error handling is as follows:

```
Try
    txtOutput.Text = CStr(oMath.Add(CInt(txt01.Text), _
        CInt(txt02.Text), _
        CInt(txt03.Text), _
        CInt(txt04.Text), _
        CInt(txt05.Text)))
Catch
    MessageBox.Show("An error occurred in the call to Add ", _
        "Add Error")
Finally
    oMath = Nothing
End Try
```

As long as no run-time error occurs, the *Try* block executes, not the *Catch* block. If an error occurs during execution of the *Try* block, the *Catch* block runs. The *Finally* block of code always runs.

This functionality is powerful because it allows you to structure your code and wrap error handling around it. The code is also simple to read and follow, and you can catch specific exceptions in addition to catching all exceptions by adding exception filters to the *Catch* statement.

You can see from this simple example that besides being powerful, structured exception handling can both improve the readability of your code and reduce the amount of code you need to write. Chapter 3 digs into exception handling in more detail and shows how to create your own exceptions.

Components, Classes, and Objects

Now let's start digging into components and classes. Back in the Visual Basic 4 through Visual Basic 6 days, we almost always thought of components and classes together. For instance, when you created an ActiveX DLL in Visual Basic 4 through 6, you were really building a component that contained one or more classes. The classes were the implementation of the code, whereas the components were the container for the classes. When you compiled the component, Visual Basic generated either a .dll or an .exe extension.

As mentioned earlier, in Visual Basic .NET, you create projects that are compiled into assemblies. Assemblies are now the .dll or .exe implementation of the project and contain the MSIL that actually gets processed by the CLR. When you build the project, you place classes or classes that are called components in your project. Ah, there it is. Now we have two types of classes.

Components and Classes

The easiest way to create any type of class is to use Visual Studio .NET. When you add a class or an item, the Add New Item dialog box shown in Figure 1-2 is displayed.

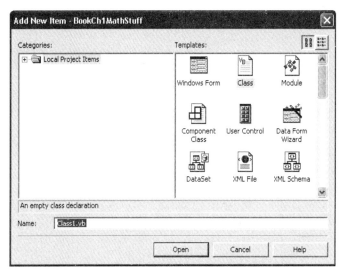

Figure 1-2   The Add New Item dialog box, which is used to add classes and other items to a Visual Studio .NET project

One type of class is a simple class, just as in Visual Basic 4 through 6. You can clearly see in the diagram the two types of classes: a simple class (Class) and a component class (Component Class). To illustrate the differences, we created two classes that contain no implementation code. The first one is a simple class named *Address*, and the code is shown here:

```
Public Class Address

End Class
```

The second one is *BusinessType* and is a component class:

```
Public Class BusinessType
    Inherits System.ComponentModel.Component

#Region " Component Designer generated code "

Public Sub New(Container As System.ComponentModel.IContainer)
    MyClass.New()

    'Required for Windows.Forms Class Composition Designer support
    Container.Add(me)
End Sub
```

```
Public Sub New()
    MyBase.New()

    'This call is required by the Component Designer.
    InitializeComponent()

    'Add any initialization after the InitializeComponent() call.

End Sub

'Component overrides dispose to clean up the component list.
Protected Overloads Overrides Sub Dispose(ByVal _
    disposing As Boolean)
    If disposing Then
        If Not (components Is Nothing) Then
            components.Dispose()
        End If
    End If
    MyBase.Dispose(disposing)
End Sub

'Required by the Component Designer
Private components As System.ComponentModel.IContainer

    'NOTE: The following procedure is required by the
    'Component Designer.
    'It can be modified using the Component Designer.
    'Do not modify it using the code editor.
<System.Diagnostics.DebuggerStepThrough()>
Private Sub InitializeComponent()
    components = New System.ComponentModel.Container()
End Sub

#End Region

End Class
```

Wow, that's quite a difference in code. Here's the practical difference. When you create a simple class, it's just that—a simple class just like the one you created in Visual Basic 4 and later versions except that it contains the *Class* statements to start and end the class definition. You can add your own constructor (the *New* procedure—more on this later), but it's still a simple class with no other features. A component class, on the other hand, is derived from the *System.ComponentModel.Component* class, meaning that it is a component class with all the features of the base *Component* class.

You first notice a difference with the component class when you create a new one in Visual Studio .NET. The new class opens with a design surface similar to that of a visual element such as Windows Forms. (See Figure 1-3.)

Why would a class have a designer? That powerful design surface can be used to visually add to the component class features such as an event log or a performance counter, as shown in Figure 1-3. It enables you to see some of the features of your class. You can even add support for the designer to your class so that your class has properties and acts just like the classes in the .NET Framework.

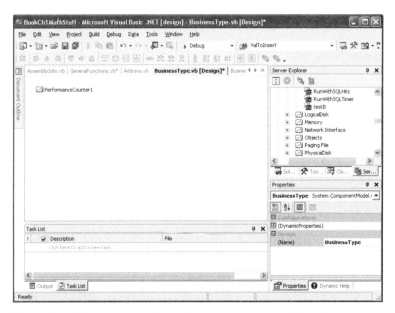

Figure 1-3   The design surface allows you to drag and drop items onto a class and to interact with the item's properties.

Class and Module Files

In Visual Basic .NET, Visual Basic files containing code, including forms, class files, and module files, always have a .vb extension. How do you distinguish the code for a class from the code for a module? You use a statement to start the code block that identifies the type of block. This is similar to the approach provided by later versions of ASP. For instance, to create a class, you use a *Class* statement like the one shown earlier:

```
Public Class Address

End Class
```

To create a module, you would use a *Module* statement:

```
Module GeneralStuff

End Module
```

Now you can see how the definition occurs. You simply use the correct statement to start the code block. You can also use a scope directive on either statement.

When you create a class in Visual Studio .NET, a single file for your new class is created and the file is given the same name as the class or module. For instance, the *Address* class is contained in Address.vb, and the *GeneralStuff* module is in GeneralStuff.vb.

You can also put more than one element in a single file. For instance, a slightly modified version of GeneralStuff.vb might look like this:

```
Public Module GeneralStuff

End Module

Class TestIt

End Class
```

This is legal and works fine. However, we prefer to keep each class or module in a separate file. This division makes the code more logical and easier to maintain.

One other note on classes and modules. Now that you have class and module statements, you must maintain those names. For instance, if you rename Address.vb in Solution Explorer (or in the Properties window), you're not renaming the class, only the file. You also need to change the class name in the code by editing the *Class* statement or by using the Properties window.

Instantiating and Using Classes

When you instantiate classes in Visual Basic .NET, you use the *New* operator. The *New* operator can be used in two ways. First, you can use the *New* operator to instantiate the class when you create a reference to it. This is handy because you have immediate access to the object. Second, you can use the *New* operator to instantiate the object after you create the reference to it. To instantiate the object at reference time, you would use this syntax:

```
Dim oAddress As New Address()
```

This statement does not instantiate the class upon the first reference to it. Instead, it instantiates the class immediately after creating it.

To instantiate the *Address* class at a point in time after you create the reference, you would use this syntax:

```
Dim oAddress As Address
oAddress = New Address()
```

The last line shows another change in the way we build applications. The *Set* keyword is no longer used to set object references because everything in the .NET world is treated as an object. This is another area in which code is simplified and standardized at the same time.

> **Note**   In the days before Visual Basic .NET, using the *New* operator when you created the reference negatively affected the performance of your applications. Happily, this effect is gone now and there should be no performance difference between the two methods other than the overhead of instantiating a class at the time of definition.

You can add classes and modules to any project. This is really cool for Web applications because now you can use modules to store standard bits of code whereas before you had to use include files. You can also create classes and then use them just like external classes. This latter approach makes it easy to create a class for use in a particular application and then migrate the class to a separate component later for general use.

Constructors and Destructors and Such

What happens when a class is instantiated? In practical terms, the class becomes an object at the point of instantiation. But how do you perform actions in your code when the class instantiates? You can add a procedure known as a *constructor* to a simple class. (Component classes automatically have constructors.) A constructor is nothing more than a subroutine named *New*. When the class is instantiated, *New* (that is, the constructor) is fired. This is a handy location for you to place your startup code, similar to a *Form_Load* event or a *Page_Load* event in a Windows Forms or Web Forms application, respectively. The following code shows a simple constructor that instantiates a new object when *New* is instantiated:

```
Public Sub New()
    Dim oAddress As New Address()
    ⋮
End Sub
```

What happens when the class is no longer used? When all the references to an object are gone, a process called *garbage collection* eventually determines that the object is no longer used, and the object is destroyed, thus freeing its memory. Just before the garbage collector destroys the object, it executes a *Finalize* procedure. A sample *Finalize* procedure is shown here:

```
Protected Overrides Sub Finalize()
    MsgBox("Finalize firing now")
End Sub
```

In practice, you wouldn't place a call to display a message box in a *Finalize* procedure, but it does serve as a good example. If you place the code to display the dialog box in a class called by a Windows Forms application, you'll see the message box fire shortly after you close the application, demonstrating how the garbage collector operates and the *Finalize* procedure is called.

You can't tell when the garbage collector will run and destroy any objects you create and then call the *Finalize* procedure. Instead, we (and the MSDN documentation) recommend that you create a method named *Dispose* in each class you create. *Dispose* should contain any code the class needs to clean up resource usage (such as closing any open files or data connections). Then any code that uses the class can call *Dispose* when it's through using the class.

You can call the *Collect* method of the garbage collector like this:

```
GC.Collect()
```

Collect causes the garbage collector to perform a collection. However, this operation is very overhead-intensive, and you shouldn't try to outguess the garbage collector. Instead, call *GC.Collect* only when you have a real reason to do so.

Structures

Structures, which are similar to classes both in their construction and in the way they behave, allow you to define your own types. Structures are value types and as such can contain values. And to some extent, structures behave like classes. However, structures differ from classes in that each of two variables defined as structures has its own copy of the data. For instance, if you define a structure named *Customer* and create variables *A* and *B* of type *Customer*, each contains its own data. Furthermore, if you then assign *A* to *C*, *C* gets a copy of the data in *A*, not a reference to *A*. Because of this behavior, structures are very useful in objects and business applications of many types.

In Visual Basic 6, you could take advantage of *user-defined types* (UDTs), which allowed you to create a special type that could be reused throughout the application. In Visual Basic .NET, structures are used instead of UDTs. Structures are much more flexible than UDTs and easier to implement.

The following code shows how to declare a simple structure with only a few properties:

```
Structure Employee
    Public CustomerID As Integer
    Public Name As String
    Public Address As String
    Public Address2 As String
    Public City As String
    Public StateProvince As String
    Public Country As String
    Public PostalCode As String
End Structure
```

You can use the structure like this:

```
Dim MyEmp As Employee
MyEmp.Address = txtInput.Text
txtOutput.Text = MyEmp.Address
```

The first line defines *MyEmp* as type *Employee*. The second line sets the *Address* of *MyEmp*, and the last line retrieves the address. This short example demonstrates how you can create essentially a lightweight object (structure) that behaves like an object with properties. This results in a structure that behaves like a class but might be more efficient. Structures are placed on the stack, whereas classes are placed on the heap when instantiated. Thus, a structure might provide better performance than a class. You'll find this out in a given application only by testing.

Structures can also have methods and raise and handle events just like classes. Then what is the difference between a class and a structure? As we mentioned earlier, when you create a variable as a type of structure, the variable contains the values assigned to it, not a reference to an object containing those values. Because of this behavior, structures don't require allocation of memory on the global heap like objects do. Structures also don't have a *Finalize* procedure like classes do, and a structure can't be inherited from.

So when should you use a structure rather than a class? Use structures when you don't need to create an extendable class and when the structure won't contain large amounts of data. For instance, if you need an object that contains several properties, you can create that object as a structure and save the overhead of a class.

Property Procedures

The syntax for property procedures has changed a bit to simplify it. Now you create one property procedure with separate *Get* and *Set* methods. The following code demonstrates this:

```
Property Street() As String
    Get
        Return mStreet
    End Get
    Set(ByVal Value As String)
        mStreet = Value
    End Set
End Property
```

As with most other tasks, Visual Studio .NET does a lot of the coding for you. To create the above procedure, you simply enter the first line and press Enter. Then Visual Studio .NET fills out the rest of the shell for the procedure, and you fill in the blanks.

Working with Methods

There are a few changes in store when working with methods (functions or subroutines). First, when you set up a parameter string for a method, the default access to the parameters is by value (*ByVal*). This means that the method can't make any changes to the values because the parameters are actually local variables in the method. You can use the *ByVal* keyword to make your code more readable, but if you omit it, the parameters will be passed by value anyway.

Second, when you return values from a function, you can do so in two ways. You can return values like you always did by setting the name of the function to the return value, as illustrated here:

```
Function Add(ByVal X As Integer, Y As Integer) As Integer
    Add = X + Y
    Exit Function
End Function
```

Or you can use a new syntax, in which the *Return* statement is used to return the value, like this:

```
Function Add(ByVal X As Integer, Y As Integer) As Integer
    Return X + Y
End Function
```

These two functions work pretty much the same way, with a couple of exceptions. When *Return* executes, it returns from the function then and there, alleviating the need for an *Exit Function* statement. The other difference comes up in your development cycle. If you take the *Add* method with the *Return* statement, you can quickly turn it into the *Multiply* function, like so:

```
Function Multiply(ByVal X As Integer,Y As Integer) As Integer
    Return X * Y
End Function
```

This illustrates the beauty of the *Return* statement. To create the *Multiply* function, we copied the *Add* function and changed *Add* to *Multiply*. Then we changed the plus sign (+) to an asterisk (*) and that was it. This approach also removes the likelihood of errors cropping up in your applications when you forget to rename the function on the assignment statement. Copying functions is now tremendously simpler using *Return*.

Another change involves optional parameters. In Visual Basic .NET, optional parameters must be the last parameters in the parameter list and they must also be set to a default value. For instance, we could modify the *Add* method to take several optional parameters, setting the default value of the third through the sixth parameter to *0*:

```
Function Add(ByVal O1 As Integer, _
    ByVal O2 As Integer, _
    Optional ByVal O3 As Integer = 0, _
    Optional ByVal O4 As Integer = 0, _
    Optional ByVal O5 As Integer = 0, _
    Optional ByVal O6 As Integer = 0) As Integer

    Add = O1 + O2 + O3 + O4 + O5 + O6
    Exit Function
End Function
```

In this case, the math statement is simple because all the missing parameters are *0* and thus can be added without even checking their values.

You also can't declare a function or a subroutine as *Static*. If you want any variables in the function or subroutine to be static, you must explicitly declare them as such.

Notice as well that you must now provide parentheses with both subroutines and functions. This makes the calling syntax quite clean. Visual Studio .NET adds the parentheses for you automatically, making it relatively easy to add the empty ones.

Overloading Properties and Methods

Now let's get down to one of our favorite new features. Visual Basic .NET supports the *overloading* of properties and methods (functions). This feature is tremendously powerful because it allows you to have multiple definitions for a single method.

For instance, consider the following three versions of the *Add* method. The only differences between them are the method's arguments.

```
Function Add(ByVal O1 As Integer, _
    ByVal O2 As Integer, _
    Optional ByVal O3 As Integer = 0, _
    Optional ByVal O4 As Integer = 0, _
    Optional ByVal O5 As Integer = 0, _
    Optional ByVal O6 As Integer = 0) As Integer

    Add = O1 + O2 + O3 + O4 + O5 + O6
    Exit Function
End Function

Function Add(ByVal X As Long, ByVal Y As Long) As Long
    Return X + Y
End Function

Function Add(ByVal X As Decimal, ByVal Y As Decimal) As Decimal
    Return X + Y
End Function
```

When you make a call to one of these methods, the particular method called will be chosen based on the parameters you feed it. Thus, which parameters you pass to an overloaded function controls which function is executed. You can now have consistent interfaces with the only difference being the properties.

You'll see the *Overloads* keyword again later in the book as we define the data layers (discussed in Chapter 4) and other classes.

Overriding Existing Methods

In addition to overloading a method, you can override it. This is useful when you create a method or a property that is the same as the one in the base class that your class is derived from. For instance, the base class might have a method named *FormatCurrency* that takes a monetary value and formats it appropriately. Now you create a new class and need to format currency differently, say, because your local government has changed its currency (such as the switch to the euro in many European countries/regions). You can use overrides on your function definition and, when another application calls *FormatCurrency* in your class, your method will be called, not the one in the base class. You can also call the base class version of a method at any time by using *Mybase* to qualify the method call.

You can also use the *NotOverridable* keyword on a method definition to prevent overriding. Likewise, you can add the *MustOverride* keyword to force overriding of the method. You'll see the *Overrides* keywords again later in the book.

Events

As in earlier versions of Visual Basic, you can create and handle events. The event creation process is fairly simple. First, in the class in which you want to fire the event, you must declare the event. Then, you must raise the event at the appropriate points in the code by using the *RaiseEvent* statement. Finally, you must wire an event handler in the client application. To illustrate, let's take a look at the *SimpleMath* class by adding an event to it.

You can see the event definition in the following code just after the class definition. The event is then raised in each version of *Add* by calling *Raise-Event*.

```
Namespace Simple
    Public Class SimpleMath
        Public Event ProcessStatus(ByVal bStatus As _
            Boolean)

        Function Add(ByVal O1 As Integer, _
            ByVal O2 As Integer, _
                Optional ByVal O3 As Integer = 0, _
                Optional ByVal O4 As Integer = 0, _
                Optional ByVal O5 As Integer = 0, _
                Optional ByVal O6 As Integer = 0) As Integer

            RaiseEvent ProcessStatus(True)
            Add = O1 + O2 + O3 + O4 + O5 + O6

            Exit Function
        End Function
        Function Add(ByVal X As Long, _
            ByVal Y As Long) As Long
            RaiseEvent ProcessStatus(True)
            Return X + Y
            Exit Function
        End Function
        Function Add(ByVal X As Decimal, _
            ByVal Y As Decimal) As Decimal
            RaiseEvent ProcessStatus(True)
            Return X + Y
            Exit Function
        End Function
    End Class
End Namespace
```

Now, let's use the event in an application. There are two ways to wire the event into the application. We can use *WithEvents* in the definition just as we have in the past:

```
Dim WithEvents oMath As New SimpleMath()
```

Then to use the event, we simply create an event handler like this:

```
Private Sub oMath_ProcessStatus( _
    ByVal bStatus As Boolean) _
    Handles oMath.ProcessStatus

    txtStatus.Text = "Add routine status: " & bStatus
End Sub
```

Now, when either implementation of *Add* completes, the event handler updates the *txtStatus* control. Of course, to create all this code, you should use Visual Studio .NET. Then you can easily create event handlers using the code editor just as you did in Visual Basic 6 and earlier versions.

In addition to *WithEvents*, you can use *AddHandler* to cause any subroutine to handle an event. Let's walk through a simple example. First, create a reference to the class:

```
Dim oMoreMath As New MoreMath ()
```

Then create a subroutine that will handle the event:

```
Private Sub MultiplyHandler(ByVal bStatus As Boolean)
    txtStatus.Text = "Multiply routine status: " & bStatus
End Sub
```

You probably noticed that this is a standard subroutine with no funny naming and no *Handles* clause at the end of the definition. We don't need the *Handles* clause because we're going to set up the event handler in our code at run time. To set up the event handler, you use the *AddHandler* keyword like this:

```
AddHandler oMoreMath.MultiplyStatus, _
    AddressOf MultiplyHandler
```

The first parameter is the name of the event being wired up. The second parameter uses *AddressOf* to point to the subroutine that will handle the event. You could remove the event handler later on by using the *RemoveHandler* keyword.

AddHandler and *RemoveHandler* are both useful because they are runtime features, not design-time features. Therefore, you can dynamically use them to add and remove event handlers in code. This is much more flexible than wiring up the handler at design time.

Interfaces and Implements

You can create separate interfaces in Visual Basic .NET using the *Interfaces* statement. Interfaces describe the signature of the class but contain no implementation code. You then use the *Implements* statement to develop a class that implements the interface. We won't use *Interfaces* in this book because we're not great fans of defining separate interfaces for classes. We prefer to create classes that are not inheritable and also create object frameworks that are inheritable. For example, the database component classes in Chapter 4 handle interaction with a database. This component is not designed to be a framework component that is extended. As such, we can mark its classes as noninheritable. A base framework class such as *CustomerBase*, however, is designed to be inherited, and we would mark it *Must Inherit*. That forces developers to properly use the database component and the *CustomerBase* component. You'll see these principles used in many of the examples throughout this book.

Shared Members

Sometimes you need either methods or properties that are shared across all instances of a class, usually when you have to obtain some type of data and make that available to all instances of the class. To accomplish this, you can use the *Shared* keyword on the definition of a method or property.

Namespaces

Namespaces are an interesting feature of all languages that the .NET Framework supports. Namespaces are a new concept to many developers, but they are really a common way to segregate items in an application. When you use a database such as Microsoft SQL Server, you can think of a particular database and its tables as two levels of a namespace. For instance, the database name might be Northwind. The Northwind database logically breaks all elements it contains into its namespace. Within Northwind, each table is another namespace that contains its own elements. You can get qualified access to any field in the database by specifying the database and table name. In fact, the database engine forces you to do this.

Now let's consider .NET. When you create a Visual Basic .NET application using Visual Studio .NET, a default namespace with the same name as the project is created for you. For instance, let's create a class library named *Math-Stuff* (by selecting File New and then Class Library) that contains a class named *SimpleMath*. Figure 1-4 shows the default namespace definition in the Project Properties General tab for the BookCh1MathStuff project.

Now let's create a client application to use this component. Add the new application project, and then in Solution Explorer, right-click the References folder in your client project and add a reference to the *MathStuff* class library. Place an *Imports* statement at the start of the file that will use the class, like this:

```
Imports MyMathStuff
```

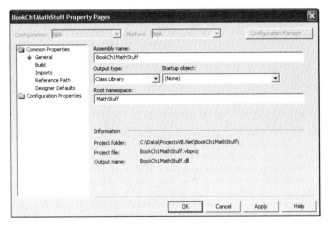

Figure 1-4   The default namespace is set in the project's Property
Pages dialog box.

Now you can use the *SimpleMath* class and its methods as follows:

```
Dim oMath As New SimpleMath()
txtOutput.Text = CStr(oMath.Add(CInt(txt01.Text), _
    CInt(txt02.Text), _
    CInt(txt03.Text), _
    CInt(txt04.Text), _
    CInt(txt05.Text)))
```

Notice that we didn't completely qualify the class name on the *Dim* statement. Because of the *Imports* statement, we can use class name without qualifying it as shown in the preceding code. Visual Studio .NET helps when you create the *Imports* statement because it will use IntelliSense to show you the available namespaces, as shown in Figure 1-5.

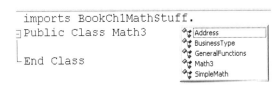

Figure 1-5   IntelliSense works with almost everything in Visual Studio
.NET, including namespaces.

You can also create your own namespaces in your applications. To create a namespace, use the *Namespace* statement to create the namespace and place other members such as classes inside the namespace. For instance, we can take the *SimpleMath* class and put it in the *Simple* namespace like this:

```
Namespace Simple
    Public Class SimpleMath

        Function Add(ByVal O1 As Integer, _
            ByVal O2 As Integer, _
            Optional ByVal O3 As Integer = 0, _
            Optional ByVal O4 As Integer = 0, _
            Optional ByVal O5 As Integer = 0, _
            Optional ByVal O6 As Integer = 0) As Integer

            Add = O1 + O2 + O3 + O4 + O5 + O6
            Exit Function
        End Function
        Function Add(ByVal X As Long, ByVal Y As Long) As Long
            Return X + Y
        End Function
        Function Add(ByVal X As Decimal, _
            ByVal Y As Decimal) As Decimal
            Return X + Y
        End Function
    End Class
End Namespace
```

Then we can change the *Imports* statement to this:

```
Imports MyMathStuff.Simple
```

Of course the .NET Framework also has many namespaces. Consider the following code:

```
Catch eos As System.IO.EndOfStreamException
    ' No action is necessary; end of stream has been reached.
Catch IOExcep As System.IO.IOException
```

These two statements also illustrate referencing properties of a class by fully qualifying them. Both exception filters are fully qualified by the *System.IO* prefix. If you added an *Imports* statement like the following, you wouldn't need the prefix:

```
Imports System.IO
```

So, you can see how namespaces can be used to segment your applications code and to make it easier to use elements of the namespaces in your applications.

Inheritance

Let's wrap up this section on components with a short discussion of inheritance. Some people think inheritance is at the heart of component design, but it's really just a part of it, although a very important part. Visual Basic was ushered into the OOP world with the introduction of Visual Basic 4 and then continued improvements with versions 5 and 6. Visual Basic didn't fully arrive into the OOP world until the introduction of Visual Basic .NET and its inheritance capabilities.

Let's look at inheritance from a practical point of view. With inheritance, you can create one class and then derive a second class from it by using the *Inherits* statement. The derived class will have the same interface as the first class. For instance, let's take the *SimpleMath* class we discussed earlier in this chapter and create another class, named *MoreMath*, that inherits from *SimpleMath*. To do this, we simply create the new class and then use the *Inherits* statement:

```
Public Class MoreMath
    Inherits MyMathStuff.Simple.SimpleMath
End Class
```

Notice that we fully qualify the path to *SimpleMath* with both the project namespace and the *Simple* namespace that contains the class.

Now, the *MoreMath* class contains no members, right? Wrong! Because it inherits *SimpleMath*, *MoreMath* looks exactly like *SimpleMath* to any applications that use it. For instance, any other application creates a reference to *MoreMath* and calls the *Add* method just as it does with *SimpleMath*. Now we can add more methods to *MoreMath*, effectively extending the functionality of *SimpleMath*, its base. You can also use events from the base class or the derived class.

Throughout the rest of the book, we'll be talking about inheritance in more detail and letting you know where to use inheritance—and where not to use it. You'll also see how object frameworks are built that are implemented through inheritance and parts of the framework that have nothing to do with inheritance. We will discuss Visual Basic .NET's OOP features in more detail in Chapter 8.

Deploying .NET Applications

To wrap up this introduction to Visual Basic .NET and components, we'll touch on how to deploy applications and the components they use. As with any other applications, Visual Basic .NET applications must have some way to find the components they use. (We discuss deployment in more detail in Chapter 14.)

Normally, you place an assembly for a single application in that application's folder structure. For instance, if you look in the MathStuff project folder, you'll find a bin folder that contains the MathStuff.dll and MathStuff.pdb files. MathStuff.dll is the assembly, and the MathStuff.pdb (program database) file contains debugging information for the assembly. The .pdb file also contains information the linker can use when debugging the assembly.

When you create an application in Visual Studio .NET that uses a component that isn't in the global assembly cache (GAC), the assembly is automatically copied to the project's bin folder. So, if you simply copy the project's bin folder, the assembly for the component is copied as well. Since the files the application needs are in the same folder, the application can run without registration. The same thing occurs with a Web application, because just like a Windows application, the Web application has a bin folder for its assemblies.

The GAC is a shared (hence the word *global*) assembly location on each system running the .NET Framework. The GAC is actually a folder hierarchy in the file system where the assemblies are located. (The folder name is Assembly and is located in the Windows folder.) There is a utility named Gacutil.exe that you can use to place assemblies in the GAC or to remove them. You shouldn't copy files into the GAC without using the proper utilities. Even better than using Gacutil.exe, you can easily build an .msi setup file using Visual Studio .NET, and then your assemblies in the .msi file will be installed when the .msi file is run. When you install the .NET Framework on a system, Windows Explorer is modified to work with the GAC. Thus, you can use it to add or remove files.

You can also use the Microsoft .NET Framework Configuration tool, found under Administrative Tools in the Start menu to manage the GAC, as shown in Figure 1-6.

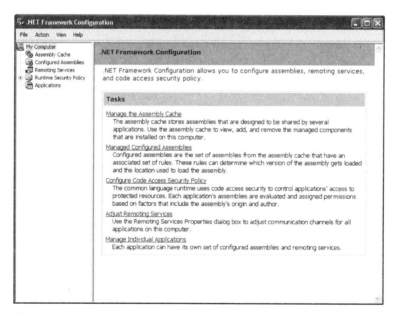

Figure 1-6   The Microsoft .NET Framework Configuration tool can be used to modify the GAC and other settings such as security policies.

You can see from this figure that this tool can also be used to manage other features of .NET applications such as assemblies, remoting services, and security.

If you have components that are shared by several applications, you can install those by creating what's called a *merge module*. Then each application's .msi file can contain the merge module, thus making sure the shared assemblies are installed.

Conclusion

We've covered a lot of ground in this chapter, touching on many items that relate to component development with Visual Basic .NET. By now, you should have some idea of what Visual Basic .NET is and how it can be used for component development. You should also be able to see that Visual Basic .NET and Visual Studio .NET are a powerful team that allow you to really dive into development quickly and efficiently.

In fact, we estimate that by using Visual Studio .NET and Visual Basic .NET, you should cut from 25 to 35 percent of the coding from a typical development process. We're seeing numbers in this range from our own applications as well as our consulting and training clients. This means you should be able to write the code faster and have less code to maintain in the future. Thus, your overall application costs should go way down.

Starting with Chapter 2, we're going to dig into object-oriented development. As mentioned earlier, the concepts and examples shown in the rest of the book are from real .NET applications that are used by thousands of users. The components in the book can also be easily customized for your applications.

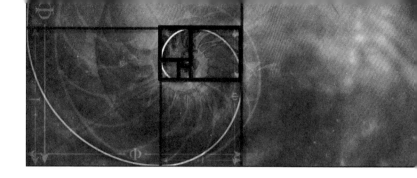

2

Architectural Options with .NET

Whenever I look at architecture and design in the software world, I remember the words my mother taught me when I was a small child about crossing a road: "Stop. Look. Listen. Go." That was a tough lesson to learn as an eager and over-zealous little guy. I'm no different as a software developer. Whenever I encounter great new technology like 38Microsoft Visual Basic .NET, I'm ready to charge ahead and code, and ask questions later. We're sure that many of you developers and programmers feel the same way. This chapter is our version of our mothers' "Stop. Look. Listen. Go." but with a different twist: "Stop. Look and learn some of the capabilities of .NET. Listen and learn architecture and design. Go and program." If you take this advice, you'll be in a better position to learn what architecture fits .NET best; where to use components, inheritance features, server controls, user controls, and so on; and how to leverage the thousands of .NET Framework classes we have access to. This chapter will help you understand these subjects. Once you've read this chapter, you'll feel comfortable choosing a flexible architecture, know what features of the .NET Framework to use where, and know some of the design options you have within .NET. As you progress through the rest of this book, you'll see how to build components that fit into the .NET Framework and how to build a complete enterprise application around it. You'll end up with many components—from server controls and user controls to user interface components, business components, and a data access component—that you can immediately reuse in your applications. What's best about these components is that they have been tested and are used in several production business applications with steep requirements for scalability, performance, and reliability.

Choosing the Right Architecture

The .NET platform is the only truly Internet-centric development platform available at this time and has been designed from the ground up with the Internet in mind. It took years and a substantial amount of money to accomplish this, but in the end it's worth the time and expense. In working with .NET since the later alpha versions, we have come to love it and, even more, to love developing and writing code again. With the .NET Framework, we can create better-performing Web and enterprise applications more easily and more quickly than we could before, and these applications meet the demands of performance, scalability, and availability.

Before delving into the various software architecture models, we want to make an analogy between building a house and developing software. The architecture of a house, as well as that of software, determines the overall structure. One underlying question that both kinds of architects ask is, "What is used where?" Before deciding on the final architecture, the architect must consider the wishes and goals of the homeowners (or clients). For a house, an architect draws up blueprints and makes changes iteratively until the homeowners are satisfied that they will be getting what they want. For software, this stage is the analysis phase, in which the design team creates the system specifications. In the analysis phase, changes are also done iteratively until the clients see that all their requirements have been considered. The next step often involves choosing the land—or with software, the software platform. Then come the foundation, the plumbing, the electrical wiring, and so on. In software, this work translates to building the framework classes, choosing the database engine, and deciding how data will move through the system. The .NET Framework handles most of these details for you, via the thousands of classes in the .NET Framework class library. (We've found it a fun challenge to find the classes within the .NET Framework that match our requirements.) At this point, the house can be built on a solid foundation using the material and building sequence specified in the architectural plans and design. At this point in software development, we plug in all the components we have chosen, customized, or written. Most of these deal with the required business rules. The user interface and output generation can be designed in parallel. Just as a contractor checks each phase of the house being built, so do software developers verify that each stage of application building goes according to plan. Because object-oriented programming (OOP) uses inheritance and components, software developers have a huge advantage over architects who design and build homes. We can reuse major parts of our applications for any other application we must build without sacrificing quality. As a matter of fact, the more we use major components for important parts of our applications, the more stable they become over time (as we improve them). Even better, with OOP and inheritance, we can pass increased stability and performance to applications that are already written and avoid major rewrites. With homes, this step would be remodeling. And we all know that remodeling can be very messy and expensive. OK, we have taken this analogy far enough.

At the risk of sounding repetitive (just as parents' instructions often are), consider the effect that choosing the right architecture and successfully carrying out the analysis and design phase have on the applications you create. Doing this work correctly at the beginning of a project leads to great applications that are hassle-free to maintain and can be extended relatively easily. If you ignore this work up front and dive right into coding, the result will often be applications that barely work, create huge maintenance nightmares, and make life a pain for us developers—definitely something we want to avoid.

Brief History of Software Architecture

In this section, we're going to offer a quick history of past and current software architecture models—from one-tier, two-tier, and three-tier architecture to the flexible *n*-tier architecture we've come to know and appreciate. We use this architecture as the basis for our own development in .NET and for the examples in this book.

One-Tier Architecture

Thinking of one-tier architecture, in which everything in the application resides in the same place, was quite the trip back in time. I personally remember writing a chess program in Germany in the late 1970s. It had to run in a total of 16 KB (kilobytes, not megabytes) of memory, and it needed graphics (just black and white dots). The platform it needed to run on was an 8088 processor and MS-DOS. It had to be written in the assembly language, and the chess pieces were described mathematically to live with the memory restrictions. It even saved games on a cassette recorder. OK, old memories aside, you see this kind of application very little now. Even development languages such as Microsoft FoxPro, Borland Delphi, and Clipper use databases that are in separate files and can have multiple accesses to get at least a two-tier architecture. Figure 2-1 shows a one-tier form.

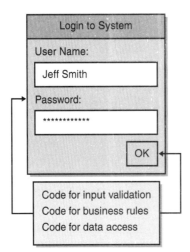

Figure 2-1   One-tier application architecture

After downloading and installing this book's companion files from *http://www.microsoft.com/mspress/books/5203.asp*, you'll find the sample files for this chapter in the Ch02 directory. Load the Architecture.sln file into Microsoft Visual Studio .NET. You can find this file in the Architecture subdirectory. The Architecture.vb form is the menu from which you can choose the different samples and is designated as the startup object of this project. The One Tier button leads to the OneTier.vb form. There isn't much to this form. The username and password are hard-coded. (Keep in mind that this example is for demonstration purposes only. We wrote the samples in this chapter to demonstrate architecture, not code.)

One-tier applications turn into huge, unmanageable behemoths. They are tough to maintain and very difficult to upgrade or change. Their deployment is also more difficult. There are very few reasons to use a one-tier application in today's development environments. We almost always separate the user interface, business logic, and database access so that even in the small applications or Windows services we develop, we don't use this architecture.

Two-Tier Architecture

The natural second step in the evolution of software architectures was the separation of the program and the data. In two-tier architecture, not only is the physical data separated, but the database engine can also be an application, such as Microsoft SQL Server or Oracle, that is optimized for data access. Figure 2-2 shows the separation we're talking about.

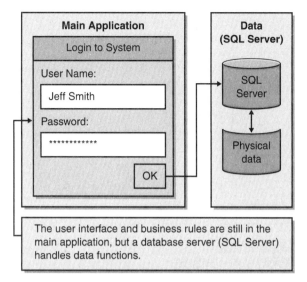

The user interface and business rules are still in the main application, but a database server (SQL Server) handles data functions.

Figure 2-2   Two-tier application architecture with data access separated

With two-tier architecture, the user interface and business rules are still mingled together, but data access is greatly improved and scalability is much higher, supporting up to several hundred concurrent users. Many users connected to the database simultaneously create a fair amount of network traffic and use server resources, especially when the client application stays connected. This traffic jam creates a bottleneck and limits performance and scalability for larger systems.

Our second example shows a typical two-tier login for an application. When the login button is clicked, a connection is made to the database, calling a *DataReader* object named *DataReaderObject*. Each row is compared to the entered username until found. Then the password is compared and access is granted. When the process is over, the connection to the database is closed. Though this example is simple, you can clearly see the two layers. With two-tier architecture, you still have to deal with the disadvantages of having lots of business-related code, even including the data connection within the user interface. Same or similar code blocks have to be repeated often, and maintaining such applications is difficult.

Many of today's applications and Web projects use this architecture, perhaps because it's relatively easy to implement. Figure 2-3 shows a slight variation of this architecture, in which stored procedures are used not only to access, manipulate, and delete data, but also to implement business rules.

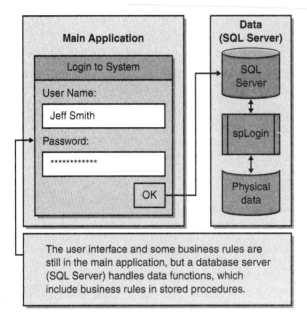

Figure 2-3   Two-tier application architecture with data access separated and stored procedures

We see this variation often, and clients have called us many times to overcome its limitations in terms of scalability and performance. Having part of the business rules in the application and the other part in SQL Server stored procedures increases the complexity of the application and makes maintaining code difficult. Using stored procedures in general is a good idea. You'll see that we make extensive use of them in our sample applications. They increase the performance of SQL Server, allowing it to do what it does best: run queries, make transactions, track indexes, and so forth. Even though simple business rules such as constraints and insert triggers are acceptable, when complex business rules are integrated into stored procedures, SQL Server has to do the kind of work it wasn't intended to do and quickly becomes a bottleneck again.

Our third example shows a typical two-tier login, but instead of iterating through a *DataReader* object on the client, the username and password are passed to a stored procedure that validates the user and returns the result. Here is the code to create the stored procedure *spLogin*:

```
CREATE PROCEDURE spLogin
    @User char(15),
    @Password char(15)
AS

DECLARE @RecordFound int
```

```
SELECT @RecordFound = Count(*)
From Employees
Where LastName = @User
AND Extension = @Password
If @RecordFound > 0
    Return(1)
Else
    Return(0)
```

This stored procedure accepts the username and password as parameters, searches for both of them, and creates the *@RecordFound* integer. When the stored procedure gets called, all processing is done on SQL Server and only the result is returned, as either a 1 for valid or 0 for invalid, depending on the record count of the *@RecordFound* variable.

Although two-tier architecture has certain advantages and is often used in today's solutions, we feel it is time to replace it with at least a three-tier approach, ideally an *n*-tier approach. In the next couple of subsections, you'll find how easily this separation is accomplished in .NET.

Three-Tier Architecture

The push to a basic three-tier architecture came rather quickly with the advent of the Internet. Microsoft Active Server Pages (ASP) allowed only scripted code in the user interface. This code had to be interpreted every time, resulting in slow response times and limited scalability. This is where Windows DNA came in. We should really say "comes in," in the present tense, since Windows DNA is still widely used and probably will be until .NET has become the application development platform of choice. The Windows DNA architecture suggests a standard three-tier development, with the presentation layer, business layer, and database layer separated. The presentation layer is written using either ASP or Win32 clients. The middle-tier and prepackaged components in this architecture are built using COM or COM+. The database layer uses SQL Server, Oracle, Microsoft Exchange Server, mainframes, or other relational database management systems (RDBMSs). The diagram in Figure 2-4 shows the separation of the three tiers. Although all three tiers are logically separated, they could run on the same server or be on three or more independent systems.

The fourth example, named ThreeTier.vb, shows this separation. It doesn't use COM+, which is a good thing because we won't have to deal with its limitations and hassles. This code shows you how easily layers are created and called and how the headaches of COM are all but gone. With this example, we're going to look at code in more detail, especially at the techniques used to create layers, to access code, and to pass data back and forth.

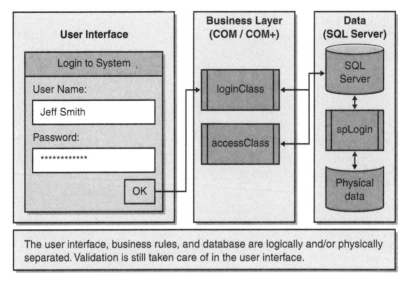

Figure 2-4 Three-tier application architecture

We'll start with the Architecture solution. It already contains the Architecture project we've been using so far. To create our tiered separation, we add a new project to the solution and name it BusinessLayer; we also rename the main class file logic.vb. The first thing you find in this class is the import of the SqlClient that we use to connect to SQL Server. Right after that is the declaration of the *BusinessLogic* namespace. Namespaces are very important in .NET since they help organize the incredible number of base classes in the .NET Framework and in our own classes and objects on top of it. (See Chapter 1 for more information about namespaces.) By default, a project has its own name as its base namespace and you can add other namespaces. In our example, we added the *BusinessLayer* namespace. When we want to call the *Security* class, we use this syntax:

```
BusinessLayer.BusinessLogic.Security()
```

By importing the namespace into the calling application, you can avoid having to specify an object's namespace:

```
Imports BusinessLayer.BusinessLogic
```

You see the code for this in the button *Click* event of the three-tier example. We only have to declare the variable as *Security()*:

```
Dim localLogin as New Security()
```

The rest of the code in our *Security* class is almost the same as in the previous two-tier example. The only difference is that we're using OOP principles of encapsulation by declaring all variables as private and creating public properties to pass the username and password before the *userLogin* function gets called. We could have done this by passing parameters to this function, but we wanted to show you encapsulation principles at work.

Let's take a quick look at the calling code in the user interface. To have access to the BusinessLayer project, we need to add a reference to it in the Architecture project. We do this in the References item of the Architecture project in Solution Explorer. With this reference added, we can create the calling code in the button *Click* event handler:

```
Imports BusinessLayer.BusinessLogic
⋮
    Private Sub btnLogin_Click(...) Handles btnLogin.Click
        Dim localValidateUser as Boolean
        Dim localLogin as New Security()
        localLogin.UserName = txtUserName.Text
        localLogin.Password = txtPassword.Text

        localValidateUser = localLogin.loginUser
        localLogin = Nothing

        ⋮
    End Sub
```

After the import of the *BusinessLogic* namespace, we just declare a variable with the *Security* class, populate the properties, and call the *loginUser* function. This will return a true or false login validation. Notice that there is no logic in the user interface anymore. There isn't even a hint of where the value comes from. The calling code in the client has no idea how results get created. The functionality of user validation is totally encapsulated in the business layer. Business logic resides in one place instead of in several places, with part in the user interface, another part in components, and still another part in the database. Applications are much easier to debug and maintain this way.

That's all there is to it. We have a three-tier application. No registry settings, no hassle of debugging—the .NET debugger follows the code from the calling code to the business layer and can even be set up to follow the code into the stored procedure. When a change is made in the business class, it's immediately available in the calling code. Another huge advantage is the capability to use the same business logic class in a Web Forms page in *exactly the same way* you used it in the Windows Forms example shown here. In contrast, Windows DNA software developed in the middle tier often has to be different for Win32 clients and ASP. The tools and programming techniques were different then; however, in .NET they are the same! If you feel eager to give the easy access to layers created in .NET a try, you can add a Web project to this solution and create a Web Forms page that collects the username and password, and then cut and paste the same code into a button server control's *Click* event. (Don't forget the *Imports* statement.) We made a detour from our discussion of architecture to show you how easily and seamlessly .NET allows us to create these tiers.

The Limitations of Windows DNA and COM

While we were writing our first Windows DNA applications, we found that theoretically, nothing is wrong with the three-tier model. In practice, however, things were a bit different. The limitations of the Windows DNA model lie not within the architecture but within the tools. Because Microsoft and other development platform providers were surprised by the Internet explosion and had to come up with development solutions quickly, they inadvertently cut corners. Besides the challenges of having to use a conglomerate of languages and techniques to write Internet applications, COM's limitations are the biggest challenge for Windows DNA. Let's take a look at the languages and tools that are or were used to create a Web application with Windows DNA:

- ASP pages: Client-side Microsoft Visual Basic Scripting Edition (VBScript)

- ASP pages: Client-side JavaScript

- ASP pages: Server-side VBScript

- ASP pages: Server-side JavaScript

- ASP pages: Hypertext Markup Language (HTML), Dynamic HTML (DHTML), Cascading Style Sheets (CSS)

- ASP pages: Extensible Markup Language (XML), Extensible Stylesheet Language (XSL)

- Client components: Microsoft Visual Basic

- Server components: Visual Basic

- Microsoft ActiveX components: C++

- Databases: Stored procedures with Transact-SQL in SQL Server

Even for the most experienced programmers, using this array of tools efficiently and effectively can be daunting. Business logic could be located in any combination of the above choices. Mastering all these languages and dealing with COM simultaneously requires a very sophisticated skill level.

Here are some of the challenges and limitations of COM:

- DLL hell created by small problems such as a slight change in a component's interface, which can render a whole component-based tier useless. Versioning is difficult, and creating a large working set of DLLs requires rocket science skills and a well-designed system approach.

■ Difficult deployment when DLL components are used on client systems.

■ Lack of interoperability with other platforms.

■ No support for inheritance natively. Inheritance features are critical to building complex application frameworks successfully. The .NET Framework, for example, is built by relying heavily on OOP and inheritance.

■ Needing to change programming models when developing for the Internet vs. other types of development.

■ State management with Internet sessions not handled automatically.

■ Visual Basic as a tool to build COM components.

    ❑ No full OOP and inheritance support.

    ❑ No multithreading.

    ❑ Limited integration with other languages.

    ❑ Poor error handling.

    ❑ No useful user interface for Internet-based applications.

These challenges show the difficulty and cost associated with creating *n*-tier applications that use COM/COM+ and pre-.NET technology.

Although three-tier architecture, with its clear separation among the user interface, the business logic, and the database, has helped us reach more highly scalable applications that are easier to maintain and upgrade, it still falls short of the best solution: the flexible *n*-tier architecture you can achieve with the .NET Framework.

Flexible *n*-Tier Architecture

Two things hamper the three-tier architecture we just discussed. First, using Windows DNA for application development quickly reveals that business rule components can't be used in the same way in ASP Web applications and other clients. Many applications therefore repeat business rules with a different interface for each client, which is not a good solution. It leads to duplicate sections of code that are harder to maintain and update. The solution to this challenge in Windows DNA was to buffer the user interface from the business layer through a facade layer. Instead of writing duplicate business rules, you wrapped their use into the facade layer and let it create the changes required by the calling client. The need for this buffer zone has dwindled in .NET but still can exist when you want to add or change business layer functions for a specific client application. An example would be to add additional security when a Web service accesses business logic.

The second challenge we face when implementing three-tier architecture is data access. We find that we often repeat data access and data manipulation code in business components when we adhere to the three-tier architecture. The problems arise when the database changes, when we find a better way to access data, or when data access technology changes. In one of our past applications, we implemented the three-tier design but left data access in the business classes. The time arrived to move to newer features of Microsoft ActiveX Data Objects (ADO) and a newer version of SQL Server. We were faced with the challenge of rewriting major portions of our business rules. With several hundred rules, this was not a small task and took longer than anticipated. Fortunately, we decided at the point of rewriting the business rules to implement a buffer layer, or facade, between the database and the main business layer. We called it the data access layer. Soon after making the switch, we found a performance-enhancing trick with ADO 2.6 that was relatively easy to implement in our data access layer. There was no need to rewrite the business rules. Figure 2-5 shows a layout of the flexible *n*-tier architecture.

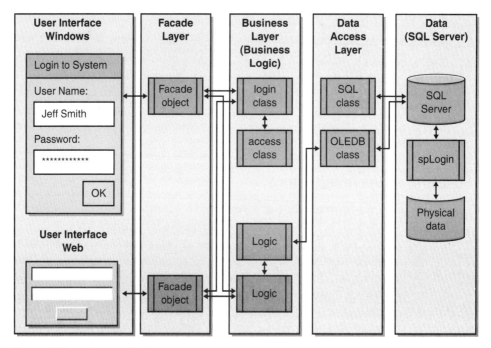

Figure 2-5 *n*-tier architecture

The *n*-Tier Architecture in Action

Our next example, FlexibleNTier.vb, shows how we implement the data access layer. (In Chapter 4, we're going to take a close look at data access methodology and the building of the data access component; for now, we'll show only how it is used in this example.) We have copied the final component into the BusinessLayer example. (It is called DataAccessLayer.dll.) To use the data access component within the BusinessLayer project, we need to create a reference to it. We do this in the References item for the BusinessLayer project in Solution Explorer. You add this specific reference by selecting the DataAccess-Layer.dll file from the Projects tab of the Add Reference dialog box. The business logic class for this example is in the LogictoDAL.vb file. We gave it the same namespace as in our previous example but changed the name of the login class to *SecurityDAL*. The *Imports* statement points to *DataAccessLayer.Data-Access*, where all the data access methods and functions reside. Looking at the code in LogictoDAL.vb reveals that there is no reference to ADO.NET and its data functions. Although the previous example's business logic contained all the required data access functions, there are none to be found here. This is possible by fully encapsulating the data access functionality within the data access component.

Here is the code used in the stored procedure:

```
CREATE PROCEDURE spLogin2
    @User char(15),
    @Password char(15),
    @Validate bit output
AS

Declare @RecordFound int

Select @RecordFound = count(*)
From Employees
Where LastName = @User
AND Extension = @Password

Select  @RecordFound

If @RecordFound > 0
    set @Validate = 1
Else
    set @Validate = 0
```

This stored procedure is slightly different from the one we used before. It sets the validation result to an output variable defined as *@Validate*. This way we don't have to return a *DataReader* or *DataSet* with a resulting table. All we get back is the output parameter containing a 1 for valid or a 0 for invalid user validation.

Here is the code for LogictoDAL.vb in its entirety:

```
Imports DataAccessLayer.DataAccess
Namespace BusinessLogic
    Public Class SecurityDAL
        Private privateConnectionString as String
        Private privateStoreProcedureName as String
        Private privateReturnOutputList as New ArrayList()

        Private privateUserName as String
        Private privatePassword as String
        Private validateUser as Boolean = False

        Public WriteOnly Property UserName() as String
            Set(ByVal Value as String)
                privateUserName = Value
            End Set
        End Property
        Public WriteOnly Property Password() as String
            Set(ByVal Value as String)
                privatePassword = Value
            End Set
        End Property

        Public Function loginUser() as Boolean
            privateConnectionString = "..."
            privateStoredProcedure = "spLogin2"
            Dim privateSQLServer as New _
                SQLServer(privateConnectionString)
            privateSQLServer.AddParameter("@User", privateUserName, _
                SQLServer.SQLDataType.SQLChar,15)
            privateSQLServer.AddParameter("@Password", _
                privatePassword, SQLServer.SQLDataType.SQLChar,15)
            privateSQLServer.AddParameter("@Validate",, _
                SQLServer.SQLDataType.SQLBit,, _
                ParameterDirection.Output)
            returnOutputList = privateSQLServer.runSPOutput( _
                privateStoredProcedureName)
            validateUser = CType(returnOutputList.Item(0), Boolean)

            privateSQLServer.Dispose()
            privateSQLServer = Nothing

            Return validateUser
        End Function
```

The *Imports* statement lets us use the data access layer's functionality without fully qualifying the *DataAccessLayer.DataAccess.SQLServer* class. We use the same namespace for the *BusinessLogic* class as before and give this class a slightly different name. Incidentally, this is a great place to mention that the only difference in the calling code of the client in this example compared to the three-tier example is the name of the calling class. You'll find this code in the FlexibleNTier.vb file's code section under the *btnLogin_Click* event handler. Instead of the previous code,

```
Dim localLogin as New Security()
```

we now call the business layer class that uses the data access layer with this:

```
Dim localLogin as New SecurityDAL()
```

Notice that the following lines of code in LogictoDAL.vb declare only the variables needed:

```
Private privateConnectionString as String
Private privateStoreProcedureName as String
Private privateReturnOutputList as New ArrayList()

Private privateUserName as String
Private privatePassword as String
Private validateUser as Boolean = False
```

These variables include the connection string, the name of the stored procedure to run, the *ArrayList* that will hold the output parameter for the stored procedure's result, the name and password to be validated, and last but not least, the variable holding the result returned. No data access variables are declared or used. The following lines of code deal with the public parameters used for this class:

```
Public WriteOnly Property UserName() as String
    Set(ByVal Value as String)
        privateUserName = Value
    End Set
End Property
Public WriteOnly Property Password() as String
    Set(ByVal Value as String)
        privatePassword = Value
    End Set
End Property
```

Next is the public function *loginUser*. This code is more interesting since it calls the data access layer:

```
Public Function loginUser() as Boolean
    privateConnectionString = "..."
    privateStoredProcedure = "spLogin2"
    Dim privateSQLServer as New _
```

(continued)

```
     SQLServer(privateConnectionString)
   privateSQLServer.AddParameter("@User", privateUserName, _
     SQLServer.SQLDataType.SQLChar,15)
   privateSQLServer.AddParameter("@Password", _
     privatePassword, SQLServer.SQLDataType.SQLChar,15)
   privateSQLServer.AddParameter("@Validate", _
     ,SQLServer.SQLDataType.sQLBit,, _
     ParameterDirection.Output)
```

Before we declare *privateSQLServer* as the *SQLServer* object with the *privateConnectionString* variable attached, we fill the connection string and name the stored procedure that it needs to call. As soon as our data access component is declared, we add parameters to be used. The data access layer provides a one-line *AddParameter* function that allows us to pass the names, type, size, value, and direction of the stored procedure. First we add the *@User* and *@Password* parameters, and then we add the *@Validate* output parameter. Notice that we have given it the *ParameterDirection.Output* direction to differentiate it from the preceding input parameters. As soon as all required parameters are defined, we call the *runSPOutput* method of the data access component:

```
returnOutputList = privateSQLServer.runSPOutput( _
   privateStoredProcedureName)
validateUser = CType(returnOutputList.Item(0), Boolean)
```

The method that runs a stored procedure that returns a list of output parameters is named *runSPOutput*. It accepts the name of the stored procedure to be executed. This method returns an *ArrayList* of output parameters. In our case, there is only one, and we pass the returned validation to the *validateUser* variable. This one was defined as of type *Boolean*. With *Option Strict* turned on, we need to do the type conversion you see in the preceding code. We promise that you'll find out later (in Chapter 4) how this data access component works. All we have left to do is dispose of this instance of the data access object and return the value to the client:

```
privateSQLServer.Dispose()
privateSQLServer = Nothing
Return validateUser
```

You can readily see how easily we implemented this four-layer example. When compared with all the work we would have had to do in Windows DNA, this almost looks too easy. In reality, it isn't that easy; it's just that the .NET Framework hides all the complexity that creates the plumbing between components in the different layers. We also get improved performance compared to COM and COM+ components. You might ask yourself why this is the case since layering increases system requirements by passing data back and forth between its layers used. The reason for this is .NET's plumbing is done natively. All the code we've written so far is supported by the common language runtime (CLR) on the lowest level of the .NET Framework. See Figure 2-6 for a closer look at the architecture of Visual Studio .NET.

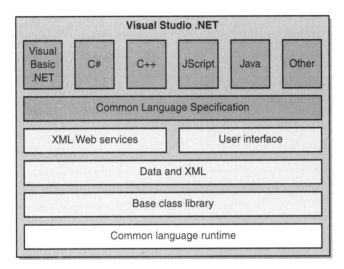

Figure 2-6   Internal architecture of Visual Studio .NET

No data marshaling is necessary to communicate through the layers in .NET. All .NET classes have their root in *System.Object*, which sits right on top of the CLR. As you can see in Figure 2-6, this is the very foundation upon which all .NET components are built. Components and classes can even be built in different managed languages, still inherit from each other, and still be used without data marshaling when communicating with each other. This is in sharp contrast to COM and COM+ layered components. Every time one of these components communicates with either the user interface or other layers and the database, data marshaling has to take place because COM+ components handle data differently from ASP or Win32 applications or even the database itself. This becomes significantly expensive in overhead, limiting both scalability and performance.

We're not trying to take potshots at Windows DNA and COM+. Very large and functioning systems are built on these technologies. But .NET is specifically designed to address the problems we've been discussing and is a better solution for your future projects. Its COM+ component support is very good and doesn't require a full replacement of your hard-earned COM+ component library. When .NET communicates with COM+ components, however, you introduce data marshaling and its overhead again. To get the best possible performance and scalability, pure .NET programming is a prerequisite.

What's Flexible About *n*-Tier Architecture?

We have no rigorous "this is what you must do" approach with the *n*-tier architecture. Use the layered approach that makes the most sense for your applications. When a facade layer isn't needed, don't use it. When you write a small program that isn't part of a large-scale enterprise application, you might use just the user interface components with business logic in their code, but still use the data access layer component for data access needs. On the other hand, you might need more layers when business logic becomes overly complex. You might even have to create a layer for asynchronous processes in your application. The point is to be flexible in your design considerations.

Years of programming experience have shown that a separation of the user interface, business logic, and database (a minimum three-tier approach) as a minimum layered architecture makes sense. Whenever we have chosen otherwise, we have ended up regretting that choice when it came to maintaining and upgrading the application.

The components and tools built for our HRnet sample application allow you to reuse them so that you can create flexible *n*-tier solutions yourself. In Chapter 4, we're going to build the data access component. It's very generic and covers most data access requirements. Although we've written it for SQL Server 7 or SQL Server 2000, you could easily adapt it to OLE DB with other data sources in mind. We have tested and fine-tuned this component in real-world, large-scale production systems. In .NET, it can be used in any of the layers and makes data access much easier than having to deal with data-related code repeatedly. You could even package it as a COM+ compatible component that could be used in ASP and Visual Basic 6. Using this component is like having a permanent data access layer for your applications. Such is the power of good components built with .NET.

From our discussion, you can see that the .NET Framework allows you to create *n*-tier applications with relative ease. Prepackaged components can fit or create these layers without the complexity and overhead previous generations of development tools required. The flexible approach of *n*-tier architectures has always made sense when designing applications but has been hard to implement until now. With the .NET Framework, you'll finally be able to design a new generation of flexible, scalable, and reusable *n*-tier applications.

Solutions Using the .NET Framework

You now know that our architecture of choice is the flexible *n*-tier solution using the .NET Framework. We next want to look at how the various .NET features fit within the different layers. Keep in mind that there is no canned solution. We'll recommend a particular approach, but .NET is flexible enough to let you customize solutions in many different ways. The approach we suggest works best for us and is the outcome of writing several .NET-only production applications in the past year. We built the HRnet sample application and all its components using the features we'll be talking about in this section.

Even though each application we create is different, we still find many features common to all our applications. For example, almost every application we have written accesses data, has a user interface, processes data, and so on. It would be a waste of time and resources to rewrite this functionality every time we create a new application. In most cases, it would also be unnecessary to create a deep class structure for this kind of functionality. Writing a component for these functions is simply the best solution. As we've already mentioned, a data access component is a good example of a reusable component. In fact, in our examples the data access component makes up the whole data access layer. Another example of a useful generic component is the security component, which we'll cover in detail in Chapter 5.

Still other common features among our applications might be our preferred user interfaces or a specific way we want the output to look. This is where visual inheritance or the use of server and user controls comes into play. In the next few sections, we'll break down into layers our suggestions for what to use where.

User Interfaces

The .NET Framework has three user interfaces to choose from: console, Windows Forms, and Web Forms. Since the console interface in .NET looks and feels like good old MS-DOS, we aren't going to cover it here.

The separation of logic and design in ASP pages has been a top request of many developers. In ASP, user interface and code were intermingled, sometimes creating hassles. ASP.NET separates logic and design in the form of *code-behind* files. The HTML and the code are each stored in separate files that get linked for execution. The code-behind file is not the place for business logic, however. This file should be used only to enhance user validation and call middle-tier objects. When you create ASP.NET pages, you have two great ways to further code reuse and inheritance. You can either create user controls or custom server controls.

User Controls and Web Forms

User controls are the reusable sections of code and content as separate ASP.NET controls. (The programming model for user controls is the same as the one used for ASP.NET pages.) We include them in an ASP.NET page and have all their functionality. You can think of user controls as include files on super steroids. They encapsulate their functionality well enough to be reused on the same ASP.NET page while presenting different data. We'll discuss a couple of tricks that enhance their usage manifold in Chapter 7, Chapter 10, and Chapter 11.

Custom Server Controls and Web Forms

Custom server controls are just like ASP.NET server controls that you create. The closest comparison with previous technology is that custom server controls are like COM controls but easier to create and use. They're precompiled and have properties, methods, and events. They can render HTML, XML, or no output at all. You'll find more information on custom server controls in Chapter 6, Chapter 10, and Chapter 11.

Which Controls Should I Use?

Both user controls and custom server controls are great choices for code reuse and OOP. The best place for user controls is in the individual applications you write. They give an application a common look and feel. We tend to use them to break common features of the user interface into pieces. Each ASP.NET page is a collection of all the user controls and the specific HTML and code it requires. User controls are not intended to be used beyond their application's boundaries. An example of a user control is a custom header we use in all Web pages for a project. Besides the HTML makeup of the header, the user control could also include custom code that gets executed whenever the control is clicked.

Custom server controls, on the other hand, are the kinds of objects we want to use across many applications. They belong to our general toolbox. We don't mean the Toolbox in Visual Studio .NET, but rather the components we generally use in all our applications. An example of a custom server control is an enhanced drop-down box with an indexed lookup feature.

Windows Forms and Visual Inheritance

In Windows Forms, we can use visual inheritance features. Visual inheritance allows us to not only inherit a class's methods and properties but its form as well. This allows us to create a basic form and inherit from it, adding controls and functionality along the way. Visual inheritance can go several layers deep. In the Ch02 sample subdirectory, you will find the VisualInheritance folder. The VisualInheritance solution shows a simple but powerful example of how visual inheritance can help build data entry pages quickly and with a common look and feel.

Because everything in .NET is an object, it's also possible to subclass visual objects such as text boxes, buttons, and so on and create your own enhanced versions.

Facade Functions

Even though the need for buffering the user interface from the business logic has decreased in .NET, there are times when wrapping the business logic into a facade layer to abstract behavior for a specific user interface is necessary. The two best choices for this are either components or specifically written classes. Chapter 9 is all about the facade layer.

Business Layer

The business layer is where we can use the new inheritance and OOP features of Visual Basic .NET the most. Business logic is the best place for creating an application-specific class framework. Most businesses have general guidelines and generic objects to work with that become more specific the closer you get to an actual implementation of an object. For example, to describe an employee of a company who works in the accounting department, you could use a class framework with class layers, as shown in Figure 2-7.

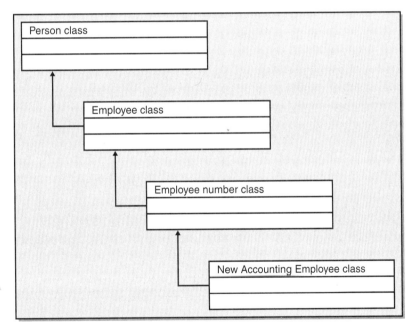

Figure 2-7   Sample class layers

Each description of an object becomes more specific to the actual used object. In this case, you create a new accounting employee object to add an employee to the accounting department. Each level that becomes more specific (deeper) adds functionality to its parent or parents and allows access to their properties, events, and methods. Such a framework of classes will typically be used only for a specific application.

In addition to a business class framework, it's possible to describe very generic repetitive business functions that require no changes when instantiated into business components for reuse across applications.

Data Access Layer

A data access component, such as the one used in our previous example, is the best solution for the data access layer. If we run across additional data access requirements the component doesn't already handle, we can enhance the component to include such additional functionality without changing or breaking existing data access functions.

Data Layer

The data layer can be any RDBMS available. ADO.NET allows the use of data objects beyond typical relational databases. It also supports XML natively. The two major data providers available for ADO.NET are SQL and OLE DB adapters. When relational database functions are required, we found SQL Server integration to work best. Systems using the .NET Framework and SQL Server 7 and SQL Server 2000 benchmark higher and scale better than any other combination available at the time this book was written.

Analysis and Design

Good software applications are the result of simple principles applied correctly. We don't want to oversimplify the complexity of creating large enterprise systems; however, adhering to these principles is what makes large systems possible. In this section, we're going to go through the steps involved in creating an enterprise application.

Step 1: System Analysis   To build a functional application, you must know its requirements, goals, and functions. In addition, you must know the workflow, the process flow, and the data flow within the system. At the end of the system analysis, you should have a system specification document. This document should provide a clear picture of what the application will accomplish and how it will do so. This plan becomes the foundation for functional and system design as well as database requirements.

Figure 2-8 shows a small excerpt of the system analysis document we created for a .NET enterprise application. Although specific tools for this step are available, we choose to create the system specification document in either Microsoft PowerPoint or Microsoft Visio Professional.

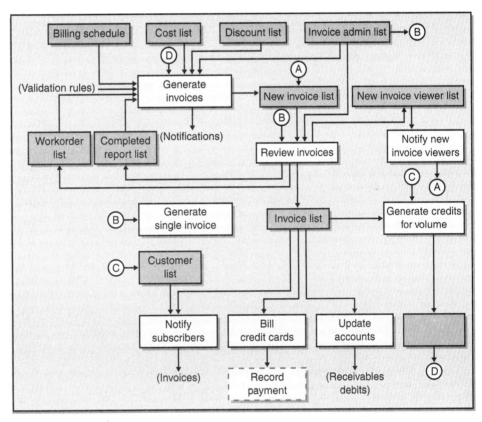

Figure 2-8   Sample system analysis document describing an invoicing business process

Step 2: Operational Specification (Modeling the Application)   Once the system specification document is available, we take these specifications and describe the operations that the application needs to fulfill. We also start defining general objects and their factions. Many different techniques are available for this step, such as Rational Rose, Visual Object Modelers' Visual UML, or the object modeling of Visio. The only challenge we see in using these tools is the learning curve associated with them. In some cases, their expense is also prohibitive. We've found that 3×5 cards and large dry-erase boards work well also. The tool or technique you use is less important than the fact that you used something to create the specifications.

Step 3: Database Design   Having the operational specifications and general objects allows you to start working on the database design. Although third-party modeling tools are available for this step, we found Visio Enterprise to be the best choice. A rapidly growing modeling technology for databases is object role modeling (ORM), which Visio Enterprise supports. ORM is a fact-based, conceptual data-modeling technique and is focused on objects and their relationships. The general description of objects from the previous step fits well with the first step of ORM database modeling. ORM modeling separates the physical storage of data from its conceptual design. This model then translates into an entity-relationship (ER) model that generates the actual database.

Step 4: Architectural Design   We covered this step in this chapter. The results of this step are the design of components, classes, class structures, and application-specific framework classes. We also decide which existing components can be used for this application. We structure them, group them, and assign them a place in the *n*-tier architecture. Objects now have specific descriptions. Process and data flow, state management, and activities have been defined in detail. The same tools we discussed in step 2 also apply in the architectural design.

Step 5: User Interface Design   We find that many good developers and programmers have limited experience or lack the ability to design user-friendly applications. This is why we always include an interface or graphical design specialist in the process. Here is where we fine-tune the look and feel of the application. The outcome of this phase is a specific definition and description for user control and server control creation.

Step 6: Write the Application   We write the application from the ground up. First come the most generic classes and components. Each one of them gets tested, and then the next higher layer is created. This write-and-test process continues until all the layers are finished. The user interface is also fine-tuned.

Step 7: Wire the Application Together   All parts of the application are wired together and tested. Stress testing shows how the application performs and reveals bottlenecks.

Obviously the preceding steps are only a high-level introduction to system analysis and design. The purpose for mentioning them is to impress upon you the need to analyze, plan, model, and design your applications before you write them. If you haven't already done so, you might resist these steps at first. Once you have overcome this resistance, you'll find the 80/20 rule applies in system design as well: 80 percent planning and 20 percent implementing will keep you from writing code 80 percent of the time that needs to be rewritten 80 percent of the time and causes you to lose 80 percent of the sleep you deserve (along with 80 percent of your hair). Any way you look at it, we urge you to try our approach and see for yourself.

Conclusion

The correct choice of architecture helps us build very large scalable enterprise applications. *N*-tier layers help us separate functionality and allow us to alter applications or add to them more easily. Maintaining existing code, user interfaces, and databases is also easier and better. Although pre-.NET technology allowed such architecture to be used, the implementation was and is far more difficult. The .NET Framework and powerful managed languages such as Visual Basic .NET allow us to write tiered applications with components, classes, application frameworks, and inheritance features both in code and in the user interface with relative ease. What helps us to achieve this goal is solid system analysis, design, and modeling.

With the knowledge of this foundation, let's create generic components and classes that we can reuse with most of the applications we have to write. Then we'll build the HRnet application using the principles of this chapter and the components created.

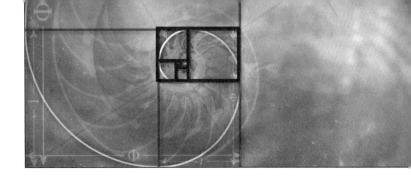

3

Exception Handling in the .NET Framework

Exception and error handling are greatly improved in Microsoft Visual Basic .NET. In fact, many Microsoft Visual Basic developers would say that anything would be an improvement over the error handling provided up through Visual Basic 6. The *On Error Goto* statement—at best unstructured, and at worst ineffective—has been the bane of many a developer's existence. The *On Error Goto* statement has made it difficult for developers to precisely identify exceptions and their sources and causes. It has also made it difficult to handle exceptions appropriately. As a result, developers have spent countless hours debugging applications under development and repairing applications in production environments. Sure, you can still use *On Error Goto* in Visual Basic .NET. However, the alternative *Try* statement is far superior in its structure and much more precise in its ability to identify specific types of errors.

Prior to the Microsoft .NET Framework, exception handling was implemented by each language. Visual Basic 6 and earlier versions have the *On Error Goto* statement and the related *Resume* statement. C++ uses the *Try* statement and the related *Catch* and *Finally* clauses in conjunction with the *Throw* statement. Other languages have their own unique exception-handling constructs. Some languages are better than others at handling exceptions. This difference in syntax and the underlying infrastructure for exception handling has made it difficult to handle exceptions between components written in different languages.

The Exceptional News on .NET

The .NET Framework introduces consistent, structured exception handling across all languages because it implements exception handling as part of the framework. This integration facilitates better handling of exceptions between components written in different languages. An exception raised in a component written in C# will be properly handled in a component written in any .NET language.

> **Note** It's important to define exception handling as viewed by the .NET development team. There's a difference between an exception and an error. An *exception* is anything that happens when an application is running that is not the expected, or normal, result. An *error* is an exception from which the application cannot automatically recover. For instance, if an application attempts to open a file and the file doesn't exist, an exception occurs. If the application handles the exception and, for example, creates the file, no error occurs. However, if the application cannot recover gracefully when the file is missing, an error has occurred. The exception-handling mechanism in the .NET Framework is intended to handle all exceptions, not just errors. That doesn't mean that every unexpected situation in your application should throw an exception.

Some exceptions might be handled with some old-fashioned defensive programming, for example, when closing a database connection. In the following code, the *State* property of the connection object is checked. No attempt is made to close the database connection unless it is currently open.

```
If connection.State <> ConnectionState.Closed Then
    connection.Close()
End If
connection = Nothing
```

In the next example, an attempt is made to open a database connection. If the connection can't be opened, ADO.NET throws an exception. The *Catch* clause in this example handles all exceptions but does nothing further about them. (We'll discuss the *Try* statement in more detail later in this chapter, in the section "The Syntax of the *Try* Statement.")

```
Try
    connection.Open()
Catch exception As System.Exception
    ' Unable to open the connection.
    ' Handle the error.
End Try
```

For the remainder of this chapter, we'll use the term *exception* to refer to any exception that is thrown by the common language runtime (CLR) or the application and must be handled by the application in some way. We'll use the term *error* to refer to exceptions that create unrecoverable situations in the execution of an application. Both will be handled through the use of exceptions as defined by the .NET Framework.

We'll also address the other issues you need to consider when implementing exception-handling objects for errors in production-quality applications, including the following:

- **Event logging and notification**   Production-quality applications must log exceptional situations and provide notification to operations staff.

- **Defining exception objects**   All exceptions are objects. The .NET Framework defines and implements an object hierarchy for exception-handling objects based on the *System.Exception* class.

- **Measurement and trend analysis**   The .NET Framework defines a set of performance objects related to exception handling that can be used to record the frequency of exceptions occurring in an application.

- **Serialization and remoting**   Using serialization in application-defined exception-handling objects enables these objects to be used remotely.

In short, the .NET Framework introduces many new concepts and capabilities for exception handling in Visual Basic .NET. In this chapter, we'll explore the most important .NET exception-handling objects.

What Is Structured Exception Handling?

The entire concept of structured exception handling originated in the object-oriented world. Languages such as C++ and Java have included structured, object-oriented error handling for some time. Fortunately, the architects of the

.NET Framework recognized a good thing when they saw it. So they designed the entire exception-handling infrastructure in the .NET Framework as a structured, object-oriented, exception-handling mechanism.

Structured Exception Handling

The term *structured* is used because exceptions must be explicitly handled by syntax (instructions) in an application's code. If it's necessary to handle one or more specific exceptions in a section of code, the code must explicitly trap those exceptions. All other exception types will be passed on to the next outer phrase for handling. If an exception is not handled by the code in the application, the CLR will handle the exception. Granted, letting the runtime handle the exception is less than graceful. It results in termination of the process after the user has been notified of the condition.

By contrast, the exception handling in Visual Basic 6 and previous versions is not structured. Once an error handler is defined in a phrase of code, every exception (error) that occurs is passed to the error handler. As with structured exception handling, it's necessary to write explicit code for each exception the application intends to handle itself. However, it's also necessary to explicitly use *Err.Raise* to pass unhandled exceptions back to the calling code. So, what's the difference?

In Visual Basic 6 and earlier, if the developer doesn't use *Err.Raise* to pass unhandled exceptions back to the caller, the application "swallows" the exception, making errors extremely difficult to identify and remedy. Proper exception handling in this environment depends on a proactive developer or the scheme fails.

In Visual Basic .NET, the CLR automatically passes along any unhandled exceptions to the calling procedure. This process continues until either the application or the CLR handles the exception. The proper handling of exceptions in the .NET Framework is passive and automatic. Without any effort on the part of the developer, no exception will ever be "swallowed" by an application. Every exception is handled either by the application—which does require some work on the part of the developer—or by the CLR.

Object-Oriented Exception Handling

The exception-handling mechanism in the .NET Framework is object-oriented because exceptions are objects. All exception objects are derived (that is, inherited either directly or indirectly) from the class *System.Exception*. The .NET Framework contains many exception classes that the CLR uses internally. When necessary, your application can also use these classes. Additionally, an application can define exception classes for its own use. These exception classes are also derived from *System.Exception*. All exception classes, whether defined by the CLR or by an application, are derived from *System.Exception*. This is an important part of the exception-handling mechanism in the .NET Framework.

The Syntax of the *Try* Statement

We've already mentioned that the *Try* statement has its roots in the object-oriented world—specifically the C++ and Java languages. The *Try* statement, along with the *Throw* statement, is at the heart of the structured exception-handling facilities in those languages.

Whereas the *Throw* statement creates an exception that must be handled, the *Try* statement identifies a block of code that might generate an exception (a *Try* clause), defines exception-handling logic for one or more types of exceptions that might arise (a *Catch* clause), and defines cleanup logic that must be executed whether or not an exception occurs (a *Finally* clause). The following code is a *Try* statement that demonstrates the basic syntax:

```
Try
    ' Statements that might cause an exception go here.
[Catch e as System.Exception]
    ' Statements to handle System.Exception go here.
[Finally]
    ' Unconditional cleanup logic goes here.
End Try
```

The *Catch* and *Finally* clauses are both optional. However, one of these two must be present in the *Try* statement or the compiler will report an error. The *Catch* and *Finally* clauses are not mutually exclusive; that is, they can both appear in the *Try* statement. Also, there might be more than one *Catch* clause to handle different kinds of exceptions.

The *Try* clause of the *Try* statement defines the block of code for which exception handling is to be enabled. The statements in the *Try* clause are executed. If the execution of any statement causes an exception, execution immediately transfers to an appropriate *Catch* clause, if one exists. After the *Catch* block executes, control is transferred to the *Finally* clause. Any statements in the *Try* clause that come after the statement that caused the exception will not be executed.

The following example is a *Try* statement consisting of a *Try* clause, several *Catch* clauses for different types of exceptions, and a *Finally* clause. The purpose of the code in this example is to open a database connection. If any exception occurs while opening the connection, the exception needs to be reported to the caller. In the *Try* clause, a single statement attempts to open the connection. The *Open* method of the connection object can raise one of several exceptions.

```
Try
    connection.Open()
Catch exception As System.InvalidOperationException
    ' Connection cannot be opened.
    Throw New OpenDBException( _
        "Unable to open database connection", _
        exception)
Catch exception As System.Data.SqlClient.SqlException
    ' Connection-level error occurred.
    Throw New OpenDBException( _
        "Connection-level error on open", _
        exception)
Catch exception As System.Exception
    ' Some other unknown error occurred.
    Throw New OpenDBException( _
        "Unknown error on open", _
        exception)
Finally
    If Not connection Is Nothing Then
        If connection.State <> ConnectionState.Open Then
            connection = Nothing
        End If
    End If
End Try
```

In this example, two types of exceptions are of interest. The first *Catch* clause handles any *System.InvalidOperationException*, which is the exception that ADO.NET throws when the *Open* method is called on a database connection that is already open. This exception is also thrown when no server is specified in the connection string. We use a custom exception class, *DBOpenException*, to report this problem to the caller. We'll discuss custom exception classes later in this chapter, in the section "Defining Exception-Handling Objects."

The next *Catch* clause handles exceptions of the type *System.Data.SqlClient.SqlException*, which is an exception class defined by the ADO.NET managed provider for SQL Server. It is thrown when a connection-level error occurs during the *Open* method. Again, we report this to the caller through *DBOpenException*.

The last *Catch* clause handles any exception of the type *System.Exception*. This is, in effect, the default *Catch* clause. It will catch any exception not caught by a previous *Catch* clause. Let's take a look at why this happens.

If you read the documentation on exceptions carefully, it states that every exception class is derived from *System.Exception*. Even though no exception of type *System.Exception* is ever thrown by the CLR (nor should one be thrown by any class library or application), by catching *System.Exception*, this second *Catch* clause will handle any exception that was not caught by any previous *Catch* clause. This is one of the nice things about living in an object-oriented world. An object can always be treated as if its type were the type of any of its ancestors. So, since every exception is derived (via inheritance) from *System.Exception*, every exception can be treated as if its type were *System.Exception*.

So, this *Catch* clause has become a catch-all for any exception other than a *System.InvalidOperationException* or *System.Data.SqlClient.SqlException*. In this way, it's not unlike the *Case Default* clause in a Visual Basic *Switch...Case* statement. The *Catch* clause also uses a custom exception class named *DBOpenException*.

When using multiple *Catch* clauses in a *Try* statement, there's an important principle to keep in mind. The *Catch* clauses should be in order from most specific to least specific. When an exception is thrown, the CLR scans the *Catch* clauses in the order they appear in the code, looking for an exception type that matches the current exception. As we see with the second *Catch* clause in the previous example, an exception type does not have to match exactly for a *Catch* clause to be executed. Any exception will match a *Catch* clause that handles *System.Exception*. If *Catch* clauses are not coded with the most specific cases first, a more general exception handler might be used to handle the exception rather than the intended specific handler.

Now let's consider another example. In this case, the first *Catch* clause handles all exceptions of type *System.Exception*. The second *Catch* clause handles exceptions of type *System.InvalidOperationException*. However, because *System.InvalidOperationException* is descended from *System.Exception*, the first *Catch* clause will handle all errors, including *System.InvalidOperationException*. The exceptions will never be handled by the second *Catch* clause—which was probably the developer's intent.

```
Try
    connection.Open()
Catch exception As System.Exception
    ' Some other unknown error occurred.
```

(continued)

```
        Throw New OpenDBException( _
            "Unknown error on open", _
            exception)
    Catch exception As System.InvalidOperationException
        ' Connection cannot be opened.
        Throw New OpenDBException( _
            "Unable to open database connection", _
            exception)
    Finally
        If Not connection Is Nothing Then
            If connection.State <> ConnectionState.Open Then
                connection = Nothing
            End If
        End If
    End Try
```

The *Finally* clause ensures that the connection object is set to *Nothing*. The *Finally* clause is always executed whether or not an exception was thrown by the connection's *Open* method.

Defining Exception-Handling Objects

Microsoft encourages developers to use the predefined exceptions in the .NET Framework before defining new exception classes. In some cases, there might be an exception class already defined in the .NET Framework class library that appropriately identifies the exceptional situation the application might encounter. In some instances, the best approach we can take is to create a new exception class. It's not feasible to assume that all potential exceptions could or should be handled by default exception classes. Thankfully, Microsoft has given developers some reasonable advice on creating new exception classes in a number of technical articles on MSDN that deal with exception handling in .NET applications.

Guidelines for Defining Custom Exception Classes

One of the first principles we need to remember about exception handling in the .NET Framework is that every exception is an object. The type (or class) of an exception object identifies the exception that has occurred, and this type must be derived from the *Sytem.Exception* class. When defining exception classes, it's strongly recommended that new classes never inherit directly from *System.Exception*. Instead, application-oriented exception classes should inherit (directly or indirectly) from *System.ApplicationException*. This is the first guideline offered by Microsoft for the creation of custom application-oriented exception classes.

> **Note**   All the exception classes defined in the .NET Framework class library are descendants of the class *System.SystemException*. Both *System.ApplicationException* and *System.SystemException* are direct descendants of *System.Exception*.

In Figure 3-1, we see the *System.ApplicationException* class in the Visual Studio .NET Object Browser. Note that several constructors are defined for this class, in particular the constructor named *New()*. This constructor is the default and takes no parameters. In this case, no additional information is passed to the constructor of exception objects. The second constructor is *New(String)*. This constructor takes one argument, a string, which will be the value of the *Message* property for the object.

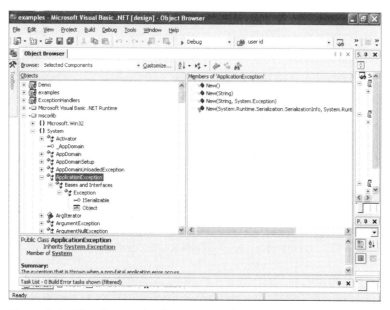

Figure 3-1   The *System.ApplicationException* object in Object Browser

Looking at *System.ApplicationException* in Figure 3-1, there doesn't appear to be any *Message* property defined for the class. However, when the Bases And Interfaces tree is expanded and the *System.Exception* class is selected (see Figure 3-2), *Message* appears as a property of this class. Since all exception classes ultimately inherit from *System.Exception*, every exception class will have a *Message* property. In fact, every exception class will have all the methods and properties listed for the *System.Exception* class, as shown in Figure 3-2.

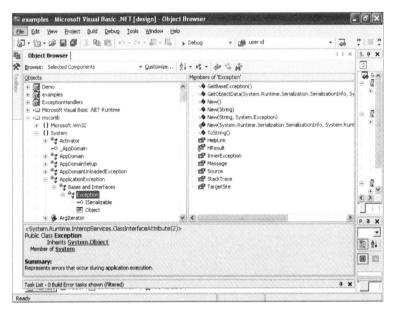

Figure 3-2   *System.Exception* in Object Browser

Another important guideline for creating custom application exception classes is that the name of the class should always end in *Exception*. If you notice, this convention is followed throughout the .NET Framework class libary: *System.Exception*, *System.SystemException*, *System.ApplicationException*, *System.Data.SQLClient.SQLException*, and so on. You would be well advised to follow this convention. Consistency makes application code more maintainable.

Finally, it's a good idea to provide properties in exception classes when additional information is useful. An example of this is adding another property to the *SQLException* class to provide more information from a specific data access layer like the one created in Chapter 4. We could add a property named *DataMethod* that returns the name of the specific method that caused the exception.

Defining a Custom Base Class for Exceptions

Upon closer inspection, it appears that some useful properties might not be present in *System.ApplicationException*. For example, there is no provision for capturing environmental information such as the date and time the exception occurred, the name of the machine on which the exception occurred, and the process ID and/or thread ID. This information might be useful in an application in which an exception occurs. So let's define a custom base class for application exceptions.

The starting point for a base exception class is its name. The name of the example base class is *VBPOBaseException*. Note that this follows the exception class naming guideline mentioned earlier. The base exception class will inherit *System.ApplicationException*, which conforms to the guidelines as well. Finally, the class will be marked as *MustInherit*. This prevents any object from being created from this class. Instead, the application will define exception classes that inherit *VBPOBaseException*. The child classes will be used to create an application-specific exception when the application code must throw an exception. The following code shows the declaration of the *VBPO-BaseException* class.

```
Public MustInherit Class VBPOBaseException
    Inherits System.ApplicationException

    Public Sub New()
        MyBase.New()
    End Sub

    Public Sub New(ByVal message As String)
        MyBase.New(message)
    End Sub

    Public Sub New(ByVal message As String, _
        ByVal innerException As System.Exception)
        MyBase.New(message, innerException)
    End Sub

End Class
```

The Base Exception Class Constructors

The constructors for any class are always procedures named *New*. All the exception classes implement four versions of the *New* constructor. In the previous example, the three standard *Public* constructors of an exception class are shown. We'll address three of these constructors now. The fourth constructor handles serialization, which we'll cover later in the section "Exception-Handling Objects and Remoting."

The first constructor in the example is the default constructor *New()*. It takes no arguments. *VBPOBaseException* implements the default constructor by simply calling the corresponding constructor for the *System.ApplicationException* class. It does this using the *MyBase* keyword. *MyBase* always refers to the

direct base class that is inherited by the class in which it is used. The following
example shows how the class might be used.

```
Class DBOpenException
    Inherits VBPOBaseException
     Public Sub New()
        MyBase.New()
    End Sub
End Class

Sub DBOpen()
    Try
        Dim connection as new SQLClient.SQLConnection(ConnStr)
        connection.Open()
    Catch exception as System.Exception
        Throw New DBOpenException()
    End Try
End Sub
```

Admittedly, this is not a real-world scenario. However, it does demonstrate the
inheritance of *VBPOBaseException* and the creation of an exception using the
new exception class, *DBOpenException*, by using the default constructor.

The next constructor for *VBPOBaseException* is *New(message)*. This constructor takes a string that becomes the value of the *Message* property of the
exception object. It is implemented and used the same way as the default *New()*
constructor except for passing the message string as a parameter. The following
example shows the use of the *New(message)* constructor:

```
Class DBOpenException
    Inherits VBPOBaseException
    ' Skip the default constructor.
    ⋮
    Public Sub New(ByVal message As String)
        MyBase.New(message)
    End Sub
End Class

Sub DBOpen()
    Try
        Dim connection as new SQLClient.SQLConnection(ConnStr)
        connection.Open()
    Catch exception as System.Exception
        Throw New DBOpenException("Unable to open database")
    End Try
End Sub
```

The last constructor in *VBPOBaseException* is the *New(message, inner-Exception)* constructor. The *message* parameter is the same as the parameter in the *New(message)* constructor. The *innerException* parameter is an exception of type *System.Exception* that will become the *InnerException* property of the new exception. The *InnerException* property is used to keep up with the original exception that caused the current exception. Every exception has an *Inner-Exception* property, so it's possible to drill down into a stack of exceptions to get to the base exception that started the whole mess. Well, you could do that, but it would probably be easier just to use the *BaseException* property of the outer exception and let it do all the work.

```
Class DBOpenException
    Inherits VBPOBaseException
    ' Skip the default constructor.
    ⋮
    ' Skip the message constructor.
    ⋮
    Public Sub New(ByVal message As String, _
        ByVal innerException as System.Exception)
        MyBase.New(message,innerException)
    End Sub
End Class

Sub DBOpen()
    Try
        connection = new SQLClient.SQLConnection(ConnStr)
        connection.Open()
    Catch exception as System.Exception
        Throw New DBOpenException( _
            "Unable to open database", _
            exception)
    End Try
End Sub
```

This example demonstrates the use of the *New(message, innerException)* constructor. Notice that the exception being handled—the one defined in the *Catch* clause—is passed as the *innerException* parameter. If the calling routine examined the *InnerException* property of the *DBOpenException* object being thrown, it would find the exception object that was thrown by ADO.NET. This might be an exception of type *SQLException, InvalidOperationException,* or some other exception type.

Adding Custom Properties to the Base Exception Class

After creating the constructors for the base exception class, the next task is to consider what custom properties might make sense for the base exception class. We'll focus our discussion on environmental information that can be extracted from the .NET Framework class library without a lot of work. That isn't to say that the information produced is insignificant—quite the contrary. In fact, it's somewhat surprising that Microsoft didn't include this kind of information in the *System.Exception* class so that the information would be included in all exceptions.

```
Private m_appDomainName As String = _
    System.AppDomain.CurrentDomain.FriendlyName
Public ReadOnly Property AppDomainName() As String
    Get
        Return m_appDomainName
    End Get
End Property
```

The application domain name will default to the name of the assembly file that started the application, for example, demo.exe. As you can see in the example, the *Property* is created as *ReadOnly*. This is because the value of the property is retrieved from the Framework class library in the initialization of *m_appDomainName*, the *Private* module-level variable that holds the property's value.

Table 3-1 shows the custom properties of *VBPOBaseException*.

Table 3-1 Custom Properties of *VBPOBaseException*

Name	Description	Source
AppDomainName	The name of the application domain for the process, usually the .exe filename.	*System.AppDomain*
AssemblyName	The name of the assembly containing the code that created the exception	*System.Reflection*
AssemblyVersion	The major and minor versions of the assembly as a string	*System.Reflection*
MachineName	The name of the machine that was running the code that created the exception	*System.Environment*
ThreadId	The thread ID of the thread that was running when the exception was created	*System.AppDomain*
ThreadUser	The name of the user who started the thread identified by *ThreadId*	*System.Threading*
TimeStamp	The date and time the exception was created	*System.DateAndTime*

The remaining properties are all handled in a similar manner, the basic difference being the name and/or type of the property and the .NET Framework property or method that is used to initialize the property. Consequently, the code for the remainder of the properties, shown here, provides a basic description of each of the properties in *VBPOBaseException*.

```
Private m_assemblyName As String = _
    System.Reflection.Assembly.GetCallingAssembly.GetName.Name
Public ReadOnly Property AssemblyName() As String
    Get
        Return m_assemblyName
    End Get
End Property

Private m_assemblyVersion As String = _
    System.Reflection.Assembly.GetCallingAssembly.GetName. _
    Version.ToString
Public ReadOnly Property AssemblyVersion() As String
    Get
        Return m_assemblyVersion
    End Get
End Property

Private m_machineName As String = _
    System.Environment.MachineName
Public ReadOnly Property MachineName() As String
    Get
        Return m_machineName
    End Get
End Property

Private m_threadId As Long = _
    System.AppDomain.GetCurrentThreadId
Public ReadOnly Property ThreadId() As Long
    Get
        Return m_threadId
    End Get
End Property

Private m_threadUser As String = _
    System.Threading.Thread.CurrentPrincipal.Identity.Name
Public ReadOnly Property ThreadUser() As String
    Get
        Return m_threadUser
    End Get
End Property
```

(continued)

```
Private m_timeStamp As DateTime = _
    New System.DateTime(System.DateTime.Now.Ticks)
Public ReadOnly Property TimeStamp() As System.DateTime
    Get
        Return m_timeStamp
    End Get
End Property
```

With the custom properties defined for *VBPOBaseException*, there is one more thing left to do. All the information contained in custom properties is useful information. However, it would be nice if we could add it all to the *Message* property so that whenever the *Message* property value is displayed, printed, or logged, all those wonderful custom property values would be included. Well, guess what? There is a very simple way to do this—override the *Message* property. The following code example shows one way of overriding the *Message* property for *VBPOBaseException*.

```
Public Overrides ReadOnly Property Message() As String
    Get
        Return MyBase.Message & _
            "(Application Domain Name: " & _
            Me.AppDomainName & _
            "; Assembly Name: " & _
            Me.AssemblyName & _
            "; Assembly Version: " & _
            Me.AssemblyVersion & _
            "; Machine Name: " & _
            Me.MachineName & _
            "; Thread Id: " & _
            Me.ThreadId.ToString & _
            "; Thread User: " & _
            Me.ThreadUser & _
            "; Time Stamp: " & _
            Me.TimeStamp & _
            ")"
    End Get
End Property
```

At this point, *VBPOBaseException* is a fairly reasonable base class for our exception-handling objects. It handles all the standard constructors, adds some very useful properties containing information about the run-time environment, and overrides the *Message* property—not bad for a day's work. That must mean that it's time to move on, right? Well, not so quickly. We still need to deal with several other issues to prepare our exception-handling module for the harsh world of production applications.

Event Logging

One of the hallmarks of world-class applications is the use of an event log to record exceptional events in the life of the application. Since this book endeavors to be practical in its application, it makes sense to add event logging capabilities to the *VBPOBaseException* class.

Thankfully, the .NET Framework provides classes for the Windows event logs. These classes make it easy to open and write to any event log, on either the local machine or a remote machine. These classes are in the *System.Diagnostics* namespace. Specifically, the *EventLog* class provides the functionality that we need. However, before diving into the code, we need to consider a couple of things.

First of all, where should the exception object log an event? For ease of illustration, the example will use the default application log. It's possible to create a custom application log, but that is outside the scope of this discussion. Next, when should the exception object record an event in the log? In this example, that decision will be left up to the exception handler. A method will be added to *VBPOBaseException* that will cause it to write to the event log. Finally, what should the exception object write to the event log? This will be the combination of the *Message* and *Stacktrace* properties. The example will also add a *Boolean* property, *IsHandled*, that defaults to *False* but can be set to *True* by the application code. This will slightly affect the contents of the message written to the event log. So, without further ado, here is the example. We have eliminated code that would be repeated from previous examples.

```
' Skip some up-front stuff.
⋮
Public MustInherit Class VBPOBaseException
    Inherits ApplicationException
    ' Skip most of the property variables, except…
    ⋮
    Private m_isHandled As Boolean = False
      ' Skip the constructors.
    ⋮
      ' Skip most of the properties, except IsHandled.
    ⋮
    Public Property IsHandled() As Boolean
        Get
            Return m_isHandled
        End Get
        Set(ByVal Value As Boolean)
            m_isHandled = Value
        End Set
    End Property
```

(continued)

```
        ' Skip most of the methods, except WriteLog.
  ⋮
    Public Overloads Sub WriteLog()
        WriteLog (EventLogEntryType.Information)
    End Sub
    Public Overloads Sub WriteLog( _
        ByVal eventType as EventLogEntryType)
        Dim msgText As New System.Text.StringBuilder()
        ' Open Application.
        msgText.Append(Me.Message)
        msgText.Append(ControlChars.CrLf)
        msgText.Append(Me.StackTrace)
        Dim ApplicationEventLog As _
            New EventLog("Application", ".", Me.AppDomainName)
        ApplicationEventLog.WriteEntry( _
            msgText.ToString,eventType)
        ApplicationEventLog.Dispose()
        ApplicationEventLog = Nothing
        msgText = Nothing
    End Sub
End Class
```

Several things in this example are noteworthy. There is a new property, *IsHandled*, that can be set by the calling application code. If *IsHandled* is *False* (the default), it's assumed the exception hasn't been handled. If the application sets this property to *True*, it's assumed the exception has been handled. In either case, this fact is included in the *Message* property of the exception object.

The *WriteLog(eventType)* method is the key to the event logging in the exception object. This method creates a reference to the application event log on the local machine (".") using *System.Diagnostics.EventLog*. The *AppDomain-Name* property, which contains the name of the process executable, is used as the source for the event. The method takes as a parameter a member of *Event-LogEntryType*, which can be *Information*, *Warning*, *Error*, *FailureAudit*, or *SuccessAudit*. The method then combines the *Message* and *StackTrace* properties from the exception object and writes them to the event log. Notice the call to the *Dispose* method of the *ApplicationEventLog* object. This is important to ensure that the resources associated with the object are released immediately.

Note that *WriteLog* is overloaded. There are two different implementations of *WriteLog* with different arguments. One version takes no arguments; the other takes an *EventLogEntryType* argument. The version that takes no argument calls the other version and passes it *EventLogEntryType.Information* as a default value. We could have used an *Optional* argument, but the coding of the method would have been a bit more obtuse. Overloading is very clear—each version of the method stands on its own.

```
Try
    example.Dispose()
    MessageBox.Show("Database closed connection!", _
        "Example")
Catch exc As ex.CloseDBException
    MessageBox.Show( _
        "Unable to open database." & ControlChars.CrLf & _
        "Message = " & exc.Message & ControlChars.CrLf & _
        "Stacktrace = " & exc.StackTrace)
    exc.IsHandled = True
    exc.WriteLog(EventLogEntryType.Error)
End Try
```

This example shows the use of the *IsHandled* property and the *WriteLog* method. After executing this code, check the event log. The results should look something like Figure 3-3. If the *IsHandled* property is *False*, the results will look like this:

```
Error! Reference source not found.
```

Figure 3-3   Event log event for a handled *VBPOBaseException* descendant

One last note on event logging: writing to the event log might not be a strong enough measure for some applications. In some cases, it might be necessary to notify operations or support personnel of the exception so that it can be remedied quickly. The subject of real-time notification is beyond the scope of this discussion. However, this is an issue that often requires some serious attention in the application and technical architectures of a system.

Exception-Handling Objects and Remoting

We need to address one final issue for *VBPOBaseException*. We need to add a bit of code to the class that supports our exception classes in a remote environment. It might seem like overkill to do this, but the process is straightforward and will prepare *VBPOBaseException*—and all of its descendants—for eventual use in a remote environment, even though that might not be a requirement at the moment. This is part of making our exception-handling objects bullet-proof.

To support remote exceptions in .NET, it's necessary to enable any exception classes for serialization. This process has three steps. First, the class must implement the *ISerializable* interface. In fact, this has already been done because *System.Exception* implements this interface. However, the code for *VBPOBaseException* does need to add the *<Serializable()>* attribute to the class definition. This is demonstrated in the following code:

```
<Serializable()> Public MustInherit Class VBPOBaseException
    ⋮
```

Second, *VBPOBaseException* must override a method from the *ISerializable* interface, *GetObjectData(serializationInfo, streamingContext)*. This method is used when the exception is serialized (deconstructed) on the server in preparation for sending to the client. In this method, any custom properties that have been added to the exception class should be saved in the serialization information. This is done with methods on the *serializationInfo* object that encode the data for serialization.

```
Imports System.Runtime.Serialization
Public Overrides Sub GetObjectData( _
    ByVal info As SerializationInfo, _
    ByVal context As StreamingContext)
    Dim MyName as String = Me.GetType.Name
    MyBase.GetObjectData(info, context)
    With info
        .AddValue(MyName & ".AppDomainName", _
            m_appDomainName, m_appDomainName.GetType)
        .AddValue(MyName & ".AssemblyName", _
            m_assemblyName, m_assemblyName.GetType)
        .AddValue(MyName & ".AssemblyVersion", _
            m_assemblyVersion, m_assemblyVersion.GetType)
        .AddValue(MyName & ".MachineName", _
            m_machineName, m_machineName.GetType)
        .AddValue(MyName & ".ThreadId", _
            m_threadId, m_threadId.GetType)
        .AddValue(MyName & ".ThreadUser", _
            m_threadUser, m_threadUser.GetType)
```

```
        .AddValue(MyName & ".TimeStamp", _
            m_timeStamp, m_timeStamp.GetType)
    End With
End Sub
```

This example shows one possible implementation of the method *VBPO-BaseException.GetObjectData*. Note the use of the *info.AddValue* method to individually add the custom properties to the serialization information. This is all that it takes to persist our custom properties in a serialized object. Note that it isn't necessary to add every custom property if the property can be reconstructed from other data after the object has been deserialized (reconstructed). In *VBPOBaseException*, every custom property has a value that would be lost if we didn't persist it. So, we have the value of each of the custom properties in the serialization information.

Third and last, *VBPOBaseException* must implement a new constructor to support serialization, *New(serializationInfo, streamingContext)*.

```
Imports System.Runtime.Serialization
' Constructor for Serialization
Protected Sub New( _
    ByVal info As SerializationInfo, _
    ByVal context As StreamingContext)
    MyBase.New(info, context)
    m_appDomainName = _
        info.GetString(Me.GetType.Name & ".AppDomainName")
    m_assemblyName = _
        info.GetString(Me.GetType.Name & ".AssemblyName")
    m_assemblyVersion = _
        info.GetString(Me.GetType.Name & ".AssemblyVersion")
    m_machineName = _
        info.GetString(Me.GetType.Name & ".MachineName")
    m_threadId = info.GetInt64(Me.GetType.Name & ".ThreadId")
    m_threadUser = _
        info.GetString(Me.GetType.Name & ".ThreadUser")
    m_timeStamp = _
        info.GetDateTime(Me.GetType.Name & ".TimeStamp")
End Sub
```

This constructor is used when the exception is deserialized at the client. Before doing anything else, it calls the serialization constructor on the base class—in this case, *System.ApplicationException*. Note that the constructor in this case is not *Public* but *Protected*. This prevents calls to this constructor except by classes that inherit *VBPOBaseException* and the serialization support in the CLR. This is important because exception classes have very strict rules concerning their creation and use. Serialization and deserialization of exception objects should almost always take place at the request of the CLR. However, when a child class is being instantiated through serialization, it's important that each exception class call the serialization constructor for its base class to ensure that the base class or base classes are properly initialized.

All of this might seem like a lot of work, but as we said earlier, the process is relatively straightforward. The CLR handles most of the work of serialization (and deserialization) on behalf of the exception class. The only requirements are that the class be attributed as *<Serializable()>*, implement *ISerializable*, override the *GetObjectData* method, and implement *New(info, context)*. *System.ApplicationException*, which is inherited by *VBPOBaseException*, implements *ISerializable*, satisfying that requirement.

In the final analysis, this seems a small price to pay to ensure that the exception-handling classes are prepared to function in a remote environment without any further work. This gives a great deal of freedom to the application implementation team to change the application architecture to support key business objectives without having to wait for changes to infrastructure components such as exception-handling classes.

Creating an Application Exception Class Hierarchy

Now that *VBPOBaseException* is complete, what next? This class was marked *MustInherit*, meaning that no exception object can ever be directly created using it. Well, the idea is to create specific exception classes for the application that inherit *VBPOBaseException*. This is fairly simple thanks to all the work we did on *VBPOBaseException*. Most of the application-specific exception-handling classes that will inherit from it will need to add little or no functionality.

Take a look at our last example. This piece of code creates a new exception-handling class named *UserLogonException*. It inherits *VBPOBaseException*, which gives the class most of its functionality. Note that it's necessary to implement four constructors corresponding to the constructors that were implemented in *VBPOBaseException*. In each case, the constructor has to do nothing more than invoke the corresponding constructor of the parent class by using the *MyBase* keyword.

```
<Serializable()> Public Class UserLogonException
    Inherits VBPOBaseException
    ' Default Constructor
    Public Sub New()
        MyBase.New()
    End Sub
    ' Constructor to set Message property
    Public Sub New(ByVal message As String)
        MyBase.New(message)
```

```
        End Sub
        ' Constructor to set Message and InnerException properties
        Public Sub New(ByVal message As String, _
            ByVal innerException As Exception)
            MyBase.New(message, innerException)
        End Sub
        ' Constructor for Serialization
        Protected Sub New(ByVal info As SerializationInfo, _
            ByVal context As StreamingContext)
            MyBase.New(info, context)
        End Sub
End Class
```

If needed, this class could now be extended, adding more custom properties and serialization support for those properties and possibly adding new methods to the exception-handling class. As with any class hierarchy in an object-oriented language, the possibilities are almost endless. The key is to implement the truly useful and leave the rest alone.

Conclusion

In this chapter, you've seen how to construct and use custom exception-handling classes in an application. The solutions comply with Microsoft's guidelines for building custom exception-handling classes: inheritance schemes, naming conventions, custom properties, and the use of serialization. The solutions also address event logging for exception-handling classes and the construction of an application-specific hierarchy for custom exception-handling classes.

In the next chapter we'll take a close look at the advantages ADO.NET offers applications. Then, we'll build a Data Access component that encapsulates most of the major functions necessary for data access. Exception handling and event logging, as we demonstrated in this chapter, are an integral part of this component.

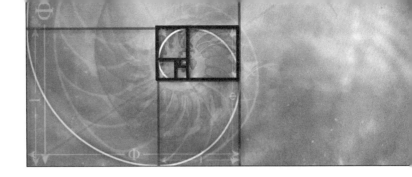

4

Implementing the Data Access Layer

Most of the applications we've written so far have had one underlying similarity—the requirement to access data and work with it. In the past, whenever we worked with different platforms, we took the time and made the effort to write a data access component, which in turn provided a data access layer. We're going to do the same throughout this chapter using Microsoft ADO.NET and Microsoft Visual Basic .NET. The biggest difference is that the Microsoft .NET Framework with Microsoft ADO.NET makes our task much easier, both in writing and then implementing the data access component. By the end of this chapter, we'll have a generic data access component that we can plug into any .NET application and use immediately. You'll not only understand how the component works but also be able to add functionality with ease.

When writing a data access component, we learn new data features of ADO.NET, write classes and methods, and continuously test and improve the code. We use performance testing to determine the best way to get things done in a test environment that duplicates large production databases. Once the component is completed, we push it into production and monitor its performance, scalability, availability, and error trapping. What we're presenting in this chapter has followed these steps. For each function, we'll explain what we did and why.

First, we'll look at ADO.NET and what it offers. We'll concentrate on the features that increase performance while allowing scalability. Then we'll design and write the data access component piece by piece. With each additional feature we'll look only at the differences between it and the features we've already discussed.

After completing our data access component, we'll discuss how to handle transactions and data concurrency, and how to use OLE DB–compliant code to access other databases such as Microsoft Access and Oracle.

After we complete the object and show you a simple two-tier example, you'll have a component that is ready to be used in *n*-tier environments. This approach fits within the architecture we discussed in Chapter 2. Finally, we'll summarize the features of our data access component so that you can easily reference it while you're applying it in your own applications. With all this in mind, let's get going.

The Power of ADO.NET

Data access has evolved over the years, and the result of this process is ADO.NET. We're very impressed with it and find it to be almost perfect as a standards-based programming model that allows us to create distributed, scalable, data-sharing applications. In the next few sections, we'll discuss the benefits of ADO.NET.

Performance

We found that ADO.NET, especially when using the Microsoft SQL Server .NET managed provider, improves data access and manipulation tremendously. This provider is tightly coupled with SQL Server by using the Tabular Data Stream (TDS), which is SQL Server's native communications protocol. Directly accessing and manipulating data can show improvements of over 50 percent compared with the other data providers and more again compared with previous ADO versions. What excites us even beyond this is the performance improvement we found while passing data through layers. We have long since switched to *n*-tier architectures, which created the need to pass data from layer to layer. Here is where ADO.NET really shines—no more costly performance hits from COM marshalling and value type conversions! Simply passing Extensible Markup Language (XML) from layer to layer has made processing overhead dwindle and performance more than double.

Scalability

With the advent of ever-growing Web sites and potentially thousands of concurrent users, we simply can't ignore scalability. The single most important reason for ADO.NET's scalability is its inherent way of handling disconnected data. In simple terms, we adhere to the *3Gs*—get in, get it (or get it done), and then get out, as fast as possible. This frees up valuable resources on the servers, such as database connections and record locks, so that the servers can handle more client requests. The *DataSet*, as we'll see shortly, fits this model of processing data. But, and this is a big but, you can still violate the principles of scalability by using some of ADO.NET's features incorrectly. This happens especially with the *DataReader* object since it needs to keep its connection open until it's done processing data.

Regarding performance and scalability, we need to understand that we can't have the best performance and best scalability at the same time; we must find an acceptable balance. For example, the best performance can be achieved through using the *DataReader*. It's wickedly fast, but since the connection has to stay open, it doesn't scale well. We need to learn which data object to use when and where.

XML Equals Interoperability

Since ADO.NET uses XML as its transportation protocol, any component or client that can handle XML can use ADO.NET components. This is a big step from applications that use proprietary data protocols and can work only with components written in the same language or communicating through COM.

Ease of Use

Though we'll increase the ease-of-use features of ADO.NET further with our data access component, ADO.NET offers a more intuitive way to work with data. One such way is the opportunity to use strongly typed data with code like

```
LastName = myDataSet.Tables("Employee").Columns("LastName").Value
```

so that it becomes

```
LastName = Employee.LastName
```

Components of ADO.NET

Figure 4-1 shows you the most important feature in ADO.NET—the separation of data access from data manipulation. The *DataSet* is designed specifically to be totally independent of the data source and any data source it can handle. The purpose of the *DataAdapter* is to be a bridge between the actual data and the *DataSet*. More on this later.

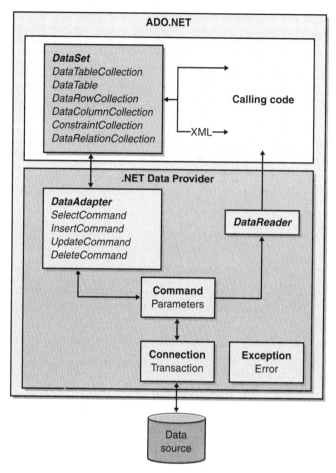

Figure 4-1   A birds-eye view of ADO.NET

Table 4-1 shows you an overview of the most important objects in ADO.NET. The *Connection, Command, DataAdapter,* and *DataReader* objects together are called the .NET data provider. There are currently a SQL Server .NET Data Provider and an OLE DB .NET Data Provider. Each contains all four objects and works similarly. They are designed to be lightweight in order to create a minimal layer between the data source and the dataset calling code. The SQL Server .NET Data Provider is fully optimized to work with Microsoft SQL Server 7 and Microsoft SQL Server 2000, whereas the OLE DB .NET Data Provider works with generic data sources. As soon as we look at the *Connection, Command,* and *DataReader* objects, we can start with our chapter examples. We use both the SQL Server and Access Northwind example databases.

We've added a few stored procedures that you can add either manually or as directed in the installation instructions in the readme.txt file. Let's look at the *Connection* object.

Table 4-1   The .NET Data Provider Objects

Object	Description
Connection	Connects to data source and has transaction capabilities
Command	Enables access to database commands to handle the following: return data, modify data, run stored procedures, and send and receive parameters
DataReader	High-performance, one-record-at-a-time data stream
DataAdapter	Bridge between data source and *DataSet*
DataSet	Disconnected, in-memory representation of data source, which contains tables as *DataTable* collections and relations as *Relations* collections

Connection Object

The simplest object we deal with is the *Connection* object. The only parameter it needs is the connection string. Here's an example. (The boldface line shows the object in action.)

```
Dim ConnectionString as String
Dim ConnectionObject as SQLConnection
ConnectionString = "data source=local; initial catalog=Northwind; " & _
    "password=  ;id="
ConnectionObject = New SQLConnection(ConnectionString)
```

In addition to using the *Connection* object as the connection to the data source, we can use it for transactions. We use SQL Server's transaction capabilities predominantly within our stored procedure, but it's good to know that we have other options. Transactions are implemented in ADO.NET by declaring a variable to hold the *Transaction* object. After we open the connection, we use the *BeginTransaction* method from the *Transaction* object. Here is the code up to this point:

```
'Declare a variable with the SQLTransaction object.
Dim TransactionObject as SQLTransaction
'Open connection.
ConnectionObject.Open()
'Start transaction-based connection.
TransactionObject = ConnectionObject.BeginTransaction
```

The next step is to define the *Command* object. (We'll discuss this object in more detail in the next section.) We enroll the *Command* object into our current transaction:

```
CommandObject = New SQLCommand(SelectStatement, ConnectionObject)
'Attach command to transaction.
CommandObject.Transaction = TransactionObject
```

Whatever data activity we handle after enrolling the *Command* object is now included in the transaction. We have the choice of either committing the changes or rolling them back. Here are both cases in code:

```
'If we commit
TransactionObject.Commit()
ConnectionObject.Close()


'If we do not want to commit
TransactionObject.Rollback()
ConnectionObject.Close()
```

After either action, we close the connection and our transaction is finished.

Command Object

You can create the *Command* object by using the *Command* constructor or the *CreateCommand* method in the *Connection* object. To generate cleaner code, we'll use the *Command* constructor. Let's enhance the previous example and include the *Command* object:

```
Dim ConnectionString as String
Dim ConnectionObject as SQLConnection
Dim CommandObject as SQLCommand
Dim SelectStatement as String
ConnectionString = "data source=local; initial catalog=Northwind; " & _
    "password=  ;id="
SelectStatement = "Select LastName, FirstName From Employees"
ConnectionObject = New SQLConnection(ConnectionString)
CommandObject = New SQLCommand(SelectStatement, ConnectionObject)
```

The boldface line shows us the *Command* object's properties we used: the SQL string to access the database and the *Connection* object we created previously. That's all there is to it—at least for the simple use of an SQL string and calling data.

Let's look at the first example included in this chapter's code samples. After you have followed the installation instructions in the readme.txt file, open the Chapter4DAL Project. You can open the code for this example in the SQL-toDataReader.aspx file in the DirectAccess folder or run the project and click the following link: "1. SQL Statement returning a DataReader." In this example, we use the *DataReader* object to get the data into a grid control. When you run this example, make sure to change the connection string with your login name and password. We also left out exception handling in the first couple of examples to make the code easier to read. (Don't worry. We'll have examples with exception handling soon.)

The SQL strings we use with the *Command* object can include parameters passed within the string or parameters that can be created from the *Command* object. This string can also include insert and update commands as well as commands that return no data at all. In general, we refrain from this approach since we prefer using stored procedures to work with our data.

More important to us is the ability of the *Command* object to accept stored procedures and execute them with or without parameters. To use the *Command* object to process stored procedrues, we have to set the *Command* object's property named *CommandType* to *CommandType.StoredProcedure*. Its default is *CommandType.Text*, with *CommandType.StoredProcedure* and *CommandType.TableDirect* as options. We don't use the *TableDirect* option very often since it returns the whole table. With *CommandType* set to *StoredProcedure*, the string we pass to the *Command* object includes the name of the stored procedure. Our second example, accessed through the link "2. Stored-Procedure without parameters returning a DataReader," is contained in SPtoDataReader.aspx, which is located in the DirectAccess folder. We've included the SQL script and instructions in readme.txt to create the stored procedures in the Northwind database. If you want to add them manually, here is the code for the first stored procedure we use:

```
CREATE PROCEDURE dbo.spGetEmployees
AS
Select LastName, FirstName, title, Birthdate, HireDate
From Employees
```

Here are the two lines to call the stored procedure without parameters:

```
Dim StoredProcedureName as String
StoredProcedureName = spGetEmployees
CommandObject = New SQLCommand(StoredProcedureName, ConnectionObject)
CommandObject.CommandType = CommandType.StoredProcedure
```

Most of the time, when we run a stored procedure, parameters need to be passed in or out of the procedure. Many stored procedures do not return any data tables, just parameters or a return value. The *Command* object supports this with the *Parameters* collection.

Example 3, accessed by clicking the link "Stored Procedure with a parameter returning a DataReader," which is contained in the SPParamstoData-Reader.aspx file in the DirectAccess folder, shows the use of the *Command* object when defining and adding a parameter to run the stored procedure. First, here is the stored procedure:

```
CREATE PROCEDURE dbo.spEmployeesbyCity
    (
    @City nVarChar(15) = "%",
    @Name nVarChar(20) = "%"
    )
AS
    Select LastName, FirstName, City
    From Employees
    Where City like @City and LastName like @Name
```

Here are the lines of code that define the parameters:

```
ParameterObject = CommandObject.Parameters.Add("@City", _
    SqlDbType.NVarChar, 15)
ParameterObject.Direction = ParameterDirection.Input
ParameterObject.Value = "London"
```

The first step for adding a parameter is to use the *Command-Object.Parameters.Add* method. This method has several parameters, including the name of the stored procedure's parameter, its data type, and its size. Its direction indicates whether this is an input or output parameter. The preceding code shows that we assign *@City* as the stored procedure's parameter name, with a data type of *SqlDbType.NvarChar* and a size of 15. It's also defined as an input parameter. Last but not least, we add the value to the parameter. When the *Command* object gets executed, the parameters will be passed or returned automatically. Table 4-2 lists the methods that you can call in the *Command* object.

Table 4-2 The *Command* Object Methods

Method	Description
ExecuteReader	This executes the *DataReader*. (This is our approach so far, but we'll offer more detail later.)
ExecuteNonQuery	An SQL statement gets executed that does not return any records. (This is good to use with stored procedures that return only parameters or nothing at all.)
ExecuteScalar	An SQL statement gets executed and returns the first row only.
ExecuteXMLReader	An SQL statement is executed and returns an XML stream.

DataReader Object

When we need performance more than scalability or when we need to work with a large result set, the *DataReader* object is the way to go. We've heard it called a *fire hose* since it's a read-only, forward-only stream of data from a database. It increases the application's performance and reduces the system requirements by having only one record at a time in memory. But it needs to have an open database connection, which limits our scalability and increases network traffic. Requiring an open connection also limits the use of the *DataReader* for *n*-tier architectures when we need to separate the layers physically. On the same system, we could pass the *DataReader* by reference; remoting is out of the question, however. Both examples we've shown so far use the *DataReader* and bind it to a *DataGrid*. Here are the specific lines of code:

```
ConnectionObject.Open
DataReaderObject = _
    CommandObject.ExecuteReader(CommandBehavior.CloseConnection)
```

When we use the *DataReader*, the connection needs to be opened before we execute it and after we iterate through it, but do not—and we repeat, *do not*—forget to close it. Open connections consume precious system resources and limit scalability. To help avoid open connections, the *ExecuteReader* method has a property option that tells the *Command* object to close the database connection automatically when the *DataReader.Close* method is called. (But the close method still needs to be called! See the second example for code implementation.) Here's one more thing about closing the *DataReader*: when you run a stored procedure that returns parameters only, the *DataReader* needs to be closed first. If this isn't done, you won't have access to the parameters returned.

When we bind the *DataReader* to the *DataGrid*, the *DataGrid* does a major job for us automatically. Normally we would have to iterate through the results one record at a time, but the *DataGrid* takes care of this for us.

DataAdapter Object

Looking back at Figure 4-1, we can see that so far we've taken the route on the right side of the diagram to get data to the calling code. As we discovered, this is the fire-and-forget-it way and is a one-way trip only. It doesn't allow data to be processed in return (other than passing parameters to a stored procedure that would use them for updating, inserting, or deleting data). We have also not yet worked in a disconnected fashion. This is where the *DataAdapter* comes in. The left side of Figure 4-1 depicts the process for handling disconnected data. The *DataAdapter* is our bridge from the actual data to the disconnected *DataSet*. This bridge is a two-way street. The *DataAdapter* fills the *DataSets* with data it passes along from the data source; actually, it passes the data it receives through the *Connection* and *Command* objects. On the way back to the data source, the *DataAdapter* can resolve changes made in the *DataSet*. Between these two processes the *DataSet* is totally disconnected from the actual data. But we'll talk more about that later.

When we instantiate the *DataAdapter*, we must pass it the *SelectCommand* property, which is the *Command* object. In the same way the *Command* object was used earlier to get data to the *DataReader*, the *Command* object retrieves the data from the data source. The actual passing of the data (like a baton passed in a relay race) happens when the *Fill* method of the *DataAdapter* is called. This is when the result fills the *DataSet*. You can see the workings of this in Example 4, the "SQL Statement returning a DataSet" link, which is implemented in the SQLtoDataSet.aspx file located in the DirectAccess folder.

```
DataAdapterObject = New SqlDataAdapter(CommandObject)
DataAdapterObject.Fill(DataSetObject, "Employees")
```

When calling the *Fill* method, we populate the *DataSet* object with a new table named Employees and the data returned from the *Command* object. The *DataAdapter* handles the creation and destruction of the connection and command objects, so there is nothing for us to do. We could explicitly create these and reuse them, but that would not fit our preferences, which you'll recall are the 3 Gs (get in, get it, get out).

If we don't name the table when using the *Fill* method, a default name will be assigned to it. We can access the table through the table collections index property as follows:

```
DataGridEmployees.DataSource = DataSetObject.Tables(0)
```

Since naming the table is supported and makes our code easier to read and debug, we prefer to give each table a name as shown in the third example. When you examine the code section of this example, you will also find that we changed the way we access the *Connection* string. Instead of having to remember its syntax or copying it back and forth, we've opted to use the *ConfigurationSettings* in the *Web.config* file. You simply add the *appSettings* element within *Web.config*, which is nothing but an XML file, and within the *appSettings* element, you create an *<add key =... entry*, as shown here:

```
<appSettings>
    <add key="Northwind" value="data source=localhost..." />
</appSettings>
```

The calling code looks like this:

```
ConnectionString = ConfigurationSettings.AppSettings("Northwind")
```

This also helps us manage all connections used within the Web application. When using Visual Basic .NET, we can create a similar file and call its content. If we feel that security is a larger issue (because although the *Web.config* file is protected from access through the Web, it's not protected from internal network access), we can create a *ConnectionStringObject* that looks at an encrypted connection string file stored on the system and pass the connection string through that object. For our examples and most applications, the web.config approach above will suffice.

In addition to the *Fill* method, the *DataAdapter* has *FillSchema* and *Update* methods. Whereas the *Fill* method creates a table and fills it with the result of the *Command* object, the *FillSchema* method just creates the empty shell of the table inside the *DataSet*. The *Update* method does exactly what it says: updates the actual data source with the changes passed from the *DataSet*.

In addition to the *SelectCommand* property mentioned earlier, the *DataAdapter* has three more properties that manage updates to the data source: *InsertCommand*, *UpdateCommand*, and *DeleteCommand*. We prefer to do updates to a SQL server database through stored procedures, but it's good to know that these options exist and that they're easily accessible in the ADO.NET *DataAdapter*.

DataSet Object

The *DataSet* object is the crown jewel of ADO.NET objects because it allows the disconnected data model we need for increased scalability and has the ability to easily pass data between tiers. In other words, the *DataSet* is stateless. That it uses XML for data transportation adds even more to its value. There is one warning, however, that we want you to be aware of and always consider: the *DataSet* is very memory hungry. It's easy to populate it with as much data as we want; however, doing so could be deadly to the memory resources on the server. Imagine 100 users opening a *DataSet* with 10,000 records each. That would mean having 1 million records in memory. Now increase that number to 1,000 users, and you have a real problem. The *DataSet* contains not only the tables and rows but also a lot of metadata, which increases its size even more. Remember our warning: Do not return huge *DataSets*! If a lot of records have to be processed, consider using the *DataReader* instead or use efficient stored procedures that handle large data jobs.

One of the ways to create tables in the *DataSet* object is through the *DataAdapter Fill* method. You've already seen this process in our last example. Examples 4 and 5 in our sample application show more variations of calling stored procedures with or without parameters. Example 4 creates the table in the *DataSet* without a name and shows how to fill the grid with the *DataSet Table* collection's index.

The *DataSet* object contains 0 or more tables. These are represented by the *DataTable* object. The *DataTableCollection* contains all the *DataTables* within the *DataSet*. Once we have a *DataTable*, it's represented by its index of the *DataTable* collection. *DataTables* themselves are represented by the *Data-ColumnCollection* and include the schema of each row in the table (like fields in a database table) and the *DataRowCollection*, which contains the data in the table (like data rows in a database table). Figure 4-2 shows the *DataSet* object and its collections and properties.

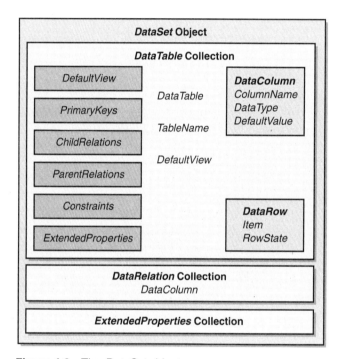

Figure 4-2 The *DataSet* object

The *DataSet* not only holds *DataTables* but can also handle primary keys, parent and child relations, constraints, and views, just like databases and tables in relational database systems. The *DataSet* can be looked upon as an in-memory copy of real tables, their relationships, and data. The only difference is that we want to work only with the data we need for our particular data functions and keep the *DataSet* as small as possible. When a *DataTable* resides in the *DataSet*, it creates a default view of this table. This view simply returns the whole *DataTable* and its data. Once we're in possession of the *DataSet*, we can create and manipulate other views.

Another way to create *DataSet* and *DataTables* is through code. We can actually create both of them programmatically. Web applications can make good use of programmatically created *DataSets* and *DataTables*. We might have a series of data entry pages that require the actual saving of data to take place after the last page is filled. An easy way to pass data from one page to the other—without having to connect and access the database until the entry needs to be saved—is to create a *DataSet* and *DataTable* with the required fields in the first page, passing them from page to page, adding data as you go, until the final page is reached. When the save method is invoked, a *Connection* object, a *Command* object, and a *DataAdapter* can then be declared and the data saved.

There's still more to the *DataSet*. It can create XML and XML Schemas that contain part or all of the *DataTable*s, their schemas, and data. It can also populate itself by reading XML. When data is changed, the *DataSet* tracks the changes and original values and lets you accept or reject the changes. If the changes are accepted, the *DataSet* can create a subset of itself, containing just the changes, and resolve the update through the *DataAdapter*. We don't have room in this chapter to go into all the details of the *DataSet*. As we build the Human Resources HRnet enterprise application in later chapters, you'll see many of the useful features the *DataSet* provides.

The ADO.NET Data Access Object

Now that we've introduced the ADO.NET components, let's put them to work in our own data access object.

Why Have a Data Access Object?

First and foremost, the data access object should make our interaction with data much easier, whether we retrieve, add, or modify it. With just a few lines of code, we should be able to accomplish what in the past could take many times the effort. We can't recall how often we've had to look up specific method syntax when working with data: did it use or not use parameters, use or not use stored procedures, return a dataset or return parameters? We lost time (and with that, money), and the situation worsened when the correct sequence of opening and closing connections got mixed up. And it could get *even worse*. What if we find that we can use a better way or improved solutions? Going back through all the code written and changing it can be a daunting task. Consistency is always a goal while writing applications. It helps us when we need to debug problems. It helps us when we need to test ways to improve performance or scalability. Adding consistency to the way we work with data might be one of the most important features of our application.

What Will the Data Access Object Do?

By writing a component, we're going to solve the problems previously mentioned while making data access a matter of only a few lines of code. And when newer and better ways come along, we simply make the changes within the component and reap the rewards everywhere. (But we're careful not to break previous functionality; otherwise, we'll stop our applications from working faster than a concrete wall stops a super-fast sports car.)

The data access object is also going to give us a consistent way of interacting with data. We'll get consistency not only within the applications but also when accessing data between ASP.NET Web Forms, Windows Forms, business classes, and even XML Web services. This is the case whether we're using Visual Basic .NET, C#, or some other language that runs under the .NET common language runtime (CLR) managed code. We're very excited about this. It might actually be possible, for a change, to remember the code for accessing data and not to have to fight with the minor code differences of the past (minor difference but major pain, I might add).

We're going to write our object specifically to access SQL Server 7 and SQL Server 2000, using the SQL Data Providers of ADO.NET. Our object will be optimized for this platform but easily transformed so that it can be used on others as well. We'll provide an example showing how simple it is to add support for other database platforms. With that said, here is the functionality we're looking for:

- Multiple constructors that are flexible for different requirements

- Simple exception handling with event logging capability

- Return of data in a variety of formats

  - As a *DataSet*

  - As a *DataReader*

  - As XML

  - As a parameter list

  - As a notification about whether a function performed correctly (not to be confused with exception handling)

- Data access from SQL Server with simple SQL statements or with stored procedures, with or without the use of parameters

Our Approach to Database Access and Usage

In general, we have to write either applications that have thousands of potential simultaneous users in the Web environment or custom applications that require very fast response times from ten to hundreds of users on an internal, non-Web-based application. Lately it's become a combination of both. Many of the new-generation applications we're writing are totally Web based and have different levels of access for intranet users, extranet users, or general Web users. The same database is accessed from these different clients simultaneously with a very high potential load. More and more companies are looking to SQL Server as the solution for their database needs. For these reasons, we're concentrating on accessing data either through SQL statements or stored procedures with either SQL Server 7 or SQL Server 2000.

Needing to get the highest possible performance while staying scalable and flexible and having a reasonable amount of security, we generally use stored procedures with SQL Server 7 or SQL Server 2000 exclusively. Whether we have to access data, add data, or modify data, we use stored procedures. We want to take advantage of what SQL Server does best: data access, data manipulation, transactions, and so forth. Now we know that some of you are thinking, "These guys are too inflexible, and think they know it all." This isn't so. We simply use what we've found and tested to be best. Yes, we're still going to build direct SQL string capability into the object. Why? Because we see good reasons for using it from time to time, such as building ad hoc data access in reports. You might even use SQL statements for adding data and updating data, even though we wouldn't encourage you to do so. The choice is yours, and the data access component lets you do either.

Implementing the Data Access Object

Let's take a look at implementing our data access component.

The Data Access Object as a Component

There are several ways we could write the component. We could just create a class or a collection of classes. We could copy these classes into every project we create, or we could move them into the global assembly cache (GAC) so that they are accessible like the .NET Framework classes. We could also write a component, implementing it just like classes, either directly or in the GAC. We chose the latter. Components are just like classes with additional functionality. A component supports a graphical design interface within the Visual Studio .NET integrated development environment (IDE). With this you get drag-and-drop access so that you can add code from the Toolbox or Server Explorer and manipulate properties in the property window. The latter is especially useful when adding performance counters or event logging, or when using message queues.

For those of you who want to build the data access component and test it as we progress through each step, you can add it to the Chapter4DAL solution as a new project and add a new component. You can leave the existing DataAccessLayer project and DataAccessObject component as is since they contain the complete code. To test your in-progress component, you just need to add its namespace and rename the calling code in our existing examples.

Open Visual Studio .NET and the Chapter4DAL solution. Select the DataAccessLayer project in Solution Explorer. Add a component to it, and name it DataTestObject.vb. Your Visual Studio .NET screen should look similar to Figure 4-3.

Figure 4-3   The new DataTestObject component in Visual Studio .NET

The DataTestObject.vb file is opened in the form designer, and it's ready for you to drag-and-drop from Server Explorer (also shown in Figure 4-3), or you can simply double-click to access the code directly. Figure 4-4 shows what this looks like and some code we've already added.

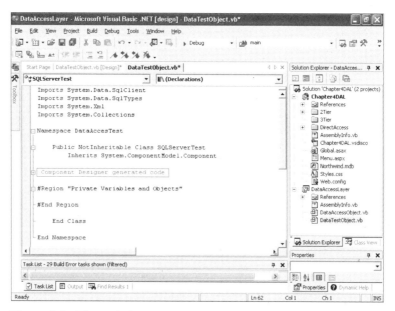

Figure 4-4   The code behind the DataTestObject component

For the moment, ignore the code generated by the Component Designer. You can see that the rest looks like a class with some added code. For our component to work correctly, we need to import several namespaces, namely the *Data.SqlClient*, *Data.SqlTypes*, *XML*, and *Collections* namespaces. We also need to give your component a namespace. Name it *DataAccessTest*. This will ensure you don't confuse it with the data access component, which is contained in the *DataAccess* namespace. To further help us avoid mixing up both components, we also changed the name of the *DataTestObject* class to *SQLServerTest*.

In addition to naming the class, we made it *NotInheritable*. We want users to instantiate this class directly. If we allow it to be inherited, we lose control of what the users can do to it. Debugging would be very complicated, and the stability of the data access object would easily be compromised. If users want changes, they will have to request them through you or whoever has control over the component.

You can also see in Figure 4-4 that we adopted the use of regions to define logical code segments. Using Visual Studio .NET's feature of collapsible regions within your code provides modularity and enhances the readability of your code.

How you want to handle these suggestions is up to you. From now on, we're going to add code and test the component step by step.

Private Variables and Objects

Our privately used variables and ADO.NET objects within the Private Variables & Objects region are divided into three general areas. The first area defines our ADO.NET objects for data access:

```
Private privateConnection as SqlConnection
Private privateCommand as SqlCommand
Private privateDataReader as SqlDataReader
Private privateXMLReader as XMLReader
Private privateSQLDataAdapter as SqlDataAdapter
Private privateDataSet as DataSet
Private privateParameterList as ArrayList = New ArrayList()
```

Most of the variables declared are ADO.NET components. The only difference is *privateParameterList*. We're going to handle passing parameters totally abstracted from the *Command* object's parameter collection. This will allow us to create parameters in the calling code without having the *Command* object initialized. We're then handling the conversion to SQL parameters internally. The *privateParemeterList* is the result of this conversion and is used in the methods that call stored procedures.

The second area of defined variables handles the connection string. The first line is familiar to you already. The other four lines allow the building of the connection string through its most important parameters: the server name, the database used, and the user's name and password.

```
Private privateConnectionString as String
Private privateServer as String
Private privateDatabase as String
Private privateUserName as String
Private privatePassword as String
```

The third area of variables defines other useful variables like the module name, a disposed flag, and a generic exception message that we pass along with other information to the calling code when exceptions occur.

```
Private privateModuleName as String
Private privateDisposedBoolean as Boolean
Private Const privateExceptionMessage as String = _
    "Data Application Error. " & _
    "Detail Error Information can be found in the Application Log"
```

Constructors

To call our data access object three different ways, we overload the constructor of this class by passing different sets of parameters into *Public Sub New()*. What we need to watch out for is not to repeat *Public Sub New()* as a constructor, since this is already done in the Component Designer Generated Code region. When we expand this region, we find an area to add additional code under the Add Any Initialization… comment. It is here we include the naming of the module:

```
privateModuleName = Me.GetType.ToString
```

The default constructor does nothing else. This means we must set the connection string by hand after we initialize the component from the calling code.

The second constructor allows us to pass the *ConnectionString* parameter. This way we can call the object with its connection string as the parameter and we don't have to set the *ConnectionString* property.

```
Public Sub New(ByVal ConnectionString as String)
    MyBase.New()
    privateConnectionString = ConnectionString
    privateModuleName = Me.GetType.ToString
End Sub
```

The final constructor accepts the connection string parameters broken into the server name, database name, username, and password. It then concatenates the connection string from this information.

```
Public Sub New(ByVal Server as String, ByVal Database as String, _
    ByVal UserName as String, ByVal Password as String)
    MyBase.New()
    privateConnectionString = "Server=" + Server + ";Database=" + _
        Database + ";UserID=" + UserName + ";Password=" + _
        Password + ";"
        privateModuleName = Me.GetType.ToString
End Sub
```

Properties

When we call the data access object without a connection string, we need to set its properties after instantiating it. We can set either the *ConnectionString* property or the individual properties that concatenate the connection string later. We're going to show only one of the properties. You can complete the rest accordingly.

```
Public Property ConnectionString() as String
    Get
        Try
            Return privateConnection.ConnectionString
        Catch
            Return""
        End Try
    End Get
    Set(ByVal Value as String)
        privateConnectionString = Value
    End Set
End Property
```

The only thing out of the ordinary in the preceding code is the *Get* block. When the calling code requests the *ConnectionString* to verify its existence, we have to catch the potential exception that it doesn't exist. We then simply return an empty string.

The First Method: Running an SQL Statement and Returning a *DataSet*

With some of the footwork done, we can now add our first method. To keep things simple, we'll add the *runSQLDataSet* method. This method accepts two parameters: the SQL string and a table name. The first of these two parameters is required; the second, the table name, is not. The result returned will be in the form of a dataset with the returning data in a datatable. Let's look at the code:

```
Public Function runSQLDataSet(ByVal SQL as String, _
    Optional ByVal TableName as String = Nothing) as DataSet
    Try
        privateConnection = _
            New SqlConnection(privateConnectionString)
        privateCommand = New SqlCommand(SQL, privateConnection)
        privateSQLDataAdapter = New SqlDataAdapter(privateCommand)
        If TableName = Nothing Then
            privateSQLDataAdapter.Fill(privateDataSet)
        Else
            privateSQLDataAdapter.Fill(privateDataSet, TableName)
        End If
        privateConnection.Close()
        Return privateDataSet
    Catch ExceptionObject as Exception
        Throw New Exception(privateExceptionMessage, ExceptionObject)
    End Try
End Function
```

The *runSQLDataSet* function is defined as a dataset. You can see that both the SQL and *TableName* strings are passed *ByVal*. *TableName* is optional and is set to *Nothing* by default. Since the *DataAdapter.Fill* method does not allow passing empty strings or nulls, we handle the optional *TableName* property in the *If Then* statement that checks for its existence and runs the *privateSQLDataAdapter.Fill* method with or without its optional *TableName* parameter. The rest of the code consists of the ADO.NET objects we've discussed and the added exception handling. Let's take a close look at how to handle exceptions specific to our data access object.

Exception Handling

In Chapter 3, we learned about exception handling. We will now use some of the principles discussed there. Let's look again at the lines of code that handle our exception:

```
Catch ExceptionObject as Exception
    Throw New Exception(privateExceptionMessage, ExceptionObject)
End Try
```

The *ExceptionObject* contains any exception raised in the *Try* block. To pass this exception to our calling code (whether it's a code-behind page in Web Forms or the code block that calls our object from Windows Forms, or it's from the middle tier), we throw a new exception to it and pass our custom message along with all the exception information. This way, the exception message of the calling code can point to the exact location the exception occurred, and there's no guessing as to which component caused the error.

Logging Exceptions

For the same reason we created our custom exception handler, we're going to add some basic event logging to our data access object. To make this work correctly, you must change the permissions in the ASPNET (aspnet_wp) account by adding it to the debugger user group. This will allow us to write custom event log sources.

First, we need to create a function that we call when we want to write information to the event logs. Here is the code within the Exception Logging region of our object:

```
Private sub LogException(ByRef ExceptionObject as Exception)
    Dim EventLogMessage as String
    Try
        EventLogMessage = "An error occurred in the following " & _
            "module: " & privateModuleName & vbCrLf & "The Source " & _
            "was: " & ExceptionObject.Source & vbCrLf & _
            "Message: " & ExceptionObject.Message
        Dim localEventLog as New EventLog("Application")
            localEventLog.WriteEntry(privateModuleName, _
            EventLogMessage, Diagnostics.EventLogEntryType.Error,55)
    Catch EventLogException as Exception
        Throw New Exception("EventLog Error: " & _
            EventLogException.Message, EventLogException)
    End Try
End Sub
```

The *LogException* function requires the *ExceptionObject* parameter. With this parameter, the information regarding the exception is available for us to write to the log. It's up to our discretion within the data access object how much we want to show. We then define and build the *EventLogMessage*. We give it the source name and the message. The boldface lines in the previous code do the actual work. First, we instantiate a new *Eventlog* that will write to the Application log. We then write the actual entry. The parameters passed are the module name and the message we just created and formatted. To make it an error message, we use the *Diagnostics.EventLogEntryType.Error* enumerator, and last but not least, we pass the *ID* parameter. When we keep track of the IDs assigned, our debugging will be much easier as we write and use many components.

Now that we have a working event log function, let's add it to the *runSQL-DataSet* function we already created. The added line is in boldface.

```
Public Function runSQLDataSet(ByVal SQL as String, Optional ByVal TableName as
String = Nothing) as DataSet
    Try
        ⋮
        Return privateDataSet
    Catch ExceptionObject as Exception
        LogException(ExceptionObject)
        Throw New Exception(privateExceptionMessage, ExceptionObject)
    End Try
End Function
```

That's all there is to it. Now let's just hope that we write good SQL statements to keep our logs nice and clean. Then again, if we don't, we'll have ample information to track and fix the errors of our ways.

What Else?

Take a minute and look at the code of our *runSQLDataSet* method. Does anything look suspicious to you? Well, we can improve upon a couple of things. First, there's no check for a valid SQL statement. Second, is there a better place for the *privateConnection.Close* method? It seems to get called only when there isn't an error. Third, how are we going to handle the disposal of our data access object?

Validating the SQL is not easy. The method will not allow the passing of a null parameter or an empty string. It will error out immediately; however, we'd like to have a better exception message passed. We can also reasonably assume that the SQL statement needs to be larger than 10 characters. The minimum SQL statement you have to pass is Select * From X, which is already 15 characters long. Here is the private subroutine in the Validations region:

```
Private Sub ValidateSQLStatement(ByRef SQLStatement as String)
    If Len(SQLStatement) < 10 Then
        Throw New Exception(privateExceptionMessage & " The SQL " & _
        "Statement must be provided and at least 10 characters long.")
    End If
End Sub
```

When the validation is called and the SQL statement is fewer than 10 characters, the data access object throws the exception that bumps immediately out of the object to the calling code and delivers the default exception message plus the preceding custom message. Here is the code modification in the data access object:

```
Public Function runSQLDataSet(ByVal SQL as String, _
    Optional ByVal TableName as String = Nothing) as DataSet
    ValidateSQLStatement(SQL)
    Try
        ⋮
    End Try
End Function
```

The second "What else?" asked us to take care of the positioning for the close connection. The current location is within the *Try* block. This causes the connection to stay open after an error occurs until the data access object is destroyed or the garbage collector finally reclaims it. The easiest way to handle this is to include a *Finally* block in our exception handler and close the connection there since the code in this block always runs, regardless of whether an exception occurs. Here is the code for this:

```
    ⋮
    Finally
        privateConnection.Close()
    End Try
End Function
```

Our third "What else?" was to take care of the *Dispose* method. Even though the garbage collector does a reasonable job cleaning up objects that have gone out of scope, we want to accelerate the process when we deal with data access. We want the fewest number of open connections and, when they must be opened, we want the duration to be as short as possible. As we discovered, the *DataReader* is the biggest culprit. Therefore, our *Dispose* method will close any open connections, and it will dispose of and finalize itself so that the garbage collector can take it out of memory immediately. It also sets the *privateDisposedBoolean* flag we previously initialized in the private variables region.

We close the connection first not only to clean up after the user, but also because the finalization of the object can't happen unless all connections are closed. The garbage collector for out-of-scope objects finalizes them and, on the next pass, disposes of them. Since we call the *Dispose* method directly, we can direct the garbage collector not to go through this time-consuming extra step. There's one trap we could get caught in: what if we call the object after it's marked for disposal but before the garbage collector releases it? For this reason we have our *privateDisposedBoolean* flag. We set it after we run the dispose subroutine. We always check the *privateDisposedBoolean* flag before we run any methods within the object. This prevents the object from being "resurrected" before the garbage collector decides to do the final cleanup. To implement this behavior, we need to overload the object's *Dispose* method and add our own functionality. Here is the code for the overloaded *Dispose* subroutine in the "Overloaded Dispose" region:

```
Public Overloads Sub Dispose()
    If privateDisposedBoolean = False Then
        Try
            privateConnection.Dispose()
        Finally
            MyBase.Dispose()
            GC.SuppressFinalize(Me)
            privateDisposedBoolean = True
        End Try
    End If
End Sub
```

After checking whether the *privateDisposedBoolean* flag is set, the *privateConnection.Dispose* method releases the connection if it hasn't been released already. Whatever the outcome (even if it fails, which would normally cause an exception), we can continue since we ignore the error in the *try* block. The *Finally* code always gets called. In this case, we call the component's full *Dispose* method and tell the garbage collector through *GC.SuppressFinalize(Me)* to ignore the finalize and release the object instead. With that done, we set the disposed flag to *true*. This way, no other call into this object can succeed while the object waits for releases, which avoids the resurrection that could take place otherwise. We have one more thing to do: we must check the *privateDisposedBoolean* flag before we run our methods.

```
Public Function runSQLDataSet(ByVal SQL as String, _
    Optional ByVal TableName as String = Nothing) as DataSet
    Try
        If privateDisposedBoolean = True Then
            Throw New ObjectDisposedException(privateModuleName, _
            "This object has already been disposed; " & _
            "you cannot reuse it.")
```

```
        End If
          ⋮
    End Try
End Function
```

The Complete Code for the *runSQLDataSet* Method

Since we're going to build the rest of the data access methods in a similar fashion as we built the *runSQLDataSet* method, we're repeating all the code we've created for it and the supporting subroutines and functions. For easy reading of the code, we've taken out all the comments you'll find in the provided data access object. Here is the *runSQLDataSet* method:

```
Public Function runSQLDataSet(ByVal SQL as String, _
    Optional ByVal TableName as String = Nothing) as DataSet
    ValidateSQLStatement(SQL)
    Try
        If privateDisposedBoolean = True Then
            Throw New ObjectDisposedException(privateModuleName, _
            "This object has already been disposed. " & _
            "You cannot reuse it.")
        End If

        privateConnection = New SqlConnection(privateConnectionString)
        privateCommand = New SqlCommand(SQL, privateConnection)
        privateSQLDataAdapter = New SqlDataAdapter(privateCommand)
        If TableName = Nothing Then
            privateSQLDataAdapter.Fill(privateDataSet)
        Else
            privateSQLDataAdapter.Fill(privateDataSet, TableName)
        End If

        Return privateDataSet

    Catch ExceptionObject as Exception
        LogException(ExceptionObject)
        Throw New Exception(privateExceptionMessage, ExceptionObject)
    Finally
        privateConnection.Close()
    End Try
End Function
```

Here is the code for the *ValidateSQLStatement* subroutine:

```
Private Sub ValidateSQLStatement(ByRef SQLStatement as String)
    If Len(SQLStatement) < 10 Then
        Throw New Exception(privateExceptionMessage & " The SQL " & _
            "Statement must be provided and at least 10 characters long.")
    End If
End Sub
```

The following code implements the *LogException* subroutine:

```
Private sub LogException(ByRef ExceptionObject as Exception)
    Dim EventLogMessage as String
    Try
        EventLogMessage = "An error occurred in the following " & _
            "module: " & privateModuleName & vbCrLf & "The " & _
            "Source was: " & ExceptionObject.Source & vbCrLf & _
            "Message: " & ExceptionObject.Message
        Dim localEventLog as New EventLog("Application")
        localEventLog.WriteEntry(privateModuleName, EventLogMessage, _
            · Diagnostics.EventLogEntryType.Error,55)
    Catch EventLogException as Exception
        Throw New Exception("EventLog Error: " & _
            EventLogException.Message, EventLogException)
    End Try
End Sub
```

And finally, here is the overloaded *Dispose* subroutine:

```
Public Overloads Sub Dispose()
    If privateDisposedBoolean = False Then
        Try
            privateConnection.Dispose()
        Finally
            MyBase.Dispose()
            GC.SuppressFinalize(Me)
            privateDisposedBoolean = True
        End Try
    End If
End Sub
```

Calling the Data Access Object's First Method

That was a lot of coding without any testing. If you're sitting on the edge of your seat eager to give this a try, we know exactly how you feel. We couldn't wait either. Compared with writing data access objects in previous versions of Visual Basic and other languages, and creating the plumbing through COM+, for example, our coding is going to be super easy. You can test and run the supplied data access object through Menu.aspx. Click the link "1. SQL With Data Access Object and returning a DataSet" under the heading Data Access Object. The code is located in the SQL2Tier.asp file, which is in the 2Tier folder of the Chapter4DAL project. Notice in the code for the SQL2Tier.aspx page that the actual data access is accomplished in only two lines:

```
Dim localSQLServer as New SQLServer(ConnectionString)
NorthwindDataSet = _
    localSQLServer.runSQLDataSet(SelectStatement, "Employees")
```

That's all there is to it! Well—almost. We have a little preparation to do. Here are the steps:

1. Import the *DataAccessLayer.DataAccess* namespace. This is where our data access object resides.

2. Declare a connection string and an SQL select statement. You have to pass to our object what you want to do, and both of these are required.

3. Declare a *DataSet*. You do not have to explicitly import the *System.Data* namespace since Visual Studio .NET does this automatically for Web applications. You need the *DataSet* for handling the returned *DataSet* unless the data access object returns XML, in which case none of the ADO.NET objects need to be instantiated.

4. Use the object.

The rest of the code we wrote is for creating a timer and for populating a label that tells us the name of the returned *DataTable*. The code includes an exception block that also gets passed to a label. To test the exception handling, cause an error by passing an incorrect SQL statement that calls for the "Employeeees" table to be searched for instead of the correct name, "Employees" table. You'll get the exception message, and when you look at the Application event log, you'll see the event message we created. Isn't programming in .NET great? We sure get excited when we compare how effortlessly we can do all this with programming on other platforms. The data access object is totally separated and in its own layer already. There are no COM+ registration, debugging, or redeployment headaches. By creating the object in its own project and referencing it in the Web application, we're ready to call its code. When we add more functionality, all we need to do is rebuild the project and voila! The changes are immediately available to us.

If you created your own DataTestObject component in the DataAccessLayer project, you're probably dying (OK, I'm overexaggerating) to give it a try. Open the SQL2Tier.aspx file in the code editor. Under the current *Imports* statement, add another statement like the one in boldface:

```
Imports DataAccessLayer.DataAccess
Imports DataAccessLayer.DataAccessTest 'Your component
```

We recommend you comment out the *Dim localSQLServer* line and add your own:

```
'Dim localSQLServer as New SQLServer(ConnectionString)
Dim localSQLServer as New SQLServerTest(ConnectionString)
```

That's all you need to do to test and run your own added component. Have fun!

Other SQL Statement Methods

We're now going to add several more methods that call SQL statements. We can do this quickly by showing you only the necessary code changes. You can look at the rest of the code and comments in the DataAccessObject.vb file.

The *runSQLDataReader* follows the same principles but returns the *DataReader* instead. Before calling the *Command.ExecuteReader* method, we must remember to open the connection. Also, the connection can't be closed in the data access component since it needs to stay open in the calling program until it has iterated through the *DataReader*. The important step to remember with this method is to close the connection in the calling code as soon as possible.

```
Public Function runSQLDataReader(ByVal SQL As String) As SqlDataReader
    'Validate the SQL String to be larger than 10 characters.
    ⋮
    Try
        ⋮
        'Set a new Connection.
        privateConnection = New SqlConnection(privateConnectionString)
        'Set a new Command that accepts an SQL statement
        'and the privateConnection.
        privateCommand = New SqlCommand(SQL, privateConnection)
        'We need to open the connection for the DataReader explicitly.
        privateConnection.Open()
        'Run the Execute Reader method of the Command Object
        privateDataReader = privateCommand.ExecuteReader
        Return privateDataReader
        ⋮
```

The *runSQL* method is like the previous *runSQLDataReader* method, but it calls *command.ExecuteNonQuery* and returns nothing. If it fails, an exception message will be called.

```
Public Function runSQL(ByVal SQL As String)
    'Validate the SQL String to be larger than 10 characters.
    ⋮
    Try
        ⋮
        'Set a new Connection.
        privateConnection = New SqlConnection(privateConnectionString)
        'Set a new Command that accepts an SQL statement
        'and the connection.
        privateCommand = New SqlCommand(SQL, privateConnection)
        'We need to open the connection for the DataReader explicitly.
```

```
privateConnection.Open()
'Run the ExecuteNonQuery method of the Command Object.
privateCommand.ExecuteNonQuery()
    ⋮
```

Stored Procedures

Since SQL Server 6.5, we've made working with data using stored procedures a standard for our development. We've talked about the reason already. Our data access object will now be expanded to handle them for us.

The First Method with Stored Procedures

The first iteration of this method creates the code necessary to run the stored procedure without any parameters and return a dataset. This isn't very helpful in real life since we have to pass input parameters to most stored procedures, either to get conditional subsets of data or to run our insert, update, and delete stored procedures. It will, however, show you how similar the code is to the *runSQLDataSet* method we examined earlier. Here is the code, with the changes in boldface:

```
Public Function runSPDataSet(ByVal SPName as String, _
    Optional ByVal TableName as String = Nothing) as DataSet
    ValidateSPStatement(SPName)
    Try
        If privateDisposedBoolean = True Then
            Throw New ObjectDisposedException(privateModuleName, _
                "This object has already been disposed. " & _
                "You cannot reuse it.")
        End If

        privateConnection = New SqlConnection(privateConnectionString)
        privateDataSet = New SqlDataSet

        privateCommand = New SqlCommand(SPName, privateConnection)
        privateCommand.CommandType = CommandType.StoredProcedure

        privateSQLDataAdapter = New SqlDataAdapter(privateCommand)
        If TableName = Nothing Then
            privateSQLDataAdapter.Fill(privateDataSet)
        Else
            privateSQLDataAdapter.Fill(privateDataSet, TableName)
        End If

        Return privateDataSet

    Catch ExceptionObject as Exception
        LogException(ExceptionObject)
```

(continued)

```
        Throw New Exception(privateExceptionMessage, ExceptionObject)
    Finally
        privateConnection.Close()
    End Try
End Function
```

Those three boldface lines are all we have to add. We run a slightly different validation for stored procedure names, and we tell the command object that this is a stored procedure. An example of this is in the Menu.aspx page, which is accessed by clicking the "1. SQL With Data Access Object and returning a DataSet" link under the "Data Access Object—Data Is Accessed Through Data Access Object In CodeBehind" heading. The implementation file SQLStoredProcedure2Tier.aspx is in the Chapter4DAL project in the 2Tier folder.

The Secret of Handling Parameters: The *AddParameter* Function

Our primary goal for the data access object is to make it easy and to have to import and use the least amount of data namespaces and ADO.NET objects. For this reason, we chose to abstract the behavior of adding parameters totally from the *Command* object's parameters collection. We also want the IntelliSense options that help us when we need to fill the required and optional parameters. The two required parameters are the parameter name and its value. We've made them the first two parameters in our *AddParameter* method, which will speed up code creation. The optional parameters are the *SQLDataType* parameter and the size and direction of the parameter. By default there are no *DataType* and no size limitations, and the direction of the parameter is set for input parameters. In addition, we want the adding of parameters to be completed in one simple command line. It took a bit of time as well as trial and error to come up with the solution.

To allow the use of our own *SQLDataTypes* when calling the *AddParameter* method, we chose to create a public enumeration of those *SQLDataTypes* we use the most. You can find this code in the Private Variables And Objects region. Here are the types we chose:

```
Public Enum SQLDataType
    SQLString
    SQLChar
    SQLInteger
    SQLBit
    SQLDateTime
    SQLDecimal
    SQLMoney
    SQLImage
End Enum
```

We put these enumerations in the order of the data types we use most often. You can also add other *SQLDataTypes* that aren't covered here.

Next we need to build the *AddParameter* method. We're going to do this step by step, in the sequence this method executes. The complete code is in the sample object. Feel free to continue building your own object if you started it as explained earlier.

```
Public Sub AddParameter(ByVal ParameterName as String, _
    ByVal Value as String, _
    Optional ByVal SQLType as SQLDataType = Nothing, _
    Optional ByVal Size as Integer = Nothing,_
    Optional ByVal Direction as ParameterDirection =
    ParameterDirection.Input)
```

Now that we have the required and optional parameters we need, we're going to fill the internal *privateParameterList*. Every time the *AddParameter* method is called, another parameter is added to our *privateParameterList*. Later this list will be converted to the *SQLCommand* parameter collection. In the same step, we can also convert our own enumerated *SQLDataTypes* to the actual SQL Server *DataTypes* supported with the types contained in *SqlCommand.ParameterCollection*. Let's continue our code:

```
Dim buildDataType As SqlDbType
'The parameter class is defined hereafter and creates a new
'Parameter of the type we want to add to the privateParameterList.
Dim buildParameter As Parameter = Nothing
Select Case SQLType
    Case SQLDataType.SQLString
        buildDataType = SqlDbType.VarChar
    Case SQLDataType.SQLChar
        buildDataType = SqlDbType.Char
    Case SQLDataType.SQLInteger
        buildDataType = SqlDbType.Int
    Case SQLDataType.SQLBit
        buildDataType = SqlDbType.Bit
    Case SQLDataType.SQLDateTime
        buildDataType = SqlDbType.DateTime
    Case SQLDataType.SQLDecimal
        buildDataType = SqlDbType.Decimal
    Case SQLDataType.SQLMoney
        buildDataType = SqlDbType.Money
    Case SQLDataType.SQLImage
        buildDataType = SqlDbType.Image
End Select
'This actually builds the parameter in the type we want.
buildParameter = New Parameter(ParameterName, Value, buildDataType,_
    Direction)
```

(continued)

```
'Now we are ready to add this parameter to our internal list.
    privateParameterList.Add(buildParameter)
End Sub
```

After defining the *buildDataType* to the *SqlDBType* that we need to use in the parameter collection, we call the class that restructures the parameter in the type we need for our collection. The *Select Case SQLType* finds the correct type to be passed. We then call the parameter class and add the freshly built parameter to our internal *privateParameterList*.

The *Parameter* class creates a new parameter object with the correct data types and passes the parameters contained in *AddParameter*'s parameters. This is the code:

```
Public Class Parameter
    Public ParameterName as String
    Public ParameterValue as String
    Public ParameterDataType as SQLDataType
    Public ParameterSize as Integer
    Public ParameterDirectionUsed as ParameterDirection

    Sub New(ByVal passedParameterName as String, _
        ByVal passedValue as String, _
        Optional ByVal passedSQLType as SQLDataType = Nothing, _
        Optional ByVal passedSize as Integer, _
        Optional ByVal passedDirection as ParameterDirection = _
        ParameterDirection.Input)
        ParameterName = passedParameterName
        ParameterValue = passedValue
        ParameterDataType = passedSQLType
        ParameterSize = passedSize
        ParameterDirectionUsed = passedDirection
    End Sub
End Class
```

At first look, this step seems to be unnecessary, but we've found that we can't circumvent it if we want to have the *AddParameter* method totally abstract from ADO.NET's *Command.Parameter* collection and its properties. After we've called our *AddParameter* method as often as needed, the *privateParameterList* in our object has a list of all of the parameters in the types we defined.

There are two more functions required. The first converts the parameters in our *privateParameterList* to actual *SQLParameters*. We'll do this when we call our stored procedure methods. This way we can use the same parameter list for more than one stored procedure. Let's look at the code:

```
Private Function ConvertParameters(ByVal passedParameter as Parameter) _
    As SqlParameter
    Dim returnSQLParameter as SqlParameter = New SqlParameter()
```

```
returnSQLParameter.ParameterName = passedParameter.ParameterName
returnSQLParameter.Value = passedParameter.ParameterValue
returnSQLParameter.SqlDbType = passedParameter.ParameterDataType
returnSQLParameter.Size = passedParameter.ParameterSize
returnSQLParameter.Direction = passedParameter.ParameterDirectionUsed
Return returnSQLParameter
End Function
```

The *ConvertParameters* function takes our parameter types and returns the equivalent *SQLParameter* collection's types as a native *SQLParameter*.

The second function we still need to add will clear the *privateParameter-List*. This is helpful if we want to instantiate the data access object once and call several different stored procedure with different parameters before we dispose of the object. The code is very simple:

```
Public Sub ClearParameters()
    Try
        privateParameterList.Clear()
    Catch parameterException as Exception
        Throw New Exception(privateExceptionMessage & _
            " Parameter List did not clear." , parameterException)
    End Try
End Sub
```

All the *ClearParameters* subroutine does is clear our internal *privateParameter-List*. It will then be immediately ready to have new parameters added.

The *runSPDataSet* Method with Parameters

Now that we have our *AddParameter* function and a way to convert our own parameter type to the one required, we can extend our *runSQLDataSet* method that uses parameters. Here is all the code, with the lines that give us access to *SQLParameters* in boldface:

```
Public Function runSPDataSet(ByVal SPName as String, _
    Optional ByVal TableName as String = Nothing) as DataSet _
    ValidateSPStatement(SPName)
    Dim privateUsedParameter as Parameter
    Dim privateParameter as SQLParameter
    Dim usedEnumerator as IEnumerator = _
        privateParameterList. GetEnumerator()
    Try
        If privateDisposedBoolean = True Then
            Throw New ObjectDisposedException(privateModuleName, _
                "This object has already been disposed. " & _
                "You cannot reuse it.")
        End If
```

(continued)

```
            privateConnection = New SqlConnection(privateConnectionString)
            privateDataSet = New SqlDataSet

            privateCommand = New SqlCommand(SPName, privateConnection)
            privateCommand.CommandType = CommandType.StoredProcedure

            Do While(usedEnumerator.MoveNext())
                privateUsedParameter = Nothing
                privateUsedParameter = usedEnumerator.Current
                privateParameter = ConvertParameters(privateUsedParameter)
                privateCommand.Parameters.Add(privateParameter)
            Loop

            privateSQLDataAdapter = New SqlDataAdapter(privateCommand)
            If TableName = Nothing Then
                privateSQLDataAdapter.Fill(privateDataSet)
            Else
                privateSQLDataAdapter.Fill(privateDataSet, TableName)
            End If

            Return privateDataSet

    Catch ExceptionObject as Exception
        LogException(ExceptionObject)
        Throw New Exception(privateExceptionMessage, ExceptionObject)
    Finally
        privateConnection.Close()
    End Try
End Function
```

We start by creating *privateUsedParameter*, *privateParameter*, and *usedEnumerator* based on *privateParameterList*. We then iterate through the *usedEnumerator*, which represents each parameter in our internal list. We convert it to an *SQLParameter* and pass it to the *privateCommand*'s parameter list. This is done in the *Do While* loop block. Once the parameters are converted and imported, the *DataAdapter* is used as before.

We're now ready to test this. Look at the StoredProcedure-Params2Tier.aspx file. It instantiates the data access object just as before but adds parameters, calls the *ClearParameter* method, and runs another method to which it adds a parameter, all with just a few lines of code:

```
Dim localSQLServer As New SQLServer(ConnectionString)
localSQLServer.AddParameter("@City", "London", _
    SQLServer.SQLDataType.SQLChar)
localSQLServer.AddParameter("@Name", "King", _
    SQLServer.SQLDataType.SQLChar)
NorthwindDataSet = localSQLServer.runSPDataSet(StoredProcedurename, _
```

```
    "FirstTable")
localSQLServer.ClearParameters()
NorthwindDataSet2 = localSQLServer.runSPDataSet( _
    StoredProcedurename, "SecondTable")
```

As you run this example, take the time to make some modifications to the *AddParameter* method or call a new one. You'll see how the IntelliSense features apply.

We now have a fully functional blueprint of an abstract data access method for stored procedures that fulfills all our design goals.

Other Stored Procedure Methods

Besides returning a *DataSet*, we want to return a *DataReader*, XML, and parameters as well as a method that returns nothing. Since there are few modifications, we will touch only on the differences.

The *runSPDataReader* method will return a *DataReader* object. Like before, we need to watch the open connection in the calling program. You can find the code for this method in the RunSPDataReader region in DataAccessObject.vb and an example of how to use it in StoredProcedureOther2Tier.aspx.

The *runSPXMLReader* method returns an XML statement as a string. When you use this method, you do not need to declare any ADO.NET objects in the calling code, not even the *DataSet* object. The calling code just needs to know how to deal with XML. When you write the stored procedures that return XML, the FOR XML clause has to be included so that it is forced into returning XML to our data access object. Here is the stored procedure *spGetEmployeesXML* that we call from the sample code:

```
ALTER PROCEDURE dbo.spGetEmployeesXML
AS
Select LastName, FirstName
From Employees FOR XML AUTO, ELEMENTS
```

You can find the code for this method in the runSPXMLReader region in DataAccessObject.vb and an example of how to use it in the same example we just discussed.

Here is the code block that runs the *XMLReader* and iterates through it to return a string:

```
privateConnection.Open()
privateXMLReader = privateCommand.ExecuteXMLReader
'Build XML String
Do Until privateXMLReader.Read = False
    privateXMLString += privateXMLReader.ReadOuterXML & "<BR>"
Loop
Return privateXMLString
```

We can create *privateXMLString*, applying any formatting options we might want. In this case, we just return the *OuterXML* and an HTML break for easy viewing in our example.

The *runSPOutput* method outputs an array list of output parameters from stored procedures. To handle these, our object will run the *command.ExecuteNonQuery* method. This is very fast, and though it doesn't create a table output, it does return our output parameters.

OLE DB Example

To demonstrate an OLE DB provider, we included the *runSQLACCESSDataSet* method, in which we're accessing an Access database with an SQL statement that returns a dataset. When you compare the code in this method with the code in the *runSQLDataSet* method, you'll find that data access with the OLE DB Data Providers is almost exactly the same as it is with the SQL Server .NET Data Providers. We haven't added an OLE DB data access object to this chapter's version. Following the same steps for creating our SQL data access object, you can easily add OLE DB data access.

Using the Data Access Object

Examples 1 through 5 in the data access object project show us the use of our object in code-behind Web pages. The same code applies in Visual Basic .NET Windows Forms and can just as easily be used in *n*-tier objects and classes. Here are the general steps to use the object:

1. Import the *System.Data* namespace. It allows us to create and pass *DataSet* objects.

2. Register the data access component.

3. Import the data access component's namespace. This is *DataAccessLayer.DataAccess*.

4. Declare and set the connection string, SQL statement, or stored procedure names. Don't forget to declare a local *DataSet* if one is passed.

5. Declare the *SQLServer* object. It resides in the *DataAccessLayer.DataAccess* namespace.

6. Call the SQLServer object's data methods, with or without parameters, and accept the results.

Let's look at the necessary code of a typical example:

```
Imports System.Data.SqlClient
Imports DataAccessLayer.DataAccess

Dim ConnectionString as String = ". . ."
Dim StoreProcedureName as String = "spEmployeesbyCity"
Dim NorthWindDataSet as DataSet

Dim localSQLServer as New SQLServer(ConnectionString)
localSQLServer.AddParameter("@City", _
    "London", SQLServer.SQLdataType.SQLChar,10)
NorthWindDataSet = localSQLServer.runSPDataSet(StoredProcedureName, _
    "EmployeeTable")
localSQLServer.Dispose()
localSQLServer = Nothing
```

That's all there is to it. Not counting declaring and setting variables, the actual data access code is in only three lines (shown in boldface).

Additional Questions About Data Access

Even though our data access component is fairly complete, there are other questions that still might be unanswered.

How Do We Handle Transactions?

We've shown that ADO.NET includes the ability to handle transactions with the *Connection* object. This might be a viable option in smaller applications. We haven't tested this with large databases involving many simultaneous users. We have, however, tested the handling of transactions in stored procedures. It works for us, even with very large databases and hundreds of simultaneous users.

What About Data Concurrency?

Just like the handling of transactions, we handle data concurrency in stored procedures. The *DataSet* and *DataAdapter* objects have powerful features that handle data concurrency. To give us an alternative option for handling data concurrency, we can simply add additional methods to our data access object.

What About Connection Pooling?

We discussed earlier that the SQL Data Providers are specifically designed to give us maximum performance with SQL Server 7 and SQL Server 2000. In creating these providers, SQL Server's TDS is used as the low-level protocol between the database and ADO.NET components. This circumvents OLE DB's session pooling capabilities. To take advantage of connection pooling, the SQL Data Providers must use the pooled components features of COM+. The SQL connection string has built-in attributes for these. You can set the connection lifetime as well as minimum and maximum pool sizes, and you can set the pooling to *true*. Here is an example:

```
connString = "server=(local)Trusted_Connection=yes;database=northwind;" & _
    "connection reset=false;" & _
    "connection lifetime=5;" & _
    "enlist=true;" & _
    "min pool size=1;" & _
    "max pool size=50"
```

Can We Use Performance Counters?

Absolutely! Just as we added event logging, we can add performance counters. You can add them programmatically or with drag-and-drop functionality from Server Explorer to the component. You will see examples of this in the HR enterprise example.

Conclusion

With a better understanding of ADO.NET, we can see that data access has made another jump in its evolutionary process from Remote Data Objects (RDO) and Data Access Objects (DAO) to ActiveX Data Objects (ADO) and then ADO.NET. ADO.NET is specifically designed to increase scalability and excels in its disconnected data manipulation capabilities. It is made of small, lightweight components that are optimized for speed. It supports XML from the ground up. *DataSets* are its crown jewel and make *n*-tier architectures simple and easy to achieve. We've shown many of ADO.NET's features in theory, code, and samples. To make data access even easier and more manageable, we abstracted ADO.NET's capabilities in a data access component. This component can be called anywhere within the .NET Framework–compatible languages. We can call it directly, pass it into the GAC, or import it into our *n*-tier application's data access layer. With integrated features such as optimized ADO.NET components, encapsulated exception handling, and enhanced disposal, data access will be easier and more flexible than before. We pay tribute to the minds that conceived and created ADO.NET to make our lives as developers easier.

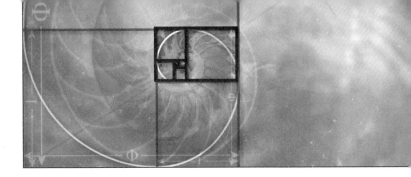

5

Implementing the Security Layer

This chapter is about application security in intranet applications. We'll go over several Microsoft .NET Framework security options, and then we'll look at how to build a security layer for our HRnet application that is flexible and thus can be used by many different applications in the enterprise. In this process, we'll review several of the various security techniques that we analyzed and discuss why we decided to use certain ones in our application.

The .NET Framework provides several technologies that can be used for security purposes. The framework features include the common language runtime (CLR) security, which all .NET applications use; other generic security features that any application can use; and finally, specific security features for Microsoft ASP.NET Web applications. All these features allow you to use the type of application security that matches your needs.

Our application has two major security requirements. We first need to be able to authenticate users. This means that we must be able to determine who a user is and whether that user has access to the application. Second, we need to be able to determine what a user can do in the application. This is known as *authorization* and is usually defined as role based authorization, the second security requirement. *Role-based authorization* describes a process in which we control a user's use of the application based upon her membership in a particular group. For instance, after a user logs in, we might determine that she belongs to a group of users known as Managers. Then we could let her use parts of the application that only the Managers group has access to. Both authentication and authorization features provide us with control over who gets in and what they can do.

To solve the security problems of authentication and authorization, we'll show you two major approaches. The first is the ASP.NET authentication system with forms authentication. This solution takes us part of the way toward meeting our requirements and can be used in purely ASP.NET applications. The second solution we'll cover is a robust custom security layer that uses part of the .NET Framework security system and works in Microsoft Windows, ASP.NET, and other scenarios, such as Windows Services and XML Web services.

Overview of Relevant .NET Security Features

Before we build the security layer, let's look at the application security features in the .NET Framework. Table 5-1 provides a short description of some of the .NET Framework security technologies.

Table 5-1   .NET Framework Security Technologies

Type	Description
Authentication	The .NET Framework provides Microsoft Internet Information Services (IIS) authentication features, forms authentication, Windows authentication, and custom authentication.
ASP.NET authentication providers	The authentication providers handle standard credential sources. For instance, the Windows authentication provider uses the standard Windows credential (NTLM or Microsoft Active Directory) source. The .NET Framework provides three standard providers for ASP.NET applications: Windows authentication, forms authentication, and Passport authentication.
Authorization	Authorization support is provided in a variety of ways. There are standard features for Windows authorization, custom authorization, COM+ authorization, and more. There is also a URL-based authorization service for allowing or denying access to specified resources (that is, URLs).

Many other features in the .NET Framework will also be useful for us. For instance, classes that provide support for the Crypto API are built in. These classes allow us to easily encrypt and decrypt data in our applications. A variety of authentication mechanisms are used in IIS and Windows applications today, including many that can be used with .NET Framework role-based security. Some of the most commonly used mechanisms are basic, digest, Passport, operating system (such as NTLM or Kerberos) features provided by IIS, or application-defined mechanisms.

The .NET authentication features are fully extensible, so we can use the built-in features that rely on the operating system, ASP.NET security, or completely customized code as part of the process.

Application Security Needs

As mentioned at the start of this chapter, the first element of security our application needs is authentication. *Authentication* is the process of discovering and verifying the identity of a principal (individual) by examining the user's credentials and validating those credentials against a credentials authority. If the authentication check is successful, the user is allowed access to the application. If authentication fails, the application can decide to allow the user to have limited access to the application or simply deny him access to the entire application.

The simplest forms of authentication are the various IIS authentication modes. If we were using Active Directory, we could simply turn on basic or integrated security in IIS. Figure 5-1 shows a simple application and its security settings. Here we've cleared the Anonymous access check box, which forces the user to be authenticated by IIS against either a local Windows account or an Active Directory account. Clicking OK after making the changes immediately forces authentication on this site with non-anonymous access.

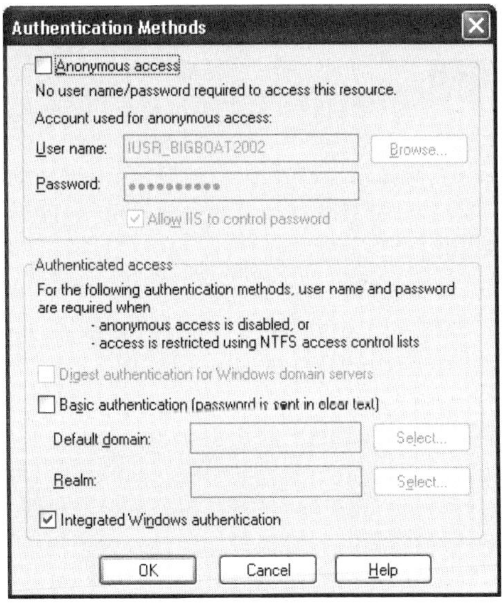

Figure 5-1   Configuring the authentication methods for IIS

However, in our HRnet application, we can't use the IIS features because we aren't using Active Directory or local Windows accounts for users. Instead, we have an employee's database that contains users in the Employees table. We will also likely have other users of the security system in other applications that are customers and not employees. Thus, we don't want to maintain Active Directory accounts for them. Instead, we need a custom authentication mechanism that allows for a custom database of user credentials.

This leads us to the authorization problem. The HRnet application we're going to build in subsequent chapters also needs the ability to control user access based on that user's role membership. We should be able to accomplish this by using a custom set of tables for the user's credentials. We need to control who has access to what based on the user's role in the organization. Since this application contains sensitive human resources information, its data must be guarded and access to it must be restricted based on the user's credentials. ASP.NET provides a number of features for authorization also, as we'll see in the section "Forms Authentication Services."

There is one further wrinkle for the application. We know we'll be using ASP.NET to build part of the application, so it will be running in a browser. Our application design also specifies that we build part of the application using Windows Forms because of the power and security that technology offers over Web-based applications. Thus, our security solution must provide for both ASP.NET Web Forms and Windows Forms.

Forms Authentication Services

The first option that appealed to us for the Web application was forms authentication. We can use—and even customize—the forms authentication security built into ASP.NET in our applications. The simplicity of this mechanism and the control it provides are compelling.

The forms authentication security model is good for many applications but not all. Let's take a look at it. You can use the forms security model by simply changing the Web.Config file and then customizing a login form. It's really simple and flexible.

Forms authentication is similar to custom authentication, which is used in many public Internet and extranet applications. Using custom authentication, you basically store user information (such as name and password) in a custom data store such as a database. When users access the application, you authenticate them against that store. Forms authentication refers to this type of system in which unauthenticated requests are redirected to an HTML form in which the user can present the logon credentials. The redirection is done using HTTP client-side redirection.

In ASP.NET forms authentication, the user typically provides credentials (username and password) and submits them via a login form. Figure 5-2 demonstrates this process. When the user sends a request for a form to IIS the first time, ASP.NET picks up the request and checks the user's credentials by asking for the authentication cookie. If the request isn't authenticated, HTTP client-side redirection is used to send that request to an authentication form (login.aspx), in which the user can supply authentication credentials. After the application (login.aspx) authenticates the request, the system issues a cookie that contains a key for reacquiring the user's identity on subsequent requests. Subsequent requests for resources that are sent to the application will contain the cookie in the request headers and will be authenticated and authorized by the ASP.NET forms engine.

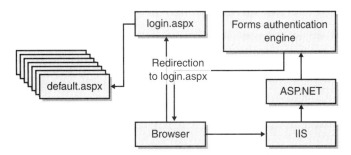

Figure 5-2   Forms authentication overview

Forms authentication is sometimes used for *personalization*—the customization of content for a known user. In some of these cases, identification is the issue rather than authentication, so a user's personalization information can be obtained simply by accessing the username.

The real benefit of forms authentication is that the ASP.NET system takes care of handling authentication on each page. Your code does not.

Creating the Forms Authentication Architecture for an Application

The easiest way to create a forms authentication system is to build a simple login form (such as login.aspx). This form will obtain the username and password, validate against a trusted data source, and call one of the methods of the *FormsAuthentication* class to authenticate the user (such as *RedirectFromLoginPage*).

RedirectFromLoginPage redirects the user to the originally requested URL, whereas the *SetAuthCookie* method simply generates the authentication cookie. After the steps of authentication are complete and the user is identified, .NET handles the remaining process. You actually turn on forms authentication and control its configuration by changing the Web.Config file.

Configuring the Application

The following code shows a sample authentication section for Web.Config. The mode attribute has been changed from *Windows* to *Forms*, and the Forms element sets the authentication parameters.

Several things are important here. First, since this is XML, the tags are case sensitive and, as a result, *Forms* is correct, but lowercase *forms* is wrong and will generate a run-time error. The *name* attribute (which controls the cookie name) has been left as the default setting. The *loginUrl* attribute points to the login page, which sits at the root level of the project. The attributes are explained in more detail later in this chapter.

```
<authentication mode="Forms">
  <forms name=".ASPXUSERDEMO"
    loginUrl="login.aspx" protection="All"
    timeout="60">
  </forms>
</authentication>
<authorization>
  <deny users="?" />
</authorization>
```

The authorization tag in this example has also been set to *?*. This will deny all anonymous users access to any resources and force the logon to occur. If you don't set this entry, users can access the site and the forms engine won't authenticate them.

The forms tag has several attributes:

■ **name** This attribute specifies the HTTP cookie to use for authentication. The default value is *.ASPXAUTH*. If multiple applications are running on a single server or a server farm and each application requires a unique cookie, you must configure the cookie name in each application's Web.Config file to provide separate cookies for each application. The easiest way to accomplish this is to create a naming scheme for your application that specifies the authentication cookie name.

- *loginUrl*   This attribute controls the URL for the login page. This is the page to which a user is redirected if no valid authentication cookie is found. The default value is *default.aspx*. We almost always use login.aspx as the name for this page.

- *protection*   This attribute controls the type of encryption that is used for the authentication cookie.

  - ❏   *All* specifies that the application uses both data validation and encryption. This causes the cookie to be encrypted and then validated in order to protect the cookie at the highest level. This option uses the configured data validation algorithm (based on the <machineKey> element). Triple-DES (*3DES*) is used for encryption if it is available and if the key is long enough (48 bytes or more). The default (and recommended) value is *All*.

  - ❏   *None* specifies that both encryption and validation are disabled. This might be useful for some applications that are using cookies only for personalization and have weaker security requirements. Using cookies in this manner is not recommended. It does provide better performance as it is the least resource-intensive way to use forms authentication. Obviously this is not a good choice for our application because we want to secure the users' credential information.

  - ❏   *Encryption* causes the cookie to be encrypted using Triple-DES or DES, but data validation is not performed on the cookie. Cookies used in this way might be subject to plaintext attacks.

  - ❏   *Validation* specifies that a validation scheme verifies that the contents of an encrypted cookie have not been altered in transit. The cookie is created using cookie validation by concatenating a validation key with the cookie data, computing a Message Authentication Code (MAC), and appending the MAC to the outgoing cookie.

- *timeout*   This attribute specifies the amount of time until nonpersistent authentication cookies expire. The value is in minutes (an integer). The default value is *30*. The timeout attribute is a sliding value, expiring at the specified number of minutes after the time the last request was received. The cookie is updated when more than half of the specified time has elapsed. This might result in a loss of precision. Persistent cookies don't time out.

- ■ ***path*** This attribute specifies the path for cookies issued by the application. The default value is a backslash (\) because most browsers are case-sensitive and won't send cookies back when there is a path case mismatch.

Forms authentication can use any authentication source. The credentials can be stored in any place such as a database or a text file. You can also place credentials in Web.Config by using the credentials tag. This allows definition of the username and password credentials within the configuration file. We don't recommend this as a general practice, and it's not the approach we took when building our HRnet application.

Creating the Credentials Store

As mentioned earlier, we use a database for our credentials. Our first step in using forms authentication was to create a data source for the credentials. This is a simple database with UserKey, UserName, Password, and EmployeeID columns. After we had a database with credentials, setting up the security was simple. Our first cut at this database architecture is shown in Figure 5-3.

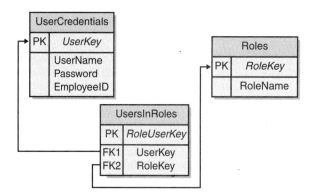

Figure 5-3   First draft of the user credential database architecture

As you can see, the main table is UserCredentials, which contains the users' credentials. This is the only table we'll use for forms authentication. The sample data for this table is shown in Table 5-2.

Table 5-2   The UserCredentials Table

UserKey	UserName	Password	EmployeedID
1	nDavolio	nDavolio	1
2	Afuller	Afuller	2
3	Jleverling	Jleverling	3
4	Fpeacock	Fpeacock	4
5	Sbuchanan	SBuchanan	5
6	Msuyama	MSuyama	6
7	RKing	RKing	7
8	Lcallahan	Lcallahan	8
9	Adodsworth	ADodsworth	9

Creating the Login Form

Next we created the login form. The resulting form is shown in Figure 5-4. You can see that the form takes a username and a password. Pretty simple.

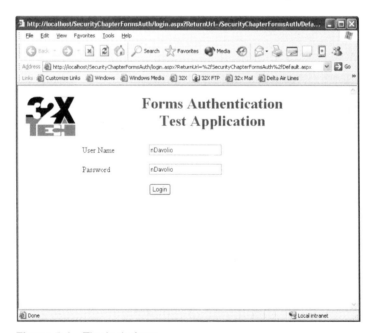

Figure 5-4   The login form

Let's take a look at the code for the form. The form is a simple Web Forms page named login.aspx. The entire HTML follows:

```
<%@ Page Language="vb" AutoEventWireup="false"
Codebehind="login.aspx.vb"
Inherits="SecurityChapterFormsAuth.Login" %>
<!DOCTYPE HTML PUBLIC "-//W3C//DTD HTML 4.0 Transitional//EN">
<HTML>
    <HEAD>
        <title>HR App Login Form</title>
        <meta content="Microsoft Visual Studio.NET 7.0"
            name="GENERATOR">
        <meta content="Visual Basic 7.0" name="CODE_LANGUAGE">
        <meta content="JavaScript"
            name="vs_defaultClientScript">
        <meta content="http://schemas.microsoft.com/
            intellisense/ie5" name="vs_targetSchema">
    </HEAD>
    <body>
    <form id="Form1" method="post" runat="server">
        <TABLE cellSpacing="1" cellPadding="1"
            width="100%" border="0">
        <TR>
            <TD style="WIDTH: 74px"><IMG src="Images/logo.GIF">
        </TD>
        <TD>
            <H1 align="center"><FONT color="#ff0066">
                Forms Authentication
            <BR>Test Application</FONT>
            </H1>
        </TD>
        </TR>
        <TR>
        <TD style="WIDTH: 74px"></TD>
        <TD>
        <TABLE style="WIDTH: 549px; HEIGHT: 123px"
            cellSpacing="1" cellPadding="1"
            width="549" border="0">
            <TR>
            <TD>User Name 
            </TD>
            <TD><asp:textbox id=" txtUserName"
                    runat="server">
                </asp:textbox>
                <asp:requiredfieldvalidator
                    id="RequiredFieldValidator1"
                    runat="server"
                    ErrorMessage="Required"
                    ControlToValidate=" txtUserName">
```

```
                </asp:requiredfieldvalidator>
                 
            </TD>
            </TR>
            <TR>
            <TD>Password
            </TD>
            <TD><asp:textbox id=" txtPassword"
                TextMode="Password"
                runat="server">
                </asp:textbox>
                <asp:requiredfieldvalidator
                    id="RequiredFieldValidator2"
                    runat="server"
                    ErrorMessage="Required"
                    ControlToValidate=" txtPassword">
                </asp:requiredfieldvalidator></TD>
            </TR>
            <TR>
            <TD></TD>
            <TD></TD>
            </TR>
            <TR>
            <TD></TD>
            <TD><asp:button id="cmdLogin"
                runat="server"
                Text="Login"></asp:button></TD>
            </TR>
            </TABLE>
            <P></P>
            <P></P>
            </TD>
            </TR>
            <TR>
            <TD style="WIDTH: 74px"></TD>
            <TD><asp:label id="lblMessage"
                runat="server" Visible="False"
                ForeColor="Red"
                Font-Bold="True"></asp:label></TD>
            </TR>
            </TABLE>
        </form>
    </body>
</HTML>
```

The only thing special about this page is the use of the validation controls to make sure the user doesn't enter blank fields. Also, the *txtPassword* control was set to a mode of *SingleLine* during testing to make it easier to determine the password entered. After testing, we switched the mode to *Password*.

The code-behind file is pure simplicity. Before the class definition are two *Imports* statements:

```
Imports System.Web.Security
Imports DataAccessLayer.DataAccess
```

Our code starts after the standard Class definition and Web Form Designer Generated Code, just before the *Page_Load* event routine with the definition of the connection string for the security database. To use this connection string, you'll need to change the *server*, *uid*, and *pwd* fields and probably the database field as well:

```
Const privateConnectionString As String = _
    "server=localhost;uid=sa;pwd=;database=SecurityCredentials"
```

Next, the *cmdLogin* event code is raised when a user clicks the Login button. You can see that this code hinges on the *CheckLogin* function used in the *If* statement. If *CheckLogin* returns *True*, the user is valid and is redirected into the application. As you can see, the call to the *RedirectFromLoginPage* method is commented out. If this line is uncommented and the following two lines are commented or taken out, after a successful login, the user will be redirected to the page she originally tried to access. The way the code is currently written, *SetAuthCookie* is called instead, and the user is redirected to default.aspx. This allows us to force the user to default.aspx when she logs in, no matter which page she tried to access. The call to *SetAuthCookie* simply writes the authentication cookie but does not cause redirection. The entire code for this procedure follows:

```
Private Sub cmdLogin_Click( _
    ByVal sender As System.Object, _
    ByVal e As System.EventArgs) Handles cmdLogin.Click
    'Next line calls CheckLogin to validate user.
    If CheckLogin(txtUserName.Text, txtPassword.Text) Then
        'If user is valid, redirect back to original
        'page and set up authentication cookie.
        'FormsAuthentication.RedirectFromLoginPage( _
        '    txtEmployeedID.Text, False)
        FormsAuthentication.SetAuthCookie(txtUserName.Text, False)
        Response.Redirect("default.aspx")
    Else
        'If user is not valid, then display error.
        lblMessage.Text = "Invalid Credentials: Please try again"
        lblMessage.Visible = True
    End If
End Sub
```

Now, let's dig into *CheckLogin*. As written, this function executes the *spCheckUserCredentials* stored procedure to determine whether the user's account and password are valid. If the call to this procedure returns a value greater than zero, the user is valid; otherwise, she isn't validated because the stored procedure didn't find a matching user.

```
If localCount > 0 Then
    localValidUser = True
End If
```

Other than this *If* statement, this procedure uses the same format as any procedure to call into the *SQLServer* database class. The code for this function is shown here:

```
Function CheckLogin( _
    ByVal localUserName As String, _
    ByVal localPassword As String) As Boolean

    Dim localCount As Integer
    Dim localDSRoles As DataSet
    Dim localdr As DataRow
    Dim i As Integer
    Dim localValidUser As Boolean

    localValidUser = False

    Dim ReturnOutPutList As New ArrayList()
    Dim ParamsStoredProcedure As String = _
        "spCheckUserCredentials"

    Try
        Dim localOutPutServer As New _
            SQLServer(privateConnectionString)

        localOutPutServer.AddParameter( _
            "@UserName", localUserName, _
            SQLServer.SQLDataType.SQLChar, 20, _
            ParameterDirection.Input)
        localOutPutServer.AddParameter( _
            "@Password", localPassword, _
            SQLServer.SQLDataType.SQLChar, 30, _
            ParameterDirection.Input)
        localOutPutServer.AddParameter( _
            "@Count", , SQLServer.SQLDataType.SQLInteger, , _
            ParameterDirection.Output)
```

(continued)

```
        ReturnOutPutList = _
            localOutPutServer.runSPOutput(ParamsStoredProcedure)

        'Get the output parameters and iterate through them.
        Dim s As String
        For Each s In ReturnOutPutList
            localCount = CInt(s.ToString)
        Next
        If localCount > 0 Then
            localValidUser = True
        End If

    Catch ExceptionObject As Exception

Finally
End Try


Return localValidUser
End Function
```

That's about it for forms authentication, but we do have a few final words. You must test this application thoroughly. For instance, if you have the persistence set to *True*, the cookies don't time out and users don't have to log back in. That might be different behavior than you want. Also, if you use the *RedirectFromLoginPage* method, you must test your application thoroughly by checking access to it via each type of page. This is necessary because users can access the site by going to any page, and that might cause problems. For example, when you have a page that depends on a *querystring* variable, the variable might not be there when the user goes directly to that page.

Authorization Features

Now that we've seen forms authentication, let's look at some of the .NET Framework authorization features. As we mentioned at the beginning of the chapter, *authorization* is a process that determines whether a user (referred to as a *principal* in the .NET Framework world) is allowed to perform a requested action. Authorization always occurs after authentication and uses information about the principal's identity to determine which resources the principal can access. The .NET Framework provides role-based security services that can be used to implement authorization.

Role-based security simply means that a user has a role of some type. In Windows security, roles are groups of users. A role simply implies that you are a member of a group and therefore have some type of role based on that membership. For instance, the HRManagers group in our example is a custom group that implies that everyone in that group has a role of a manager in the human resources department. You could, of course, create roles that are more task oriented, such as DataInput, which implies that a person can only enter data.

Authorization Types in the .NET Framework

Business applications often provide access to data or resources based on credentials supplied by the user. Typically, applications check the role of a user and provide access to resources based on that role. The CLR provides support for role-based authorization based on a Windows account or a custom identity. You can use a variety of credential sources in your applications, ranging from Windows or Active Directory to custom authorization. As discussed earlier in this chapter, we also need other credential sources such as a database. Luckily, the .NET Framework provides those mechanisms, as we will see later in the section "The Security Layer."

Role-based security in the .NET Framework supports three kinds of principals:

- *Generic principals* represent users and roles that exist independent of Microsoft Windows NT, Microsoft Windows 2000, Microsoft Windows XP, or Microsoft Windows .NET Server users and roles. For instance, these principals might represent users that come from a database credential store.

- *Windows principals* represent Windows users and their roles (or their Windows or Active Directory groups). A Windows principal can impersonate another user, which means the principal can access a resource on a user's behalf while presenting the identity that belongs to that user.

- *Custom principals* can be defined by an application in any way necessary for that particular application. They can extend the basic notion of the principal's identity and roles.

Working with Role-Based Authorization

The .NET Framework role-based security supports authorization by making information about the principal, which is constructed from an associated identity, available to the current thread. The identity, along with the principal it helps to define, can be based on a Windows account or can be a custom identity unrelated to a Windows account.

Your code can use the identity and principal objects to access information about users. The authorization code is the same for Web and Windows applications. Two sets of classes are provided, one for Windows and Active Directory security, and another for custom security solutions. The custom authentication and authorization objects are *GenericIdentity* and *GenericPrincipal*. The Windows authentication and authorization objects are *WindowsIdentity* and *WindowsPrincipal*.

Let's take a quick look at a sample. We use the following code in a Windows Forms application's *Form_Load* event handler to determine whether a user is a manager. If he is part of the Managers Windows group, the *pnlManagers* panel is visible. If he isn't, the panel isn't visible.

```
If CheckRole("Managers") Then
    pnlManagers.Visible = True
End If
```

The *CheckRole* function does all the authorization checking and returns *True* or *False*. Let's look at *CheckRole*. The function takes only one parameter, the role identifier:

```
Function CheckRole(ByVal sRoleName As String) _
    As Boolean
```

The next two lines create variables used by the function:

```
Dim sDomain As String, i As Integer
Dim sFullPath As String
```

Now for the fun: the next line retrieves the current identity for the user and stores it into an identity object.

```
Dim MyIdentity As WindowsIdentity = _
    WindowsIdentity.GetCurrent()
```

Next, a new *WindowsPrincipal* object is created with the *WindowsIdentity* that we just created.

```
Dim MyPrincipal As New WindowsPrincipal(MyIdentity)
```

The next two lines first create a *Boolean* variable to hold the role status and then pull the username for the user and store it in *IdentName*:

```
Dim bInAdministrators As Boolean
Dim IdentName As String = MyIdentity.Name
```

We find the location of the forward slash (\) in the username and retrieve the domain or machine name. This is necessary for the *IsInRole* method later.

```
i = IdentName.IndexOf("\")
sDomain = IdentName.Substring(0, i)
```

Now, the full path name of the user group is created by concatenating the machine or domain name with the role name.

```
sFullPath = sFullPath.Concat(sDomain, "\", sRoleName)
```

We can finally go after the role by calling the *IsInRole* method. This method returns *True* if the user is in that role or *False* otherwise:

```
bInAdministrators = MyPrincipal.IsInRole(sFullPath)
```

If the user was not in the role specified, we also check to see whether the user is an Administrator on the system and, if so, authorize him:

```
If bInAdministrators = False Then
    bInAdministrators = _
        MyPrincipal.IsInRole(WindowsBuiltInRole.Administrator)
End If
```

Notice that we use *WindowsBuiltInRole.Administrator* as the role indicator. You must use this enumeration to check for built-in roles. If you try to use *Administrator* or *Administrators* as a string, the check won't work. The other enumerations for built-in roles are shown after the end of this function.

Finally, we can return *bInAdministrator* and end the function:

```
    Return bInAdministrators
End Function
```

The built-in role enumerations are listed here:

- *AccountOperator*
- *Administrator*
- *BackupOperator*
- *Guest*
- *PowerUser*
- *PrintOperator*
- *Replicator*
- *SystemOperator*
- *User*

For ASP.NET applications, you can also create a handler for the *Authorize-Request* event in global.asax. You could also create your own HTTP module to handle security. Likewise, you can wrap some of the .NET Framework functions in a class library to implement custom methods that you can access.

The .NET Framework also allows you to make assignments declaratively at the method level. With the availability of method-level role assignments, you can secure components and interfaces that were designed without security in mind. If the methods themselves are not securable with declarative role assignments, you might need to do programmatic role checking. Keep security in mind when deciding how to factor business functionality through methods. Otherwise, you could be forced to add security-related code at the last minute.

URL Authorization

ASP.NET applications are special cases because they are based on HTTP and HTML and thus share the good and bad of those technologies. URL authorization is designed to allow you to restrict a user's access to a folder or files. URL authorization is performed by the *URLAuthorizationModule* class, which maps users and roles to pieces of the URI namespace. This module implements both positive and negative authorization assertions—that is, the module can be used to selectively allow or deny access to arbitrary parts of the URI namespace for certain sets, users, or roles. This allows you to authorize access to particular URLs based on user or role IDs.

The *URLAuthorizationModule* class is available for use at any time. To use it, you need only place a list of users and roles in the <allow> or <deny> elements of the <authorization> section of a configuration file.

You can map either user accounts or roles to Windows users if you are using IIS Authentication. When doing so, simply set a domain or server name prefix to the username or role. For instance, if the Engineers role maps to the Engineers group in the MyCo domain, the authorization will appear like this:

```
< authorization><Allow user= "Ken"
    roles= "MyCo\Engineers"/>
<deny users= "*"/></authorization>
```

The question mark in the following code represents anonymous users and thus forces users to log on:

```
< authorization>
    <deny users= "?"/>
</authorization>
```

The Security Layer

Now that we've examined several security options, let's consider what we do in our HRnet application. As mentioned earlier, our application has several security requirements:

- Support for both ASP.NET and Windows applications

- A custom credentials database, using SQL Server for now (shown in Figure 5-3)

- Username, password, and role information

These simple requirements led us to make choices. We could have used any of the technologies discussed so far, but for one reason or another they did not fit exactly right. For instance, ASP.NET would allow us to use custom authentication, but it doesn't work with Windows applications. Therefore, we needed a more generic technology. Enter our security layer.

Microsoft anticipated application needs that went beyond the standard ways they integrated security into ASP.NET and the .NET Framework. To accommodate these needs, they created generic credentials classes. A developer can use these classes to create a custom security system that provides easy-to-use role-based security. The first task we faced was trying to design a component that met these needs and didn't require lots of developer work. Our first thought was to create the security layer and have ASP.NET developers simply place code to check the login status at the top of each page. This approach is fraught with problems because it places the responsibility on the developer to work out the security on each page and include it. We figured that there must be a better way, and luckily there is. The architecture we decided on is shown in Figure 5-5.

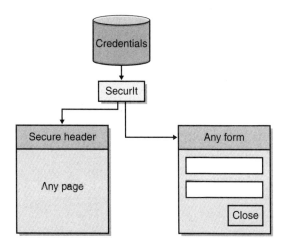

Figure 5-5   The security architecture for HRnet

Figure 5-5 shows our security layer implemented by the SecurIt component. This component is the only part of the application that actually touches the credentials in the database. The Web application and the Windows application don't go directly to the database. The Windows application shown in Figure 5-5 can also talk directly to the SecurIt component. Because the Windows application is stateful, it can simply create a reference to the component locally and hold on to it until the application ends. The Web application can't and therefore must use some type of intermediate storage.

Another factor comes into play at this point, which we mentioned earlier. The Windows application can rely on a single starting point for the application, whereas the Web application can be started from any page. Figure 5-5 shows our solution to this. We created a secure ASP.NET server control that checks the user's credentials. If the user is not logged in, this control redirects the user to the login page. All the developer needs to do is put the header on the page and the page is secure. We can also easily create an audit program that searches a Web site and makes sure that all pages in the site contain the header control. Besides, developers want to use the header because it implements the header part of the UI, which includes the page's image and its title. As you can see, including the header in each page isn't extra work.

The resulting system is nice and simple. Both application types can use the SecurIt component, and the front end for developers is simple and requires only a minimum amount of coding.

Creating the SecurIt Component

The first step in creating the SecurIt component is to add a component class named *SecurIt* to your project. Then delete the default class (*class1*) in the new project and add a new class named *UserSecurity*. This is the class that does the bulk of the security work.

Next add the following three *Imports* statements just before the *Class* statement:

```
Imports DataAccessLayer.DataAccess
Imports System.Security.Principal
Imports System.Web
Public Class UserSecurity
    Inherits System.ComponentModel.Component
```

Now expand the generated code region and find the constructor with no parameters:

```
Public Sub New()
    MyBase.New()
```

```
This call is required by the Component Designer.
InitializeComponent()

'Add any initialization after the InitializeComponent() call.
```

Add the following lines just before the *End Sub* statement. The first line in the *Try* block sets the *privateModuleName* variable.

```
Try
    privateModuleName = Me.GetType.ToString
```

The next line grabs the *HTTPContext* object if the class is running in a Web application. If the context object is set, the *If* block picks up the *UserName* and an array of roles from the *Session* object:

```
_context = HttpContext.Current
If _context.Session("UserName") <> "" Then
    privateUserName = _context.Session("UserName")
    privateUserRoles = _context.Session("Roles")
    InstantiateCredentials()
End If
```

An exception generated here indicates that the component is not in a Web application, and we can ignore the error but set *_context* to *Nothing*:

```
Catch
    _context = Nothing
End Try
```

The rest of the code in this region is generated by Microsoft Visual Studio .NET for the component designer.

Next we added a region titled Private Variables And Objects:

```
#Region " Private Variables and Objects"
```

The next two lines of code define variables that reference the generic security classes we mentioned earlier. The *GenericIdentity* class will represent a logged-in user, and the *GenericPrincipal* class will represent groups the user belongs to. Both of these objects will have their properties set in code by the SecurIt component. The other definitions are used by the SecurIt component.

```
Private privateUserIdendity As GenericIdentity
Private privateUserPrincipal As GenericPrincipal
Private privateDisposedBoolean As Boolean
Private privateModuleName As String
Private privateConnectionString As String = _
    "Server=LocalHost ;Database=SecurityCredentials;" & _
    "User ID=SecurGetIt;Password=xyl23ddz;"
Dim _context As HttpContext
```

(continued)

```
Private privateUserRoles(30) As String
Private privateUserName As String
Private Const privateExceptionMessage As String = _
    "Security layer Error. Detail Error Information " & _
    "can be found in the Application Log"

#End Region
```

The next region defines public members:

```
#Region "Public Properties and Objects"
```

The first property is used to retrieve the *UserName* and is read-only:

```
Public ReadOnly Property UserName() As String
    Get
        Return privateUserName
    End Get
End Property
```

The next property is an array and is used to return an array of roles the user belongs to:

```
Public ReadOnly Property Roles() As Array
    Get
        Return privateUserRoles
    End Get
End Property

#End Region
```

The next region contains the private functions:

```
#Region "Private Functions"
```

The first function in this section is *GetRolesFromDatabase*. This function is called by the *Login* function and takes the username as an argument. Then it retrieves the role names from the credentials database and returns them in a *DataSet*:

```
Private Function GetRolesFromDatabase(ByVal sUserName As _
    String) As DataSet
    Dim localDSOutput As DataSet
    Dim ParamsStoredProcedure As String = "spRolesForUser"
    Try
        Dim localOutPutServer As New _
            SQLServer(privateConnectionString)

        localOutPutServer.AddParameter( _
            "@UserName", sUserName, SQLServer.SQLDataType.SQLChar, _
            20, ParameterDirection.Input)
```

```
        localDSOutput = _
            localOutPutServer.runSPDataSet(ParamsStoredProcedure)

        Return localDSOutput
    Catch ExceptionObject As Exception
        LogException(ExceptionObject)

    Finally
    End Try
End Function
```

The next function creates the identity for the user.

```
Private Sub InstantiateCredentials()
    Try
```

The next line instantiates the *GenericIdentity* class and sets it to the user:

```
privateUserIdendity = _
    New GenericIdentity(privateUserName)
```

This line instantiates the *GenericPrincipal* class and sets it to the roles contained in the *privateUserRoles* array:

```
privateUserPrincipal = _
    New GenericPrincipal(privateUserIdendity, _
    privateUserRoles)
```

The rest of the code in this function cleans up the *Try…Catch* block and ends the function:

```
    Catch ExceptionObject As Exception
        LogException(ExceptionObject)
        Throw New Exception("An error occurred " & _
            "setting credentials")
    End Try
End Sub
```

The *SaveState* function performs a simple task. It stores the username and the user's roles in session variables named *UserName* and *Roles*:

```
Private Sub SaveState()
    If Not IsNothing(_context) Then
        context.Session("UserName") = privateUserIdendity.Name
        _context.Session("Roles") = privateUserRoles
    End If
End Sub
```

Within this region is a second region (Logging) that contains the logging functions:

```
#Region " Logging"
```

The first log function is *LogException* and is the same as the one from Chapter 4, so we won't repeat it here. We copied the *LogStatus* function from the *LogException* function and redesigned it slightly so that we could write messages that were status messages and not errors. The main changes are highlighted in bold here:

```
Private Sub LogStatus(ByRef localReason As String)

Dim EventLogMessage As String       'This is the Message we will
                                     'pass to the log.

Try
    'Create the Message to be passed from the exception.
    EventLogMessage = "An event occured in the following " & _
        "module: " & privateModuleName & _
        " The reason was: " & localReason & vbCrLf

    'Define the Eventlog as an Application Log entry.
    Dim localEventLog As New EventLog("Application")
    'Write the entry to the Application event log,
    'using this Module's name.
    localEventLog.WriteEntry(privateModuleName, _
        EventLogMessage, EventLogEntryType.Information, 56)
    Catch EventLogException As Exception
        Throw New Exception(privateExceptionMessage & _
            " - EventLog Error: " & EventLogException.Message, _
            EventLogException)
    End Try

End Sub
#End Region
#End Region
```

Next we created the Public Methods region:

```
#Region "Public Methods"
```

As you would expect, the first method is *Login* and logs the user in. This method returns *True* when the user's credentials are valid and *False* when they are invalid.

```
Public Function Login( _
    ByVal localUserName As String, _
    ByVal localPassword As String) As Boolean
```

The first few lines define variables for the function and set the return value to *False*:

```
Dim localCount As Integer
Dim localDSRoles As DataSet
```

```
Dim localdr As DataRow
Dim i As Integer
Dim localValidUser As Boolean

localValidUser = False
```

Next, an array is defined to contain the stored procedure output, and the name of the stored procedure output is set:

```
Dim ReturnOutPutList As New ArrayList()
Dim ParamsStoredProcedure As String = "spCheckUserCredentials"
```

If the *privateUserName* variable is already set, the user is logged in and the function returns *True*—no sense hitting the database if it isn't necessary.

```
If privateUserName <> "" Then
    localValidUser = True
    Return localValidUser
End If
```

The *Try* block is then started. The first few lines simply set up the call to the data access layer from Chapter 4 and execute the stored procedure.

```
Try

    Dim localOutPutServer As New _
        SQLServer(privateConnectionString)

    localOutPutServer.AddParameter( _
        "@UserName", localUserName, _
        SQLServer.SQLDataType.SQLChar, _
        20, ParameterDirection.Input)
    localOutPutServer.AddParameter( _
        "@Password", localPassword, _
        SQLServer.SQLDataType.SQLChar, 30, _
        ParameterDirection.Input)

    localOutPutServer.AddParameter( _
        "@Count", , SQLServer.SQLDataType.SQLInteger, , _
        ParameterDirection.Output)

    ReturnOutPutList = _
        localOutPutServer.runSPOutput(ParamsStoredProcedure)
```

Now the fun starts. At this point, we've executed the stored procedure and have the return values. Now we can grab the output parameters and iterate through them. In this case, there is only one return value, and if it is greater than zero, the user is valid.

```
Dim s As String
For Each s In ReturnOutPutList
    localCount = CInt(s.ToString)
Next
If localCount > 0 Then
```

Now that we have a valid user, we can set the return value to *True*, set the username (*privateUserName*) variable, and grab the roles by calling *GetRolesFromDatabase*.

```
localValidUser = True
privateUserName = localUserName
localDSRoles = GetRolesFromDatabase(localUserName)
```

Next, we simply loop through the *DataSet* containing the roles and load them into the *privateUserRoles* array.

```
i = 0
For Each localdr In localDSRoles.Tables(0).Rows
    privateUserRoles(i) = _
        Trim(localdr("RoleName"))
    i += 1
Next
```

Finally, we redimension the array to the number of roles.

```
ReDim Preserve privateUserRoles(i - 1)
```

Now we call *InstantiateCredentials* to build the principal objects.

```
InstantiateCredentials()
```

Finally, the *SaveState* function is called to store the credentials, and then the procedure cleanup is performed.

```
        SaveState()

    End If

Catch ExceptionObject As Exception
    LogException(ExceptionObject)
Finally
End Try

Return localValidUser
End Function
```

The *Logout* function is pure simplicity. It takes an optional reason and logs out the user by clearing the session variable and killing the objects. If a reason is supplied, it's logged.

```
Public Function Logout(Optional ByVal localReason _
    As String = "") As Boolean
    Dim localLogoutOk As Boolean

    Try
        If localReason <> "" Then
            LogStatus("Logout " & localReason)
        End If

        If Not IsNothing("_context") Then
            _context.Session("UserName") = ""
            _context.Session("Roles") = ""
            privateUserPrincipal = Nothing
            privateUserIdendity = Nothing
        End If
    Catch ExceptionObject As Exception
        localLogoutOk = False
    End Try
    Return True
End Function
```

The next function is *CheckRole*, which takes a role name as a string parameter and returns *True* when the user is in that role or *False* when the user is not. The role in boldface in the following code shows the call to the *IsInRole* method to check the user's group membership:

```
Public Function CheckRole( _
    ByVal localRoll As String) As Boolean
    Dim localValidRoll As Boolean = False

    If privateDisposedBoolean = True Then
        Throw New ObjectDisposedException(privateModuleName, _
        "This object has already been disposed, you cannot" & _
        " reuse it.")
    End If

    Try
        localValidRoll = _
            privateUserPrincipal.IsInRole(localRoll)
    Catch exc As Exception
    End Try

    Return localValidRoll
End Function
#End Region
```

The only other code in the SecurIt component is the *Dispose* function, which is the same as the *Dispose* functions used in classes in previous chapters.

Now it's time to test the security layer. Of course, we created a simple interface to test it once it compiled cleanly. Then we placed debug statements in the *Login* and *CheckRole* functions and stepped through them. The following output is from the Command window during the debugging process of the security layer. First, you can see that we're testing the values of the *localString-Array* to determine the role defined in element zero. Second, the *IsInRole* method checks the current user against the roles defined. Finally, the last line shows *False* because Clerk is not a valid role:

```
>? localStringArray(0)
"Manager"
>? localPrincipal.IsInRole("Manager")
True
>? localPrincipal.IsInRole("Clerk")
False
```

So far, that's it for the security layer. Now let's create the missing piece for the Web applications and then see how the security layer is used in both Web and Windows applications.

Creating the Secure ASP.NET Header

The first step in creating the header was to create a new project of type Class Library, because ASP.NET server controls are simply components (class libraries). Once the class project was created, we began building the header. The header is actually pretty simple. It has two properties: a text string for the header text and an image path for the logo. Most of the code deals with the security aspects related to the SecurIt component. Figure 5-6 shows the projected layout of the home page for the Web application and the page header.

As you can see from Figure 5-6, the header has an image in the top left corner and the title text is centered. The HTML for the header is shown here:

```
<P><TABLE id="TableHeader" cellSpacing="1"
    cellPadding="1" width="100%" border="0">
    <TR>
        <TD style="WIDTH: 118px">
            <IMG src="/SecurityChapterWebApp/Images/logo.GIF">
        </TD>
        <TD><H1 align="center"><FONT color="red">Home Page</FONT></H1>
        </TD>
    </TR>
</TABLE>
</P>
```

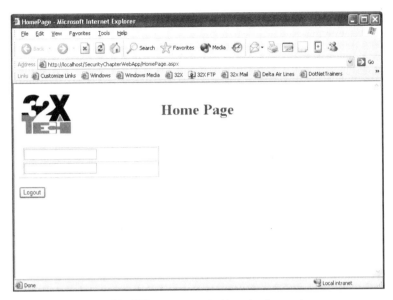

Figure 5-6   The ASP.NET server control header for each page

As you can see, this simple HTML represents the header in an HTML table. The question is, how do we put this into the magic ASP.NET server control? This turns out to be pretty straightforward. First, let's walk through the code for the control.

The project name for the server control project is *SecHeaderControl*. Figure 5-7 shows the General page in the Property Pages dialog box for the project.

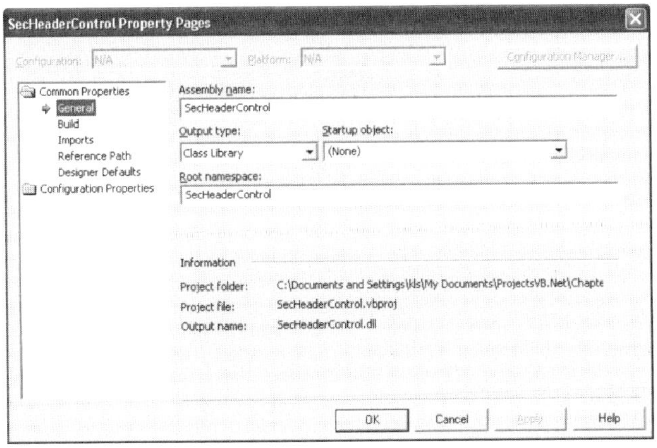

Figure 5-7   General settings for the SecHeaderControl project

Next, rename Class1.vb to SecHeader.vb, and change the class name on the *Class* statement. Then add the following *Imports* statements to the class:

```
Imports System.ComponentModel
Imports System.Web.UI
Imports System.Web
Imports System.Drawing.Design
```

Now add the *Designer* attribute to the class definition as shown in the next section of code. The reference to *SecHeaderDesigner* defines the designer class for the control. We'll cover this class at the end of this section.

```
<Designer(GetType(SecHeaderDesigner))> _
Public Class SecHeader
```

Since this class is a server control, it will inherit from the *WebControl* class in the .NET Framework. To accomplish this, we need to add the following *Inherits* statement:

```
Inherits System.Web.UI.WebControls.WebControl
```

The next three lines dimension variables:

```
Dim _text As String = "Default Header"
Dim _imagepath As String
Dim _TroubleOut As String
```

Next, we're going to add the two public properties. The first of these is the *Text* property and is created with the following two *Property* procedures. The attributes before the property procedures control how the property behaves.

```
<Bindable(True), Category("Appearance"), _
    DefaultValue("Default Header")> _
Property [Text]() As String
    Get
        Return _text
    End Get

    Set(ByVal Value As String)
        _text = Value
    End Set
End Property

<Bindable(True), Category("Appearance"), DefaultValue(""), _
    Editor(GetType(System.Web.UI.Design.ImageUrlEditor), _
    GetType(UITypeEditor))> _
Property [ImagePath]() As String
    Get
        Return _imagepath
    End Get
```

```
        Set(ByVal Value As String)
            _imagepath = Value
        End Set
    End Property
```

The previous code shown in boldface wires in the *ImageUrlEditor*. This editor allows the user of the control to browse for an image and then returns the image path.

The heart of the server control is the *Render* method. ASP.NET calls this method when the page is rendered to generate the controls output. Therefore the HTML we looked at earlier is output by this method.

The header for the *Render* method looks like this:

```
Protected Overrides Sub Render( _
    ByVal output As System.Web.UI.HtmlTextWriter)

    output.Write("<TABLE id=""TableHeader"" " & _
        "cellSpacing=""1"" cellPadding=""1"" " & _
        "width=""100%"" border=""0"">")
    output.Write("<tr>")
    output.Write("<TD style=""WIDTH: 118px""><IMG " & _
        "src=""" & ResolveUrl(ImagePath) & """></TD>")
    output.Write("<TD>")
    output.Write("<H1 align=""center""> " & _
        "<FONT color=""red"">" & [Text] & _
        "</FONT></H1>")
    output.Write("</TD>")
    output.Write("</TR>")
    output.Write("</TABLE>")
    'output.Write(_TroubleOut)

End Sub
```

The first boldface line outputs the part of the table with the image. Notice the call to *ResolveUrl(ImagePath)*. The *ResolveUrl* method takes a relative image path and renders it as an absolute path. This allows our control to properly display images when the control is hosted in pages that are in different folders.

The second boldface line outputs the header text. The *[Text]* entry outputs the text that the user of the control specifies. *Text* is in square brackets ([]) because it is a reserved word. The last line in *Render* is commented out. This line is used to output a text string during debugging of the control. Creating the debugging string is not shown in the text of this chapter but is in the source file.

The main work in this control is done in the *New* constructor. The first few lines create a variable for the context object and set a reference to the current *HttpContext*.

```
Public Sub New()
    Dim _context As HttpContext
    Try
        _context = HttpContext.Current
    Catch
        Exit Sub
    End Try
```

If the code reaches the next line and the *_context* is *Nothing*, the control is running in design mode and the code exits the constructor. If you don't insert the exit code, the control won't render correctly because it will try to run the security code in design view.

```
If _context Is Nothing Then
    Exit Sub
End If
```

Next, we instantiate the security component.

```
Dim oUser As SecurIt.UserSecurity
Try
    oUser = New SecurIt.UserSecurity()
```

At this point, the security layer will contain the user credentials if they are logged in. The following line simply checks the *UserName* property and, if it's blank, sends the user to login.aspx. You have two choices for transferring control to the login page. The *Reponse.Redirect* method (commented out in the next code snippet) actually sends a request to the browser to perform the redirection. Instead of *Redirect*, you can use *Server.Transfer*, as shown in the next boldface line. We prefer *Server.Transfer* because it performs the transfer without sending anything to the user. Plus, the user will still see her original URL in the Address line of the browser and won't see the URL for the Login page.

```
If oUser.UserName = "" Then
    '_context.Response.Redirect("login.aspx")
    _context.Server.Transfer("login.aspx")
End If
```

Finally, the code cleans up the *Try…Catch* block and ends the class.

```
    Catch exc As Exception
        Throw New Exception( _
            "An error occurred redirecting to login page", exc)
    End Try
End Sub
End Class
```

The last thing we need to create for the control is the designer class. Simply add a new class to the project and name it *SecHeaderDesigner*. Then add the following *Imports* statements:

```
Imports System
Imports System.IO
Imports System.Web
Imports System.Web.UI
Imports System.ComponentModel
Imports System.Web.UI.Design
```

Next, add the *Inherits* statement after the *Class* statement:

```
Public Class SecHeaderDesigner
    Inherits ControlDesigner
```

The only method in this class is *GetEmptyDesignTimeHtml*. This method is called when no properties have been set for the control.

```
Protected Overrides Function GetEmptyDesignTimeHtml() As String
    Return "No title (text) has been set for the header control"
End Function


End Class
```

Save and build the project. Fix any typing errors, and you're ready to test. Now add the control to the Toolbox by right-clicking the Toolbox, clicking Customize Toolbox in the shortcut menu, and then clicking the .NET Framework Components tab and clicking Browse. Find your control's DLL, double-click it, and click OK.

Using the SecurIt Layer

Implementing the security layer in an application involves only a few steps. First, we set a reference to the SecurIt component's DLL. This copies the DLL into the project structure.

Let's first use the security layer in an ASP.NET application. Once you've created the application and added a reference to the security layer, create a home page and a login page. The login page should have two text boxes, one for the username and one for the password. The entire HTML for our login.aspx is shown here:

```
<TABLE id="Table1" cellSpacing="1" cellPadding="1" width="100%"
    border="0">
    <TR>
        <TD style="WIDTH: 118px"></TD>
```

(continued)

```html
        <TD>
        <H1 align="center"><FONT color="red">
            Login Form</FONT></H1>
        </TD>
    </TR>
    <TR>
        <TD style="WIDTH: 118px"></TD>
        <TD>
            <TABLE id="Table2" cellSpacing="1" cellPadding="1"
                width="300" border="0">
                <TR>
                    <TD>Username</TD>
                    <TD><asp:textbox id="txtUsername"
                            runat="server">nDavolio</asp:textbox>
                        <asp:RequiredFieldValidator
                        id="RequiredFieldValidator1" runat="server"
                        ErrorMessage="Please enter your user name"
                        ControlToValidate="txtUsername">
                        </asp:RequiredFieldValidator></TD>
                </TR>
                <TR>
                    <TD>Password</TD>
                    <TD><asp:textbox id="txtPassword"
                        runat="server"
                        TextMode="Password">nDavolio
                        </asp:textbox>
                        <asp:RequiredFieldValidator
                            id="RequiredFieldValidator2"
                            runat="server"
                            ErrorMessage=
                            "Please enter your password"
                            ControlToValidate="txtPassword">
                        </asp:RequiredFieldValidator></TD>
                </TR>
                <TR>
                    <TD>Valid</TD>
                    <TD><asp:textbox id="txtValid" runat="server"
                        Width="65px"></asp:textbox></TD>
                </TR>
            </TABLE>
            <P><asp:button id="cmdLogin" runat="server"
                Text="Login"></asp:button></P>
            <P></P>
        </TD>
    </TR>
    <TR>
        <TD style="WIDTH: 118px"></TD>
        <TD></TD>
    </TR>
</TABLE>
```

The *txtValid* text box is used only in testing mode when the *Redirect* line is commented out. The only code in this page is the dimension line before the *Page_Load* event handler.

```
Dim oUser As New SecurIt.UserSecurity()
```

And here is the code in the *cmdLogin Click* event:

```
oUser = New SecurIt.UserSecurity()
txtValid.Text = oUser.Login(txtUsername.Text, txtPassword.Text)
oUser.Dispose()
oUser = Nothing
Response.Redirect("HomePage.aspx")
```

This code performs the login and redirect operations. Of course, the last line could have used *Server.Transfer* instead of *Response.Redirect*. It's your choice. That's it. Now developers can use this login page and only have to drop a header on their pages to make the security system work.

The HomePage also has a Logout button to allow users to exit the application. The *Click* event for this button contains the following code:

```
Dim oUser As SecurIt.UserSecurity
oUser = New SecurIt.UserSecurity()

oUser.Logout("Normal")

oUser.Dispose()
oUser = Nothing

Response.Redirect("login.aspx")
```

The code for the Windows application is essentially the same as that for the Web application. The Windows form has two text boxes and a button just like the Web application. The form also has two other text boxes that allow the user to check a role or display the roles the user is a member of. The code for the form is shown here:

```
Dim oUser As New SecurIt.UserSecurity()

Private Sub cmdLogin_Click(ByVal sender As System.Object, _
    ByVal e As System.EventArgs) Handles cmdLogin.Click
    txtValid.Text = oUser.Login(txtUsername.Text, _
    txtPassword.Text)
End Sub

Private Sub cmdCheckRole_Click( _
    ByVal sender As System.Object, ByVal e As _
    System.EventArgs) Handles cmdCheckRole.Click
    Dim localValidRole As Boolean
```

(continued)

```
        localValidRole = oUser.CheckRole("Manager")

        txtRoles.Text = "Manger = " & localValidRole
End Sub

Private Sub cmdGetRoles_Click(ByVal sender As System.Object, _
    ByVal e As System.EventArgs) Handles cmdGetRoles.Click

        Dim privateUserRoles() As String
        Dim i As Integer

        privateUserRoles = oUser.Roles

        For i = 0 To UBound(privateUserRoles)
            txtListOfRoles.Text &= privateUserRoles(i) & vbCrLf
        Next
End Sub
```

You can see from the boldface line in the preceding code how the roles are retrieved and placed into an array.

Conclusion

So what is left to do with the component in this chapter? Our next step is to encrypt the passwords (because they go into the database) and then apply the same encryption process to a user's password when checking authentication. This requires only a bit more code in the security component, but it also requires an application to maintain the user credentials. In the real world, we would implement an application to manage the user credentials, making it easy on users. The other thing we would do is place the security component in COM+. This would allow us to secure the component with an ACL and provide it with access to the event log without allowing other users or prying eyes to dig into the component and dig out constants, which can be done with just about any executable that isn't secure. All code, not just .NET applications, must deal with this issue.

You can see from the coverage in this chapter that the .NET Framework offers a tremendous number of security options. We didn't cover Code Access or Evidence Security, which are two other powerful security options for your applications. They come into play whether or not you intentionally employ them, because all .NET code uses these two mechanisms.

In the next chapter, we move on to the next phase of building our HRnet application, in which we create the generic client handlers for the Web portion of it.

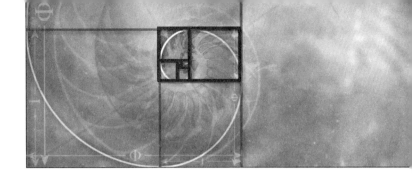

6

Implementing Generic Web Client Handlers

Recently I attended a Microsoft ASP.NET and Microsoft Visual Basic .NET seminar. One of the attendees must have misread the subject matter, because he said that he was converting his Web site to ASP (not to ASP.NET—someone at his company must have been sleeping). He asked the speaker whether using design-time controls was a good idea, since they looked like a "great object-oriented way to do things." The response—from the audience, not the speaker—was a high-volume, reverberating "No way!" Even though many folks thought this outburst was funny, those of us who have tried to use design-time controls (DTCs) with ASP didn't think so. DTCs worked, but only half the time; and when they did work, they made the applications extremely slow. We abandoned using them almost instantly. So why are we talking about DTCs? Well, we're not trying to put them down; however, the hesitancy they created in developers to trust server-side controls could prevent you from using the server and user controls in ASP.NET. Worse yet, not using them would be a tremendous shame because server-side controls in ASP.NET are extremely powerful and fast, and they allow you to create Web applications similar to traditional application development tools such as prior versions of Microsoft Visual Basic.

ASP.NET supports different kinds of server controls. HTML server controls are HTML control counterparts with added server-side functionality. Since they are provided mostly for compatibility reasons, we won't cover them here. Another kind of controls provided in ASP.NET are ASP.NET server controls. They have a rich set of properties, events, and methods and are what DTCs should have been. They are fully server-side controlled and render HTML output. They are compiled and extremely fast. They are also built with browser-independence in mind. You can recognize them easily because they are called in HTML with the ASP prefix. An example of a button would look like this:

```
<asp:Button id="Button1" runat="server" Text="Button"></asp:Button>
```

Although we won't go into detail about how ASP.NET server controls work, you'll learn quite a bit about them in the course of this book. Microsoft has given us the ability to write our own server controls from scratch that are just like the ones Microsoft provides. And we can build upon the default controls that ship with ASP.NET.

The ability to create new server controls or build upon existing ASP.NET controls helps us overcome many of the limitations imposed by Web development. A simple example of these limitations is the ASP.NET TextBox control. It lacks a lot of the behaviors that TextBox controls have in other development platforms such as Visual Basic, Microsoft Visual FoxPro, or Delphi. With ASP.NET's ability to enhance this control's default behaviors, we can add functions such as automatic highlight on focus and automatic creation of name tags for the control. We can also integrate these custom controls into the Visual Studio .NET Toolbox, making them available in a drag-and-drop fashion like ASP.NET intrinsic controls. This type of code reuse is very powerful and allows us to build large and complex Web applications much faster than we might ever have thought possible.

In addition to server controls, ASP.NET supports user controls. You could call user controls "include files on steroids"; however, this label doesn't really do them justice. User controls give us much greater abilities than include files ever have.

We're going to explain both user and server controls in detail. We're also going to create useful controls of both types. In the process, you'll learn how to plan for them, create them, and use them. We'll also explain how to incorporate them in your design As in all our chapters, you'll end up being able to reuse directly the controls we provide or change them quickly for your own application's needs.

User Interface Options with ASP.NET

User interface options have changed dramatically over the last couple of years, even more so for Web applications. Let's take a quick look at the past and the present states of user interface options and speculate about what the future might bring.

The Past

Code reuse in traditional ASP was quirky to say the least. Thank goodness for progress. You can only appreciate the good after you've worked with the bad. Include files were used heavily. Since the script engine processes all include files into one continuous page along with the actual ASP page, the result could get very large. And large means slow, especially in an interpreted environment such as ASP. We also saw developers trying to build an object-oriented hierarchy of include files. One include file called another that called another that called another—you get the idea. This not only created slow interpreted code but also caused maintenance nightmares—experiences we would rather forget. Include files also could not be loaded dynamically, and there was no way to expose properties, events, and methods. There was no encapsulation, so you could use the same include file several times on one page, each creating a slightly different result.

Enough about include files. You could also accomplish code reuse with the *server.execute* command. This command embedded code into the calling ASP page's content at the same place the command was called. Properties had to be passed with query strings. This solution created challenges similar to those we saw with include files. Another way to create user interface–related reusable code was with ActiveX controls. Unfortunately, ActiveX controls were browser-dependent, needed to be downloaded to the client, and created a lot of security issues. You could also reuse client-side code using Java Script libraries, which we still can use in ASP.NET today. We had no other options, so we used each of these techniques, depending on application requirements and our desire to reuse code to save time and energy.

The Present

ASP.NET lets us use include files just as ASP did. We might not recommend using them, but doing so is available and supported. Java Script libraries are still usable and sometimes the only options for enhancing browser-independent client functionality.

ASP.NET provides us with HTML server controls and ASP.NET server controls. We mentioned earlier that HTML server controls are really nothing more than standard HTML functions with added server-side functionality. ASP.NET server controls, on the other hand, give us much more control in a way similar to controls in Visual Basic, FoxPro, and so on. We've shown that ASP.NET server controls are prefixed with *<ASP:…runat="server">*. We have a lot of these server-side controls available to us right out of the box. Figure 6-1 shows a hierarchy of these controls.

Although the list of available server-side controls is extensive, it will become apparent that there are not enough. Microsoft's task isn't to provide a control for every possible application. Component vendors and you as a developer can create additional server controls. The term we would like to use for these controls is *custom server controls*. It is the most descriptive label we know and allows us to distinguish the controls from supplied default server controls. We mentioned that there are three ways to create custom server controls. Figure 6-2 shows an example of each way.

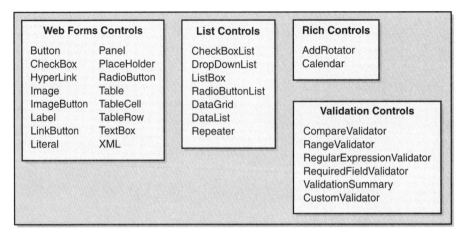

Figure 6-1 Server controls shipped with ASP.NET

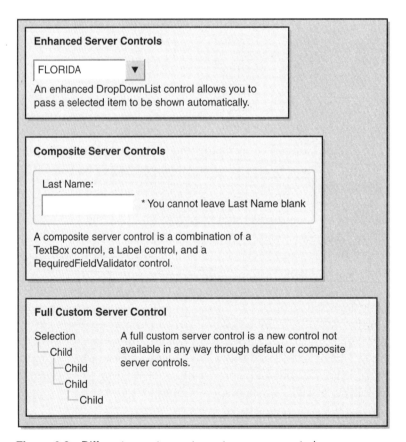

Figure 6-2 Different ways to create custom server controls

User controls are also very powerful. They behave just like ASP.NET Web Forms applications (or at least part of them), but they do so in an encapsulated object-oriented way.

The Future

Even though we don't have a crystal ball to show what the future will bring, we predict an abundance of third-party controls—many are already available. You'll also be able to use the server controls we introduce in this chapter. You'll be able to create your own collection of enhanced server controls that you can use in future applications. Take the OOP approach for user interface controls as well as business logic code, and soon you'll be rewarded with a large supply of custom user controls for your applications.

Choosing Between User Controls and Custom Server Controls

Both user controls and custom server controls allow code reuse for the user interface and code implementation. You could achieve the same outcome with either control in most cases, but both have distinctive advantages and disadvantages. For this reason, we need to compare the two types of controls and decide in which circumstances each is more appropriate. Table 6-1 shows a comparison of the two types of controls.

Table 6-1   Comparison of User Controls and Custom Server Controls

User Control	Custom Server Control
Compiled at run time	Precompiled
HTML design	No visual design; HTML needs to be declared programmatically
ASP.NET page model with code behind	Component model
Needs ASP.NET .aspx page to exist	Can be used in ASP.NET .aspx pages, user controls, or other custom server controls
No design-time interface (Only a box representing the user control is visible on an .aspx page.)	Has design-time and run-time interface (Even with no properties or data, a design-time look-alike is visible on an .aspx page.)
Cannot be added to the Toolbox	Can be added to the Toolbox (using drag and drop).
Cannot be traced by itself, only as part of an ASP.NET .aspx page	Not applicable

Typically, when we present both control options in .NET seminars, the attitude of developers is to adopt one or the other, whichever they feel more comfortable using. Those who have used Visual Basic, ASP, and HTML a lot seem to gravitate toward user controls. Those who have used C++ and Java and have developed components before tend to prefer custom server controls. It's natural to use what we're familiar with, but we recommend that you look at the best use for each type of control. The small learning curve associated with this examination will return great results.

Let's look at the main differences. First, a custom server control is precompiled, which gives it component-like behavior. When designed correctly, it looks, acts, and feels just like an ASP.NET built-in server control such as a Text-Box or a Label control. A user control, on the other hand, is compiled at run time. When the compiler finds the register directive in an .aspx page that points to a user control, it compiles the control before it inserts its content into the .aspx page.

The second major difference between these two control types is that when using user controls, you have the ability to create HTML in a designer. You don't have this option with custom server controls. Even though creating HTML programmatically is relatively simple, not being able to create HTML in the designer is a major reason you wouldn't use custom server controls. In our opinion, this issue makes the decision of when to use which control easier. Let's take a closer look at the decision process.

We'll cut to the chase right away and explain which control to use in one sentence: user controls are best when you create reusable user interface components for one specific application. Custom server controls are best for small and distinctive user interface options that can be used across many applications. We'll clarify this a bit with bad examples for each.

Here's the first example. You want to enhance a TextBox control, giving it a different background color set by a property that you set only once in the application. You decide to do this with a user control. This isn't a good solution. Dropping user controls into your Web Forms page wherever a text box is needed and seeing only a gray box at design time, as well as not being able to access their properties, would be a minor nightmare.

Instead of creating a user control for this enhanced TextBox control, you should create a custom server control based on the TextBox control and set its default properties to the chosen color. After implementing it and adding it to the Visual Studio .NET Toolbox, all you would need to do is drag and drop it on a Web Forms page whenever you want to use the enhanced TextBox custom server control.

Now here's the second example. You need address information for customers, vendors, banks, employees, and so on and decide to write a full address section in a custom server control. This solution isn't good either because you spend a lot of time programmatically creating the right look and function of the address section and then testing it. After including the address server control in the Visual Studio .NET Toolbox, you find that you used it for only one application. Even though the next application you work on requires addresses, these addresses need to look different, and you can't use the custom server control that cost you so much time and effort. This is a great example of when to user controls. You can quickly create and implement the HTML for the reusable address by using the same design features you have in Web Forms applications. For the next application, you simple copy the user control to it and make the changes required. Table 6-2 summarizes what we just discussed and provides a few more reasons you would use each type of control.

Table 6-2   Guidelines for Using a User Control vs. a Custom Server Control

User Control	Custom Server Control
Within one application	Across many applications
Reusable parts of user interface that would normally be part of Web Forms pages	Small and distinct user interface options such as enhancements to ASP.NET's default server controls
Ability to leverage individual cache settings (can be done for each user control)	Leverage templating
Not applicable	Package and sell controls

Each type of control is very powerful when used correctly; however, you can multiply their usability when you combine them. Using a custom server control in a user control is just as easy as using one in a Web Forms page. Doing so gets you the best of both worlds.

Building User Controls

The user control we're going to build now will be used in Web Forms pages within HRnet. It's the address user control and encapsulates standard information needed when entering addresses. During its creation, we're going to cover all the important principles you need to consider when creating user controls.

The Microsoft .NET Framework SDK documentation has the best definition for user controls we've seen: "A user-authored server control [fancy words for user control] enables an ASP.NET page to be reused as a server control." Indeed, user controls have the same object model as ASP.NET pages. Those of you who gave .NET a try in Beta 1 and later versions might remember that user controls were actually called "pagelets." That was quite descriptive. We guess it wasn't sophisticated enough to be used in the final version. The only differences between Web Forms pages and user controls are in the requirements of user controls to be embedded in a Web Forms page. You can't run or trace a user control by itself; it needs to be registered and used in a Web Forms page. This makes sense since user controls don't have *<HTML>...</HTML>* or *<FORM>...</FORM>* tags. The *<HTML>...</HTML>* tags can be used only once. Also, a user control needs to be within the Web Forms page's *<FORM>...</FORM>* tags to be part of the page's event driven model. User controls can be created by extracting parts of an .aspx page, adding the control directive, and changing the extension to .ascx or by using Visual Studio .NET, which gives you the control's structure and .ascx extension automatically (you can still copy and paste HTML into it).

The Basics of User Controls

Let's look at the sample files for this chapter. Open the UserandServerControls solution. In the UserControls directory, you'll find the Address.ascx user control. Open it—by default it will be in design view. You can see that it looks like a normal Web Forms page. Switch to the HTML view. Here is a portion of the HTML:

```
<%@ Control Language="vb" AutoEventWireup="false"
   Codebehind="Address.ascx.vb" Inherits="UserandServerControls.Address"
   TargetSchema="http://schemas.microsoft.com/intellisense/ie5" %>
<TABLE id="Table1" cellSpacing="1" cellPadding="1" width="100%" border="0">
   ⋮
```

Instead of the *@ Page* directive, user controls use the *@ Control* directive followed by the other standard directives for code-behind pages. Immediately after the *@ Page* directive, normal HTML starts defining the content. As we discussed before, there are no *<HTML>* or *<FORM>* tags, just the HTML that makes up the page. The user control also has a code-behind file that behaves exactly like the code-behind file of an .aspx Web Forms page.

How is this user control used in a Web Forms page? Look for the Address-Control.aspx page, and open it in design view. Figure 6-3 shows the page.

User controls have no design-time behavior, and they represent themselves only with a gray box that contains their names, similar to Button controls. Switch to HTML view to look at the control's registration and calling code. Here is the beginning code for this page:

```
<%@ Register TagPrefix="uc1" TagName="Address"
  Src="UserControls/Address.ascx" %>
<%@ Page Language="vb" AutoEventWireup="false"
  Codebehind="AddressControl.aspx.vb"
  Inherits="UserandServerControls.AddressControl"%>
<!DOCTYPE HTML PUBLIC "-//W3C//DTD HTML 4.0 Transitional//EN">
  ⋮
    <TD>
      <P align="center">
        <uc1:Address id="Address1" runat="server"></uc1:Address>
    </TD>
  ⋮
```

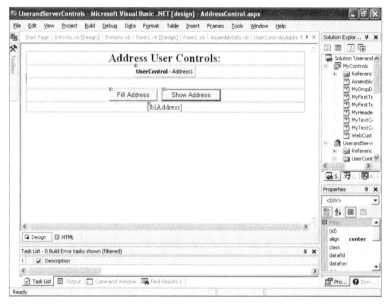

Figure 6-3   Web Forms page with custom user controls in design view

In the first line, we find the *@ Register* directive, which tells the compiler to include the user control when compiling this page. Next we define the *Tag-Prefix*. It separates the ASP.NET built-in controls (their *TagPrefix* is ASP) from user and custom server controls. By default, Visual Studio .NET uses *uc1*, which can be replaced with anything you want. Next is the *TagName*, which is this user control's name used in the page. The source is the absolute or relative path to the actual user control source files. The user control is registered and can now be used in the page. A bit farther down in the HTML, you find the code that brings the control to life:

```
<uc1:Address id="Address1" runat="server"></uc1:Address>
```

You use both the *TagPrefix* and *TagName* we defined. Giving the user control an ID is rather important. In the same way we can drop many TextBox controls onto a Web Forms page, we can have more than one of the same user controls on the page as well, with different unique IDs. First right-click the AddressControl.aspx page in Microsoft Solution Explorer, and then click Build And Browse on the shortcut menu. You'll see one address. Now add the following line of code after *</uc1:Address>*:

```
<uc1:Address id="Address2" runat="server"></uc1:Address>
```

When you click Build And Browse again, you'll see two addresses.

User controls can be registered either by HTML declarations or by dragging and dropping them onto the Web Forms page. When you use drag and drop, you must do so from Microsoft Solution Explorer, using the specific user control you want to place onto a Web Forms page. The control gets placed where you pointed and, if not registered on the page already, the *@ Register* directive is automatically added with the default .NET tag names.

Go ahead and click Build And Browse for the AddressControl.aspx Web Forms page. At run time, the user control is inserted into the Web Forms page. The result is shown in Figure 6-4.

Figure 6-4   Web Forms page with address user control at run time

Now that we have the basics out of the way, we can take a look at how we get access to a user control's properties and methods and, last but not least, its event model.

Properties of User Controls

The two choices for accessing a user control's properties are to either declare public variables or use property objects. When called, either of these two choices can be set declaratively or programmatically. We don't recommend using public variables since it's against good object-oriented programming (OOP) principles. Even though using public variables uses less code, it's best not to start bad habits. Let's look at the properties we declared for our Address.ascx user control:

```
'Property definitions used in the Address User Control

Public Property Header() As String
    Get
        Return lblHeader.Text
    End Get
    Set(ByVal Value As String)
        lblHeader.Text = Value
    End Set
End Property
Public Property Street() As String
    Get
        Return txtStreet.Text
    End Get
    Set(ByVal Value As String)
        txtStreet.Text = Value
    End Set
End Property
Public Property Suite() As String
    Get
        Return txtSuite.Text
    End Get
    Set(ByVal Value As String)
        txtSuite.Text = Value
    End Set
End Property
Public Property City() As String
    Get
        Return txtCity.Text
    End Get
    Set(ByVal Value As String)
        txtCity.Text = Value
    End Set
End Property
Public Property State() As String
    Get
        'Return the Value (not text) of Selected Item
        Return lstStates.SelectedItem.Value
```

(continued)

```
          End Get
      Set(ByVal Value As String)
          'Search for Value of States to be displayed
          Dim n As Integer
          For n = 1 To lstStates.Items.Count
              If lstStates.Items(n).Value.ToString = Value Then
                  lstStates.SelectedIndex = n
                  Exit For
              End If
          Next
      End Set
  End Property
  Public Property Zip() As String
      Get
          Return txtZip.Text
      End Get
      Set(ByVal Value As String)
          txtZip.Text = Value
      End Set
  End Property
```

The *Header*, *Street*, *Suite*, *City*, and *Zip* public property definitions in the preceding code behave the same way. They set the equivalent TextBox control's *Text* properties when their values are set, and they return the same values. An exception is the *State* property; it requires a bit more work. Before we explain its functionality, you need to look at the code-behind page of our Address.ascx user control. When the page loads the first time, a *DataSet* containing state information with both *short* and *long* state values (CA for California) is returned and bound to the *lstStates* DropDownList control. Since *ViewState* is also automatically handled in user controls, postbacks automatically contain the information without having to go back to the database. Here's the code that loads the state information:

```
Private Sub Page_Load(ByVal sender As System.Object, _
    ByVal e As System.EventArgs) Handles MyBase.Load
    'Put user code to initialize the page here
    'First Time Around --> Get the States Data
    If Not IsPostBack Then
        Dim statesDataSet As DataSet
        'Call Data Access Layer and Get States Table
        Dim StatesInformation As New SQLServer("data source=" & _
            "CPU-TENOTEBOOK;initial catalog=HRnet;password=;" & _
            "persist security info=True;user id=sa;" & _
            "workstation id=CPU-TENOTEBOOK;packet size=4096")
        Dim privateSQLStatement As String = _
            "Select * from States Order by States.st_name"
        statesDataSet = StatesInformation.runSQLDataSet( _
            privateSQLStatement, "States")
```

```
            StatesInformation.Dispose()
            StatesInformation = Nothing
            'Fill states DropDownList Control
            '(Value is CA, Text is California)
            lstStates.DataSource = statesDataSet
            lstStates.DataTextField = "st_name"
            lstStates.DataValueField = "st_short"
        End If
        Page.DataBind()
End Sub
```

Let's get back to the *States* public property definition. Here is the code again:

```
Public Property State() As String
    Get
        'Return the Value (not text) of Selected Item
        Return lstStates.SelectedItem.Value
    End Get
    Set(ByVal Value As String)
        'Search for Value of States to be displayed
        Dim n As Integer
        For n = 1 To lstStates.Items.Count
            If lstStates.Items(n).Value.ToString = Value Then
                lstStates.SelectedIndex = n
                Exit For
            End If
        Next
    End Set
End Property
```

The *Get* property (what is returned to the calling Web Forms page) simply returns the List control's current selected item's value. Notice that the value is the state's short name. In databases we like to save the states' short names instead of the long names, but we want to display their full names in the DropDownList control. The *Set* property (what can be set by the calling Web Forms page but can also be left empty) is another matter and a bit more involved. The ASP.NET DropDownList control has a deficiency. It has no built-in method or property to set a default value for the current row in its list to be displayed. We have to do this ourselves. If you followed the descriptions of custom server controls closely, you probably had the same thought we had: let's create a custom server Drop-DownList control adding this feature. That's exactly what we'll do later in this chapter in the section "Enhanced ASP.NET DropDownList Server Control."

For now we have to iterate through all the values in this list control until we find a match to the value we passed. Once we find it, we set the selected index and voila! The DropDownList control shows the default value we set in the user control's calling page.

Now let's look at both ways to set the properties we defined in the user control. First we'll set the *Header* property declaratively in the HTML that defines the control. Change the code in AddressControl.aspx to the following:

```
<P align="center"><ucl:address id="Address1" Header="Home Address"
    runat="server"></ucl:address></P>
```

By inserting *Header="Home Address"*, you set this property while calling the user control. This behavior is similar to passing parameters to subroutines and functions.

Second, we'll set properties programmatically from the calling page's code-behind file. There are some prerequisites you need to know to make this possible. Remember that user controls are not precompiled DLLs, so they don't simply give our code-behind file access to their properties and methods—the code-behind file doesn't know about the user control yet. You can discover a user control's properties and methods in one of two ways. The first and less preferable approach is to use the reflection capabilities in .NET, which can detect properties, events, and methods at run time. This approach is necessary only when the user control isn't compiled. We won't cover this option.

When you use Visual Studio .NET to create user controls, you can simply build them after you create or change them. When this is done, you can set a reference to them in the calling Web Forms' code-behind file. This is the second approach and our preferred way to gain access to user controls' properties, events, and methods. Here is the code that sets this reference:

```
Protected Address1 As Address
```

You need to add this code for each user control called in the page. *Address1* references the specific user control's ID. As soon as you add this line of code, *Address1*'s properties, public methods, and public variables are available, as you can see in the following lines of code:

```
Private Sub btnGetAddress_Click(ByVal sender As System.Object, _
    ByVal e As System.EventArgs) Handles btnGetAddress.Click
    User Control's Properties are set
    Address1.Street = "123 Fourth Ave"
    Address1.Suite = "101"
    Address1.City = "Los Angeles"
    Address1.State = "CA"
    Address1.Zip = "11111-2222"
End Sub
```

Each user control used in a Web Forms page needs its own reference, even if the same user control is used over and over again. Each user control's ID must have a line of reference.

Run this example, and click the Fill Address button. Clicking the button invokes the preceding code, which populates the Address.ascx user controls. By the way, clicking that button also runs the code we wrote to set the correct state in the DropDownList control.

Next, we included a Show Address button. Here is the code it calls:

```
Private Sub btnShowAddress_Click(ByVal sender As System.Object, _
    ByVal e As System.EventArgs) Handles btnShowAddress.Click
    'Read from User Control's Properties
    lblAddress.Text = Address1.Street + " " + Address1.Suite + "<BR>"
    lblAddress.Text += Address1.City + ", " + Address1.State + _
        " " + Address1.Zip
End Sub
```

Instead of setting the properties of Address.ascx, we call their values into the *lblAddress* Label control. Notice that the state is in its short form, CA, for California, whereas the user control reads the full name.

The next example, AddressControl2.aspx, shows how the same Address.ascx user control can be called two times in the same form, each time with its own separate properties, events, and methods. This ability is very powerful and allows full encapsulation of the control, just like .NET's OOP features in the rest of its framework. Each iteration of the user control has its own internal state of properties, settings, and data, and each handles its own methods and events. You can test this in this example by clicking all the buttons, changing data, clicking again, and so on. Notice that we had to declare the second user control, even when it calls the same control:

```
Protected Address1 As Address
Protected Address2 As Address
```

To gain access to properties, events, and methods, you must declare each instance of a user control. Don't forget these lines of code. It isn't automatically added by Visual Studio .NET. Forgetting them has caused us a couple of hours of wondering and searching why user controls suddenly didn't work correctly anymore.

Methods of User Controls

To access methods, we have to fulfill the same requirements we discussed for user control properties. To call a method, either the method has to be declared public or we have to call a property that in turn calls a method. (We did the latter with the *State* property in our previous example.)

We want our user control to have the ability to save its state, not only internally, which it does automatically within the controls used, but also externally, calling the *SaveAddressState* and *GetPreviousState* methods from the Web form that calls it. We have added the following two public subroutines to AddressMethods.ascx to provide this functionality:

```
Public Sub SaveAddressState()
    Session("Address") = txtStreet.Text
    Session("Suite") = txtSuite.Text
    Session("City") = txtCity.Text
    Session("State") = lstStates.SelectedItem.Value
    Session("Zip") = txtZip.Text
End Sub
Public Sub GetPreviousState()
    If Not Session("City") Is Nothing Then
        Street = CType(Session("Address"), String)
        Suite = CType(Session("Suite"), String)
        City = CType(Session("City"), String)
        State = CType(Session("State"), String)
        Zip = CType(Session("Zip"), String)
    End If
End Sub
```

First we need to mention that this isn't a production-ready sample. It simply demonstrates accessing methods within user controls. We would handle this functionality in an object specific to the instantiation of a user control. The preceding code would not allow full encapsulation and would work only for one instance of the user control. *SaveAddressState* simply passes the user control's address values to session variables, whereas *GetPreviousState* checks for the availability of the session and then inputs the saved values. Notice that we save the returned information using the user control's properties and not its specific TextBox or DropDownList control. Saving the information to the property allows us to use the information to provide additional functionality such as setting the correct state in the *States* DropDownList control.

AddressControlEvents.aspx is the Web Forms page that uses our enhanced AddressEvents user control. In its code-behind file, we call the two subroutines we added through button click events:

```
Private Sub btnSaveState_Click(ByVal sender As System.Object, _
    ByVal e As System.EventArgs) Handles btnSaveState.Click
    AddressMethods1.SaveAddressState()
End Sub

Private Sub btnRestoreState_Click(ByVal sender As System.Object, _
    ByVal e As System.EventArgs) Handles btnRestoreState.Click
    AddressMethods1.GetPreviousState()
End Sub
```

As you can see, calling the subroutines is a simple and clean process. You can test the added behavior by adding an address of your own, clicking Save User Control State, making changes to the address, and then clicking Restore User Control State to return your saved settings.

Event Bubbling in User Controls

User controls handle the events of their controls just as Web Forms pages do. This means that we need to handle these events within the user control. We need to know that none of these events will be visible to the calling .aspx page. User controls also encapsulate events within themselves. Each instantiation of the same user control on one page handles its own event handling.

If the calling page doesn't receive events from its user controls, how do we go about letting the page know that a certain event occurred? We do this by using *event bubbling*. User controls can raise events, allowing us to pass events that need to go to the calling page by setting up and raising a user control event.

We'll illustrate event bubbling by adding the capability to notify the calling Web Forms page when any of the Address user control's fields change. The user control we use for this example is AddressEvents.ascx; it is used by the AddressControlBubbling.aspx page. Let's take a look at the user control's code-behind page first:

```
Dim AddressSender As Object
Dim AddressE As EventArgs
Public Event AddressChanged(ByVal AddressSender As Object, _
    ByVal AddressE As EventArgs)
```

After defining a new event sender and new event arguments, we create a new event definition for this user control. Notice that this is a public event, so the calling page can access the event definition. The preceding lines of code can be anywhere in the user control's class structure. We prefer to put them with the other control's definitions, near the beginning of the class.

Farther down in the code-behind page, you find the lines of code that raise the event:

```
Private Sub txtStreet_TextChanged(ByVal sender As System.Object, _
    ByVal e As System.EventArgs) Handles txtStreet.TextChanged
    ContentChanged()
End Sub
Private Sub txtSuite_TextChanged(ByVal sender As System.Object, _
    ByVal e As System.EventArgs) Handles txtSuite.TextChanged
    ContentChanged()
End Sub
```

(continued)

```
    ⋮
Sub ContentChanged()
    'Let's raise the event
    RaiseEvent AddressChanged(AddressSender, AddressE)
End Sub
```

Each TextBox or DropDownList control's *Change* event gets redirected to the *ContentChanged* subroutine. Here we raise our *AddressChanged* custom event that we declared earlier.

Now let's look at AddressControlBubbling.aspx and see how it handles the event passed by the user control. The first necessary change is in the declaration of the user control in the .aspx code-behind page. It can no longer be declared simply as this:

```
Protected AddressEvents1 As AddressEvents
```

We need to add the *WithEvents* keyword to allow the user control's event processing within the calling .aspx page:

```
Protected WithEvents AddressEvents1 As AddressEvents
```

Now we're ready to provide an event handler that takes care of the public events of the user control:

```
Private Sub AddressEvents1_Change(ByVal sender As System.Object, _
    ByVal e As System.EventArgs) Handles AddressEvents1.AddressChanged
    lblChangeMessage.Text = "The Address had a changed"
End Sub
```

This event handler is very similar to the ones created automatically when you want to handle a button click event or a change event. It has the sender and *e* parameters and the *Handles* keyword. The code in boldface shows that we want to handle the *AddressChanged* event of the AddressEvents1 user control. The definition is specific to the user control's ID. This allows events to be encapsulated within a user control, just as properties can. When you test this example, you can use the Fill Address and Show Address buttons, and then make a change in the address. Click the Show Address button again, and the Change event bubbles up to the form and is shown in a specific label. Click the Show Address button one more time, and the event disappears. Why? No changes were made between the first and second button clicks.

The ability to bubble up an event from individual controls in a user control or to create user control–specific events is one of its strengths and allows us to create well-defined, functioning user controls.

Dynamically Loaded User Controls

There is one more powerful feature of these controls we haven't yet discussed, and we'll tackle it in this section. We've found the option to load user controls dynamically into Web Forms .aspx pages to be one of the most useful features in ASP.NET. This feature allows us to create much more flexible user interfaces, bringing interaction with Web pages to a new level. Before user controls, achieving a high level of interaction was either impossible or very difficult and code-intensive. To demonstrate this great feature, we're going to allow a Web Forms page to call the AddressEvents.ascx user control a total of three times to allow the entering of a business address, home address, or emergency contact address. The form's name is MultiAddressControl.aspx. We recommend that you take a close look at the code and follow along carefully.

Before adding controls dynamically to an .aspx page (which can be done with any ASP.NET Web control, not only user controls), we need to do a bit of setup work. First, we need to be able to access the .aspx form's properties, events, and methods from its code-behind page. Second, we want to be able to place the controls anywhere on the page, even when they're created dynamically. If we don't take care of the first step in our setup, we simply can't add dynamic controls, and if we don't take care of the second step, the controls will be added to the end of the form, which might not fit into our design and might look terrible. Fortunately, the power of .NET comes to help. Let's solve these challenges, one step at a time.

Adding Controls Dynamically

To place controls dynamically on a Web Forms page, we need to access the page's properties, events, and methods from the code-behind page. For this reason, we need to create a reference to the Web Forms page. Here's the code that can be placed anywhere within the class definition of this page. As mentioned earlier, we recommend you place this near the top of the class.

```
'First, we need to reference the Form on this .aspx page
Protected multiAddress As System.Web.UI.HtmlControls.HtmlForm
'Second, we need to declare all possible User Controls by the name
'we give them
Protected WithEvents BusinessAddress1 As AddressEvents
Protected WithEvents HomeAddress1 As AddressEvents
Protected WithEvents EmergencyAddress1 As AddressEvents
```

The name *multiAddress* needs to match the ID of the form:

```
<form id="multiAddress" method="post" runat="server">
```

The user control is declared as an HtmlForm in the *System.Web.UI.HtmlControls* namespace. This gives us programmatic access to the form. To access the user controls with events, we also must define and name any of the potential user controls we will call in the page. This is important for getting full access to their properties, events, and methods. Even when a specific user control or one of the same user controls with a different name does *not* get called, the control needs to be predefined since its definition cannot be created dynamically. We'll call the same user control named AddressEvents with up to three different contexts: a business address, a home address, and an emergency address. You can do this in any combination.

We're now ready to add user controls dynamically. In the MultiAddress-Control.aspx sample Web form, we choose three CheckBox controls to determine which user control will be loaded dynamically. Here's the code that determines whether a CheckBox is selected and needs to load a user control:

```
'Check to see which addresses are required
If chkBusiness.Checked = True Then
    btnGetAddress.Visible = True  'Toggle BusinesssAddress Button
    ' Load the Control
    BusinessAddress1 = _CType(LoadControl _
        ("UserControls\AddressEvents.ascx"), AddressEvents)
    BusinessAddress1.ID = "BusinessAddress1"
    BusinessAddress1.Header = "Business Address"
    multiAddress.Controls.Add(BusinessAddress1)
    btnGetAddress.Visible = False
End If
```

We already defined *BusinessAddress1* in the previous lines of code and need to add the specific control. This is done using the *LoadControl* command with the location of the AddressEvents.ascx file. Notice that we use the *CType* function to allow *option strict* to be turned on. Now that the user control is loaded, we can give that control its ID (which is necessary to access it later in the code-behind page), and we can pass the header. Passing the header is equivalent to passing properties declaratively in HTML. Now that the control is loaded, has an ID, and has its properties set, we can add it to the .aspx form's control collection using *multiAddress.Controls.Add(BusinessAddress1)*. The user control is now added to the Web Forms page and we have full code-behind access to its properties, events, and methods. The only problem with this implementation is the placement of dynamically called controls—at the end of the form. Let's take care of this next.

Placing Dynamically Added Controls

The amount of thought put into ASP.NET technology becomes apparent when you see the next solution: placeholders. You can drop as many placeholders on a Web Forms page as you like. As long as you don't assign anything to them, they disappear. But you can place any ASP.NET default server control, user control, or custom server control into one of the PlaceHolder controls dynamically. Here is the HTML for our page with the placeholders in boldface:

```
<TABLE id="Table1" cellSpacing="1" cellPadding="1" width="100%"
   align="center" bgColor="whitesmoke" border="0">
   <TR>
      <TD>
         <P align="center"><STRONG><FONT size="5">
         Address User Controls:</FONT></STRONG></P>
      </TD>
   </TR>
   <TR>
      <TD>
         ⋮
         <P align="center">
         <asp:label id="lblAddress" runat="server"></asp:label><BR>
         <asp:PlaceHolder id="PlaceHolder1"runat="server">
         </asp:PlaceHolder><BR>
         <asp:PlaceHolder id="PlaceHolder2" runat="server">
         </asp:PlaceHolder><BR>
         <asp:PlaceHolder id="PlaceHolder3" runat="server">
         </asp:PlaceHolder><BR>
         <asp:Label id="lblChangeMessage" runat="server"></asp:Label>
         </P>
      </TD>
   </TR>
⋮
```

In the preceding HTML, you can see that we put the Placeholder controls exactly where we wanted. Once the Placeholder controls are added, we can dynamically add any control to them. In our case, we add the user control we just created to a Placeholder control. Here is the code. (The assignment to the Placeholder control is in boldface.)

```
'Check to see which addresses are required
If chkBusiness.Checked = True Then
   btnGetAddress.Visible = True  'Toggle BusinesssAddress Button
   ' Load the Control
   BusinessAddress1 = _CType(LoadControl _
      ("UserControls\AddressEvents.ascx"), AddressEvents)
   BusinessAddress1.ID = "BusinessAddress1"
```

```
      BusinessAddress1.Header = "Business Address"
      multiAddress.Controls.Add(BusinessAddress1)
      PlaceHolder1.Controls.Add(BusinessAddress1)
      btnGetAddress.Visible = False
End If
```

Feel free to move the Placeholder controls somewhere else and see how the user controls realign themselves accordingly.

That's all there is to it. The rest of the code in the MultiAddressControl.aspx sample is for testing and event handling. You can look at the code and compare it to previous samples.

We've taken a quick but detailed tour into user controls, showing how useful they can be. Now that you understand how to build and implement them, including accessing their properties, events, and methods from code-behind pages and dynamically loading them anywhere on a Web Forms page, you have a great tool for OOP in user interfaces. We've built a flexible and powerful address user control that we use in the HRnet application. (More on this in Chapter 14.)

Building Custom Server Controls

As flexible as user controls can be for individual Web applications, custom server controls can be just as capable and even more so, both for individual and universal Web applications. We've already discussed where and when to use custom server controls. Here are the three major choices you have when creating them:

- **Full custom server control**   A full custom server control builds whatever outcome is required from scratch. It inherits from *System.Web.UI.WebControls.WebControl*. You can create any properties, events, and methods you want and show any output, both in design and run-time views, or show no output at all. This is the default setting when you create a custom server control in Visual Studio .NET, and we'll create our first control this way, covering every required step in detail.

- **Enhanced, or derived, custom server control**   An enhanced, or derived, custom server control is based on a default ASP.NET server control or on another custom server control. It inherits all properties, events, and methods from its parent, and you can add your own properties, events, and methods—a behavior very similar to inheritance in Visual Basic .NET. Major features and behaviors of these controls come from their parents. You simply add features or change existing ones.

■   **Composite server control**   A composite server control groups several existing server controls: default, full, or enhanced custom server controls. It interconnects functionality and dependability of these controls, exposing all or defined properties, events, and methods. Composite server controls are very similar to user controls. When we design them, we must be extremely careful not to make them too specific. Doing so would limit their value, hampering the most important reason for having them: reuse.

The Basics of Full Custom Server Controls

Because a code template for a full custom server control is created by default in Visual Studio .NET, we'll use it for our first server control example and explain its general behavior. We've found a code template to be of great help, even for advanced users. The sample files for our custom server controls are in C:\Build-OOP\Ch06\MyControls. You can either add this project into your environment or create a new project with a name such as MyNewControls. Make sure you set the correct path and select Web Control Library in the Add New Project dialog box, as shown in Figure 6-5.

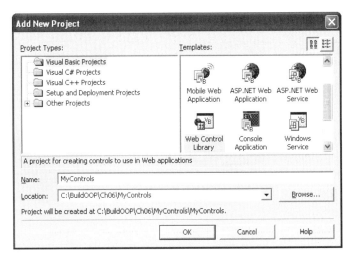

Figure 6-5   Adding a new WebControl library with a specific location

Even though the new project is added to our solution, we still have to create a reference to it in our Web application in order to use the compiled custom server controls. If you're adding your own MyNewProject project, add a reference to the UserandServerControls project now. We're now ready to use our newly created controls directly.

A look at the newly created MyControl (or MyNewControl) project shows that a default WebCustomControl1.vb has been created. We won't change this control so that we can look back at its default behaviors. Here is the full code segment for it:

```
Imports System.ComponentModel
Imports System.Web.UI
<DefaultProperty("Text"), ToolboxData("<{0}:WebCustomControl1 runat=server>
    </{0}:WebCustomControl1>")> Public Class WebCustomControl1
    Inherits System.Web.UI.WebControls.WebControl
    Dim _text As String
    <Bindable(True), Category("Appearance"), DefaultValue("")>
    Property [Text]() As String
        Get
            Return _text
        End Get
        Set(ByVal Value As String)
            _text = Value
        End Set
    End Property
    Protected Overrides Sub Render(ByVal output As
        System.Web.UI.HtmlTextWriter)
        output.Write([Text])
    End Sub
End Class
```

Registering and Calling a Custom Server Control

Before getting into more detail, let's run this example in a Web Forms page. It won't be very exciting, but it will teach us the fundamentals of server controls. Create a new .aspx page using flow layout, and give it a name. We named the page MyFirstCustomServerControl.aspx.

Just like user controls, custom server controls need to be registered. Here is the HTML code for registering the control:

```
<%@ Register TagPrefix="MyC" Namespace="MyControls"
    Assembly="MyControls" %>
```

Compare this to user control registration:

```
<%@ Register TagPrefix="uc1" TagName="Address"
    Src="UserControls/Address.ascx" %>
```

The @ *Register* and the *TagPrefix* are treated the same. Notice, however, that the *TagName* that defines the user control isn't used to define the custom server control. Instead of being called by a specified *TagName*, the custom server control is called directly with its class name within a namespace that resides in a Web control library project. This is why the next two directives point to the namespace used in a specific assembly instead of the physical source file, as is the case with user controls. Now call the specific custom server control we just created. Here's the HTML code that needs to be within the Form statement:

```
<MyC:webcustomcontrol1 id="WebCustomControl1" runat="server"
      Text="I am working"></MyC:webcustomcontrol1>
```

When you switch to Design View, you'll already see the text "I Am Working." We'll offer you more on design time behavior shortly, but for now, build and browse MyFirstCustomServerControl.aspx. We agree that this example won't win the Nobel prize, but you did build and implement a server control in just a few minutes.

The Custom Server Control Class

Let's look at the code in WebCustomControl1.vb in more detail:

```
Imports System.ComponentModel
Imports System.Web.UI
<DefaultProperty("Text"), ToolboxData("<{0}:WebCustomControl1 runat=server>
      </{0}:WebCustomControl1>")> Public Class WebCustomControl1
      Inherits System.Web.UI.WebControls.WebControl
```

After referencing the two system namespaces, we create a public class with the name for our custom server control—in this case, it defaults to WebCustomControl1. We inherit this class from the *WebControl* base class in the *System.Web.UI.WebControls* namespace. This gives us a lot of default server control behaviors. Notice that the class has added attributes. These attributes are used by Visual Studio .NET and are not required to run server controls. The first attribute defines a default property named *Text*. This property becomes visible in the Visual Studio .NET Properties window. The second attribute defines the tag XML, which will be placed in the page when you drag and drop the control to a Web Forms page. The definition of the XML tag is within the *Toolbox-Data* attribute. The {0} represents the *TagPrefix* defined in the *<% @ Register %>* directive. When drag and drop is used, Visual Studio .NET automatically creates the register directive and injects the *ToolboxData* attribute's XML tag defined earlier into the Web Forms page. If no other *TagPrefix* was defined, *cc1,cc2,cc3*, and so on are used by default. The default behavior can be changed using an assembly-level attribute named *TagPrefixAttribute*. Here is the line of code inserted after the *Imports* statements:

```
Imports System.ComponentModel
Imports System.Web.UI
<Assembly: TagPrefix("MyControls", "MyCustomControls")>
  ⋮
```

Remember that this is an assembly-level attribute and will be used for all custom server controls within this project, even though you might define it in only one control. This attribute could also be transferred into the *AssemblyInfo* class contained in the AssemblyInfo.vb file of the Web control library project. Enough about the *TagPrefix* for now. In case you're wondering how custom server controls are added to the Toolbox, we'll cover this a bit later in this chapter.

Within the control's class body, a private variable *_text* is created along with a property definition. Again, you find attributes added to the *Text* property. Here is the line of code defining the *Text* property and its attributes:

```
Dim _text As String
<Bindable(True), Category("Appearance"), DefaultValue("")>
    Property [Text]() As String
    Get
        Return _text
    End Get
    Set(ByVal Value As String)
        _text = Value
    End Set
End Property
```

Attributes are used heavily with custom server controls. Table 6-3 shows some of the more common ones.

Table 6-3   Common Attributes for Custom Server Controls

Attribute	Value	Description
Bindable	*Boolean*	Visual Studio .NET will or will not display this control in the Databindings dialog box.
Browsable	*Boolean*	Visual Studio .NET will or will not display this control in the designer.
Category	*String*	Defines the category in which this property will be displayed in the Properties window.
DefaultProperty	*String*	Specifies the default property selected in the Properties window when a server control is selected.
DefaultValue	*String*	The default value
Description	*String*	The text here is displayed in the description box in the Properties window.

We can see from the preceding code that the *Text* property is declared as bindable in the Databindings dialog box. The *Text* property will show itself in the Appearance category and is an empty value by default.

The next block of code in the WebCustomControl1 custom control creates the output.

```
Protected Overrides Sub Render(ByVal output As _
    System.Web.UI.HtmlTextWriter)
    output.Write([Text])
End Sub
```

The *Render* method is defined in the control base class. Since the output in a full custom server control must be created by itself, the *Render* method must be overridden. In the default example, the overriding is done in the preceding lines of code and defined as *HtmlTextWriter*. The *HtmlTextWriter* class provides rich HTML formatting capabilities that allow us to create well-formed HTML, manage attributes, and include styles. Let's have a little fun with our first server control. Comment out the preceding lines of code, and include the following lines if you create your own example or uncomment them if you use our example:

```
Protected Overrides Sub Render(ByVal output As HtmlTextWriter)
    output.AddStyleAttribute("color", _
        System.Drawing.ColorTranslator.ToHtml(System.Drawing.Color.Red))
    output.AddStyleAttribute("font", "Italic")
    output.AddStyleAttribute("font-family", "Arial")
    output.RenderBeginTag("H3")
    output.Write([Text])
    output.RenderEndTag()
End Sub
```

Once you do this, rebuild the MyControls project. When you switch to the design view of MyFirstCustomServerControl.aspx, you see the changes; you see them as well when you click Build And Browse on the file's shortcut menu.

Design-Time and Run-Time Views in Custom Server Controls

The behavior we've seen so far allows both design-time and run-time views to show the same information. Both views exhibit the same behavior because the *ControlDesigner* class calls the control's *Render* method to generate the HTML for the Visual Studio .NET design view. By changing the *ControlDesigner* class, you can display different design-time information from the control's run-time behavior. (More on this later in this chapter when we explain composite server controls.)

State Handling in Custom Server Controls

Last but not least, when you build a full custom server control, you have to handle state information yourself. You can do this easily using the Web Forms *ViewState* capabilities. You'll find the sample MyHeaderLabel.vb custom server controls in the MyControls project. State information is taken care of within the property definition. Here are the lines of code to handle state information for the *Text* property:

```
<Bindable(True), Category("Appearance"), DefaultValue("")>
    Property [Text]() As String
    Get
        Return CType(ViewState("Text"), String)
    End Get
    Set(ByVal Value As String)
        ViewState("Text") = Value
    End Set
End Property
```

The *ViewState* value of the property is set when the property is passed in. When we return (*Get*) the value, we make sure to pass the new value of the *View-State("Text")* variable. We could have accessed the *ViewState* directly; however, we advise you, as always, to use properties for encapsulation. Our MyCustom-Controls.apsx example shows the MyHeaderLabel server control in action. We set its *Text* property only one time; the internal *ViewState* takes over from then on:

```
If Not IsPostBack Then
    'Fill Heading
    MyHeaderLabel1.Text = "My Custom Server Controls"
    ⋮
```

The Visual Studio .NET Toolbox and Custom Server Controls

Visual Studio .NET makes it easy to add your custom server controls to the Toolbox. Let's see how this is done. We want to add our new controls to the Toolbox available to us in the design view for the Web Forms page. Open one of the previous example's Web Forms pages in design view. In the Toolbox, you'll find the tabs for Data, WebForms, Components, HTML, and so on. You can add a custom tab and name it by right-clicking the Toolbox and then clicking Add Tab on the shortcut menu. We've chosen the name Custom Server Controls for our additional tab. You can realign the tabs using drag and drop. Now you need to add the custom server controls we created. Right-click the new tab, and click Customize Toolbox on the shortcut menu to open the Customer Toolbox dialog box. Click the .NET Framework Components tab in the dialog box and browse to the location of your control's DLL. The default installation location for the MyControls.dll file is the C:\BuildOOP\Ch06\MyControls\MyControls\bin folder. After the new controls are accepted (all controls in the DLL will be selected by default), they will appear as choices in the new Toolbox tab, named with their class names. You're now ready to use the custom server controls in the same way you used default ASP.NET controls, with full drag-and-drop support. When you add a new control to an existing DLL, you have to follow this procedure to import the new control.

Enhanced or Derived Custom Server Controls

Even though we find full custom server controls helpful, we've found it very useful to enhance existing ASP.NET server controls. Creating derived server controls is relatively easy. Instead of inheriting from *System.Web.UI.WebControls.WebControl*, we inherit from the actual control, such as Button, TextBox, or DropDownList. As mentioned previously, we found a little deficiency in the DropDownList control and will enhance it in our first example.

Enhanced ASP.NET DropDownList Server Control

Our first derived custom server control is named MyDropdownList.vb in the MyControls project. What is the deficiency with the default DropDownList control? Well, unlike the Windows Forms counterpart, you cannot simply select a specific value in the DropDownList as a default value. We ran into this problem earlier in this chapter when we looked at user controls for address entries. Whenever we wanted to fill a State DropDownList with existing information, we had to set this information by creating custom code in each control—an acceptable solution when you use only a small number of these controls in a Web application, but if DropDownList controls are common in your user interface, creating custom code becomes cumbersome and does not agree with the high OOP standards of .NET. This is where enhanced, or derived, custom server controls come to the rescue. Let's dive right into the code for this example. Here is the entire code for the MyDropDownList server control:

```
Imports System.ComponentModel
Imports System.Web.UI
<DefaultProperty("Text"),
ToolboxData("<{0}:MyDropDownList runat=server></{0}:MyDropDownList>")>
Public Class MyDropDownList
    Inherits System.Web.UI.WebControls.DropDownList
    Dim localValue As String
    <Bindable(True), Category("Appearance"), DefaultValue("")>
    Property [Text]() As String
        Get
            Return Me.SelectedItem.Value
        End Get
        Set(ByVal Value As String)
            localValue = Value
            'Search for Value of States to be displayed
            Dim n As Integer
            For n = 1 To Me.Items.Count
                If Me.Items(n).Value.ToString = Value Then
                    Me.SelectedIndex = n
                    Exit For
```

(continued)

```
          End If
        Next
      End Set
    End Property
End Class
```

Compared line by line to the default WebCustomControl1.vb control we discussed earlier, the MyDropDownList server control looks very similar. As we mentioned, one of the main differences between controls is the parent class they inherit. Full custom server controls inherit from *System.Web.UI.WebControls.WebControl*, whereas the derived MyDropDownList server control inherits from the ASP.NET DropDownList control class *System.Web.UI.WebControls.DropDownList*.

By inheriting the ASP.NET DropDownList control class, we inherit all the DropDownList control's properties, events, and methods—even the *ViewState*. We can therefore concentrate on only the changes or additions we need for the functionality we desire. If the default *Text* property isn't set, we want the control to return the first item. If it indeed is set, we want our custom server control to find its value for us and set the index automatically so that the correct value is automatically displayed for us. All required changes to make this happen are in the *Text* property definition. Here's the code again, first for the *Get* property (passed from the control to the calling page):

```
<Bindable(True), Category("Appearance"), DefaultValue("")>
Property [Text]() As String
    Get
    Return Me.SelectedItem.Value
    End Get
    ⋮
```

When we pass a value from the DropDownList control, it has to be defined as the value of the selected item because we are dealing with a collection. The property set (the value passed from the calling page to the control) requires the majority of modifications:

```
    ⋮
    Set(ByVal Value As String)
        localValue = Value
        'Search for Value of States to be displayed
        Dim n As Integer
        For n = 1 To Me.Items.Count
            If Me.Items(n).Value.ToString = Value Then
                Me.SelectedIndex = n
                Exit For
            End If
        Next
    End Set
End Property
```

We have to search for the specific index of the collection of data that represents the DropDownList control. We do this by counting through each item in the collection, comparing its value with the passed value. If we find a matching value, the index is set to it and the count is stopped. If it isn't found, the first index is automatically chosen. That's all we have to do to enhance ASP.NET's DropDownList control. This is almost too easy—let's see how it works. Look at and run the MyCustomControls.aspx Web Forms page. Figure 6-6 shows the resulting screen of the MyDropDownList custom server control used three times on the same Web Forms page.

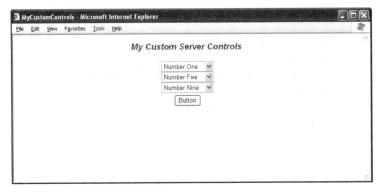

Figure 6-6   MyDropDownList custom server control used three times in the MyCustomControls.aspx Web Forms page

The first control has no specific default value. The second and third controls have a specific default value: Number Five and Number Nine, respectively. These are set programmatically in the calling Web Forms code-behind page, as follows:

```
Private Sub Page_Load(ByVal sender As System.Object, _
    ByVal e As System.EventArgs) Handles MyBase.Load
    'Put user code to initialize the page here
    If Not IsPostBack Then
        'Let's Fill an Arraylist with some value for databinding
        Dim localList As New ArrayList()
        localList.Add("Number One")
        localList.Add("Number Two")
        localList.Add("Number Three")
        localList.Add("Number Four")
        localList.Add("Number Five")
        localList.Add("Number Six")
        localList.Add("Number Seven")
        localList.Add("Number Eight")
        localList.Add("Number Nine")
        localList.Add("Number Ten")
```

(continued)

```
        MyDropDownList1.DataSource = localList
        MyDropDownList2.DataSource = localList
        MyDropDownList3.DataSource = localList
        Page.DataBind()
        MyDropDownList2.Text = "Number Five"
        MyDropDownList3.Text = "Number Nine"
    End If
End Sub
```

As you can see in the preceding lines of code, all you have to do to set a default value is pass the value to our new server control's *Text* property.

So far, this control works great and as intended. We found a minor inconsistency that we'd like to show you so that you can be aware of it. Look at the MyCustomControlBeware.aspx Web Forms page. It's almost an exact copy of the previous example, however, the third MyDropDownList control's item collection isn't set programmatically; it is set declaratively instead. Here is the HTML for this (we used the Visual Studio .NET DropDownList property builder):

```
<ccl:MyDropDownList id="MyDropDownList3" runat="server">
   <asp:ListItem Value="One">One</asp:ListItem>
   <asp:ListItem Value="Two">Two</asp:ListItem>
   <asp:ListItem Value="Three">Three</asp:ListItem>
   <asp:ListItem Value="Four" Selected="True">Four</asp:ListItem>
   <asp:ListItem Value="Five">Five</asp:ListItem>
</ccl:MyDropDownList>
```

Looking at the code in HTML view, you'll notice that the *asp:ListItem* declarations are underlined in red and have the following error message: "The active schema does not support the element asp:listitem." Even though the code works at run time, design-time elements seem to have a problem with our derived server control. We don't quite understand why this is the case since we inherited fully from the ASP.NET built-in DropDownList control. When you set the items collection programmatically, which is the preferred way, you don't run into this inconsistency. You can also ignore the warning since the code is running correctly. Another option would be to create an item custom server control that would be called instead.

Highlighting the Selected Textbox Server Control

Let's create another derived server control that adds a feature to the TextBox control that we might be accustomed to in other programming languages: the highlighting of a text box when it has focus.

The solution to automatic highlighting is a perfect example of a derived server control and the power of OOP. We have to handle only those changes we want. The sample control we created is MyTextBoxHighlight.vb, and it is used in the MyTextBoxHighlight.aspx Web Forms page. Here is the code for MyTextBoxHighlight.vb:

```vb
Imports System.ComponentModel
Imports System.Web.UI
Imports System.Drawing
<DefaultProperty("Text"), ToolboxData( _
    "<{0}:MyTextBoxHighlight runat=server></{0}:MyTextBoxHighlight>")> _
    Public Class MyTextBoxHighlight
    Inherits System.Web.UI.WebControls.TextBox
    Private privateHighlightColor As Color
    'Highlight Color Property
    <Bindable(True), Category("Appearance"), DefaultValue("")> _
        Property HighlightColor() As Color
        Get
            Return privateHighlightColor
        End Get
        Set(ByVal Value As Color)
            privateHighlightColor = Value
        End Set
    End Property
    Protected Overrides Sub Render(ByVal output As HtmlTextWriter)
        'Check if a BackColor is defined, if not make it white
        Dim privateNormalBackColor As Color = Me.BackColor
        If privateNormalBackColor.Equals(Color.Empty) Then
            privateNormalBackColor = Color.White
        End If
        'Check if a color definition is given, if not, make it the same
        'as the background
        If privateHighlightColor.Equals(Color.Empty) Then
            privateHighlightColor = Me.BackColor
        End If
        'Translate System Color values to HTML
        Dim usedHighlight As String = _
            ColorTranslator.ToHtml(privateHighlightColor)
        Dim usedNormalBackColor As String = _
            ColorTranslator.ToHtml(privateNormalBackColor)

        'Add style attributes to the control
        Me.Attributes("OnFocus") = "style.background='" & _
            usedHighlight & "'"
        Me.Attributes("OnBlur") = "style.background='" & _
            usedNormalBackColor & "'"
        'Now run the Textbox's default rendering
        MyBase.Render(output)
    End Sub
End Class
```

The code in boldface highlights some of the important areas we want to discuss in more detail. Notice that we added *System.Drawing* to the *Imports* statement. We'll use the .NET color definitions for our *HighlightColor* property. Next you see that we inherit from the *TextBox* class directly, thus inheriting all its properties, events, and methods. Next we define the *HighlightColor* property. It's of the type *System.Drawing.Color*. When you see the property in its windows, you'll have access to the .NET color picker automatically. (We love .NET and integrations such as this one with the color picker.) Next we had to override the control's *Render* method. Now we add the highlight color as well as other features. We check for the setting of our derived Textbox's *BackColor* property:

```
Dim privateNormalBackColor As Color = Me.BackColor
If privateNormalBackColor.Equals(Color.Empty) Then
    privateNormalBackColor = Color.White
End If
```

If the *BackColor* property is empty, we assign white to it (the default behavior would make it transparent), otherwise we set our internal *BackColor* to the property's *BackColor*. Why? When our control gains focus, we set the *HighlightColor* property to the selected highlight color, but when we lose focus again, we must set it back to what it was. If the *BackColor* property was empty, the color is white, if not, the color is set back to whatever was found in *Me.BackColor*.

Next, we check whether a *HighlightColor* value was chosen. If it was, we don't need to do anything; however, if no value was chosen, *HighlightColor* must be the same as *BackColor*. We handle this in the next few lines of code:

```
If privateHighlightColor.Equals(Color.Empty) Then
    privateHighlightColor = Me.BackColor
End If
```

Our next chore is to convert the *System.Drawing.Color* values to HTML values. Again, .NET aids us in doing this with the *ColorTranslator* function found in *System.Drawing*:

```
Dim usedHighlight As String = _
    ColorTranslator.ToHtml(privateHighlightColor)
Dim usedNormalBackColor As String = _
    ColorTranslator.ToHtml(privateNormalBackColor)
```

After all this preparation work, we can actually apply the highlight in both the *OnFocus* and *OnBlur* style. We do this by adding the correct attributes to the *MyTextHighlight* class as follows:

```
Me.Attributes("OnFocus") = "style.background='" & _
    usedHighlight & "'"
Me.Attributes("OnBlur") = "style.background='" & _
    usedNormalBackColor & "'"
'Now run the TextBox's default rendering
MyBase.Render(output)
```

Adding attributes is straightforward and simple. We use the *Me.Attribute("xyz")* command, with *xyz* representing the correct names. We add the background style for both the *OnFocus* and *OnBlur* events. And last but not least, we call the default rendering method that takes care of both design-time and run-time rendering of controls.

In the MyTextHighlight.aspx Web Forms page, we added this control several times, adding different highlights or no highlight at all.

Additional Steps for a Production Control

What else could we have done with this control? To make it ready for production, we would have checked for the browser type before adding the style attributes. Instead of adding style attributes, we could have written Java Script and added it to the control or to a Java Script file we referenced. We also could have included properties and code for highlighted foreground and background colors.

Adding Java Script to Custom Server Controls

There are two ways to add Java Script to custom controls. The first way is through the *Page.RegisterStartupScript* method. You use this method when you want to create Java Script for the control. When you want to add Java Script that can be accessed by other script code, you use another method named *Page.RegisterClientScriptBlock*. Both methods have two string parameters: the name of the script block and the script itself. We didn't supply a sample for Java Script functionality. Here's the code you would include in your custom control to add a Java Script block:

```
Protected Overrides Sub OnPreRender(e as EventArgs)
    Dim privateJavaScript as String
    privateJavaScript = "<script language='JavaScript'. ..>
        </script>"
    MyBase.OnPrerender(e)
    Page.RegisterStartupScript(GetType(ClassName).FullName, _
        privateJavaScript)
End Sub
```

You can see that we chose the first method discussed, *Page.RegisterStartupScript*. The *OnPreRender* method is a great place for adding Java Script.

Notice that we run the *OnPreRender* base class code first, then add the Java Script registration to ensure that we don't conflict with the base class's requirements and instantiation sequence. In the overridden *Render* method, you then add an attribute similar to the ones we showed you earlier in the highlighted TextBox server control. If you defined an *OnMouseOver(this)* function in the preceding Java Script, you need to add the following line of code to the control's attributes:

```
Protected Overrides Sub Render(output as HtmlTextWriter)
    output.AddAttribute("onmouseover","OnMouseOver(This)")
    MyBase.Render(output)
End Sub
```

Composite Server Controls

Arguably one of the best ways to create usable custom server controls is to combine several existing ASP.NET default controls into one super-enhanced control. You could say that composite controls are most like custom user controls. You can create composite server controls that look and feel exactly like user controls. They are, however, compiled and can be used in a drag-and-drop fashion, just like ASP.NET default server controls. They can also show themselves at design time, and when more than one of the same controls is used on the same Web Forms page, each one registers itself in the code-behind page. (You might remember that this wasn't the case with custom user controls.) Server controls, however, have no visual designer. Remember also that we recommend creating custom server controls that are usable across multiple platforms. If you put too many controls into a single control, the control becomes too specific and reusability might be limited.

To show you the power of composite server controls, we'll first create an enhanced custom TextBox control similar to the one available to us in other languages such Visual Basic 6 and Microsoft Visual FoxPro. When this control, which we named MyLabelTextBox, is used within a Web Forms page, you can add a label on the top or at the left side of the control (it is always aligned properly), or you can choose to have no label at all. Once we create this new composite server control and show how it works, we'll add functionality.

Wouldn't it be nice to have a simple property that can be set to activate a required field validation, data type validation, or both, without having to add validation controls to the Web Forms page? This is exactly what we're going to do with our MyLabelTextBox. When we're finished, we'll have a super-enhanced TextBox with many additional features.

Composite ASP.NET MyLabelTextBox Server Controls

Let's get started with the first step of our MyLabelTextBox server control. Even though its implementation is similar to that of the previous server controls, you need to be aware of some important differences. First we'll show you the all the code for the control:

```
Imports System.ComponentModel
Imports System.Web.UI
Imports System.Web.UI.WebControls
<DefaultProperty("Text"), _
    Designer(GetType(MyControls.MyFirstControlDesigner)), _
    ParseChildren(True), PersistChildren(False), _
    ToolboxData("<{0}:MyFirstTextControl _
    runat=server></{0}:MyFirstTextControl>")> _
    Public Class MyFirstTextControl
    Inherits System.Web.UI.WebControls.WebControl
    Implements INamingContainer
    Dim _text As String
    Dim _label As String
    Dim _showLabel As Boolean
    Dim _Left As Boolean
    'Text Box's Text Value Property
    <Bindable(True), Category("Appearance"), DefaultValue("")> _
        Property [Text]() As String
        Get
            Return _text
        End Get
        Set(ByVal Value As String)
            _text = Value
        End Set
    End Property
    'Label's Text Value Property
    <Bindable(True), Category("Appearance"), DefaultValue("")> _
        Property Label() As String
        Get
            Return _label
        End Get
        Set(ByVal Value As String)
            _label = Value
        End Set
    End Property
    'Show Label Boolean Property
    <Bindable(True), Category("Behavior"), DefaultValue("")> _
        PropertyShowLabel() As Boolean
        Get
```

(continued)

```
                Return _showLabel
            End Get
            Set(ByVal Value As Boolean)
                _showLabel = Value
            End Set
        End Property
        'Position Label Property
        <Bindable(True), Category("Behavior"), DefaultValue("")> _
            Property Left() As Boolean
            Get
                Return _Left
            End Get
            Set(ByVal Value As Boolean)
                _Left = ValueEnd Set
            End Property
        'Initialize the Control's Members
        Private textBox1 As TextBox          'textBox is defined
        Private label1 As Label              'label is defined
        'Create Child Controls
        Protected Overrides Sub CreateChildControls()
            textBox1 = New TextBox()         'textbox is instantiated
            textBox1.ID = "textBox1"
            textBox1.Text = Text
            label1 = New Label()             'label is instantiated
            label1.ID = "lablel1"
            label1.Text = Label
        'First way to add Server Controls to this Composite Server Control
            If _showLabel = True Then        'Do we need to show the label?
                If _Left = True Then         'What is the alignment?
                    'Left
                    Controls.Add(label1)
                    Controls.Add(New LiteralControl(" "))
                    Controls.Add(textBox1)
                Else                         'Right
                    Controls.Add(New LiteralControl("<Div align=left>"))
                    Controls.Add(label1)
                    Controls.Add(New LiteralControl("<BR>"))
                    Controls.Add(textBox1)
                    Controls.Add(New LiteralControl("</Div>"))
                End If
            Else
                Controls.Add(textBox1)       'Just the TextBox
            End If
        End Sub

        'Returns Controls
        Public Overrides ReadOnly Property controls() As ControlCollection|
            Get
                EnsureChildControls()
```

```
        Return MyBase.Controls
      End Get
   End Property
End Class
```

The first change from normal server controls that you'll see is in the imports area:

```
Imports System.ComponentModel
Imports System.Web.UI
Imports System.Web.UI.WebControls
```

The line in boldface is an additional import that helps us to get to ASP.NET's default server controls such as TextBox or Label controls. The next major difference lies in the attribute area before defining the class:

```
<DefaultProperty("Text"), _
    Designer(GetType(MyControls.MyFirstControlDesigner)), _
    ParseChildren(True), PersistChildren(False), _
    ToolboxData("<{0}:MyFirstTextControl _
    runat=server></{0}:MyFirstTextControl>")> _
    Public Class MyFirstTextControl
```

To allow for design-time behavior, we need to add the *DesignerAttribute*. It defines the class that will override the *GetDesignTimeHTML* method. We override this method because we must instantiate the ASP.NET server controls at design time. The default behavior of *GetDesignTimeHTML* isn't enough to handle design-time viewing. (We'll look at the MyFirstControlDesigner file shortly.) In addition to *DesignerAttribute*, you can see *ParseChildrenAttribute* and *PersistChildrenAttribute*. When *ParseChildrenAttribute* is set to true, nested elements (XML elements) in the custom server control's tags are treated as child controls instead of properties—when the control is used declaratively. In our example, we want this to be the case. When the *PersistChildrenAttribute* is set to *True*, the child controls in the custom server control are persistent as nested inner controls. Since we don't want this behavior, we set it to *False*.

The next addition comes after the class definition and inheritance statement:

```
Public Class MyFirstTextControl
Inherits System.Web.UI.WebControls.WebControl
Implements INamingContainer
```

When we use the same custom server control more than once in the same Web Forms page, we need to make sure that all child controls have unique IDs; otherwise all controls would represent the same properties, events, and methods, which wouldn't be very useful. This is where the *System.Web.UI.INamingContainer* interface comes in. When implemented, the ASP.NET page framework creates a new naming scope under that control.

Next we set internal variables and declare their properties:

```
Dim _text As String
Dim _label As String
Dim _showLabel As Boolean
Dim _Left As Boolean
'Text Box's Text Value Property
<Bindable(True), Category("Appearance"), DefaultValue("")> _
    Property [Text]() As String
    Get
        Return _text
    End Get
    Set(ByVal Value As String)
        _text = Value
    End Set
End Property
'Label's Text Value Property
:
```

For this example, we need the TextBox control's *Text* property, the Label controls *Text* property, and two switches that define whether the label should be shown and, if so, where. Notice that we don't need to take care of state management in the TextBox and Label controls. This behavior is inherited.

The next piece of code is the heart of composite server controls:

```
'Initialize the Control's Members
Private textBox1 As TextBox          'textBox is defined
Private label1 As Label              'label is defined
'Create Child Controls
Protected Overrides Sub CreateChildControls()
    textBox1 = New TextBox()          'textbox is instantiated
    textBox1.ID = "textBox1"
    textBox1.Text = Text
    label1 = New Label()              'label is instantiated
    label1.ID = "lablel1"
    label1.Text = Label
'First way to add Server Controls to this Composite Server Control
    If _showLabel = True Then          'Do we need to show the label?
        If _Left = True Then           'What is the alignment?
            'Left
            Controls.Add(label1)
            Controls.Add(New LiteralControl(" "))
            Controls.Add(textBox1)
        Else                           'Right
            Controls.Add(New LiteralControl("<Div align=left>"))
            Controls.Add(label1)
            Controls.Add(New LiteralControl("<BR>"))
            Controls.Add(textBox1)
```

```
        Controls.Add(New LiteralControl("</Div>"))
      End If
   Else
      Controls.Add(textBox1)          'Just the TextBox
   End If
End Sub
```

We need to override the *CreateChildControls* method since we define our own controls. After declaring variables that represent the TextBox and Label controls, we are ready to override *CreateChildControls*. We then declare the new controls, giving them IDs and setting the correct properties: the server control's *Text* property to the TextBox control's *Text* property, and the server control's *Label* property to the Label control's *Text* property. After we declare the controls used, we can render them in two ways.

The first way is to implement them with *Controls.Add*. We add controls based on the settings of our *ShowLabel* and *Left* alignment properties. The syntax is simple. Calling the *Controls.Add(xyz)* method adds the controls, where *xyz* represents either a declared server control or a new LiteralControl control. We use LiteralControls to add HTML when needed. Incidentally, besides ASP.NET default server controls, you can add other custom server controls to composite server controls.

Next, we override the *Controls* method:

```
'Returns Controls
Public Overrides ReadOnly Property controls() As ControlCollection
    Get
        EnsureChildControls()
        Return MyBase.Controls
    End Get
End Property
```

We override this method to determine whether the server control contains child controls, and in our case it does. If the *EnsureChildControls* method doesn't find the child controls, it calls the *CreateChildControls* method to ensure their existence.

The second way to render our control is by overriding the *Render* method. When we use *Render*, the *Controls.Add* implementation can be omitted. Here is the code that yields the same results:

```
'Second way to add server controls to this composite server control
Protected Overrides Sub Render(ByVal output As _
    System.Web.UI.HtmlTextWriter)
    If _showLabel = True Then          'Is label to be shown?
        If _Left = False Then          'Is label top or left?
            output.Write("<Div align=left>")
            label1.RenderControl(output)
```

(continued)

```
            output.Write("<BR>")
            textBox1.RenderControl(output)
            output.Write("</Div>")
        Else
            label1.RenderControl(output)
            output.Write(" ")
            textBox1.RenderControl(output)
        End If
    Else
        textBox1.RenderControl(output)
    End If
End Sub
```

Each control has a *RenderControl* method. All we need to do is call it and direct its output, which creates the control's HTML through the *HtmlTextWriter* class. Generic HTML can be added with the *output.Write* method.

The answer to which of the two controls is preferable isn't an easy one. We find that the second method behaves somewhat better in design-time views, however, the first method is better to use when controls like validation and other logical controls have to be added.

OK, we might be getting really excited to try the new control, but we want to implement the custom control designer for our design-time view. The code for this resides in the MyFirstTextControlDesigner.vb file. Here is the code in its entirety:

```
Imports System.ComponentModel
Imports System.ComponentModel.Design
Imports System.Diagnostics
Imports System.Web.UI
Imports System.Web.UI.Design
Public Class MyFirstControlDesigner
    Inherits ControlDesigner
    Public Overrides Function GetDesignTimeHtml() As String
        Dim control As MyFirstTextControl = CType(Component, _
            MyFirstTextControl)
        Dim childControls As ControlCollection = control.Controls
        Return MyBase.GetDesignTimeHtml
    End Function
    Public Overrides Sub Initialize(ByVal component As IComponent)
        If Not TypeOf component Is MyFirstTextControl Then
            Throw New ArgumentException("Component must be a " & _
            "MyFirstTextControl", "component")
        End If
        MyBase.Initialize(component)
    End Sub
End Class
```

Before we run this example, we need to import the *System.Web.UI.Design* namespace. This isn't available by default in Visual Studio .NET. Therefore you need to add *System.Design* to the Reference area of your custom server control's project—the MyControls project in our case. The *GetDesignTimeHtml* method allows design-time rendering of controls. In the case of derived controls, this rendering will happen automatically. In the case of composite controls, no default design-time rendering happens since the *GetDesignTimeHtml* method does not know about the controls in the composite control. We have to tell it that they exist. This is why we first declare a variable (named *control* in our case) as the actual composite server control (our MyFirstTextControl). Once the control is declared, we can get to its child controls collection, which we return to *GetDesignTimeHtml* and that in turn renders the controls in Visual Studio .NET's design view. Next, we override the *Initialize* method. We do this only in order to check that the calling control is indeed *MyFirstTextControl*.

Now that we're ready for testing, let's open the MyTextBox.aspx Web Forms page in design view. Figure 6-7 shows the design-time view of our composite control.

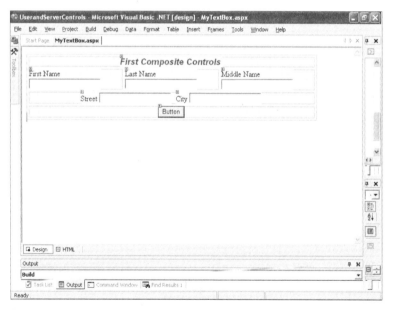

Figure 6-7   Design-time view of the MyFirstTextControl composite server control

Take the time to run this Web Forms page. Figure 6-8 gives us the run-time view. Notice the accuracy of the design-time behavior by comparing Figure 6-7 and Figure 6-8.

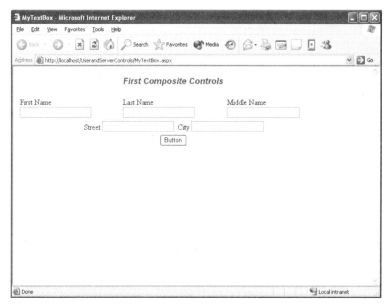

Figure 6-8 Run-time view of the MyFirstTextControl composite server control

When you're back in design view, look at the Properties window for one of the MyFirstTextControl controls. You'll find the properties we added. When you switch to HTML view, you can see how the properties are set declaratively:

```
<TR>
  <TD>
    <ccl:myfirsttextcontrol id="MyFirstTextControl1" runat="server"
      ShowLabel="True" Label="First Name" Left="False">
    </ccl:myfirsttextcontrol>
  </TD>
  <td>
    <ccl:myfirsttextcontrol id="Myfirsttextcontrol8" runat="server"
      ShowLabel="True" Label="Last Name" Left="False">
    </ccl:myfirsttextcontrol>
  </td>
  <td>
    <ccl:myfirsttextcontrol id="MyFirstTextControl2" runat="server"
      ShowLabel="True" Label="Middle Name" Left="False">
    </ccl:myfirsttextcontrol>
  </td>
</TR>
```

Enhanced Composite ASP.NET MyLabelTextBox Server Controls

Now that we've covered the basics, let's build an enhanced version of the control. We had the goal to add both required field and data type validation to our composite server control. The file for the finished version is MyTextControl.vb, and the custom design-time control is MyTextControlDesigner. In this section, we include the MyTextControl.vb file in its entirety with additions shown in boldface. The MyTextControlDesigner.vb file is almost the same as the previous file used and does not warrant repeating. Since we're not doing anything radically new, the code should be self-explanatory. Here is the code for the MyText-Control file:

```
Imports System.ComponentModel
Imports System.Web.UI
Imports System.Web.UI.WebControls

'Defaults are set and a Designer is chosen for Design View
<DefaultProperty("Text"), _
    Designer(GetType(MyControls.MyTextControlDesigner)), _
    ParseChildren(True), PersistChildren(False), _
    ToolboxData("<{0}:MyTextControl runat=server> _
    </{0}:MyTextControl>")> _
    Public Class MyTextControl
    Inherits System.Web.UI.WebControls.WebControl
    Implements INamingContainer
    Dim _text As String
    Dim _label As String
    Dim _showLabel As Boolean
    Dim _Left As Boolean
    Dim _requiredField As Boolean
    Dim _requiredFieldMessage As String
    Dim _datavalidationrequired As Boolean
    Dim _datavalidation As ValidationDataType

    'Text Box's Text Value Property
    <Bindable(True), Category("Appearance"), DefaultValue("")> _
        Property [Text]() As String
        Get
            Return _text
        End Get
        Set(ByVal Value As String)
            _text = Value
        End Set
    End Property
    'Label's Text Value Property
    <Bindable(True), Category("Appearance"), DefaultValue("")> _
        Property Label() As String
```

(continued)

```
        Get
            Return _label
        End Get
        Set(ByVal Value As String)
            _label = Value
        End Set
End Property
'Show Label Boolean Property
<Bindable(True), Category("Behavior"), DefaultValue("")> _
    Property ShowLabel() As Boolean
        Get
            Return _showLabel
        End Get
        Set(ByVal Value As Boolean)
            _showLabel = Value
        End Set
End Property
'Position Label Property
<Bindable(True), Category("Behavior"), DefaultValue("")> _
    Property Left() As Boolean
        Get
            Return _Left
        End Get
        Set(ByVal Value As Boolean)
            _Left = Value
        End Set
End Property
'Required Field Validator
<Bindable(True), Category("Behavior"), DefaultValue("")> _
    Property RequiredField() As Boolean
        Get
            Return _requiredField
        End Get
        Set(ByVal Value As Boolean)
            _requiredField = Value
        End Set
End Property
'Required Field's Error Message
<Bindable(True), Category("Behavior"), DefaultValue("")> _
    Property RequiredMessage() As String
        Get
            Return _requiredFieldMessage
        End Get
        Set(ByVal Value As String)
            _requiredFieldMessage = Value
        End Set
End Property
'DataType Validator
```

```vb
<Bindable(True), Category("Behavior"), DefaultValue("")> _
    Property DataType() As Boolean
    Get
        Return _datavalidationrequired
    End Get
    Set(ByVal Value As Boolean)
        _datavalidationrequired = Value
    End Set
End Property
'DataType check
<Bindable(True), Category("Behavior"), DefaultValue("")> _
    Property ValidationDataType() As ValidationDataType
    Get
        Return _datavalidation
    End Get
    Set(ByVal Value As ValidationDataType)
        _datavalidation = Value
    End Set
End Property
'Initialize the Control's Members
Private textBox1 As TextBox          'textBox is defined
Private label1 As Label              'label is defined
'Required field validaton
Private validator1 As RequiredFieldValidator
'Data type valiation
Private validator2 As CompareValidator
'Create Child Controls
Protected Overrides Sub CreateChildControls()
    label1 = New Label()             'label is instantiated
    label1.ID = "lablel1"
    label1.Text = Label
    textBox1 = New TextBox()         'textbox is instantiated
    textBox1.ID = "textBox1"
    textBox1.Text = Text
    'Check for Required Field Message
    If Len(_requiredFieldMessage) < 1 Then
        _requiredFieldMessage = "This Field cannot be left empty."
    End If
    'Check for required data type - make it string if nothing else
    If _datavalidation = Nothing Then
        _datavalidation = ValidationDataType.String
    End If
    'validator1 is instantiated.
    validator1 = New RequiredFieldValidator()
    validator1.ID = "requiredfield1"
    validator1.ControlToValidate = "textBox1"
    validator1.Text = "!"
    validator1.ErrorMessage = _requiredFieldMessage
```

(continued)

```
validator1.ToolTip = validator1.ErrorMessage
validator1.Display = ValidatorDisplay.Dynamic
validator2 = New CompareValidator()
validator2.ID = "datatype1"
validator2.ControlToValidate = "textBox1"
validator2.ErrorMessage = "Invalid Data Type - " & _
    datavalidation.ToString & "is required Try again"
validator2.ToolTip = validator2.ErrorMessage
validator2.Display = ValidatorDisplay.Dynamic
validator2.Operator = ValidationCompareOperator.DataTypeCheck
validator2.Type = _datavalidation
If _showLabel = True Then        'Is label to be shown?
    If _Left = False Then        'Is label top or left?
        Controls.Add(New LiteralControl("<Div align='left'"))
        Controls.Add(label1)
        Controls.Add(New LiteralControl("<BR>"))
        Controls.Add(textBox1)
        If _requiredField = True Then            'Is this required?
            Controls.Add(New LiteralControl(" "))
            Controls.Add(validator1)
        End If
        If _datavalidationrequired = True Then   'Data Validation?
            Controls.Add(validator2)
        End If
        Controls.Add(New LiteralControl("</DIV>"))
    Else
        Controls.Add(label1)
        Controls.Add(New LiteralControl(" "))
        Controls.Add(textBox1)
        If _requiredField = True Then    'Is this required?
            Controls.Add(New LiteralControl(" "))
            Controls.Add(validator1)
        End If
        If _datavalidationrequired = True Then  'Data Validation?
            Controls.Add(validator2)
        End If
    End If
Else
    Controls.Add(textBox1)
    If _requiredField = True Then            'Is this required?
        Controls.Add(New LiteralControl(" "))
        Controls.Add(validator1)
    End If
    'Do data validation?
    If _datavalidationrequired = True Then
        Controls.Add(validator2)
```

```
            End If
        End If
    End Sub
    'Returns Controls
    Public Overrides ReadOnly Property controls() As ControlCollection
        Get
            EnsureChildControls()
            Return MyBase.Controls
        End Get
    End Property
End Class
```

We urge you to take a few minutes and play with the MyEnhancedText-Box.aspx Web Forms page. This will help you to get more familiar with the properties and methods we enhanced for the MyTextControl server control.

Events and Custom Server Controls

Handling events in composite server controls is as easy as it is for user controls. The control can handle events raised by its own children. You provide event handling methods and attach delegates to the events raised by the child controls. Let's say you add a Button control to a custom server control and want to handle its Click event. Here is the code that you would insert into the *CreateChildControls* method:

```
Dim btn1 as New Button
btn1.Text = "Click"
AddHandler btn1.Click, AddressOf btn1_Click
Controls.Add(btn1)
```

When you define the Button control, you simply add the *AddHandler* call and give it an address of the event handler method. This specified event handler will then be used to respond to the actual event, and the handler code can be anywhere in the control class structure:

```
Private Sub btn1_Click(Sender as Object, E as EventArgs)
    'Process Click event Code here
    ⋮
End Sub
```

In addition to handling child control events, you can also raise custom events from the control itself. Let's say you want to let the calling form know when a TextBox has changed. First we would define a public event in the control's class as follows:

```
Public Event Change(Sender as Object, E as Eventargs)
```

Next, we create a *Subroutine* that handles internal on-change events that in return raise the public event we just defined:

```
Protected Sub OnChange(E as EventArgs)
    RaiseEvent Change(Me, E)
End Sub
```

When this subroutine is run, an event argument is passed on. The specific custom server control then raises our public event and passes a reference to itself.

Now, let's create a TextBox control with change event handling:

```
Dim txtBox1 as New TextBox
txtBox.ID = "textBox1"
AddHandler txtBox1.TextChanged, AddressOf txtBox1_Change
Controls.Add(txtBox1)
```

Once we have supplied *TextChanges* to *AddHandler* and given it a method address, we can process the event as shown here:

```
Private Sub txtBox1_Change(Sender as Object, E as EventArgs)
    OnChange(EventArgs.Empty)
End Sub
```

So what happens if *txtBox1* has a change event? First, since we gave it a handler with *txtBox1_Change* as the address, the *txtBox1_Change* subroutine just defined is called. It in return calls the *OnChange* subroutine with an empty event argument. This subroutine then raises our public Change event, which is handled in the Web Forms page by our control. Feel free to experiment with this code. You'll see samples of it in Chapter 11 and Chapter 14.

Using Windows Forms Controls

In the same way we can create custom server controls for Web Forms, in .NET, we can create custom server controls for Windows Forms pages. Creating Windows Forms controls is very similar to creating Web Forms controls. So it should come as no surprise that you have the same three choices when creating Windows Forms controls that you have with custom Web server controls:

■   **Full custom controls**   Full custom controls inherit from the *Control* class in the *System.Windows.Forms* namespace. All logic, including drawing information on a Windows form, must be implemented. Instead of overriding the *Render* method in Web Forms application, the Windows form control has an *OnPaint* method. There is no visual designer available, so you draw the output using code.

- **Inherited, or derived, controls**   Inherited, or derived, controls are built upon the specific control that we want to add or change, just like Web server controls.

- **Composite controls**   Composite controls are built upon the *User-Control* control in the *System.Windows.Forms* namespace. The great advantage you have in creating this type of control is the visual-designer surface. When you start a Windows control library project, you'll be greeted with a designer surface. Drag and drop allows you to add other Windows Forms controls. Then you're ready to add properties and custom code. Even though this process creates a Windows server control, you'll feel more like you're creating a Web Forms user control.

We've provided a small sample that shows how a custom server Windows Forms control is created and called. You'll find it in the C:\BuildOOP\CH06 directory\ WindowsFormControl subdirectory. Open the WindowsFormControl.sln project file. You'll find the ItWorks.vb file and the SimpleSample.vb windows form. Here is the code for the ItWorks file:

```
Imports System.ComponentModel
Imports System.Windows.Forms.Control
Public Class ItWorks
    Inherits Control
    Protected Overrides Sub OnPaint(ByVal e As PaintEventArgs)
        'Paint the Text property on the control
        Dim rect As Rectangle = New RectangleF(ClientRectangle.X, _
            ClientRectangle.Y, ClientRectangle.Width, _
            ClientRectangle.Height)
        e.Graphics.DrawString(Me.Text, Font, _
            New SolidBrush(ForeColor), rect)
    End Sub
End Class
```

When you look at this code, the similarity with Web Forms server controls is very apparent. We call the class, inherit from the *Control* class, and then override the *OnPaint* method. Notice that we draw a rectangle with a given height and that the *DrawString* method defines the text that will be drawn.

Now let's take a look at the code page of the SimpleSample.vb Windows form. After importing the control's namespace (in our case *WindowsFormControl*), we can add our new control:

```
'Required by the Windows Form Designer
Private components As System.ComponentModel.Container
Private WithEvents itworks As itworks
Private WithEvents HostApp As System.Windows.Forms.Form
```

In the lines shown in boldface, we declared both the Windows form and the ItWorks control as variables so that we can access them later. The *Initialize-Component* method is the place we need to add our custom control. This is also the place code is added for standard Windows Forms controls when we drag and drop them onto the form:

```
Private Sub InitializeComponent()
    Me.components = New System.ComponentModel.Container()
    Me.itworks = New ItWorks()
    itworks.Dock = System.Windows.Forms.DockStyle.Fill
    itworks.Size = New System.Drawing.Size(600, 450)
    itworks.TabIndex = 0
    itworks.Text = "Hi - This control works"
    Me.AutoScaleBaseSize = New System.Drawing.Size(5, 13)
    Me.Text = "Control Example"
    Me.ClientSize = New System.Drawing.Size(600, 450)

    Me.Controls.Add(itworks)
End Sub
```

After creating a new instance of ItWorks, we can set its properties including the text we want it to show. Thereafter we define the size of the Windows form and its properties. With this done, we can add our control to the page with the familiar *Me.Control.Add("xyz")* call that adds the *xyz* control to the Windows form.

If you take a close look at the SimpleSample.vb Windows form, you'll also find some definitions we added in the constructor of the ItWorks control:

```
Public Sub New()
    MyBase.New()
    HostApp = Me
    'This call is required by the Windows Forms Designer.
    InitializeComponent()
    itworks.Font = New Font(Control.DefaultFont.FontFamily, 14, _
        FontStyle.Bold)
End Sub
```

The *Font* function is inherited from the *Control* class that the ItWorks control was derived from. Again, this is a great example of OOP at work.

We've offered only a small introduction to custom Windows Forms controls, however, we have found them to be very similar to Web Forms server controls. Taking syntax changes in considerations, you can apply most principles taught in this chapter to Windows Forms controls.

Conclusion

Custom user controls and custom server controls are very powerful OOP tools for the user interface. We've learned how and when to use each type of control, and we've shown you with production-ready samples how we turn this approach into reality. The level of detail we covered will allow you to use our sample controls immediately in your applications or modify them. We find that both types of controls allow us to build Web applications faster than ever before. (We're going to cover rapid application development (RAD) in Chapter 14.) Sure, ActiveX controls achieved a lot, but they were much more limiting than those we can develop using .NET, ASP.NET, and Visual Basic .NET. You'll see the sample controls we created used in future chapters when we continue our development of the HRnet application.

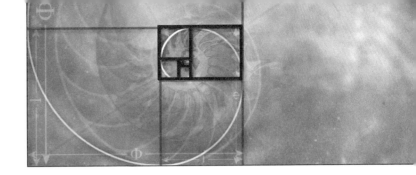

7

Implementing the Menu Handlers

Menu structures and navigation can lead to heated debates and disagreements. If we put 10 Web and application designers in the same room and gave them a set of criteria, there's a good chance we'd get 10 different recommendations for implementing menu and navigation structures. Arguments for why different solutions would be better would fly back and forth, with no apparent end to the discussion in sight. You might think that the statement "beauty is in the eye of the beholder" would apply; however, we aren't just talking about the look of an application. We're talking about ease of use, ease of self-discovery, and effectiveness when designing a menu and navigation structure. In this chapter, we'll present a flexible solution to these challenges. We'll give you more than one specific menu-handling solution. While we create our recommended menu and navigation components, we'll go into enough detail to enable you to easily modify and adjust them to your own liking. Many companies, including Microsoft, have spent large amounts of money and time researching ease of use in Microsoft Windows and Web applications. Windows applications have been around a lot longer than Web applications, and standard features such as those used since the release of Microsoft Office 2000 have been adopted. We won't concentrate on these, but we'll show one menu sample for Windows Forms at the end of this chapter that will give you an idea of how easy menu creation with Microsoft Visual Basic .NET Windows Forms is. There are fundamental differences in navigating Windows and Web applications. Because of the growing need to create Internet and intranet Web applications, we'll concentrate on Web Forms solutions, combining the power of Microsoft ASP.NET and Visual Basic .NET.

Our main objectives for this chapter are to provide you with simple, reusable menu and navigation objects that are as browser-independent as possible and provide a fully data-driven menu and navigation structure for Web applications. We want you to have a good understanding of how these objects are created so that you can either use them as is or modify them for your particular requirements.

A Bit of Menu Strategy

Before delving into the creation of our menu and navigation components, let's take a look at two Web sites that have good menu and navigation features. Microsoft's own *msn.com* Web site is well designed and easy to navigate. Figure 7-1 shows its home page, with its tabbed menu bar on the top for main subjects and additional navigation bars for related subjects on the left.

Figure 7-1   MSN home page

We've seen many Web sites that are overly complex and hard to navigate. Even some of the most skilled among us get lost trying to find information. You might have had similar experiences.

Let's look at another Web site that has good menu and navigation features. Figure 7-2 shows the Web site for InfoLink Screening Services, Inc. This site was created entirely with .NET.

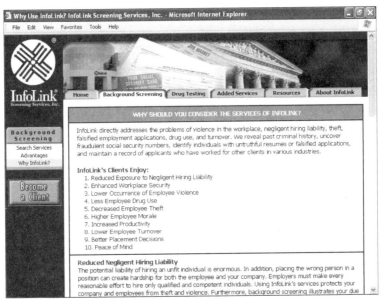

Figure 7-2   Menu and navigation structure of the InfoLink Screening Services Web site

We had the opportunity to build this Web page and thank the company for letting us use these pictures as examples for this chapter. The tabs on the main menu represent the major subject areas. Each of the main menu choices contains its own subchoices within the navigation bar on the left. This approach is especially well suited for the creation of data-driven menu and navigation structures such as those shown in Figure 7-2. Figure 7-3 shows the data-driven part of the InfoLink Screening Services Web site after secure login. Again, the tabbed main menu on top represents the major menu choices. The left navigation bar represents entry points for data entry screens and reports. More choices are given using a numbered structure within the page itself. This approach is simple and straightforward and makes it easy for users to navigate the Web site.

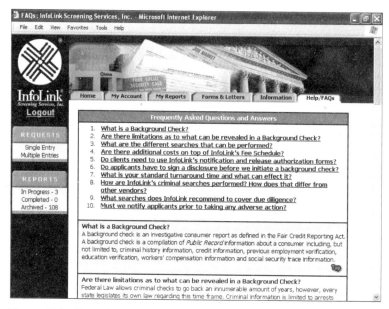

Figure 7-3 Data-driven menu structure of the InfoLink Screening Services Web site

Our Approach to Designing Effective Menus

We can summarize our approach up front with the *K.I.S.S* principle: Keep It Simple, Stupendous. (Note our little modification at the end.) We want our menu and navigation structure to live up to the following requirements:

- Be easy to use.

- Be self-explanatory.

- Have a relatively shallow structure. Deep ongoing navigation structures get everybody lost in no time.

- Be data driven.

- Look good.

- Have simple implementation.

- Use .NET components.

General Menu Interface

The results of visualizing the menu and navigation structures we've reviewed so far are illustrated in Figure 7-4.

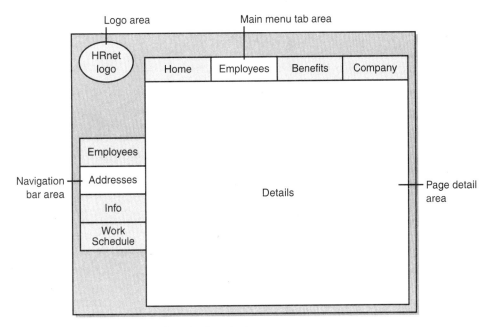

Figure 7-4   HRnet menu and navigation design

The screen is divided into four visual and functional areas:

- **Logo area**   In addition to the providing the logo, we can include functionality such as returning to the Home page when the logo is clicked. We can also include logout features, which we'll discuss in Chapter 10.

- **Main menu tab area**   The main menu tab area contains the central navigation control of the Web application. All other navigation bars have their roots in this tabbed menu. We recommend that the home page be the first tab on the main menu.

- **Navigation bar area**   The navigation bar is the second level of our menu and navigation structure. We're keeping the menu hierarchy one level deep. Although we've seen menu trees that can go several layers deep, we aren't recommending this approach. Trees easily become too wide. Following a deep tree of navigation choices also tends to become complex and hides information as well as confuses visitors.

- **Page detail area**   The page detail area is where the actual Web information or data-driven information is placed.

Our four-area approach makes it easier to create reusable page templates that allow data-driven navigation and page creation. We'll see this fully implemented in Chapter 10.

Using more than two levels in a menu is a bit more challenging. One of the options available is to use a page with tabs within the page detail area. Figure 7-5 shows how this style can be implemented.

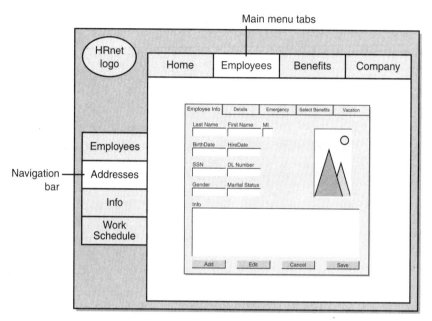

Figure 7-5   HRnet menu and navigation design details

General Menu Functionality

We want the components that represent our navigation structure to be as powerful and flexible as possible. In addition to being able to stand alone, we want our components to be able to link to their respective parent controls. Users need to be able to use the main menu bar without accessing other menus. On the other hand, when combined with a side navigation bar, the menu bar can control both the visibility and availability of the navigation bar tabs. For example, when the main menu Home tab is clicked, the side navigation bar isn't visible. When a user selects the Employees tab, the side navigation bar becomes visible and the subchoices for the Employees tab become visible automatically. Naturally, this needs to be fully data driven. The developer has to do nothing more than use the components, create the menu and submenu structure, and create the detail pages—our components will do the rest. We want several data options available.

■ **Created component**   At the initialization time of the application, the menu structure can be passed to our component in a fashion that is similar to the way parameters are passed to stored procedures. Each main menu or navigation bar item is a one-line entry into the component. Each also defines dependency and visibility. The component, in return, creates a table structure that is used to control navigation.

■ **Data tables**   Instead of creating the table structure on the fly as described in the preceding bullet, previously designed data tables can be passed and used.

■ **XML structures**   In addition to the choices just discussed, an XML structure, representing the full schema and data of the required data tables, can be passed and used.

We also want to be able to set font colors and sizes, the tab's background and foreground colors, hover capabilities, ToolTips, and the size of the tab in the component. Figure 7-6 shows what we'll ultimately achieve in this chapter.

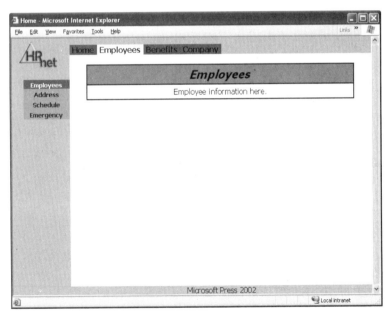

Figure 7-6   HRnet's data-driven menu and navigation bar

Creating Menu and Navigation Bar Objects

While we create HRnet's menu and navigation bar objects, we'll present you with as much detailed information as possible. We want to make sure that you can follow both our thought processes and programming techniques so that you can leverage the information to modify the structure and functionality for your own applications.

.NET Technology Used

ASP.NET intrinsic server controls offer several advantages for our menu bar. They create browser-independent code, have additional controlling features available that can be accessed declaratively or in code, and are controlled on the server. The two most likely candidates to use for navigation are the Hyperlink server control and the LinkButton server control. The challenge in implementing either one lies in the difficulty of run-time data binding for the hierarchy of controls that needs to be created on the fly. Neither control has a *DataSource* property. This is where ASP.NET's DataList server control comes to the rescue. When we embed either the Hyperlink or LinkButton server control within another control that allows data binding, each can be indirectly bound to that control's data. This little trick allows us to proceed with our data-driven navigation with relative ease. Our first example, SimpleLinkButton.aspx, which is in the LinkButton subdirectory of this chapter's sample application, shows a simple implementation of this strategy. Since this strategy is the foundation of all our navigation controls, we'll examine it first.

To start, let's look at the code-behind page. When the page is first rendered, we create a data table with our required fields and bind it to the DataList. We need this table to show you how to indirectly bind data to the LinkButton control. Here's the code that creates the table and adds the first row:

```
Private Sub Page_Load(ByVal sender As System.Object, _
    ByVal e As System.EventArgs) Handles MyBase.Load
    'Put user code to initialize the page here.
    If Not IsPostBack Then
        'Create the MainMenuTable and fill it with examples.
        Dim menuTable As New DataTable("MainMenuTable")
        Dim menuColumn As DataColumn
        Dim row As DataRow
        menuColumn = menuTable.Columns.Add("MenuID", _
            System.Type.GetType("System.Int32"))
        menuColumn = menuTable.Columns.Add("MenuTabName", _
            System.Type.GetType("System.String"))
        menuColumn = menuTable.Columns.Add("MenuTabTip", _
```

```
        System.Type.GetType("System.String"))
    menuColumn = menuTable.Columns.Add("MenuTabURL", _
        System.Type.GetType("System.String"))
    menuColumn = menuTable.Columns.Add("HasNavBar", _
        System.Type.GetType("System.Boolean"))

    'First Entry - The Home Tab
    row = menuTable.NewRow
    row("MenuID") = 1
    row("MenuTabName") = "Home"
    row("MenuTabTip") = "Our Home Page"
    row("MenuTabURL") = "Home.aspx"
    row("HasNavBar") = False
    menuTable.Rows.Add(row)
    ⋮
    MainMenuList.DataSource = menuTable
    MainMenuList.DataBind()
```

This table structure includes all the information necessary for each tab control. It includes its name, ToolTip information, target URL, and even a *Boolean* entry that specifies whether the item has a navigation bar associated with it. This *Boolean* will be used in later examples.

Now let's look at the HTML code for this example. Although DataList controls can be controlled through property pages, we recommend that you don't use property pages at this time. You'll be able to better understand the DataList control's internal functionality by knowing what's going on in the HTML.

```
<asp:DataList id="MainMenuList" RepeatDirection="Horizontal"
    runat="server">
    <ItemTemplate>
        <asp:LinkButton ID="idMenuLink"
            ToolTip='<%# Container.dataitem("MenuTabTip")%>'
            Text='<%# Container.dataitem("MenuTabName")%>'
            CommandArgument='<%# Container.dataitem("MenuTabURL") %>'
            Runat="Server">
        </asp:LinkButton>
    </ItemTemplate>
</asp:DataList>
```

There are a couple of noteworthy items in this code. The DataList control is by default arranged vertically. Therefore, we have to set *RepeatDirection* within the *asp:DataList* element as *Horizontal*. Next we need a template within the DataList that allows us to include a LinkButton control. It is within the declaration of the LinkButton control that we can include data-binding features that carry from the DataList to the LinkButton. The next bit of code shows these data-binding features in boldface. We've repeated part of the preceding code.

```
<asp:LinkButton ID="idMenuLink"
    ToolTip='<%# Container.dataitem("MenuTabTip")%>'
    Text='<%# Container.dataitem("MenuTabName")%>'
    CommandArgument='<%# Container.dataitem("MenuTabURL") %>'
    Runat="Server">
</asp:LinkButton>
```

We are binding the *Container* object's *dataitem* information to specific parts of the LinkButton control. In the case of the ToolTip, this is in the MenuTabTip field of the menuTable, which is bound to the *MainMenuList* DataList control. The *Text* attribute represents the menu's tab name. What makes it possible to create a server-side LinkButton *Click* event and pass to it the URL we want to use is the LinkButton's *CommandArgument*. Its contents are not shown on the page but rather passed with the *ItemCommand* event. The code for this is in this example's code-behind page:

```
Private Sub MainMenuListItemCommand(ByVal source As Object, _
    ByVal e As System.Web.UI.WebControls.DataListCommandEventArgs) _
    Handles MainMenuList.ItemCommand
    MainMenuList.SelectedIndex = e.Item.ItemIndex
    lblMessage.Text = "Menu Index = " & e.Item.ItemIndex
    lblMessage.Text += " URL Target = " & e.CommandArgument.ToString
    'Response.Redirect(e.CommandArgument.ToString)
End Sub
```

The most important feature the DataList provides us while using the Link-Button control is the *ItemCommand* event. We define the subroutine that handles the *Click* event of our DataList control by binding the *DataListCommandEventArgs* of our *MainMenuList.Itemcommand* object.

```
Private Sub MainMenuListItemCommand(ByVal source As Object, _
    ByVal e As System.Web.UI.WebControls.DataListCommandEventArgs) _
    Handles MainMenuList.ItemCommand
    ⋮
```

This event handler provides us with two of the most important parameters we need. First, it provides us with the *ItemIndex* of the DataList that was clicked. This allows us to pass the state of the *Menu* to the application later. Second, we get the *CommandArgument* that was assigned to the DataList. In our case, this is the URL of the page to which we will redirect the browser. To make testing our SimpleLinkButton.aspx page easier, we're not redirecting it but rather writing the output to a label named *lblMessage*.

```
lblMessage.Text = "Menu Index = " & e.Item.ItemIndex
lblMessage.Text += " URL Target = " & e.CommandArgument.ToString
```

One more item of interest is the DataList's *SelectedIndex* property. With it we can set which *Item* of the DataList is currently selected. We've put the following line within the preceding code block so that the selection stays with the DataList item that was clicked:

```
MainMenuList.SelectedIndex = e.Item.ItemIndex
```

Now it's time to test our simple menu page. Granted, it doesn't look great yet, but it has the underlying functionality we want:

- It's fully data driven and builds itself on the fly.

- It uses .NET components.

- It handles its own state.

- It allows redirection to other pages.

Now let's give this example the look and functionality we want. Our second example, BetterLinkButton.aspx, is the result of fine-tuning our DataList control. The changes are purely visual and none of the code's functionality has changed. We're using the help of style sheets and available options in the DataList control. Here is the style sheet we attached to the file. It affects both the HTML body and the LinkButton.

```
<style>
    A.menutext { FONT-WEIGHT: bold; FONT-SIZE: 12pt; MARGIN-LEFT: 5px;
        COLOR: navy; MARGIN-RIGHT: 5px; TEXT-DECORATION: none }
    A.menutext:hover { COLOR: blue; TEXT-DECORATION: none }
    A.menutext:visited { COLOR: navy; TEXT-DECORATION: none }
    A.menutext:hover { COLOR: blue; TEXT-DECORATION: none }
    A.menutext:visited:hover {text-decoration: none; color: blue}
    BODY { FONT-WEIGHT: normal; FONT-SIZE: 10pt; MARGIN: 0px;
        WORD-SPACING: normal; TEXT-TRANSFORM: none; FONT-FAMILY: Tahoma,
        Arial, Helvetica, Sans-Serif; LETTER-SPACING: normal;
        BACKGROUND-COLOR: #aec1eb }
</style>
```

Although the HTML body will take the style changes automatically, we need to let the DataList know which style to use:

```
<asp:LinkButton ID="idMenuLink" cssclass="menutext" . . .
```

The part of the style sheet that gives the LinkButton's text its font, font color, and hover colors is *menutext*. Notice that we took away the underlines and made visited links behave like standard links. We don't want the typical behavior of a link button, which gives us different colors for visited and nonvisited links and uses underlines. Notice also that we gave the links a slightly different color for hover behavior. Experiment with these settings to give you a feel for how much you can influence the LinkButton's look.

Next we want to change the background color of the clicked item within the DataList control. This will give it the look of a tab control. Fortunately, the available features of the DataList control allow us to do this easily. We create two templates within the DataList—the ItemStyle and SelectedItemStyle templates—shown here:

```
<SelectedItemStyle BackColor="White"></SelectedItemStyle>
<ItemStyle BackColor="#3366FF"></ItemStyle>
```

Feel free to experiment with this code also. You can always reset the values. In addition to the *BackColor* property, you can set many other properties to change selected and unselected behavior. Later in this chapter, we'll show you how to set these properties at run time, not declaratively as we did in the preceding code blocks.

We now have the foundation for the rest of our menu code sections. Before turning this example into a reusable custom user control, we want to explain why we used the LinkButton server control versus the Hyperlink server control. We've found that the Hyperlink server control works just like a standard HTML hyperlink—within the browser, it passes control from one Web page to another. This makes it impossible for us to force a server roundtrip. The LinkButton control allows us to use a server roundtrip and execute additional code before calling a server-side redirect to another page. This is important to us because it allows us to set the state information within the control itself—in this case, the state information is the index of the button clicked, so we can have it automatically selected in the page we are navigating to. In addition, this state information allows us to query the information for the Menu tables later. We can look for the state information of the menu and navigation bar separately or together. This will allow the proper state information to be returned regardless of whether we use the main menu bar on its own or combine it with the side navigation bar. If we didn't set this state information before redirecting, we would have to come up with a way for each page inside our Web application to identify itself to the menu controls. This isn't desirable. To encapsulate menu and navigation functionality into our components, the component itself must handle its state information.

Designing the Control

When we look at our last example, we might be tempted to storm ahead and create a custom user or server control right away. But let's consider the advice from Chapter 2 and design the control first.

We're going to start with the needed data tables and structure. Both examples we showed previously already contain a data table for the main menu. We can take its structure and enhance it. Table 7-1 has the MainMenuTable structure.

Table 7-1   MainMenuTable

Field Name	Field Type	Allows Nulls	Index
MenuID	*Integer*	No	Primary key
MenuTabName	*String*	No	
MenuTabTip	*String*	Yes	
MenuTabURL	*String*	No	
HasChild	*Boolean*	No; default is *False*	

We have added a primary key as the MenuID and defined required fields. To allow the MainMenuTable to control visibility over its children, we're going to create a one-to-many relationship between it and the NavBarTable. Table 7-2 shows its structure.

Table 7-2   NavBarTable

Field Name	Field Type	Allows Nulls	Index
NavBarID	*Integer*	No	Primary key
MenuID	*Integer*	No	Foreign key
NavBarName	*String*	No	
NavBarTip	*String*	Yes	
NavBarURL	*String*	No	
HasChild	*Boolean*	No; default is *False*	

Both Table 7-1 and Table 7-2 will be created in a MenuData component that we'll add shortly. In this component, we'll also create the relationship for these tables. Adding other layers can be done by adding tables with the same structure as the NavBar table, linking them as one-to-many each time. Remember that we recommend a navigation structure that is only two or three levels deep.

After the MenuData component, we'll move our existing MainMenu into a custom user control and add state management functionality. We'll put this control into a template and use this template for the Home, Employee, Benefits, and Company pages that we're actually creating as a mini menu-driven application.

Once we've moved and tested this example, we're going to add generic features such as colors, fonts, sizes, and selected and nonselected backgrounds to the MenuData component and the custom user control.

Now that the main menu tabbed bar is completed, we can follow the same steps to create a vertical navigation bar. You'll quickly see that the principles guiding creation of the vertical navigation bar are the same as those for the main menu tabbed bar, but we need to add additional state and menu data-handling options. Let's get on with the work.

The MenuData Component

Some of this component's functionality, which we call the MenuData component in the MenuData subdirectory of this chapter's sample application files, is the same as the functionality for our data access component, which we discussed in Chapter 4. Allowing custom exception logging and changing the dispose behavior is always on our list of options to implement. In this example, we haven't implemented public constructors because we're going to handle only one way of initializing and using the component. The MenuData component creates the MenuData dataset that contains the menu and navigation bar's controlling data that gets created by calling methods—similar to the way parameters are added to our data access component. Each time a method gets called with its parameters attached, that method creates another entry in one of the menu data tables.

When the MenuData component is initialized, we first create the structure of our tables, as shown in the following code in the Component Designer Generated Code region:

```
Public Sub New()
    MyBase.New()
    'This call is required by the Component Designer.
    InitializeComponent()
    'Add any initialization after the InitializeComponent() call
    'Create the dataset structure
    privateDataSet = CreateMenuDataSet()
End Sub
```

We added the boldface lines to call the *CreateMenuDataSet* function, which returns the structure of our tables to the *privateDataSet* object within this component. It's within the *privateDataSet* object that we save the entries for our menu and navigation structure. In the end, we return the entries from our component.

Here's some code that shows you how we created the tables and their links:

```
Function CreateMenuDataSet() As DataSet
    Dim privateMenuDataSet As New DataSet("MenuTables")
    Dim privateMenuTable As New DataTable("MainMenuTable")
    'Define the Menu DataTable.
    Dim privateMenuColumn As DataColumn

    Try
        privateMenuColumn = privateMenuTable.Columns.Add("MenuID", _
            System.Type.GetType("System.Int32"))
        privateMenuColumn.AllowDBNull = False
        privateMenuColumn = privateMenuTable.Columns.Add( _
            "MenuTabName", System.Type.GetType("System.String"))
        privateMenuColumn.AllowDBNull = False
        ⋮

    Catch tableMenuException As Exception
        Throw New Exception(privateExceptionMessage & _
            " Main Menu Table creation error.", tableMenuException)
    End Try

    Dim privateNavTable As New DataTable("NavTable")
    Dim privateNavColumn As DataColumn
    Try
        privateNavColumn = privateNavTable.Columns.Add("MenuID", _
            System.Type.GetType("System.Int32"))
        privateNavColumn.AllowDBNull = False
        privateNavColumn = privateNavTable.Columns.Add("NavBarId", _
            System.Type.GetType("System.Int32"))
        privateNavColumn.AllowDBNull = False
        ⋮
    Catch tableNavException As Exception
        Throw New Exception(privateExceptionMessage & _
            " NavBar Table creation error.", tableNavException)
    End Try

    privateMenuDataSet.Tables.Add(privateMenuTable)
    privateMenuDataSet.Tables.Add(privateNavTable)
    Try
        privateMenuDataSet.Relations.Add("MenuNav",
```

(continued)

```
                        privateMenuDataSet.Tables("MainMenuTable").Columns( _
                        "MenuID"), _
                        privateMenuDataSet.Tables("NavTable").Columns("MenuID"))
                Return privateMenuDataSet
            Catch linkException As Exception
                Throw New Exception(privateExceptionMessage & _
                    " One-to-many Link could not be created.", linkException)
            End Try
        End Function
```

The first few lines create the dataset and data tables with individual fields. We define each field's data types and identify which ones are required. After creating the fields, we add them to the dataset and then create a relationship. The structure within this example creates the tables for a main menu and a child NavBar. If you need to provide more levels in your menu, simply add another table that links to the NavTable for each additional layer.

In the next part of our MenuData component, we create the menu tables, one line at a time. Let's look at the code in more detail. It's in the AddMainMenuItems & AddNavBarItems regions within the component:

```
Public Sub AddMainMenuParameter(ByVal MenuID As Integer, _
    ByVal MenuTabName As String, _
    ByVal MenuTabURL As String, _
    ByVal HasChild As Boolean, _
    Optional ByVal MenuTabTip As String = Nothing)
    'Now get the Menu Table.
    Dim usedMenuTable As DataTable
    Dim addRow As DataRow
    Try
        usedMenuTable = privateDataSet.Tables("MainMenuTable")
        addRow = usedMenuTable.NewRow
        addRow("MenuID") = MenuID
        addRow("MenuTabName") = MenuTabName
        addRow("MenuTabURL") = MenuTabURL
        addRow("HasChild") = HasChild
        addRow("MenuTabTip") = MenuTabTip
        usedMenuTable.Rows.Add(addRow)
    Catch addMainMenuException As Exception
        'Use the private LogException function to log an exception.
        LogException(addMainMenuException)
        'The exception is passed to the calling code.
        Throw New Exception(privateExceptionMessage & _
            " Adding a record to the Main Menu Table failed.", _
            addMainMenuException)
    End Try
End Sub
```

Adding one menu or NavBar item at a time is achieved by calling a public subroutine with the parameters required for each table row. The only things to watch for are using correct data types and placing optional parameters at the end. (Don't forget to set the optional parameter to something; in this case, something ended up being *Nothing*.)

```
Public Sub AddMainMenuParameter(ByVal MenuID As Integer, _
    ByVal MenuTabName As String, _
    ByVal MenuTabURL As String, _
    ByVal HasChild As Boolean, _
    Optional ByVal MenuTabTip As String = Nothing)
```

When we call the subroutine, it calls up the correct menu data table and adds a new row. Then it enters the passed parameters into this row and saves them to the *MainMenuTable* DataTable:

```
usedMenuTable = privateDataSet.Tables("MainMenuTable")
addRow = usedMenuTable.NewRow
addRow("MenuID") = MenuID
addRow("MenuTabName") = MenuTabName
addRow("MenuTabURL") = MenuTabURL
addRow("HasChild") = HasChild
addRow("MenuTabTip") = MenuTabTip
usedMenuTable.Rows.Add(addRow)
```

This way, we can add row by row to the menu tables. The *AddMainMenu-Parameter* subroutine adds rows to the MainMenu data table, and the *Add-NavBarParameter* subroutine adds them to the NavBar data table. The only difference is in the passed parameters and data fields.

Our MenuData component is now ready for its first tests, even though we'll include additional features, such as setting color and font choices, later in this chapter in the section "The Navigation Bar Custom User Control." The Menu-DataTestForm.aspx file within the LinkButton directory calls the MenuData component, adds records for both tables, and returns both tables displayed in generic DataGrids. This way we can test the data's correctness. We can also test the functionality of the component. Let's take a quick look at how this component gets used. You start by importing the *MenuData* namespace, which contains the *MenuDataServer* class:

```
Imports MenuNavigation.MenuData
```

In the *Page_Load* event handler for the page, we call the MenuData component and add the menu items. Here's the code in its entirety:

```
Private Sub Page_Load(ByVal sender As System.Object, _
    ByVal e As System.EventArgs) Handles MyBase.Load
    'Put user code to initialize the page here.
```

(continued)

```
Dim menuTable As DataTable          'Declare a menuTable.
Dim navTable As DataTable           'Declare a NavBar Table.
'Call the MenuTable component and add info to the Main Menu Table.
Dim localMenuTables As New MenuDataServer()
localMenuTables.AddMainMenuParameter(1, "Home", "Home.aspx", _
    False,"Our Home Page")
localMenuTables.AddMainMenuParameter(2, "Employees", _
    "Employees.aspx", True, "All about Employees")
localMenuTables.AddMainMenuParameter(3, "Benefits", _
    "Benefits.aspx", True, "Our Company's Benefits")
localMenuTables.AddMainMenuParameter(4, "Company", _
    "Company.aspx", False)
'Get the menuTable from the returning dataset.
menuTable = localMenuTables.GetMenuDataSet.Tables("MainMenuTable")
'Add info to the NavBar Table.
localMenuTables.AddNavBarParameter(2, 1, "2nd Tab whatever", _
    "whatever.aspx", False)
localMenuTables.AddNavBarParameter(2, 2, "2nd Tab whatever2", _
    "whatever2.aspx", False)
localMenuTables.AddNavBarParameter(3, 1, "3rd Tab whatever", _
    "whatever3.aspx", False)
navTable = localMenuTables.GetMenuDataSet.Tables("NavTable")
localMenuTables.Dispose()            'Call Dispose on the object.
localMenuTables = Nothing            'Make sure it is out of scope.
'We assign the returned table to our MainMenu DataList.
MainMenuGrid.DataSource = menuTable
MainMenuGrid.DataBind()
'We assign the returned table to our MainMenu DataList
NavBarGrid.DataSource = navTable
NavBarGrid.DataBind()
End Sub
```

We also need to create a variable for the *MenuDataServer* class:

```
Dim localMenuTables As New MenuDataServer()
```

Then we can add the menu items, as shown here:

```
localMenuTables.AddMainMenuParameter(1, "Home", "Home.aspx", _
    False,"Our Home Page")
localMenuTables.AddMainMenuParameter(2, "Employees", _
    "Employees.aspx", True, "All about Employees")
⋮
```

Once we add all the menu items we want, we set locally defined tables (DataTables declared in the code-behind pages that use menus) as the result by calling the *MenuData* object's *GetMenuData* function. This returns a dataset containing all tables created. This is the reason we have to define the specific table within the dataset we want, as shown here:

```
'Get the menuTable from the returning dataset.
menuTable = localMenuTables.GetMenuDataSet.Tables("MainMenuTable")
navTable = localMenuTables.GetMenuDataSet.Tables("NavTable")
```

Last but not least, we assign the returned local tables to the DataGrid and bind it:

```
MainMenuGrid.DataSource = menuTable
MainMenuGrid.DataBind()
```

In our next example from DataLinkButton.aspx, the same principles are used to create a fully data bound menu navigation bar. Instead of linking to other pages, we are showing the menu item's index and the target of the page we would have called up. Please take the time to play with this code and add a couple of menu lines. You can readily see that we have full control over what the menu does and doesn't show. We can even create conditions within the page load event that can choose different sets of menu tabs based upon criteria such as role or permission information.

The Main Menu Custom User Control

Instead of copying the menu HTML and code-behind page into each page within our Web applications, we're now going to create this control as an ASP.NET custom user control. We'll do this in an experimental fashion first, before we create higher levels of independence and encapsulation.

The examples used in the next few paragraphs are in the MenuTabs subdirectory. We assume you know how to create and use custom user controls. The MainMenuTest.ascx file contains the user control that provides the main menu tab functionality. When you look at its HTML, you'll see that is exactly like the code in our previous example. The DataList and the LinkButton, with their respective data-binding techniques, are used in exactly the same way. The differences lie within the code-behind page.

First, we don't want to create the tables for menu and navigation data every time we refresh a page or navigate to another one. For this reason, we're creating a session variable for the menu tables. Each time the MainMenuTest user control is called, it checks for its availability and either creates the session variable or uses it. Here's the code:

```
If Session("MainMenuTable") Is Nothing Then
    'Call MenuTable Component and add info to the Main Menu Table.
    Dim localMenuTables As New MenuDataServer()
    localMenuTables.AddMainMenuParameter(1, "Home", _
        "/MenuNavigation/MenuTabs/Home.aspx", False, "Our Home Page")
    localMenuTables.AddMainMenuParameter(2, "Employees", _
        "/MenuNavigation/MenuTabs/Employees.aspx", True, _
```

(continued)

```
            "All about Employees")
        localMenuTables.AddMainMenuParameter(3, "Benefits", _
            "/MenuNavigation/MenuTabs/Benefits.aspx", True, _
            "Our Company's Benefits")
        localMenuTables.AddMainMenuParameter(4, "Company", _
            "/MenuNavigation/MenuTabs/Company.aspx", False)
        menuTable = localMenuTables.GetMenuDataSet.Tables("MainMenuTable")
        Session("MainMenuTable") = menuTable
        localMenuTables.Dispose()          'Calls Dispose on the object.
        localMenuTables = Nothing          'Make sure it is out of scope.
Else
    menuTable = CType(Session("MainMenuTable"), DataTable)
End If
```

We don't want to get into a lengthy discussion about session variables. In the old ASP days, using session variables was less desirable since scalability was severely limited. Fortunately, ASP.NET doesn't have the same restrictions, and more options for session variables are available. Still, you have to create a balance between performance and scalability. Whichever technique you use, that balance is still a factor. If you want only performance, scalability will suffer—and vice versa. We'll cover the challenge of scalability and performance in more detail in Chapter 11.

Second, we need to take care of state management in our custom user control. Since we're navigating from page to page, we need to pass the position of the selected menu tab to the next page. Again, we've opted to do this within a session variable. We check whether the *MainMenuIndex* session variable is already created. If it is, we set the DataList's index to the value passed in the session variable. Otherwise, we create the session variable and set it to 0. This will set the first tab to be activated. (We assume that's the one you want to use as the default; if you don't, just set it to the one you want to use as a default.)

```
If Session("MainMenuIndex") Is Nothing Then
    MainMenuList.SelectedIndex = 0
    Session("MainMenuIndex") = 0
Else
    MainMenuList.SelectedIndex = CInt(Session("MainMenuIndex"))
End If
```

Using a session variable will introduce another behavior we need to be aware of. If the session times out, session variables disappear and the client is thrown back to the main menu option. This is actually a benefit when compared to timeout or connection-lost error messages.

One more thing we can't forget is to set the state of the menu upon tab selection. When a specific tab is clicked, the state management session variable we created in the preceding code needs to be set. This is done in the MenuList *ItemCommand* as follows:

```
Private Sub MainMenuList_ItemCommand(ByVal source As Object,
    ByVal e As System.Web.UI.WebControls.DataListCommandEventArgs) _
    Handles MainMenuList.ItemCommand
    MainMenuList.SelectedIndex = e.Item.ItemIndex
    Session("MainMenuIndex") = e.Item.ItemIndex
    Response.Redirect(e.CommandArgument.ToString)
End Sub
```

With the MainMenuTest user control ready to go, we can now create an actual data-driven menu and the pages it will navigate to. You'll find the Home.aspx page for this example in the MenuTabs subdirectory. Run the Home.aspx file and see how the menu tab navigates from page to page. When you examine the Home.aspx, Employees.aspx, Benefits.aspx, and Company.aspx pages, you find that there is no additional code in the code-behind page. The state management is totally independent from the actual Web pages. All you need to do to use the custom user control is drop it into the Web pages. Looking back at Figure 7-4, you can see that we've already created the logo area, the main menu tab area, and the page detail area and are ready to add the vertical navigation bar.

The Navigation Bar Custom User Control

Before we get to the actual navigation bar, we have to make some changes to the main menu user control. The examples we use in the next few paragraphs are in the MenuNavCombo subdirectory. The main menu user control is contained in the MainMenu.ascx file. The menu control is very similar to the one we've already used. One change we made was to move the code that generates the menu tables out of the custom user control. This further encapsulates the main menu user control and allows it to be used more generically. Notice the page load section of code in the MainMenu.ascx code-behind page:

```
Imports MenuNavigation.LocalMenuData
    ⋮
Private Sub Page_Load(ByVal sender As System.Object, _
    ByVal e As System.EventArgs) Handles MyBase.Load
    Dim menuData As New DataSet()
    Dim menuTable As New DataTable()
    If Session("MenuData") Is Nothing Then
        Dim getLocalMenu As New MenuDataClass()
        menuData = getLocalMenu.getMenuDataSet
        Session("MenuData") = menuData
        menuTable = menuData.Tables("MainMenuTable")
    Else
        menuTable = CType(Session("MenuData"), _
            DataSet).Tables("MainMenuTable")
```

(continued)

```
    End If
    ⋮
End Sub
```

We no longer create the *MenuData* dataset line by line within this code-behind page. Instead we call the *MenuDataClass* within the *MenuNavigation.LocalMenuData* namespace. It in return fills out the required menu dataset, which is passed back into the main menu custom control. From here it's loaded into the *MenuData* session variable. Notice that we load the whole dataset into this session variable, not just the specific MainMenu data table. The *MainMenu* dataset contains all tables required for navigation. Since we are in the main menu user control, we now extract the specific MainMenu table from the dataset:

```
menuTable = menuData.Tables("MainMenuTable")
```

If the session variable for the *MenuData* dataset already exists, we simply extract the MainMenu data table directly:

```
menuTable = CType(Session("MenuData"),DataSet).Tables( _
    "MainMenuTable")
```

Let's take a quick look at the MenuDataClass.vb file within the MenuNavigation directory. The file defines the *LocalMenuData* namespace and within it the *MenuDataClass* class we just called in the preceding user control. This class encapsulates the menu creation. It calls the MenuDataServer component, passes the parameters that create menu and navigation tables, and returns the whole *MenuData* dataset. Separating this code from the user control gives us the encapsulation we wanted. It also simplifies the creation of business logic that returns different menu and navigation structures based on permission and access levels of individuals logging into an application or creating other kinds of navigation customization. Here's the code in the MenuDataClass.vb file:

```
Imports MenuNavigation.MenuData
Imports System.Data
Namespace LocalMenuData
Public Class MenuDataClass
    Public Function getMenuDataSet() As DataSet

        'Call MenuTable Component and add info to the Main Menu Table.
        Dim localMenuTables As New MenuDataServer()
        localMenuTables.AddMainMenuParameter(1, "Home", _
            "/MenuNavigation/MenuNavCombo/Home.aspx", False, _
            "Our Home Page")
        localMenuTables.AddMainMenuParameter(2, "Employees", _
            "/MenuNavigation/MenuNavCombo/Employees.aspx", True, _
            "All about Employees")
```

```
        localMenuTables.AddMainMenuParameter(3, "Benefits", _
            "/MenuNavigation/MenuNavCombo/Benefits.aspx", True, _
            "Our Company's Benefits")
        localMenuTables.AddMainMenuParameter(4, "Company", _
            "/MenuNavigation/MenuNavCombo/Company.aspx", False)
            'Add info to the NavBar Table
        localMenuTables.AddNavBarParameter(2, 1, "Address", _
            "/MenuNavigation/MenuNavCombo/Address.aspx", False)
        localMenuTables.AddNavBarParameter(2, 2, "Schedule", _
            "/MenuNavigation/MenuNavCombo/Schedule.aspx", False)
        localMenuTables.AddNavBarParameter(2, 3, "Emergency", -
            "/MenuNavigation/MenuNavCombo/Emergency.aspx", False)
        localMenuTables.AddNavBarParameter(3, 1, "Listing", _
            "/MenuNavigation/MenuNavCombo/Listing.aspx", False)
        Return localMenuTables.GetMenuDataSet
        localMenuTables.Dispose()        'Dispose the object
        localMenuTables = Nothing        'Make sure it is out of scope
    End Function
End Class
End Namespace
```

The other difference we find in this control is within the *MainMenuList ItemCommand*. In addition to setting the *SelectedIndex* for the DataList and keeping its state in the *MainMenuIndex* session variable, we also want to pass the state of the navigation bar. This we do by creating and setting the *NavBarIndex* session variable. You might wonder why it's set to 100. Well, whenever a user clicks a main menu tab, there shouldn't be anything selected by default in the corresponding child navigation bar. Setting the *ItemIndex* of the navigation bar to 100 allows the navigation bar user control to highlight any available choices. (We assume that you won't present more than 99 subchoices therein. If you do, increase the number to 1000.)

```
Private Sub MainMenuList_ItemCommand(ByVal source As Object,
    ByVal e As System.Web.UI.WebControls.DataListCommandEventArgs)
    Handles MainMenuList.ItemCommand
    ainMenuList.SelectedIndex = e.Item.ItemIndex
    Session("MainMenuIndex") = e.Item.ItemIndex
    Session("NavBarIndex") = 100
    Response.Redirect(e.CommandArgument.ToString)
End Sub
```

We're now ready to get the navigation bar user control working. The example file is navbar.ascx. The first thing you'll notice after opening it up in Visual Studio .NET is its vertical alignment and a Menu LinkButton on top. We also included an HTML table that allows us to align the returning LinkButton controls better and create a common width. Before getting into this control's code, we'd like to explain why we added a Menu link button as a header to the navigation bar. First, by synchronizing the name of the current main menu tab with the header of the side navigation bar, users aren't likely to get confused about where they are. Although this is a good reason, we have an even better one. If users started using the navigation bar and wanted to return to the main page of a specific tab, they would have to click the already selected main menu tab. This functionality is not as intuitive as we would like, so we also synchronize the behavior of the Menu button to return users to the main page of the selected tab. Try the example by running the home.aspx file in the MenuNav-Combo subdirectory and see for yourself.

Now let's examine the code-behind page of Navbar.ascx. The first part of the page-load event loads the correct tables into the local dataset as well as both the *menuData* and *navTable* tables. You might ask why we go through the effort of also returning the main menu's table, not just the navigation table. Well, we do this because we need to investigate the current selected main menu tab's data to see whether it allows for a navigation bar. We also need its information to set the Menu DataLink button that we described earlier. Here is the code:

```
Private Sub Page_Load(ByVal sender As System.Object, _
    ByVal e As System.EventArgs) Handles MyBase.Load
    'Put user code to initialize the page here.
    Dim menuData As New DataSet()
    Dim menuTable As New DataTable()    'Create a DataTable Instance
    Dim navTable As New DataTable()
    If Session("MenuData") Is Nothing Then
        Dim getLocalMenu As New MenuDataClass()
        menuData = getLocalMenu.getMenuDataSet
        Session("MenuData") = menuData
        menuTable = menuData.Tables("MainMenuTable")
        navTable = menuData.Tables("NavTable")
    Else
        navTable = CType(Session("MenuData"), DataSet).Tables( _
            "NavTable")
        menuTable = CType(Session("MenuData"), _
            DataSet).Tables("MainMenuTable")
End If
```

Just as we did with the MainMenu user control, we're looking for the existence of the *MenuData* dataset session. If it's not available, we create it; otherwise, we just use it. Just as before, we load the menuTable and the navTable.

Next, we need to implement the code that determines whether the NavBar user control is visible. This information is in the *menuTable* DataTable. We get to it through the ADO.NET table select statement. At the same time that we return the HasChild table cell that determines visibility, we also return the main menu selected tab's name and URL. This will go into the Menu header of the control. Here's the code:

```
Dim privateNavBarSelected As Boolean
Dim selectString As String = "MenuID =" & CType(Session _
    ("MainMenuIndex"), Integer) + 1
Dim selectRow() As DataRow = menuTable.Select(selectString)
privateNavBarSelected = CType(selectRow(0)("HasChild"), Boolean)

Menu.Text = CType(selectRow(0)("MenuTabName"), String)
Menu.CommandArgument = CType(selectRow(0)("MenuTabURL"), String)
If privateNavBarSelected = False Then
    MyBase.Visible = False
    Exit Sub
Else
    MyBase.Visible = True
End If
```

The *selectString* is created as an ADO.NET SQL statement. In this case, it will set the MenuID to the main menu's index plus 1. We needed to add the 1 to adjust for the DataList being 0-based, whereas the main menu table is 1-based. The next row creates a new variable named *selectRow* as a DataRow and applies the *selectString* SQL statement:

```
Dim selectRow() As DataRow = menuTable.Select(selectString)
```

We now have the table row that represents the data for the selected tab in the main menu. Its *HasChild* field contains the *Boolean* that specifies whether the navigation bar is visible. We use the value returned from the *HasChild* field later to mark the navigation bar as visible or invisible. Since we already have the whole row representing the main menu tab's data, we are assigning the name and URL to the Menu header of the user control. This is the code for it:

```
Menu.Text = CType(selectRow(0)("MenuTabName"), String)
Menu.CommandArgument = CType(selectRow(0)("MenuTabURL"), String)
```

Now we determine the user control's visibility. The property is easily available in *MyBase.Visible*. Should it be invisible, we set the property to *False* and exit the subroutine right away. There's no reason to continue further processing. Otherwise, we set *MyBase.Visible* to *True* and continue.

All we have left to do is limit the navigation choices for the NavBar to only those rows in the navTable that correspond to the selected menu tab. We do this by creating a view from the navTable and filter it to the selected menu tab's MenuID number. We're still carrying this in the *selectString* variable we used just a couple of lines of code ago. Here's how this is done:

```
Dim navTableView As DataView = navTable.DefaultView
navTableView.RowFilter = selectString
NavBarList.DataSource = navTable.DefaultView
NavBarList.DataBind()
```

The code for implementing this functionality is astoundingly simple. After creating the *DefaultView* for the navTable as *navTableDefaultView*, we just apply the *selectString ("MenuID=xxxx")* as a row filter. Then we bind the *navTable.DefaultView* to the DataList, and voila! That's all there is to it!

The rest of the code is the same as the code we've seen for the MainMenu user control. It handles the state management for the user control. Let's take the menu and navigation user controls for a test run. Home.aspx in the MenuNav-Combo subdirectory will get the sample started. Try all combinations of available items on the main menu tabs and navigation tabs. (Don't forget to click the side navigation bar header after browsing some of its items—it will return you to the main menu tab's page.)

Now we're going to look at a couple more usability tricks. To create all the pages in this example, we used the Home.aspx as a template, copied it, and renamed it. (We also fixed the name problem in the code-behind pages, because renaming only changes the .aspx file and not its @ *Page* directive with the *inherits="xxx"* statement.) After we had the new page, we changed its main content and added its name to the *MenuDataClass* class in the proper menu and navigation tabs.

The look and feel of the user controls come from a combination of style sheets and declarative settings inside the user controls. We looked previously at both of these. Ultimately, we'd like to set these as data items returned from the MenuData component and use them just like the menu and navigation tables. We'll show you an example of this. In the previous example's NavBar.ascx user control, open the code-behind page and remove the comment character from the following lines of code:

```
'NavBarList.ItemStyle.BackColor = Color.Yellow
'NavBarList.ItemStyle.Font.Italic = True
'NavBarList.SelectedItemStyle.BackColor = Color.LightSeaGreen
'NavBarList.SelectedItemStyle.Font.Italic = True
'NavBarList.SelectedItemStyle.BorderWidth.Pixel(1)
'NavBarList.SelectedItemStyle.BorderStyle = BorderStyle.Ridge
```

Now try the example again. Yes, we agree it's ugly, but it makes the point.

Other Options for User Controls

Although our existing user controls work well, there are some more things we could do.

■ **Turn the MainMenu and NavBar custom user controls into server controls**   After conversion to server controls, both the main menu and navigation controls could be used across several applications and applied using drag-and-drop capability. We still recommend dropping them into application-specific custom user controls. Doing so adds the look and feel for that application to the custom user control, which you can then use within a template for the application. (More on application templates in Chapter 10.)

■ **Create more abstraction by adding all color, font, highlighting, and background and foreground colors to another table in the MenuData component**   We've given you a good starting point to implement this. If it becomes important that you need this abstraction, follow the process we covered and add this functionality to your controls. Make sure that you assign default properties to these.

■ **Enhance the MenuData component to accept existing menu navigation tables or XML**   Adding additional public constructors to the MenuData component that handle each specific instance can do this. For example, the constructor for passing data would allow the passing of the required tables, which would then be validated in the MenuData component and assigned to the same internal dataset that returns the menu and navigation structures.

■ **Create additional layers of navigation**   Following the strategy of one-to-many tables and linking one menu to another allows you to go as deep as you can go. Just remember, the deeper the navigation structure, the more confused the user gets.

■ **Add graphics options to the main menu tabs**   The task of adding graphic buttons becomes a bit more daunting since you have to create functions that will take a bitmap and stretch or compress it based on the length of the tabs used. This will have to be done on the fly as the components create the navigation structure. A workaround for this might be to find the maximum length needed for the tabs, forcing them to the same width, and passing only one graphic for selected and unselected tabs. Although we've worked with such code, going into more detail now would be beyond the scope of this book.

■ **Use Microsoft Internet Explorer Web controls**   Microsoft is offering Web controls that give you much of the functionality we've built into our controls. They're not as abstract and as easy to bind to data, but they are an alternative. We've found that we need more control than they offer. You've learned the internal working of this chapter's controls and are able to create much more flexible solutions with our controls than you would be able to create with the Internet Explorer Web controls. For this reason, we haven't included any samples using them.

A Visual Basic .NET Windows Forms Example

Although this chapter and book concentrate on Visual Basic .NET component solutions for Web applications, we want to look at a simple Windows Forms menu example. Creating these types of programs has become much easier than previous versions of Visual Basic allowed. Figure 7-7 shows the result of our efforts.

Figure 7-7 Windows Forms menu example

Our Visual Studio .NET example solution WindowsFormsMenu is in the Visual Basic subdirectory of this chapter's sample applications. Start the solution and look at the ByHand.vb form. We created this form by using the menu tool at design time. Drag and drop a MainMenu component from the Toolbox, click the text property, and add items below and to the right of the first choice. Visual Basic .NET creates the accompanying code in the Windows Form Designer Generated Code region. When the user double-clicks a menu item, an event handler is created for the item's *Click* event. Here's the sample code for a *Click* event handler:

```
Private Sub MenuItem2_Click(ByVal sender As System.Object, _
    ByVal e As System.EventArgs) Handles MenuItem2.Click
    'This is the click event for the Address.
```

```
        Dim callAddress As New Address()
        callAddress.Show()
    End Sub
```

When the user chooses the Address item of the menu, a new form opens.

Another way to create Windows Forms menus is programmatically. A sample of this is in the ProgramTest.vb file. Let's look at the code-behind page:

```
Private localMainMenu As MainMenu
Private localMenuItem As MenuItem
Public Sub CreateMenu()
    localMainMenu = New MainMenu()
    localMenuItem = New MenuItem("&Employees", _
        New System.EventHandler(AddressOf Me.MenuSelect))
    localMenuItem.MenuItems.Add("&Address", _
        New System.EventHandler(AddressOf Me.MenuSelect))
    localMenuItem.MenuItems.Add("&Schedule", _
        New System.EventHandler(AddressOf Me.MenuSelect))
    localMenuItem.MenuItems.Add("Eme&rgency")
    localMainMenu.MenuItems.Add(localMenuItem)
    ' Set the form's menu to the menu you have just created.
    Me.Menu = localMainMenu
End Sub
```

First, we need to create instances of *MainMenu* and *MenuItem* variables. Then we create a new MainMenu item and assign it a name and, in this case, an event handler.

```
localMenuItem = New MenuItem("&Employees", _
    New System.EventHandler(AddressOf Me.MenuSelect))
```

Now we're ready to add subitems to the *MenuItem* we just created. We need to do this by calling the *MenuItems.Add* method, which is followed by the name and the event handler:

```
localMenuItem.MenuItems.Add("&Address", _
    New System.EventHandler(AddressOf Me.MenuSelect))
```

Thereafter we add these items to the MainMenu and set the current form's Menu structure to the MainMenu we created. Here's the specific code for this:

```
localMainMenu.MenuItems.Add(localMenuItem)
'Set the form's menu to the menu you have just created.
Me.Menu = localMainMenu
```

This takes care of the look and feel of the menu. Now we need to assign the event handler. Actually, this step should come before the *CreateMenu* subroutine; otherwise, you'll see underlines pointing to errors in *System.Event-Handler(AddressOfMe.MenuSelect)*. Don't forget this when you create this type of menu structure yourself. Here's the assigned *MenuSelect* event declaration that causes a message box to open when clicked:

```
Protected Sub MenuSelect(ByVal sender As Object, _
    ByVal e As System.EventArgs)
    MessageBox.Show("You Clicked a Menu Button")
End Sub
```

We've decided to show the programmatic functionality of adding a menu by letting a button's *Click* event handler call the preceding subroutine and create the menu structure on the fly. Try out the code and click the Employees, Address, or Schedule menu items.

We want to take this example and abstract it by encapsulating it in a way that is similar to the way we encapsulated Web Forms classes shown previously in this chapter. The code is in the Programmatically.vb file. When you look at the code-behind page for this file, you'll see very little additional code. First we create the event handler for the menu, even though the menu creation is in another class file.

```
Protected Sub MenuSelect(ByVal sender As Object, _
    ByVal e As System.EventArgs)
    MessageBox.Show("You Clicked a Menu Button")
End Sub
```

The code that actually calls the *MenuTest* class, which creates the menu, is hidden within the Windows Form Designer Generated Code region. You'll find the code after the "Add any initialization…" comment in the constructor for this page:

```
Public Sub New()
    MyBase.New()
    'This call is required by the Windows Form Designer.
    InitializeComponent()
    'Add any initialization after the InitializeComponent() call
    Dim localMenu As New MenuTest()
    Me.Menu = localMenu.getMenuStructure
End Sub
```

This code calls the *MenuTest* class. Before using it, we need to include the statement *Imports WindowsFormsMenu.GetMenuTest*. The *MenuTest* class has a single function named *getMenuStructure* that returns the menu as a MainMenu type that is assigned to *Me.Menu* of this page. In this example, the menu is created while the form instantiates. This makes it easy to use the form as a base form from which other forms in the application can inherit, all of them automatically receiving, or better said, inheriting the same menu structure.

Let's take a look at the *MenuTest* class we created. Here's the code in its entirety:

```
Namespace GetMenuTest
Public Class MenuTest
    Private privateMainMenu As MainMenu
    Private privateMenuItem As MenuItem
    Protected Sub MenuSelect(ByVal sender As Object, _
        ByVal e As System.EventArgs)
        MessageBox.Show("You Clicked a Menu Button")
    End Sub
    Public Function getMenuStructure() As MainMenu
        privateMainMenu = New MainMenu()
        privateMenuItem = New MenuItem("&Employees")
        privateMenuItem.MenuItems.Add("&Address",
        New System.EventHandler(AddressOf Me.MenuSelect))
        privateMenuItem.MenuItems.Add("&Schedule")
        privateMenuItem.MenuItems.Add("Eme&rgency")
        privateMainMenu.MenuItems.Add(privateMenuItem)
        privateMenuItem = New MenuItem("&Benefits")
        privateMenuItem.MenuItems.Add("&Listing")
        privateMainMenu.MenuItems.Add(privateMenuItem)
        privateMenuItem = New MenuItem("&Company")
        privateMainMenu.MenuItems.Add(privateMenuItem)
        Return privateMainMenu
    End Function
End Class
End Namespace
```

The code for this is straightforward, using the functionality we previously added to this class in the form's code-behind page. You might wonder why we re-created the *MenuSelect* event handler, even though this class doesn't handle events. The reason is to prevent errors from occurring within this file when we assign event handling to specific menu items. It's also required if you want to have the same event handler in the calling form's code.

We now have a functioning, data-driven Windows Form menu structure. We could take it to the next level by creating the MenuClass menu items by using database features similar to those in our previous Web Forms examples.

Conclusion

Menu and navigation functionality is an important part of any Windows or Web application. Creating a structured way to navigate through pages is important and makes our applications easy to use. It's even more important to create data-driven components that automatically create the menu and navigation structure of our applications. This allows us to tie our applications together quickly and consistently. Menu selection and sequence can easily be changed, and additional pages can be integrated as well. Even more critical is the ability to create, without a lot of complicated code, role-based menu and navigation structures that manage access and the availability of menu and navigation items. Because of our efforts, we have standard reusable components that take care of our menu and navigation needs. We explained their creation in enough detail to allow you to immediately implement them in your applications or modify them to your specific needs.

In this and previous chapters, we created general, usable objects and components. In the next chapter, we will explore the process of creating a business layer. This is the focal point of application-specific functions and processes.

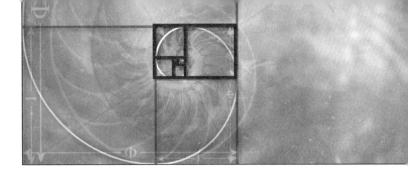

8

Implementing the Business Layer

In Chapter 4, we discussed what was needed to design and implement the data layer, starting with the theoretical and progressing to the practical. In this chapter, we'll look at the importance of consolidating many of your application's business rules into a layer that acts as the gatekeeper between how the data is stored and how it is presented and formatted for user interaction. Let's start with a discussion of the importance of business rules and then expand on the Chapter 1 treatment of the object-oriented features of Microsoft Visual Basic .NET. Then we'll spend the balance of the chapter designing and creating the business object portion of the business layer for the HRnet sample application.

Why Do We Need a Business Layer?

As you know, business rules constitute the way an organization governs itself and are contained in a company's policies and procedures. Being relatively fluid by nature, a company's business rules need to be easy to locate and maintain.

At first thought, it might seem that having a business layer would be almost bloatware for the application. Why would we build a bunch of objects to process business rules? The answer is scalability and resource management. By allowing the business layer to function as the gateway, you free the other layers to focus on their respective services—by design.

Let's expand a little further on the benefits of using a business layer. The business layer is a buffer that guards access to the resources (the data layer) that the client requests (directly or through the facade layer), so the application is eminently more scalable. You might recall that a major flaw of two-tier systems that are designed and developed for enterprise-level applications is that each client has a one-to-one correspondence with its respective resource connections.

Another benefit of using a business layer is the flexibility it provides. Once the business layer has been developed and tested, components can be reused for many form factors at the presentation layer, regardless of whether the application is for a browser, a Microsoft Smartphone, a Pocket PC, or a Microsoft Xbox. Changes can be made to the particular user interface without having an impact on the business layer, and vice versa.

By centralizing the business logic in a given layer instead of having it widely dispersed in the client, an application is also much more manageable, allowing for easier maintenance of the business components. Of course, a logical question would be, "How do you determine which logic or objects are in which layers?" We'll answer that a bit later in the chapter.

Business layers also allow us to more effectively tune the application by separating and moving the processing for various rules to different locations, either at the specific component level or at the database level, by using stored procedures. By processing rules as early as possible, we can maximize performance and proper resource allocation.

Designing Generic Business Objects

A *business object* can be defined as a mechanism that exposes information based on a given set of criteria. When designing business objects, it's crucial to understand the related business processes so that you can effectively model them as part of the design process. Once you understand the processes and the rules, you can then use a pattern as part of the design. A *pattern* is a reusable set of directions for implementing processes and exposing them as classes. For more information on the basics of design and architecture, check out the *.NET Architecture Center* at *http://msdn.microsoft.com/architecture/*.

In designing business objects, it's also important to decide on and adhere to a consistent architectural structure. In our case, the business layer is functionally modeled on the following structure, similar to the other layers within HRnet. Each layer is divided into objects, with each object further divided into regions for better maintainability and organization. The main regions within the business layer are listed in Table 8-1.

Table 8-1   **Regions Within Business Layer Objects**

Region Name	Description
Public constructors	Custom constructors and related functionality
Private variables and objects	Variables and objects needed for business rules functionality
Private functions	Functions related to internal business layer processing
Public properties	All property functionality for the class
Public methods	All public methods for the class
Exception logging	Any exception logging or related processing

> **Note**   All the regions listed in Table 8-1 are included in each business layer class, but some (such as exception logging), which are purely for documentation purposes, are empty except for comments to signify inherited functionality.

Another consistent structure within a business layer object is the method set for accessing each entity through the data layer. In dealing with the corresponding stored procedures in the database, we use the following method functionality for specific data access scenarios:

- Get all active related records.

- Get a specific record.

- Add (Insert) a new record.

- Save (Update) a specific record.

- Update "Active" status for a specific record.

Correspondingly, we've also instituted similar functionality and naming conventions at the stored procedure level in the following format for a given entity:

- *usp_GetEmployeeBenefits*

- *usp_GetEmployeeBenefit*

- *usp_InsertEmployeeBenefit*

- *usp_UpdateEmployeeBenefit*

- *usp_UpdateEmployeeBenefitActiveStatus*

We'll explore the implementation details for both levels later in the chapter. Let's continue to keep things at the overview level by examining some of the sample application business rules to see how they interact with the deeper layers of the architecture.

Determining Business Rules

In our sample application, several business rules shook out during the requirements gathering and design phases of the project. As mentioned in the preceding section, a business rule governs how the business is run, and many business rules are outlined on sticky notes stuck on computer monitors. That might sound funny, but there's some truth to it. An example of a rule might be the amount a company charges for shipping. Each sales specialist might have a table listing a shipping fee based upon the total dollar amount of an order.

In analyzing your business, ask yourself the following questions:

- **What are our business rules?** Determining the rules will help shape the logic for your business layer.

- **Where is the best place to implement our business rules?** Figure out whether the best place to implement your particular business rules is in the presentation layer, the business layer, or the data layer. Business rules generally belong in the business layer, but at times it makes sense to use a database constraint or stored procedure, or even a user input validation routine to help implement a business rule.

- **What is the background of our maintenance personnel?** Knowing the programming language background of the developers—for example, are they Web developers, database programmers, or application developers?—and the people who will be maintaining the application should play a role in where the logic is implemented.

Consider the more specific example of sensitive human resources information. One of the most important rules for our HRnet application is the access structure:

- Only HR managers, clerks, and HR payroll clerks have access to all information.

- Manager-level company personnel can view all information but can't make changes.

- Employees are restricted to only name and extension.

Another rule deals with calculating the benefit eligibility date based on the number of days after the hire date. This number changes from benefit to benefit, so it must be calculated when a new benefit is added for a given employee.

Interacting with the Security Layer

To implement the business rules just mentioned, we need the functionality of both the security layer and the data access layer. Let's implement the authentication rules based on the roles that are currently assigned to a given employee. As we discovered in Chapter 5, we can use the functionality within the security layer to determine the role information necessary to set the appropriate information access level.

As we'll talk about later in the chapter, we can use either the employee username and password or the security object to fulfill this requirement. Once we have that information, we can retrieve the roles and set the level. If the username and password are provided, we can use the logon method of our security object to retrieve the roles:

```
PrivateEmpRoles.Login(sUserName, spassword)
```

After we have the role information, we check each role (by using a For Each loop) and set the appropriate access level.

```
For Each sRole In PrivateEmpRoles.Roles()

    Select Case sRole

        Case "HRManager", "HRClerk", "HRPayrollClerk"
            PrivateAccessLevel = BLAccessLevel.BLFullAccess

        Case "Manager", "FactorySupervisor", "QAManager"
            PrivateAccessLevel = BLAccessLevel.BLManagerAccess

        Case Else
            PrivateAccessLevel = BLAccessLevel.BLRestrictedAccess

    End Select
```

Once the highest level is set, we can exit the loop.

```
    If PrivateAccessLevel = BLAccessLevel.BLFullAccess Then Exit For

Next
```

After setting the appropriate access level, we exit the subroutine. Each time a method in the business layer is accessed, the level is checked to ensure proper authentication and a corresponding status message is set. The following sample is an example of code that performs this function:

```
If AccessLevel = BLAccessLevel.BLManagerAccess Or _
    AccessLevel = BLAccessLevel.BLRestrictedAccess Then

    PrivateStatusInfo = _
        "Access level is restricted from the requested information"
    Exit Sub

Else

    PrivateStatusInfo = "Access Granted"

End If
```

> **Note**   We created an enumeration for the access levels to enhance readability. This is always a good idea when working with numeric values that will be checked throughout the application.
>
> ```
> Public Enum BLAccessLevel
>     BLFullAccess = 1
>     BLManagerAccess = 2
>     BLRestrictedAccess = 3
> End Enum
> ```

In the same manner, let's examine how the business rules for the sample application can be enforced through the functionality of the data access layer.

Interacting with the Data Access Layer

In the HRnet sample application, the business and data layers work closely together. In this section, we'll explore the rationale for and implementation of this interaction.

Building and Determining Queries Based on Business Rules

The placement of business logic is sometimes a controversial subject in our industry. The object-oriented camp wants to use the data store as the only place to hold state information, and the data-focused camp wants all or most of the logic implemented in SQL. Regardless of your perspective, there can be no doubt that stored procedures in some form are useful when implementing business logic. In the implementation of the HRnet application, the business layer relies heavily on stored procedures. Thus, it also relies on the data access layer to assist in enforcing the business rules, taking advantage of the performance benefits that stored procedures provide when compared with SQL statements. Stored procedures also assist with scalability; because they are precompiled, they don't utilize resources for excessive periods of time. As a side note, if we cared not a whit for scalability and focused only on performance, our best bet would undoubtedly be a client/server implementation with stored procedures exclusively. For *n*-tier business logic implementations, there are three choices for rule placement: the presentation layer, the business layer, and the data layer.

Let's examine the chosen technique for rules enforcement by focusing on how restricted access for employees is implemented. Let's keep in mind the pattern we discussed earlier in the chapter as we walk through the following code samples. The following example illustrates the functionality that can be exposed based on the input parameter's data. Instead of restricting employee information, you could also use this technique to handle a United States ZIP Code (numeric) or an international postal code (alphanumeric), with the implementation details being transparent to the user.

Notice in the following code sample that one of two stored procedures is called based on the access level. The first one, *usp_getEmployeesRestrictedView*, returns just the employee name and extension along with an appropriate status message that can be accessed via the object's *StatusInfo* property.

```
Public Function GetCompanyEmployees(ByVal CompanyID As Integer) _
    As DataSet
    Dim localDSOutput As DataSet
    Dim ParamsStoredProcedure As String
    Try
        Dim localOutPutServer As New SQLServer(PrivateConnectionString)

        If AccessLevel = BLAccessLevel.BLRestrictedAccess Then

            ParamsStoredProcedure = "usp_getEmployeesRestrictedView"
            PrivateStatusInfo = "Employee access level is restricted to " _
                & "Employee name and extension."

        Else

            ParamsStoredProcedure = "usp_getEmployees"
            PrivateStatusInfo = "Access Granted"

        End If
```

After that, it's just a simple matter of using the data access layer, just as we learned to do in Chapter 4. We first add the company ID for a parameter, and we then call the *runSPDataSet* method to retrieve the requested information. Finally, if there are no exceptions, we return the dataset to the calling procedure, as shown here:

```
    localOutPutServer.AddParameter( _
        "@CompanyId", CompanyID, _
        SQLServer.SQLDataType.SQLInteger, ,_
        ParameterDirection.Input)

    localDSOutput = _
        localOutPutServer.runSPDataSet(ParamsStoredProcedure)
    localDSOutput.Tables(0).TableName = "Employees"

    Return localDSOutput
Catch ExceptionObject As Exception
    LogException(ExceptionObject)

Finally
End Try


End Function
```

We discussed earlier the model for accessing data through the business layer. Let's look at how that model is implemented, starting with the get all instances (in this case, benefits):

```
Public Function GetCompanyBenefits() As DataSet

    If AccessLevel = BLAccessLevel.BLRestrictedAccess Then
        PrivateStatusInfo = "Access level is restricted " & _
            "from the requested information"
        Exit Function
    End If

    Dim localDSOutput As DataSet
    Dim ParamsStoredProcedure As String = "usp_getBenefits"

    Try
        Dim localOutPutServer As New _
            SQLServer(PrivateConnectionString)

        localDSOutput = localOutPutServer.runSPDataSet( _
            ParamsStoredProcedure)

        localDSOutput.Tables(0).TableName = "Benefits"
```

```
        Return localDSOutput

    Catch ExceptionObject As Exception
        LogException(ExceptionObject)

    Finally
    End Try


End Function
```

Building on what we've learned, we expose the functionality for updating information. Notice that we use save instead of update to more readily model the accompanying user action. The following example shows the update method example within the *Company* class:

```
Public Sub SaveCompanyBenefit(ByVal BenefitId As Integer, _
    ByVal active As Boolean, ByVal Name As String, _
    ByVal Category As String, ByVal daystoeligibility As Boolean, _
    ByVal Description As String)


    If AccessLevel = BLAccessLevel.BLManagerAccess Or _
        AccessLevel = BLAccessLevel.BLRestrictedAccess Then
        PrivateStatusInfo = "Access level is restricted from " & _
            "the requested information"
        Exit Sub
    Else
        PrivateStatusInfo = "Access Granted"
    End If

    Dim localDSOutput As ArrayList
    Dim ParamsStoredProcedure As String

    Try
        Dim localOutPutServer As New SQLServer(PrivateConnectionString)

        localOutPutServer.AddParameter( _
            "@BenefitID", BenefitId, SQLServer.SQLDataType.SQLInteger, _
            , ParameterDirection.Input)

        localOutPutServer.AddParameter( _
            "@Name", Name, SQLServer.SQLDataType.SQLChar, 50, _
            ParameterDirection.Input)

        localOutPutServer.AddParameter( _
            "@Category", Category, SQLServer.SQLDataType.SQLChar, 50, _
            ParameterDirection.Input)
```

(continued)

```
        localOutPutServer.AddParameter( _
            "@DaysToEligibility", daystoeligibility, _
            SQLServer.SQLDataType.SQLInteger, , _
            ParameterDirection.Input)

        localOutPutServer.AddParameter( _
            "@Description", Description, _
            SQLServer.SQLDataType.SQLNText, , ParameterDirection.Input)

        ParamsStoredProcedure = "usp_UpdateBenefit"

        localDSOutput = _
            localOutPutServer.runSPOutput(ParamsStoredProcedure)

    Catch ExceptionObject As Exception
        LogException(ExceptionObject)

    Finally
    End Try

End Sub
```

We've saved the data, but now how do we create a new entity? Once again, we use the functionality of the underlying data layer to assist us. The following example shows the insert method example within the *Company* class:

```
Public Function AddCompanyBenefit(ByVal active As Boolean, _
    ByVal Name As String, ByVal Category As String, _
    ByVal daystoeligibility As Integer, ByVal Description As String) _
    As Integer

    If AccessLevel = BLAccessLevel.BLManagerAccess Or _
        AccessLevel = BLAccessLevel.BLRestrictedAccess Then
        PrivateStatusInfo = "Access level is restricted from " & _
            "the requested information"
        Exit Function

    Else
        PrivateStatusInfo = "Access Granted"
    End If

    Dim localDSOutput As ArrayList
    Dim ParamsStoredProcedure As String = "usp_insertBenefit"

    Try

        Dim localOutPutServer As New SQLServer(PrivateConnectionString)
```

```
        localOutPutServer.AddParameter( _
            "@Active", CInt(active), SQLServer.SQLDataType.SQLBit, _
            , ParameterDirection.Input)

        localOutPutServer.AddParameter( _
            "@Name", Name, SQLServer.SQLDataType.SQLChar, 50, _
            ParameterDirection.Input)

        localOutPutServer.AddParameter( _
            "@Category", Category, SQLServer.SQLDataType.SQLChar, 50, _
            ParameterDirection.Input)

        localOutPutServer.AddParameter( _
            "@DaysToEligibility", daystoeligibility, _
            SQLServer.SQLDataType.SQLBit, , ParameterDirection.Input)

        localOutPutServer.AddParameter( _
            "@Description", Description, _
            SQLServer.SQLDataType.SQLNtext, , ParameterDirection.Input)

        localOutPutServer.AddParameter( _
            "@BenefitId", , SQLServer.SQLDataType.SQLInteger, , _
            ParameterDirection.Output)

        localDSOutput = _
            localOutPutServer.runSPOutput(ParamsStoredProcedure)
        'Return the Id of newly created record
        Return CInt(localDSOutput.Item(0))

    Catch ExceptionObject As Exception
        LogException(ExceptionObject)

    Finally
    End Try

End Function
```

If you wanted to load and then expose properties from within your application, you would call a procedure. The following example shows how the read-only properties are loaded through the use of the data access layer within the *Company* class:

```
Private Sub LoadProperties()
    Dim localDSOutput As ArrayList
    ' load up the properties used for employee stats
    Dim ParamsStoredProcedure As String = _
        "usp_GetEmployeeEmploymentStatusCounts"
```

(continued)

```
      Try
          Dim localOutPutServer As New _
              SQLServer(PrivateConnectionString)
          localOutPutServer.AddParameter( _
              "@FullTime", , SQLServer.SQLDataType.SQLInteger, , _
              ParameterDirection.Output)
          localOutPutServer.AddParameter( _
              "@PartTime", , SQLServer.SQLDataType.SQLInteger, , _
              ParameterDirection.Output)
          localOutPutServer.AddParameter( _
              "@TempTime", , SQLServer.SQLDataType.SQLInteger, , _
              ParameterDirection.Output)

          localDSOutput = _
              localOutPutServer.runSPOutput(ParamsStoredProcedure)

          With localDSOutput
              PrivateFulltimeNumber = CInt(.Item(0))
              PrivateParttimeNumber = CInt(.Item(1))
              PrivateTemptimeNumber = CInt(.Item(2))
          End With

      Catch ExceptionObject As Exception
          LogException(ExceptionObject)

      Finally
      End Try
  End Sub


  'The constructors are inherited from general and the read-only properties
  'are loaded locally as part of added functionality
  Public Sub New(ByVal sUserName As String, ByVal spassword As String)
      MyBase.New(sUserName, spassword)
      LoadProperties()
  End Sub
  Public Sub New(ByVal objSecurit As SecurIt.UserSecurity)
      MyBase.New(objSecurit)
      LoadProperties()
  End Sub
```

The following example shows how the read-only properties are implemented within the *Company* class:

```
#Region "Public Properties"
    Public ReadOnly Property FullTimeNumber() As Integer
        Get
            FullTimeNumber = PrivateFulltimeNumber
        End Get

    End Property
    Public ReadOnly Property PartTimeNumber() As Integer
        Get
            PartTimeNumber = PrivateParttimeNumber
        End Get

    End Property
    Public ReadOnly Property TempTimeNumber() As Integer
        Get
            TempTimeNumber = PrivateTemptimeNumber
        End Get

    End Property
    Public ReadOnly Property VacationNumber() As Integer
        Get
            VacationNumber = PrivateVacationNumber
        End Get

    End Property
    Public ReadOnly Property SickNumber() As Integer
        Get
            SickNumber = PrivateSickNumber
        End Get

    End Property
    Public ReadOnly Property MaternityNumber() As Integer
        Get
            MaternityNumber = PrivateMaternityNumber
        End Get

    End Property
#End Region
```

Get-Related Stored Procedures

The remainder of the get-related stored procedures and their corresponding parameters are listed in Table 8-2 for your reference as you learn about the sample application.

Table 8-2 Some HRnet Get-Related Stored Procedures and Related Parameters

Stored Procedure Name	Parameters
usp_GetBenefit	BenefitID
usp_GetBenefits	none
usp_GetCompanies	none
usp_GetCompany	CompanyID
usp_GetCompanyActiveNews	CompanyID
usp_GetCompanyPreviousNews	CompanyID
.usp_GetDepartment	DepartmentID
usp_GetDepartments	none
usp_GetEmergencyInfo	EmployeeID
usp_GetEmergencyInfoContact	EmployeeID, EmergencyID
usp_GetEmployee	EmployeeID
usp_GetEmployeeBenefit	EmployeeID, BenefitID
usp_GetEmployeeBenefits	none
usp_GetEmployeeBirthdays	CompanyID
usp_GetEmployeeEmployment-StatusCounts	FullTime output, PartTime output, TempTime output
usp_GetEmployees	CompanyID
usp_GetEmployeesRestrictedView	CompanyID
usp_GetEmployeeStatus	EmployeeID, FullTime output, PartTime output, TempTime output
usp_GetEmployeeStatusCounts	VacationTime output, SickTime output, MaternityTime output, FullTime output, PartTime output, TempTime output
usp_GetHireSource	HiresourceID
usp_GetHireSources	none
usp_GetNews	CompanyID, NewsID
usp_GetPosition	PositionID
usp_GetPositions	none
usp_GetStatus	none
usp_GetStatusDetail	StatusID
usp_GetTitle	TitleID
usp_GetTitles	none
usp_GetWorkSchedule	WorkscheduleID
usp_GetWorkSchedules	none

Insert-Related Stored Procedures

The insert-related stored procedures and their corresponding parameters are listed in Table 8-3.

Table 8-3   HRnet Insert-Related Stored Procedures and Related Parameters

Stored Procedure Name	Parameters
usp_InsertBenefit	*Active bit, Name nvarchar(50), Category nvarchar(35), DaysToEligibility int, Description ntext, CreatedBy int, BenefitID int* output
usp_InsertCompany	*Name nvarchar(50), Address nvarchar(60), City nvarchar(15), Region nvarchar(15), PostalCode nvarchar(15), Country nvarchar(15), MainPhone nvarchar(24), OtherPhone nvarchar(24), Fax nvarchar(24), EMail nvarchar(50), FederalTaxID nvarchar(25), UnemploymentID nvarchar(25), StateTaxID nvarchar(25), DefaultPayPeriod char(1), Comments ntext, DateCreated datetime, CreatedBy int, CompanyID int* output
usp_InsertCompanyNews	*CompanyID int, Active bit, NewsDate datetime, NewsSubject nvarchar(25), NewsInfo ntext, CreatedBy int, NewsID int* output
usp_InsertDepartment	*Name nvarchar(50), Description ntext, Active bit, CreatedBy int, DepartmentID int* output
usp_InsertEmergencyInfo	*EmployeeID int, Main bit, Contact nvarchar(50), EMail nvarchar(50), Address nvarchar(60), City nvarchar(15), Region nvarchar(15), PostalCode nvarchar(15), Country nvarchar(15),*
	HomePhone nvarchar(24), OtherPhone nvarchar(24), DayNightAny int, Comments ntext, CreatedBy int, EmergencyID int output

(continued)

**Table 8-3 HRnet Insert-Related Stored
Procedures and Related Parameters** *(continued)*

Stored Procedure Name	Parameters
usp_InsertEmployee	*CompanyID int, PositionID int, TitleID int, HireSourceID int, WorkScheduleID int, Active bit, LastName nvarchar(20), FirstName nvarchar(10), MI nvarchar(1), Salutation nvarchar(10), NickName nvarchar(15), SSN char(11), DriversLicense nvarchar(20), PrivateEmail nvarchar(35), CompanyEmail nvarchar(35), Address nvarchar(60), City nvarchar(15), Region nvarchar(15), PostalCode nvarchar(15), Country nvarchar(15), HomePhone nvarchar(24), Extension nvarchar(4), Gender char(1), Ethnicity nvarchar(1), MaritalStatus nvarchar(1), BirthDate datetime, InterviewDate datetime, HireDate datetime, FulltimeDate datetime, LastVacationDate datetime, VacationEarned int, VacationTaken int, VacationStartDate datetime, VacationDuration int, SickDays int, MaternityLeaveDate datetime, MaternityDays int, NextReviewDate datetime, TerminationDate datetime, TerminationType char(1), COBRA bit, Notes ntext, ReportsTo int, CreatedBy int, EmployeeID int* output
usp_InsertEmployeeBenefit	*EmployeeID int, BenefitID int, Active bit, EffectiveDate datetime, CreatedBy int, EmployeeBenefitID int* output
usp_InsertHireSource	*Active bit, Name nvarchar(50), Contact nvarchar(50), Details ntext, CreatedBy int* *HireSourceID int* output
usp_InsertPosition	*DepartmentID int, Name nvarchar(50), Description ntext, Active bit, Status int, PayStatus int, StartPay money, CreatedBy int, PositionID int* output
usp_InsertStatus	*Description ntext, CreatedBy int, StatusID int* output

Table 8-3   HRnet Insert-Related Stored Procedures and Related Parameters *(continued)*

Stored Procedure Name	Parameters
usp_InsertTitle	*Active bit, Name nvarchar(50), Description ntext, DateCreated datetime, CreatedBy int, TitleID int* output
usp_InsertWorkSchedule	*Sunday bit, SundayStart datetime, SundayEnd datetime, Monday bit, MondayStart datetime, MondayEnd datetime, Tuesday bit, TuesdayStart datetime, TuesdayEnd datetime, Wednesday bit,WednesdayStart datetime, WednesdayEnd datetime, Thursday bit, ThursdayStart datetime, ThursdayEnd datetime, Friday bit, FridayStart datetime, FridayEnd datetime, Saturday bit, SaturdayStart datetime, SaturdayEnd datetime,CreatedBy int, WorkscheduleID int* output

Update-Related Stored Procedures

The update-related stored procedures and their corresponding parameters are listed in Table 8-4.

Table 8-4   HRnet Update-Related Stored Procedures and Related Parameters

Stored Procedure Name	Parameters
usp_Updatebenefit	*BenefitID int, Name nvarchar(50), Category nvarchar(35), DaysToEligibility int, Description ntext, ModifiedBy int*
usp_UpdateBenefitActiveStatus	*BenefitID int, Active bit*
usp_UpdateCompany	*CompanyID int, Name nvarchar(50), Address nvarchar(60), City nvarchar(15), Region nvarchar(15), PostalCode nvarchar(15), Country nvarchar(15), MainPhone nvarchar(24), OtherPhone nvarchar(24), Fax nvarchar(24), EMail nvarchar(50), FederalTaxID nvarchar(25), UnemploymentID nvarchar(25), StateTaxID nvarchar(25), DefaultPayPeriod char(1), Comments ntext, ModifiedBy int*

(continued)

**Table 8-4 HRnet Update-Related Stored
Procedures and Related Parameters** *(continued)*

Stored Procedure Name	Parameters
usp_UpdateCompanyNews	*NewsID int, CompanyID int, NewsSubject nvarchar(25), NewsInfo ntext, ModifiedBy int*
usp_UpdateCompanyNewsActiveStatus	*NewsID int, CompanyID int, Active bit*
usp_UpdateDepartment	*DepartmentID int, Name nvarchar(50), Description ntext, Active bit, ModifiedBy int*
usp_UpdateDepartmentActiveStatus	*DepartmentID int, Active bit*
usp_UpdateEmergencyInfo	*EmployeeID int, EmergencyID int, Main bit, Contact nvarchar(50), EMail nvarchar(50), Address nvarchar(60), City nvarchar(15), Region nvarchar(15), PostalCode nvarchar(15), Country nvarchar(15), HomePhone varchar(24), OtherPhone nvarchar(24), DayNightAny int, Comments ntext, ModifiedBy int*
usp_UpdateEmployee	*EmployeeID int, CompanyID int, PositionID int, TitleID int, HireSourceID int, WorkScheduleID int, LastName nvarchar(20), FirstName nvarchar(10), MI nvarchar(2), Salutation nvarchar(10), NickName nvarchar(15), SSN char(11), DriversLicense nvarchar(20), PrivateEmail nvarchar(35), CompanyEmail nvarchar(35), Address nvarchar(60), City nvarchar(15), Region nvarchar(15), PostalCode nvarchar(15), Country nvarchar(15), HomePhone nvarchar(24), Extension nvarchar(4), Gender char(1), Ethnicity nvarchar(1), MaritalStatus nvarchar(1), BirthDate datetime, InterviewDate datetime, HireDate datetime, FulltimeDate datetime, LastVacationDate datetime, VacationEarned int, VacationTaken int, VacationStartDate datetime, VacationDuration int, SickDays int, MaternityLeaveDate datetime, MaternityDays int, NextReviewDate datetime, TerminationDate datetime, TerminationType char(1), COBRA bit, Notes ntext, ReportsTo int, ModifiedBy int*
usp_UpdateEmployeeActiveStatus	*EmployeeID int, Active bit*
usp_UpdateEmployeeBenefit	*EmployeeID int, BenefitID int*
usp_UpdateEmployeeBenefitActiveStatus	*EmployeeID int, BenefitID int, Active bit*

Table 8-4   HRnet Update-Related Stored Procedures and Related Parameters *(continued)*

Stored Procedure Name	Parameters
usp_UpdateHireSourceActiveStatus	*HireSourceID int, Active bit*
usp_UpdateHireSources	*HireSourceID int, Active bit, name nvarchar(50), Contact nvarchar(50), Details ntext, ModifiedBy int*
usp_UpdatePosition	*PositionID int, DepartmentID int, Name nvarchar(50), Description ntext, Status int, PayStatus int, StartPay money, ModifiedBy*
usp_UpdatePositionActiveStatus	*PositionID int, Active bit*
usp_UpdateStatus	*StatusID int, Description ntext, ModifiedBy int*
usp_UpdateTitle	*TitleID int, Name nvarchar(50), Description ntext, ModifiedBy int*
usp_UpdateTitleActiveStatus	*TitleID int, Active bit*
usp_Updateworkschedule	*WorkscheduleID int, Sunday bit, SundayStart datetime, SundayEnd datetime, Monday bit, MondayStart datetime, MondayEnd datetime, Tuesday bit, TuesdayStart datetime, TuesdayEnd datetime, Wednesday bit, WednesdayStart datetime, WednesdayEnd datetime, Thursday bit, ThursdayStart datetime, ThursdayEnd datetime, Friday bit, FridayStart datetime, FridayEnd datetime, Saturday bit, SaturdayStart datetime, SaturdayEnd datetime, ModifiedBy int*

Object-Oriented Features of Visual Basic .NET

Let's continue the Chapter 1 discussion of object-oriented features to set the stage for the techniques used in HRnet.

Constructors Revisited

When you instantiated a class in Microsoft Visual Basic 6, the *Class_Initialize* event was the first event raised. This event contained code that needed to be run during the instantiation process for the class instance.

However, there was no way in Visual Basic 6 to pass parameters to *Class_Initialize*. If a class instance required some parameters to complete processing, a custom method or property had to be implemented to pass that information into the class.

In Visual Basic .NET, the class has a kind of method, called a *constructor*, named *New*. The *New* method is the first code executed in a new instance of a Visual Basic .NET class, just as *Class_Initialize* was the first code run in Visual Basic 6.

Since *New* is a method, it can have parameters. When you create a *New* method for one of your classes in Visual Basic .NET, you can give it any parameters you like (or none, if it doesn't need any). Such a constructor is sometimes called a *parameterized constructor*.

If the *New* method has parameters, you must supply those parameters when an object is declared and instantiated. For example, suppose a class named *Customer* has a *New* method that requires a customer ID, as in this case:

```
Public Sub New(ByVal sUserName As String, ByVal spassword As String)
    MyBase.New()
    Try
        privateModuleName = Me.GetType.ToString

        VerifyAccess(sUserName, spassword)

    Catch ExceptionObject As Exception
        LogException(ExceptionObject)

    Finally
    End Try
End Sub
```

For such a class, you must supply the username and password at instantiation. Here's an example:

```
Dim objCompany As New Company(strUserName, StrPassword)
```

This generates an instance of the *Customer* class with the appropriate security credentials.

> **Tip** In the same way you could omit the *Class_Terminate* event for a class in Visual Basic 6, you can leave out the *New* constructor in Visual Basic .NET. If you don't include the constructor, no code in the class is run during instantiation.

Overloading

Methods do have one significant new feature in Visual Basic .NET. Multiple versions of the same method can exist in a class as long as each version has a different argument list. This feature is called *method overloading*. Let's take a look at how this is used within HRnet's business layer.

Within the *General* class, we must ensure that only appropriate personnel have access to sensitive data. The *VerifyAccess* method needs to accept either the security object created at login or the username and password to properly authenticate and set the appropriate data access level. In addition, we have different logic flow for these two types. To create the needed functionality, we create two versions of the *VerifyAccess* method, each with its own logic for data display. To utilize the overloaded functionality, we use the *Overloads* keyword. Here are high-level code fragments showing the declaration of both versions of the *VerifyAccess* method:

```
Private Overloads Sub VerifyAccess(ByVal sUserName As String, _
    ByVal spassword As String)

    ⋮
End Sub
Private Overloads Sub VerifyAccess(ByVal EmpRoles _
    As SecurIt.UserSecurity)
    ⋮
End Sub
```

For methods to be eligible for overloading, there must be some difference in the parameter list. The difference can be in the number of parameters, the parameter types, or both.

Without the ability to overload, creating the necessary functionality previously mentioned would have needed considerably more complex techniques. Separate verification routines could be created with different names, one for the security object and one for the username or password combination. Another technique involves the use of optional parameters, but it would be extremely important to coordinate both the order and type of parameters. Overloaded methods provide a more straightforward approach than separate verification routines and optional parameters.

When using the Microsoft .NET Framework, you'll see that many of its classes contain overloaded methods. An overloaded method is noted in the IntelliSense window. An example of IntelliSense support for an overloaded method is shown in Figure 8-1.

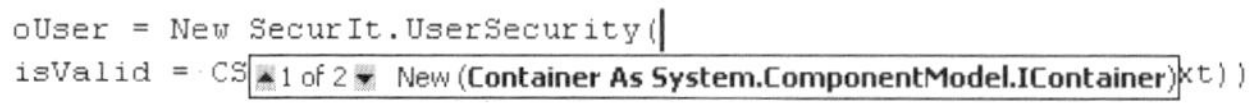

```
oUser = New SecurIt.UserSecurity(|
isValid = CS[▲ 1 of 2 ▼] New(Container As System.ComponentModel.IContainer)kt))
```

Figure 8-1   IntelliSense for an overloaded method

In Figure 8-1, notice the part of the screen indicated by the black navigation arrows that state 1 Of 2. This part of the IntelliSense ToolTip window is informing you that the method being accessed is the first of two overloaded methods. The up and down arrows on the side of the 1 Of 2 statement enable you to move through the corresponding overloaded choices and receive parameter information for each.

Overloaded Constructors

Now let's combine a couple of concepts discussed in this section: overloading and constructors. We learned that methods can be overloaded (multiple versions of the same method that use different parameters). We also discovered that a constructor is nothing more than a method with a special name. (A constructor, by the way, can also be overloaded.) Therefore, multiple *New* methods in a class can be created, each having a different parameter list. These are known as *overloaded constructors*.

> **Note**   There is a small difference between overloaded methods and their counterparts, the constructors. To overload a normal method, you must declare all versions of that method with the *Overloads* keyword. Conversely, the *Overloads* keyword is not used when declaring constructors.

For example, in the HRnet sample application, we created our *General* class so that we can either pass in the username and password or the security object to verify access. Our two constructors for the employee and company classes now look like this:

```
Public Sub New(ByVal sUserName As String, ByVal spassword As String)
    MyBase.New()
    Try
        privateModuleName = Me.GetType.ToString

        VerifyAccess(sUserName, spassword)

    Catch ExceptionObject As Exception
        LogException(ExceptionObject)
```

```
        Finally
        End Try
    End Sub

    Public Sub New(ByVal objSecurit As SecurIt.UserSecurity)

        MyBase.New()

        Try
            privateModuleName = Me.GetType.ToString
            VerifyAccess(objSecurit)
        Catch ExceptionObject As Exception
            LogException(ExceptionObject)

        Finally
        End Try
    End Sub
```

Now we can instantiate an employee with this code:

```
Dim NWemployee As new employee(sUsername, Password)
```

Or we can instantiate using the security object with this code:

```
Dim NWemployee As new employee(objSecurIt)
```

Although you can have as many overloaded constructors as you want, you should keep the number down to what you really need, which can be a big help to those who consume your classes. Remember that just because you can doesn't mean you should!

Inheritance in HRnet

We discussed inheritance in Chapter 1. Now let's focus on how it's used within the sample application. Using inheritance, we create a base class named *General* that contains all the generic business object functionality. This includes verifying access (as previously discussed), properties for communicating the data access level and status, and exception logging.

From the *General* class, we created subclasses for both employee and company. Each subclass inherits all the functionality from the base class. Subclasses would therefore have properties for access level and status without having any code for them. When a subclass designates that it inherits from the *General* base class, it instantly possesses the *entire* object interface of the base class. You might be thinking, "So what? I can do that in Visual Basic 6 by defining an interface and implementing it!" It's true that you could inherit the interface in this manner in Visual Basic 6 (interface inheritance), but in Visual Basic .NET, inheritance also includes all the logic behind properties and methods! For example, the *General* base class has validation logic to set the appropriate access based on the security context, and now all the subclasses also have this functionality.

Subtype-specific functionality is then added to the subclass. For example, each subclass inherits its constructors from the *General* class. However, the *Company* class needs properties to report employee demographics to the facade layer and higher-level layers. We load the properties in a function that is called in the inherited constructor of the *Company* subclass. Therefore, the special properties and methods (and the associated logic) specific to the company subtype are encapsulated in this one subclass.

If you're new to object-oriented concepts, you'll need some time to get used to them. However, once you're comfortable with OOP, you'll undoubtedly see that many common programming needs are much easier to solve with these capabilities. Now let's examine the syntax for using inheritance in Visual Basic .NET code.

In Chapter 1, we discussed the conceptual nature of inheritance. Now, let's revisit the syntax used to handle inheritance. Earlier in the chapter, you learned about the class definition in Visual Basic .NET. Let's apply that to our *Employee* class:

```
Public Class Employee
    ' Public Methods
    Public Sub SaveEmployeeMethod()
        'use data access layer
    End Sub
End Class
```

In HRnet, we want *Employee* to be a subclass of a generic utility class. As we discussed earlier in the chapter, doing that would give *Employee* all the capabilities of the base class. Then we would just add the functionality that needed to be specific to *Employee*.

Let's examine our generic utility class named *General* (once again at a high level):

```
Public MustInherit Class General
    'General class is the business layer base class.
    'Responsible for verifying identity and
    'proper access levels and exception logging.
```

Notice the *MustInherit* keyword here. When this attribute is used with a class, it indicates that the class can't be instantiated directly—it must be inherited before the subclass can be instantiated.

```
#Region "Public Constructors"
Public Sub New(ByVal sUserName As String, ByVal spassword As String)
```

```
    MyBase.New()
    Try
        privateModuleName = Me.GetType.ToString

        VerifyAccess(sUserName, spassword)
    Catch ExceptionObject As Exception
        LogException(ExceptionObject)


    Finally
    End Try
End Sub

Public Sub New(ByVal objSecurit As SecurIt.UserSecurity)

    MyBase.New()
    Try
        privateModuleName = Me.GetType.ToString
        VerifyAccess(objSecurit)
    Catch ExceptionObject As Exception
        LogException(ExceptionObject)


    Finally
    End Try
End Sub
#End Region
```

Now let's look at the overloaded *VerifyAccess* method. Once again, we can accept either the username and password or the security object.

```
Private Overloads Sub VerifyAccess(ByVal sUserName As String, _
    ByVal spassword As String)
    Dim sRole As String

    PrivateEmpRoles.Login(sUserName, spassword)


    For Each sRole In PrivateEmpRoles.Roles()

        Select Case sRole

            Case "HRManager", "HRClerk", "HRPayrollClerk"
                PrivateAccessLevel = BLAccessLevel.BLFullAccess

            Case "Manager", "FactorySupervisor", "QAManager"
                PrivateAccessLevel = BLAccessLevel.BLManagerAccess

            Case Else
                PrivateAccessLevel = BLAccessLevel.BLRestrictedAccess
```

(continued)

```
                    End Select
                    'Once highest level is set, we can leave
                    If PrivateAccessLevel = BLAccessLevel.BLFullAccess Then _
                        Exit For

            Next
        End Sub

        Private Overloads Sub VerifyAccess(ByVal EmpRoles As _
            SecurIt.UserSecurity)

            Dim sRole As String
            For Each sRole In EmpRoles.Roles()

                Select Case sRole

                    Case "HRManager", "HRClerk", "HRPayrollClerk"
                        PrivateAccessLevel = BLAccessLevel.BLFullAccess

                    Case "Manager", "FactorySupervisor", "QAManager"
                        PrivateAccessLevel = BLAccessLevel.BLManagerAccess

                    Case Else
                        PrivateAccessLevel = BLAccessLevel.BLRestrictedAccess
                End Select
                If PrivateAccessLevel = BLAccessLevel.BLFullAccess Then _
                    Exit For

            Next
        End Sub
```

Here are the properties that the *Employee* and *Company* subclasses will inherit:

```
Public ReadOnly Property AccessLevel() As Integer
    Get
        AccessLevel = PrivateAccessLevel
    End Get

End Property

Public ReadOnly Property StatusInfo() As String
    Get
        StatusInfo = PrivateStatusInfo
    End Get
End Property
```

To make *Company* a subclass of *General*, we use the *Inherits* keyword. *Company* will look like this:

```
Namespace BusinessLayer

    Public Class Company
        Inherits BusinessLayer.General
        ⋮
    End Class
```

Note the third line in this code. Once *Company* has this line added, it instantly gains all the functionality of the *General* class. Suppose we now declare an instance of *Company* with the following line:

```
Dim objX As New BusinessLayer.Company("nDavolio", "nDavolio")
```

Checking IntelliSense for *objX* reveals that *objX* has a property named *AccessLevel*. When that property is accessed, no code runs in the *Company* class. Instead, code runs in the *General* class, because that's where the *AccessLevel* property is.

The *Company* class also gains its constructors (the *New* methods) by inheriting them from the *General* class. When the preceding line of code executes, the *New* subroutine in *General* executes and performs the necessary setup logic.

In several cases, a subclass property or method might be required to do a limited amount of specialized tasks, while allowing the remainder of the work to be completed by the equivalent property or method in the base class. This can be done by referring to the base class with the *MyBase* keyword, as we saw in the inherited constructor example earlier.

```
Mybase.New(sUserName,Password)
```

Conclusion

In this chapter, we discussed the importance of the business layer in creating component-based applications. We also examined the importance of consolidating many of the application's business rules into a layer that acts as the gatekeeper between how the data is stored and how it's presented and formatted for user interaction. Next, we revisited and expanded key concepts such as overloading, constructors, and inheritance, and we explained how these concepts were implemented in the business layer. In the next chapter, we'll continue the journey by moving into the next layer in our sample application, the facade layer.

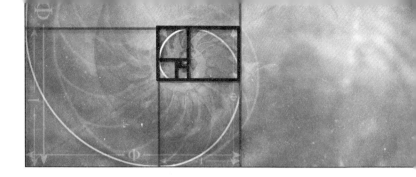

9

Implementing Facade Layers

Back in Chapter 2, we touched on the concept of a facade but didn't really dig into it, so let's do that now. The easiest way to understand how a facade works in your code is to use an analogy, for example, the facade in an old Western town. The buildings in these towns were usually simple structures. To add interest to them, facades were applied to their faces. Consider Figure 9-1.

Figure 9-1   How a facade affects the look of a building but does not impact the function

At the top of Figure 9-1, you can see the basic building with its standard "interface." Let's say the owner of the building wants a nicer look and feel, like the building at the bottom of Figure 9-1. All the owner needs to do is add to the front of the building a false layer that has the interface design of the desired look. Voila! Now the building has a facade.

Facades make even more sense for buildings that are manufactured in factories. For instance, a manufacturer can create a standard store that has an internal and external configuration, and then apply a facade to the store to make it a particular type. That makes it easy to reuse the same type of store over and over but provide a different look for each store.

Advantages of Facade Layers and Applications

Let's apply the facade concept to our applications. Why would you create a facade layer in the first place? The facade layer is basically an abstraction of a business object. For instance, consider our HRnet sample application, which has an *Employee* business object. This object has the following methods:

- *GetEmployees*
- *GetEmployeeByID*
- *GetEmployeeByName*
- *GetEmployeeState*

Now, suppose we complete our application and deploy it using this *Employee* object and others. At some point, we need to write another application for the distribution department, and this application needs information about employees as well. But not only does it need the information supplied by the current *Employees* object, it also needs the following methods:

- *GetEmployeesByVendorContactID*
- *GetEmployeesBySkillID*

There are several approaches to adding these other methods to the application. We could simply add them in the user interface, but that would be messy. Adding them to the user interface splits the code between the business objects and the user interface, which harkens back to the spaghetti code days. We could also modify the underlying *Employee* object, but that would require changing the object used by other applications and retesting and deploying the object. Again, this could be messy because it involves changing the object used by other applications.

Enter the concept of a facade. How about creating an object named *EmployeeDistribution*? We can derive this object from the *Employees* object and add the new functionality in the new object. Now our application can use

EmployeeDistribution and obtain the same functionality of the underlying *Employee* object plus the functionality that our application needs. And it requires no changes to the underlying *Employee* object.

Intuitively, you might think that it doesn't make sense to add this abstract layer, but it does allow flexibility in the use of the underlying objects. Such flexibility can be useful in situations like the one just mentioned, and it can be handy when you create an application that others will use. For instance, many commercial applications can be customized by the companies that buy them. I might buy a distribution application and then customize it to integrate with my existing applications. By using facade layers, I can tie in this customization at the facade layer, not at the business layer. Upgrades to customized applications become easier to implement.

The derivation of the facade layer from the underlying business object uses inheritance. Inheritance is simple because you use one statement in the facade layer to inherit from the business object, and automatically the facade layer picks up the interfaces and logic in the business object. This is a far cry from other versions of Microsoft Visual Basic, in which we had to create a class that basically re-created each underlying method, eventually calling each underlying method from the facade layer. You could also create facade layers with interface inheritance, but this was just about as time-consuming. Now with Microsoft Visual Studio .NET, the facade is implemented with only a few lines of code and thus becomes very useful.

Designing the Facade Layers

The first step in creating any facade layer (an object in this case) is to examine the business object the facade will use. You also must look at the application that is using the facade object. What happens when you create an application from scratch and it isn't obvious that you'll need a facade class? In most cases, it's a good idea to create a facade class on top of all your business objects. In the past, this approach added a bit of overhead to the application because of all the code required to create the facade layer. Now with .NET, very little additional code is necessary because the code from the underlying business object is inherited directly. As a result, there's no need to instantiate the business object or use marshaling or other techniques to communicate between objects. Creating the facade class isn't likely to add any performance penalties. Plus, it will be there when you need it so that you can make changes at the facade layer without changing the business objects.

Now, what do we mean by using the facade layer in the design? To illustrate, we created the design shown in Figure 9-2.

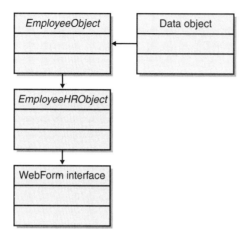

Figure 9-2   The *EmployeeHRObject* class provides a facade for the *EmployeeObject* class.

As you can see in Figure 9-2, the facade layer simply sits between the business objects and the user interface (and even other components such as XML Web services). The view of the facade layer depends on your perspective. For instance, in design view, the facade seems to sit between the business object, because the developer works with the facade layer, and the user interface or other layers. In execution, the facade layer really becomes a wrapper around the business object, because you interact with facade objects rather than business objects.

Typically we don't use facade layers between the business layers and underlying layers such as the data layer. This is not to say that facade layers are never used in those areas—we just didn't implement them there because our requirements didn't really need them. If we'd felt we'd needed a level of indirection between our business objects and the data layer, we could have implemented a facade layer. But in practice, we've found that business applications almost never change the backend database once the application is up and running. Therefore, we didn't worry about placing a facade layer over the data layer.

In Figure 9-2, you can see that the business objects are hooked into the facade layer and that the facade layer is hooked into the user interface. This arrangement makes building and implementing the application very straightforward, and maintaining it easy. If changes need to be made to pull information or perform tasks specific to the HRNet sample application, we can put this functionality in the facade layer and not touch the *EmployeeObject*. This lets us change the functionality without impacting in any way other applications that use the *EmployeeObject*.

Building the Facade Objects

Now let's take a look at how to implement the facade objects. The inheritance features in the Microsoft .NET Framework make this process very simple. First, we're going to look at a simple business object, the *EmployeeObject*. This business object has only a few methods that return data from the underlying database, keeping the amount of code in this chapter to a minimum. The class has the following public methods:

■   *GetEmployeeByID*

■   *GetEmployeeByName*

■   *GetEmployeesByDepartment*

■   *GetEmployees*

■   *GetTodaysBirthDayEmployees*

■   *GetEmployeeState*

Each method definition is shown in boldface in the following code. The entire code for the class that implements these methods is shown here.

```
Imports DataAccessLayer.DataAccess
Public MustInherit Class EmployeeObject

#Region " Private Variables and Objects"
    Private privateDisposedBoolean As Boolean
    Private privateModuleName As String
    'In production applications, you should put connection strings
    'in a secure location such as the Registry
    Private privateConnectionString As String = _
        "Server=LocalHost ;Database=northwind;" & _
        "User ID=sa;Password=;"
    Private Const privateExceptionMessage As String = _
        "Employee Object error. Detail Error Information " & _
        "can be found in the Application Log."
    Dim privateSQLServer As SQLServer
#End Region
#Region "Public Constructors"
Public Sub New()

    privateSQLServer = New _
        SQLServer(privateConnectionString)
End Sub
#End Region
```

(continued)

```vb
#Region "Public Functions"
Function GetEmployeeByID(ByVal EmployeeID As Integer) _
    As DataSet
    Dim ParamsStoredProcedure As String = _
        "spGetEmployeeByID"
    Dim NorthwindDataSet As DataSet

    Try
        'Check to see if this object has already been disposed.
        If privateDisposedBoolean = True Then
            Throw New _
                ObjectDisposedException(privateModuleName, _
                "This object has already been disposed. " _
                "You cannot reuse it.")
        End If

        privateSQLServer.ClearParameters()

        privateSQLServer.AddParameter( _
            "@EmployeeID", EmployeeID, _
            SQLServer.SQLDataType.SQLInteger, , _
            ParameterDirection.Input)

        NorthwindDataSet = _
            privateSQLServer.runSPDataSet( _
            ParamsStoredProcedure, "EmployeeByID")

    Catch ExceptionObject As Exception
        Throw New Exception( _
            privateExceptionMessage, ExceptionObject)
    End Try

    Return NorthwindDataSet
End Function

Function GetEmployeeByName(ByVal LastName As String, _
    ByVal FirstName As String) As DataSet
    Dim ParamsStoredProcedure As String = _
        "spGetEmployeebyName"
    Dim NorthwindDataSet As DataSet

    Try
        'Check to see if this object has already been disposed.
        If privateDisposedBoolean = True Then
            Throw New ObjectDisposedException( _
                privateModuleName, _
                "This object has already been disposed. " & _
                "You cannot reuse it.")
        End If

        privateSQLServer.ClearParameters()
```

```
        privateSQLServer.AddParameter( _
            "@LastName", LastName, _
            SQLServer.SQLDataType.SQLChar, 20, _
            ParameterDirection.Input)
        privateSQLServer.AddParameter( _
            "@FirstName", FirstName, _
            SQLServer.SQLDataType.SQLChar, 10, _
            ParameterDirection.Input)

        NorthwindDataSet = _
            privateSQLServer.runSPDataSet( _
            ParamsStoredProcedure, "EmployeeByName")

    Catch ExceptionObject As Exception
        Throw New Exception( _
            privateExceptionMessage, ExceptionObject)
    End Try

    Return NorthwindDataSet
End Function

Function GetEmployeesByDepartment( _
    ByVal DepartmentID As Integer) As DataSet
    Dim ParamsStoredProcedure As String = _
        "spGetEmployeeByDepartment"
    Dim NorthwindDataSet As DataSet

    Try
        'Check to see if this object has already been disposed.
        If privateDisposedBoolean = True Then
            Throw New ObjectDisposedException(privateModuleName, _
            "This object has already been disposed. " & _
            "You cannot reuse it.")
        End If

        privateSQLServer.ClearParameters()

        privateSQLServer.AddParameter( _
            "@DepartmentID", DepartmentID, _
            SQLServer.SQLDataType.SQLInteger, , _
            ParameterDirection.Input)

        NorthwindDataSet = _
            privateSQLServer.runSPDataSet( _
            ParamsStoredProcedure, "EmployeeByDepartmentID")

    Catch ExceptionObject As Exception
        Throw New Exception(privateExceptionMessage, _
        ExceptionObject)
    End Try
```

(continued)

```
        Return NorthwindDataSet

End Function


Function GetEmployees() As DataSet
    Dim ParamsStoredProcedure As String = "spGetEmployees"
    Dim NorthwindDataSet As DataSet
    Try
        'Check to see if this object has already been disposed
        If privateDisposedBoolean = True Then
            Throw New ObjectDisposedException( _
            privateModuleName, _
            "This object has already been disposed. " & _
            "You cannot reuse it.")
        End If

        privateSQLServer.ClearParameters()

        NorthwindDataSet = _
            privateSQLServer.runSPDataSet( _
            ParamsStoredProcedure, "Employees")
    Catch ExceptionObject As Exception
        Throw New Exception( _
            privateExceptionMessage, ExceptionObject)
    End Try

    Return NorthwindDataSet
End Function


Function GetTodaysBirthDayEmployees() As DataSet
    Dim ParamsStoredProcedure As String = _
        "spGetTodaysBirthDayEmployees"
    Dim NorthwindDataSet As DataSet
    Dim BirthDayMonth As Integer, BirthDayDay As Integer

    BirthDayMonth = Month(Now)
    BirthDayDay = Day(Now)

    Try
        'Check to see if this object has already been disposed.
        If privateDisposedBoolean = True Then
            Throw New ObjectDisposedException( _
                privateModuleName, _
                "This object has already been disposed. " & _
                "You cannot reuse it.")
        End If

        privateSQLServer.ClearParameters()
```

```
        privateSQLServer.AddParameter( _
            "@BirthDayMonth", BirthDayMonth, _
            SQLServer.SQLDataType.SQLInteger, , _
            ParameterDirection.Input)
        privateSQLServer.AddParameter( _
            "@BirthDayDay", BirthDayDay, _
            SQLServer.SQLDataType.SQLInteger, , _
            ParameterDirection.Input)

        NorthwindDataSet = _
            privateSQLServer.runSPDataSet( _
            ParamsStoredProcedure, "EmployeeByTodaysBirthDay")

    Catch ExceptionObject As Exception
        Throw New Exception( _
            privateExceptionMessage, ExceptionObject)
    End Try

    Return NorthwindDataSet
End Function


Function GetEmployeeState(ByVal EmployeeID As String) As String
    Dim ReturnOutPutList As New ArrayList()
    Dim localOutputString As String
    Dim ParamsStoredProcedure As String = _
        "spGetEmployeeStateProvince"
    Try
        'Check to see if this object has already been disposed
        If privateDisposedBoolean = True Then
            Throw New ObjectDisposedException( _
                privateModuleName, _
                "This object has already been disposed. " & _
                "You cannot reuse it.")
        End If

        privateSQLServer.ClearParameters()

        privateSQLServer.AddParameter( _
            "@EmployeeID", EmployeeID, _
            SQLServer.SQLDataType.SQLInteger, .
            ParameterDirection.Input)
        privateSQLServer.AddParameter( _
            "@Region", , _
            SQLServer.SQLDataType.SQLChar, 15, _
            ParameterDirection.Output)
        ReturnOutPutList = _
            privateSQLServer.runSPOutput(ParamsStoredProcedure)
            'Get the output parameters and iterate through them.
        Dim s As String
```

(continued)

```
            For Each s In ReturnOutPutList
                localOutputString &= s.ToString
            Next
        Catch ExceptionObject As Exception
            Throw New Exception(privateExceptionMessage, _
                ExceptionObject)
        End Try

        Return localOutputString
    End Function

#End Region

#Region "Dispose"
    Public Overloads Sub Dispose()
        'First we see if dispose has already been called;
        'if not, we proceed.
        If privateDisposedBoolean = False Then
            Try

            Catch

            Finally
                'If needed, call the full dispose method of this component.

                'Now we prevent the Garbage Collector from having to
                'take 2 passes.
                GC.SuppressFinalize(Me)
                'Setting the dispose flag will allow us to differentiate
                'between disposal and garbage collection so that we don't
                'resurrect the object inappropriately.
                privateDisposedBoolean = True
            End Try
        End If
    End Sub
#End Region
End Class
```

The class definition in the previous code (shown in boldface) has the *Must-Inherit* attribute applied:

```
Public MustInherit Class EmployeeObject
```

MustInherit causes the class to be an inheritable class only. In other words, you can't instantiate it directly. We want this behavior because to implement the facade layer, we're going to inherit from the business object. In this case, we inherit from the *EmployeeObject* class. The rest of the code implements the *EmployeeObject* business object. The code uses the data access layer presented in earlier chapters.

The *EmployeeHRObject* Facade Class

To create the facade layer for the *EmployeeHRObject* class for the HRnet sample application, we create a new class library project named EmployeeHRFacade-Layer and then add a single class named *EmployeeHRObject*. Here's the code for this class:

```
Public Class EmployeeHRObject
    Inherits EmployeeLayer.EmployeeObject

End Class
```

Now, you're probably wondering why we went through this trouble. The reason is to allow us to customize the facade layer later and not worry about modifying the underlying business object. That makes it easy to customize the application. Another nice benefit of this approach is that the facade layer automatically picks up changes to the *EmployeeObject*. For instance, suppose you create the simple *EmployeeObject* here and use it to start designing your facade layer. Later, another developer adds a rich set of methods to this object. Now your facade layer can pick up those changes automatically. Of course, the changes only float up to the facade layer when the dynamic-link library (DLL) containing the updated *EmployeeObject* is either copied to the global assembly cache (GAC) if it resides there or replaces the existing DLL. Now, let's extend the diagram by adding another facade layer, as shown in Figure 9-3.

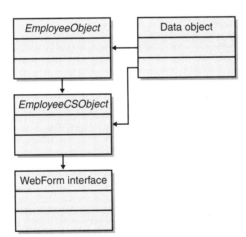

Figure 9-3   An additional facade for the *EmployeeObject* is added for another application

Figure 9-3 shows how the *EmployeeObject* is now simply wired to the *EmployeeCSObject*, which is the facade object for the customer service application.

If the customer service application needs more employee functionality, the functionality can be implemented in the facade layer, the *EmployeeCSObject* class. Let's try this out by making some modifications.

Before we modify the facade layer, let's take one more look at the simple facade layer we just created. Here we want to flesh out the class just a bit so that it is more in line with our standard architecture. The result follows:

```
Public Class EmployeeHRObject
    Inherits EmployeeLayer.EmployeeObject
#Region " Private Variables and Objects"
    Private privateDisposedBoolean As Boolean
    Private privateModuleName As String
    Private Const privateExceptionMessage As String = _
        "Employee Object error. Detail Error Information " & _
        "can be found in the Application Log."

#End Region
#Region "Public Constructors"
Public Sub New()
    privateModuleName = Me.GetType.ToString
End Sub
#End Region

#Region "Public Functions"

#End Region
End Class
```

As you can see, the facade layer should have the same structure as any other class. The following code implements things like the private variables such as *privateModuleName*, region blocks, and the *Dispose* method:

```
Public Class EmployeeHRObject
    Inherits EmployeeLayer.EmployeeObject
#Region " Private Variables and Objects"
    Private privateDisposedBoolean As Boolean
    Private privateModuleName As String
    Private Const privateExceptionMessage As String = _
        "Employee Object error. Detail Error Information " & _
        "can be found in the Application Log."

#End Region
#Region "Public Constructors"
Public Sub New()
    privateModuleName = Me.GetType.ToString
End Sub
#End Region
```

```
#Region "Public Functions"

#End Region

#Region "Overloaded Dispose"
Public Overloads Sub Dispose()
    'First we see if dispose has already been called;
    'if not, we proceed.
    If privateDisposedBoolean = False Then
        Try

        Catch

        Finally
            'If needed, call the full Dispose method of this component
            MyBase.Dispose()
            'Now we prevent the Garbage Collector
            ' from having to take 2 passes.
            GC.SuppressFinalize(Me)
            'Setting the dispose flag will allow us to check between
            'disposal and garbage collection so that we don't resurrect
            'the object inappropriately.
            privateDisposedBoolean = True
        End Try
    End If
End Sub
#End Region
End Class
```

As you can see in the code, the facade layer structure is just like any other class. You could create a template from this structure and use it to start any facade layer.

EmployeeCSObject Facade Class

Now we can create another facade class for another application, in this case a customer service application. This facade object adds another method to extract customers and employees that are in the same region. For instance, we could look up all customers in the state of Washington and pull out all the employees in that same state or region. This capability could be useful for anything from a special customer event to a sales call. The process of turning an object into different objects is called *polymorphism*. This term means the underlying base class (the business object) can take on different forms. The different forms are implemented by the derived classes (such as *EmployeeCSObject*) and take on new behaviors through their additional methods and properties. The code is shown here:

```vb
Imports DataAccessLayer.DataAccess
Public Class EmployeeCSObject
    Inherits EmployeeLayer.EmployeeObject

#Region " Private Variables and Objects"
    Private privateDisposedBoolean As Boolean
    Private privateModuleName As String
    Private privateConnectionString As String = _
        "Server=LocalHost ;Database=northwind;" & _
        "User ID=sa;Password=;"
    Private Const privateExceptionMessage As String = _
        "Employee Object error. Detail Error Information " & _
        "can be found in the Application Log."
    Dim privateSQLServer As SQLServer
#End Region
#Region "Public Constructors"
Public Sub New()
    privateModuleName = Me.GetType.ToString

    privateSQLServer = New SQLServer(privateConnectionString)
End Sub
#End Region

#Region "Public Functions"
Function GetEmployeesInCustomerRegion( _
    ByVal Region As String) As DataSet
    Dim ParamsStoredProcedure As String = _
        "spGetCustomerEmployeeMatchingRegion"
    Dim NorthwindDataSet As DataSet

    Try
        privateSQLServer.ClearParameters()

        privateSQLServer.AddParameter( _
            "@Region", Region, _
            SQLServer.SQLDataType.SQLChar, , _
            ParameterDirection.Input)

        NorthwindDataSet = _
            privateSQLServer.runSPDataSet( _
            ParamsStoredProcedure, "EmployeesAndCustomers")

    Catch ExceptionObject As Exception
        Throw New Exception( _
            privateExceptionMessage, ExceptionObject)
    End Try
```

```
    Return NorthwindDataSet
End Function

#End Region

#Region "Overloaded Dispose"
Public Overloads Sub Dispose()
    'First we see if dispose has already been called;
    'if not, we proceed.
    If privateDisposedBoolean = False Then
        Try

        Catch

        Finally
            'If needed, call this component's Dispose method.
            MyBase.Dispose()
            'Now we prevent the Garbage Collector from
            'having to make 2 passes.
            GC.SuppressFinalize(Me)
            'Setting the dispose flag will allow us to check between
            'disposal and garbage collection so that we don't resurrect
            'the object inappropriately.
            privateDisposedBoolean = True
        End Try
    End If
End Sub
#End Region
End Class
```

Conclusion

This chapter demonstrated how simple facade layers can isolate the business objects you create from the applications that use those objects. The result is an application that is much easier to create and to maintain. You can customize a facade layer without touching the underlying business object. That lets you add features without breaking running code. You can always make changes to that code later by moving working code from a facade object into a business object. And as you have seen, if you move a method from the facade object to a business object that a facade implements, you don't need to make any other changes because the new methods will be picked up through inheritance in the facade object. Amazing!

What you have witnessed in this chapter is polymorphism, which we defined earlier. Chapter 10 will show you some really cool things that you can do with the user interface and how using other OOP features make your life easier.

10

Creating the User Interface Template

In all the years we've been designing and creating software applications, we've always sought the Holy Grail of programming—code reuse. Don't confuse this idea with "code builders" such as the builders available in Visual Studio .NET and third-party programs. Such builders try to do the programming for you. Many of them create user interfaces for you, and mostly you end up with nothing but a jumbled mess of code that is usable only for prototyping. Unfortunately, a lot of people have gotten burned trying to use applications created through builders, only to find out they had to start over again. When we talk about code reuse, we mean the kind of functionality you get from object-oriented programming (OOP). The support for OOP in .NET is fantastic—second to none compared to previous generations of development tools. Despite this unprecedented opportunity, you'll discover that full inheritance and OOP aren't always easily achieved, especially when you need to create Web Forms applications. A good mixture of components, classes, user controls, and server controls allows us to come closer to reaching the goal of code reuse. In this chapter, we'll talk about the creation of user interface (UI) templates and Windows Forms built with visual inheritance. We'll share our experience in creating several pure .NET solutions, explaining what worked and what didn't. We'll also create the template for our HRnet application, using some of the previous chapter's objects, such as menu components. We wrote most of HRnet with Microsoft ASP.NET Web Forms and used Microsoft Visual Basic .NET components and classes to create the functionality. We created some of HRnet with Visual Basic .NET Windows Forms using visual inheritance. With these Windows Forms, we're going to provide support and maintenance data. Obviously, we also could have written these support functions using Web Forms pages, but we want to show you templated functionality both ways.

In brief, our main objectives for this chapter are to create a fully functional Web Forms template with the menu structure for the HRnet application. With the introduction of visual inheritance, we'll build a set of application-specific base class Windows Forms. We'll show you examples of how to use each of them with the HRnet application.

Since we're now going to build part of the HRnet application that we'll use for the rest of this book, we need to take a closer look at the application's design and functional specifications.

HRnet Sample Application Specifications

When we decided to include parts of production applications in this book, many ideas came to mind. Our ideas ranged from creating a typical Web shopping cart application to a .NET version of Northwind. We decided to take many of the features and functionality of our existing .NET applications and combine them into HRnet because they have been used and tested in large-scale production applications. Also, our business was in need of a custom human resources (HR) application that would be part of our intranet and extranet. In addition, we felt that common HR functions are familiar to many programmers. The principles used in the HRnet application illustratre every feature of .NET we wanted to cover in this book.

HRnet Application Architecture

HRnet follows the principles illustrated in Chapter 2 and is created using a flexible *n*-tier architecture, as described in Table 10-1.

Table 10-1   MainMenuTable

Tier	Description
User interface	The main application is created with Web Forms technology. Some maintenance is handled with Windows Forms.
Facade	This tier uses Visual Basic .NET classes.
Business	General business rules are handled by Visual Basic .NET classes and components, as shown in Chapter 8. XML Web Services use additional facades to buffer general rules.
Data access	This tier uses the custom data access layer component created in Chapter 4.
Data	This tier uses Microsoft SQL Server 7 or Microsoft SQL Server 2000 as a back end.

HRnet Application Functionality

Now we're going to look at some of the functions we want to include in the HRnet application. Once we have a list of these functions, we can create the UI template.

Security

We implement system authentication and role-based authorization as described in Chapter 5. Both intranet and extranet users have to log on to the system. Once authenticated, the roles assigned to users determine which screens the users can access and what level of detail is available. To keep our example simple, we'll show only three roles. The first role is the executive, who has full access to everything. The second role is the HRManager, who has limited access to and limited visibility of detail data screens. The third role is the employees, who have even more limitations in visibility and almost no access to detail screens. Figure 10-1 shows the design of the Login page.

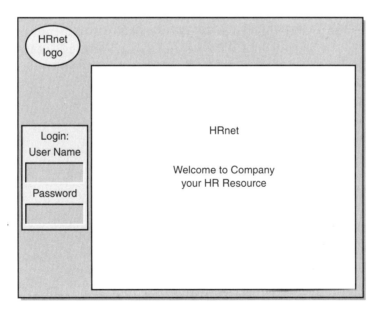

Figure 10-1   HRnet Login page design

Home Page

After a user is logged on to the system, the Home page provides summary information to that user. Besides the current date and time, the current month's employee birthdays are presented. (We show only the month and day, and not the year, to protect the employees' privacy.) Company-related news is also presented. In addition, an XML Web service is "consumed." The XML Web service used is the current weather for the company's location. Figure 10-2 shows the layout design of the HRnet Home page.

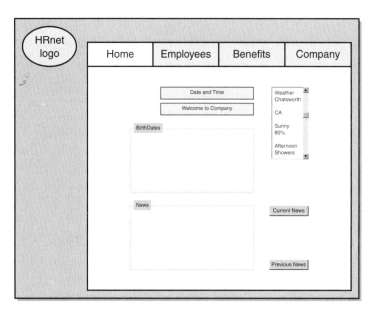

Figure 10-2 HRnet Home page design

Employees

When entering the employee area, we want to provide the user with a quick view of the company's employee status: How many full-time, part-time, and temporary employees do we have? Who is sick, on vacation, or on parental leave? Figure 10-3 shows the design of this screen's layout.

We also want to provide detailed information about our employees. Besides home address and emergency information, we want to know all important dates, from being hired to leaving the company, and also information such as social security numbers, birth dates, and payroll-related data. We want to handle benefits as well—it's important to find out each employee's eligibility and which benefits they have chosen. We also need to track each employee's work schedule and vacation information. One way to handle this information is in a tabbed form, as shown in Figure 10-4.

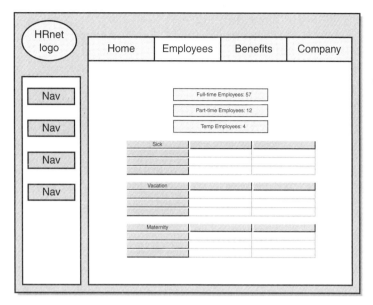

Figure 10-3   HRnet Employee summary page design

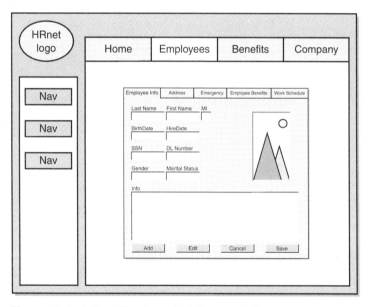

Figure 10-4   HRnet Employee Detail page design

General Company and Supporting Data

In addition to employee information, we need to track company information and provide input for other supporting data, such as positions, titles, departments, hiring sources, and available benefits. Even though this information can be managed with Web Forms pages, we decided to use Windows Forms. We'll show you a way to bring these Windows Forms into a Web application.

Menu and Navigation Structure

Now let's design the main menu and navigation bar structure. This structure will give us the necessary information to create the *MenuDataClass* and modify it for the roles used. Here is the navigation structure, with main menu items in italics:

- **Home**   The Home page has no navigation bar. It gives general company-related information.

- **Employees**   The Employee page has a navigation bar. This page gives a summary of the status of the company's employees.

    ❑   *Employee List* lists all employees.

    ❑   Details shows selected employee details such as birth date, social security number, important dates, and vacation.

    ❑   Address Selected shows employee's address information.

    ❑   Emergency Info shows selected employee's emergency information.

    ❑   Benefits Selected shows employee's chosen benefits.

    ❑   *Work Schedule* shows selected employee's work hours.

    ❑   *My Info* shows specific employee information for the logged-on employee.

- **Benefits**   The Benefits page has a navigation bar. The page provides the general rules on company benefits.

    ❑   Health Available shows health plans.

    ❑   Disability Available shows disability plans.

    ❑   401K Available shows 401K plans.

    ❑   Education Available shows education support.

- ❑   Other shows other benefits.

- ❑   Add allows the user to add new benefits.

- ■   **Company**   The Company page has a navigation bar and gives the company's general information. Pages are pulled from Windows Forms.

  - ❑   News Items shows current news items and allows the user to look at past news items.

  - ❑   Departments shows the company's departments.

  - ❑   Positions shows the company's positions.

  - ❑   Job Titles shows the company's job titles.

To allow different access for the three specific roles we have chosen, we limit general users to only those main menu and navigation bar items we emphasized with italics. Executives will see and have access to all items.

The HRnet application uses not only Web Forms pages for its user interface but also Windows Forms. Figure 10-5 shows an example of a Windows Forms page that we created with the visual inheritance features we discuss later in this chapter.

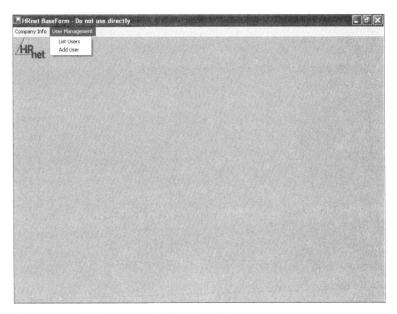

Figure 10-5   HRnet menu in Windows Forms

Creating the HRnet Web Template

In this section, we'll examine the Web template's layout and also take a detailed look at the template files.

The Web Template Layout

When you look at the previous figures in this book, you find an underlying visual design for our HRnet Web application. When we created our menu handlers in Chapter 7, we used a similar layout. Let's take a closer look at the layout of the template in Figure 10-6.

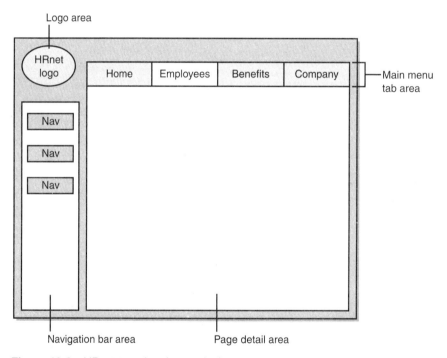

Figure 10-6   HRnet template layout design

The screen is divided into four visual and functional areas: the logo area, the main menu tab area, the navigation bar area, and the page detail area.

Logo Area

Some Web applications have links to the Home page when the logo is clicked. Because we don't like this behavior, we don't implement it in HRnet. Instead, we encapsulate the logo in a custom user control and add functionality, including a logoff option. This option is a good way to add more security to applications. In addition to the logoff option, we have a default session timeout. Whenever a page is accessed, the custom logo user control checks whether the session has timed out. If it has, it redirects to the logon page. This allows us to circumvent nasty error messages and tighten security. Another addition we will implement in the logo area is the link to our security and login component.

Main Menu Tab Area

The main menu tab is the central navigation control of the Web application. All other navigation bars have their root in this tabbed menu. Our previously designed Home page will be the default page. The main menu tab will also be controlled through the role-based logon, where the Benefits and Company tabs will be available only for administrators.

Navigation Bar Area

The navigation bar is the second level of our menu and navigation structure. We are keeping it one-level deep. It's also controlled through role-based logon. We'll improve its look and feel over what we saw in Chapter 7.

Page Detail Area

The detail area is where the actual Web information, or data-driven information, is placed. Whenever a new page needs to be inserted, we simply copy the template, rename it (more on that shortly), and integrate it into the navigation database. When this is done, we have two choices for implementing the detail area: we can simply put HTML and ASP.NET controls onto the page directly, or we can create custom user controls that we insert into the detail area.

Our approach to screen design makes it easier to create reusable page templates that allow fully data-driven navigation and page creation. We don't use framesets in any of our Web applications. A clever table layout gives us similar features without the added complexity of having to handle a frameset with multiple frames.

The Web Template Files

Figure 10-7 shows the template for the HRnet application. Look at the layout and you'll see its similarity with Figure 10-6. Since we're implementing user controls, you can't see their graphical representation. They are instead represented by boxed areas with the name UserControl-Controlname.x. Keep in mind that user controls don't show themselves at design time. Their output turns to HTML only at run time. (Refer to Chapter 6 for a discussion of the pros and cons of user controls versus server controls.)

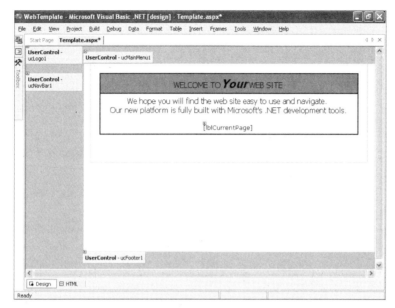

Figure 10-7 HRnet template in design view

The first three visual areas in Figure 10-6 are represented by custom user controls. We included an additional user control named *ucFooter1* that handles our copyright and Contact Us Web pages. The fourth visual area in Figure 10-6 represents the template's detail area. Here we present the major information for each specific page by replacing the HTML in the template. Notice that we placed a label server control named *lblCurrentPage* in the template's detail area. This label will help us test the menu and navigation controls by representing the tab index of the selected menu and navigation tabs. When the pages are loaded, both the *MainMenuIndex* and *NavBarIndex* session variables are retrieved and shown.

```
Private Sub Page_Load(ByVal sender As System.Object, ByVal e As _
    System.EventArgs) Handles MyBase.Load
    lblCurrentPage.Text = "Menu Session = " & Session( _
        "MainMenuIndex") & " Tab Session = " & Session("NavBarIndex")
End Sub
```

This chapter's sample files are in the WebTemplate Web application in the Ch07 directory. Before we go into the details of our template and what support files are required, take the time to compile and run the template.aspx file. You'll see some default behavior we gave the template to test it before we start using it in our Web application.

To test our template and its functionality, we need to make sure that we have all supporting components and files available. When you create a new

Web application, you need to include these files in your project. We added four folders to the WebTemplate sample: the Company folder, the Images folder, the UserControl folder, and the Menu folder. The Company folder includes the ContactUs.aspx and Copyright.aspx files. These are used only in the ucFooter1.ascx user control. If you omit this control, you don't need to include the Company folder or its contents.

Next, we added the Images folder. You might need one for your Web application anyway. Here you find our logo, the HRnet.jpg file, and a spacer.gif file that we use occasionally. The logo and spacer are part of the ucLogo.ascx user control.

Since we use user controls regularly, we always include the UserControl folder. To make our template work correctly, both the logo and footer controls are located here.

The most important folder we added is the Menu folder. It includes both the main menu and navigation bar custom user controls as well as the MenuDataClass.vb file that builds or calls the menu and navigation bar data. We separated these user controls into the menu folder to make our Web application easier to maintain. Don't forget to include a reference to the *MenuData* component in your project. It's required for building the menu and navigation tables and needs to be referenced before we look at the *MenuDataClass*. In it you'll find code for a default menu and navigation structure. Each menu and navigation entry calls the template.aspx Web form. This allows us to test menu functionality immediately, without having to add additional pages. Here is the code for this default behavior:

```
'Dim this code out and use your own instead.
'Add info to the Menu Table.
Dim localMenuTables As New MenuDataServer()
localMenuTables.AddMainMenuParameter(1, "Home", _
    "/WebTemplate/Template.aspx", False, "Our Home Page")
localMenuTables.AddMainMenuParameter(2, "Tab2", _
    "/WebTemplate/Template.aspx", True)
localMenuTables.AddMainMenuParameter(3, "Tab3", _
    "/WebTemplate/Template.aspx", True)
'Add info to the NavBar Table.
localMenuTables.AddNavBarParameter(2, 1, "Tab2-Nav1", _
    "/WebTemplate/Template.aspx", False)
localMenuTables.AddNavBarParameter(2, 2, "Tab2-Nav2", _
    "/WebTemplate/Template.aspx", False)
localMenuTables.AddNavBarParameter(2, 3, "Tab2-Nav3", _
    "/WebTemplate/Template.aspx", False)
localMenuTables.AddNavBarParameter(3, 1, "Tab-Nav1", _
    "/WebTemplate/Template.aspx", False)
'End Dim. Place your code here.
```

This code simply creates three main menu items. For the second and third main menu items, the code creates additional *NavBar* tabs. After commenting out this code, you can create your own menu structure or call different classes that create your menu structure based on roles or other business rules. You might want to refer to Chapter 7 to review how to change the look and feel of the main menu and navigation custom user controls. We already set the colors and fonts that we prefer for HRnet.

Now that we've taken care of all the supporting files, let's examine the template.aspx files in more detail. The first area of interest is in the HTML Header's Style section:

```
<style>
    A.menutext {FONT-WEIGHT: bold; FONT-SIZE: 11pt; MARGIN-LEFT: 5px;
        COLOR:   navy; MARGIN-RIGHT: 5px; TEXT-DECORATION: none}
    A.menutext:hover {COLOR: blue; TEXT-DECORATION: none}
    A.menutext:visited {COLOR: navy; TEXT-DECORATION: none}
    A.menutext:hover {COLOR: skyblue; TEXT-DECORATION: none}
    A.navbartext {FONT-WEIGHT: bold; FONT-SIZE: 10pt; MARGIN-LEFT:
        5px; COLOR: navy; MARGIN-RIGHT: 5px; TEXT-DECORATION: none}
    A.navbartext:hover {COLOR: black; TEXT-DECORATION: none}
    A.navbartext:visited {COLOR: navy; TEXT-DECORATION: none}
    A.navbartext:hover {COLOR: black; TEXT-DECORATION: none}
    BODY {FONT-WEIGHT: normal; FONT-SIZE: 10pt; MARGIN: 0px;
        WORD-SPACING: normal; TEXT-TRANSFORM: none;
        FONT-FAMILY: Tahoma, Arial, Helvetica, Sans-Serif;
        LETTER-SPACING: normal; BACKGROUND-COLOR: #aec1eb}
</style>
```

From Chapter 6, recall that the *A.menutext* and *A.navbartext* are styles that manage the font, size, and color of the main menu and navigation bars. In the body of our Web pages, we defined our preferred font and its size, spacing, and background color. More important is the definition of the margin as 0 pixels, which allows the full background to be used. We also mentioned earlier that we don't use framesets. Instead, the rest of our template.aspx page is divided into tables and cells. Here is the important part of the HTML code:

```
<TABLE id="tblMain" cellSpacing="0" cellPadding="0" width="100%"
    border="0">
    <tr>
        <td vAlign="top" align="middle" width="125" rowSpan="2">
            <ucl:uclogo id="ucLogo1" runat="server"></ucl:uclogo>
            <ucl:ucnavbar id="ucNavBar1" runat="server">
            </ucl:ucnavbar>
        </td>
        <td vAlign="bottom" align="left" height="35">
            <ucl:ucmainmenu id="ucMainMenu1" runat="server">
            </ucl:ucmainmenu>
```

```
            </td>
        </tr>
        <tr>
            <td vAlign="top" bgColor="#ffffff" height="480">
                <!------- Detail Screen starts here ------->

                <!------- Detail Screen ends here ------->
            </td>
        </tr>
        <tr>
            <td style="WIDTH: 81px"> </td>
            <td align="middle">
                <P align="left">
                <uc1:ucfooter id="ucFooter1" runat="server">
                </uc1:ucfooter></P>
            </td>
        </tr>
</TABLE>
```

How you lay out the screen is a matter of preference and might vary from application to application. We chose this layout because it fits our requirements for navigation and standardization. Whatever layout you choose in your applications, the availability of both the *MainMenu* and *NavBar* user controls is important, as is the availability of the *Logo* user control and a detail area. You can see that the page detail resides within a table cell. For easy implementation, we marked the detail area of the page with a script comment block: *<!- - - Detail screen starts / ends here - - ->*. Within this block, we create the page's detail that itself will be contained in an additional table. We find this arrangement works best and is flexible enough to allow our HTML and graphic designers some creativity because it leaves enough room for art and graphics. At the same time, the template gives our Web application structure and consistency.

Starting the HRnet Application

Now that we know how to create templates for our Web applications, we're going to start the HRnet sample application. You'll find the example files in the HRnet directory, separated from the samples belonging to specific chapters. We're going to build HRnet one step at a time. Even though we provide you with the complete HRnet sample, we recommend that you create this application from scratch, following the steps we present. Doing so will help you understand the process we follow in this book, enabling you to more easily and quickly apply the principles presented to your own applications. In Chapter 14, we summarize this process and add all the functionality we created.

First start a new Web application in Visual Studio .NET, name it HRnet, and copy the template.aspx and support files we mentioned previously into the correct directories. (Don't forget to register the components we'll use, such as the *MenuData* component, the data access layer, and security components.) Now we're ready to add our designed menu structure and create the Home page.

In a completed sample, MenuDataClass.vb file, all menu and navigation items point to correct .aspx files. When you create the application step by step, you won't have all the .aspx Web Forms pages available; however, we still want the menu structure to be complete. For this reason, we point all nonexistent .aspx Web pages that we defined in the menu structure but haven't yet created to template.aspx. This allows us to continue testing our application, including the menu structure, without having to have all files available. Here is the code that you should have in the MenuDataClass.vb at this stage, representing our designed menu and navigation structure. (Remember that the code in HRnet looks different.)

```
Imports MenuData.MenuData
Imports System.Data
Namespace LocalMenuData
Public Class MenuDataClass
    Public Function getMenuDataSet() As DataSet
        'Add info to the Main Menu Table.
        Dim localMenuTables As New MenuDataServer()
        localMenuTables.AddMainMenuParameter(1, "Home", _
            "Template.aspx", False, "HRnet Home Page")
        localMenuTables.AddMainMenuParameter(2, "Employees", _
            "Template.aspx", True, "Employee Information")
        localMenuTables.AddMainMenuParameter(3, "Benefits", _
            "Template.aspx", True, "Available Benefits")
        localMenuTables.AddMainMenuParameter(4, "Company", _
            "Template.aspx", True, "Company Information")
        'Add info to the NavBar Table.
        localMenuTables.AddNavBarParameter(2, 1, "Employee List", _
            "Template.aspx", False, "List all Employees")
        localMenuTables.AddNavBarParameter(2, 2, "Details", _
            "Template.aspx", False, "Specific Employee's Information")
        localMenuTables.AddNavBarParameter(2, 3, "Address", _
            "Template.aspx", False, "Specific Employee's Address")
        localMenuTables.AddNavBarParameter(2, 4, "Emergency Info", _
            "Template.aspx", False, _
            "Specific Employee's Emergency Info")
        localMenuTables.AddNavBarParameter(2, 5, "Benefits", _
            "Template.aspx", False, _
            "Specific Employee's Chosen Benefits")
        localMenuTables.AddNavBarParameter(2, 6, "Work Schedule", _
```

```
            "Template.aspx", False, "Specific Employee's Work Schedule")
        localMenuTables.AddNavBarParameter(2, 7, "My Info", _
            "Template.aspx", False, "Specific Employee's Work Schedule")
        localMenuTables.AddNavBarParameter(3, 1, "Health", _
            "Template.aspx", False, "List Health Benefits")
        localMenuTables.AddNavBarParameter(3, 2, "Disability", _
            "Template.aspx", False, "List Disability Benefits")
        localMenuTables.AddNavBarParameter(3, 3, "401K", _
            "Template.aspx", False, "List Retirement Benefits")
        localMenuTables.AddNavBarParameter(3, 4, "Education", _
            "Template.aspx", False, "List Education Benefits")
        localMenuTables.AddNavBarParameter(3, 5, "Other", _
            "Template.aspx", False, "List Education Benefits")
        localMenuTables.AddNavBarParameter(3, 6, "Add", _
            "Template.aspx", False, "List Education Benefits")
        localMenuTables.AddNavBarParameter(4, 1, "News Items", _
            "Template.aspx", False, "Current and Archived News")
        localMenuTables.AddNavBarParameter(4, 2, "Departments", _
            "Template.aspx", False, "Our Company's Departments")
        localMenuTables.AddNavBarParameter(4, 3, "Positions", _
            "Template.aspx", False, "Our Company's Positions")
        localMenuTables.AddNavBarParameter(4, 4, "Job Titles", _
            "Template.aspx", False, "Our Company's Job Titles")
        Return localMenuTables.GetMenuDataSet
        localMenuTables.Dispose()      'Dispose the object.
        localMenuTables = Nothing      'Make sure it is out of scope.
    End Function
End Class
End Namespace
```

This code represents the full menu structure of HRnet. When we add the security information in Chapter 11, you'll see that the code in the MenuData-Class.vb file changes to accommodate role-based security.

The HRnet Home Page

Let's now use the template for the first time and create the Home page. We'll repeat the same process for every Web page we create. Immediately following the creation of the Home page, we'll discuss some of the advantages and disadvantages of templating Web pages this way. We'll explore one other way we've found to create Web Forms templates programmatically.

Even though the process is simple, let's take a closer look. After selecting the template.aspx file, copy and paste it into the directory of your choice. In this example, copy the file into the main HRnet directory. Notice that the file automatically renamed itself to Copy of template.aspx (unless it was moved to a different folder, in which case its name would stay the same). You'd think that simply renaming this file should suffice, but this isn't the case, as you'll find out very quickly. Rename Copy of template.aspx to Home.aspx. (Right-click the file and click Rename on the shortcut menu.) After accepting the new name, everything looks fine until you open the new file. You are greeted with the following Microsoft Developer Environment error: "The file failed to load in the Web Forms designer. Please correct the following error, then load it again: The designer could not be shown for this file because none of the classes within it can be designed." Imagine how surprised we were the first time we saw this error. We figured out quickly why things didn't work as expected. Click the OK button, and both the Home.aspx and Home.aspx.vb file (which is the code-behind file for the corresponding .aspx page) are opened. Looking at the resulting code reveals what went wrong:

```
<%@ Page Language="vb" AutoEventWireup="false"
    Codebehind="Home.aspx.vb" Inherits="HRnet.Template" %>
```

This code within Home.aspx shows that renaming the file worked only for the .aspx file and its code-behind page. It didn't create the correct inheritance structure. We don't want to inherit from the template file but rather from the new Home.aspx file. Replace *Inherits="HRnet.Template"* with *Inherits= "HRnet.Home"* and save the file.

Now let's take a look at the Home.aspx.vb file. It duplicates the class named *Template*. Duplicate classes are not allowed in the same namespace.

```
Public Class Template
    Inherits System.Web.UI.Page
```

Just replace *Template* with the new class name for this page, which is its name: *Home*. After saving this file, you can close both the Home.aspx and Home.aspx.vb files. If you reopen Home.aspx again, it will behave itself as it should, and it will be ready to use. Take the time to change the form and give it a welcome area or other features.

We don't know whether the behavior resulting from copying Web Forms pages was by design or was simply overlooked by the ASP.NET team. Suffice it to say that you now know how to get around this problem.

We also found another little gotcha that you should know about in case you want to use the same name for a Web page in a different directory within the same application. Giving the file the same name in a different directory works fine with the .aspx part of the file, but its code-behind file will have problems. Since code-behind files are classes, you can't have two of the same class name in the same namespace. (Remember that a project uses its own name by default as a namespace.) To circumvent this problem, you can call the

.aspx file and its code-behind files the same name; however, you have to change the class description.

Consider this example of two Web pages with the same name in different directories (not used in our code examples). You have a Home.aspx page in the root directory. Its page directive in Home.aspx is as follows:

```
<%@ Page Language="vb" AutoEventWireup="false" Codebehind="Home.aspx.vb"
    Inherits="HRnet.Home" %>
```

In the Home.aspx.vb code-behind file, the class is defined like this:

```
Public Class Home
```

If you now want another Home.aspx file in a subdirectory of this Web application, you can create the Home.aspx file from the template. In its page directive, you need to inherit from a different file to avoid a conflict with the first home Web page. Here is a sample page directive for the second Home page:

```
<%@ Page Language="vb" AutoEventWireup="false"
    Codebehind="Home.aspx.vb" Inherits="HRnet.Home1" %>
```

Here is its accompanying code-behind file:

```
Public Class Home1
```

Now that we have our Home Page, we want to add it to the menu structure. In the MenuDataClass.vb file, change the line of code that directs the home page from the template.aspx to Home.aspx as follows:

```
localMenuTables.AddMainMenuParameter(1, "Home", "/HRnet/Home.aspx", _
    False, "HRnet Home Page")
```

You're now ready to run HRnet with the new Home page. Right-click Home.aspx, click Build And Browse on the shortcut menu, and see your Home Page in action. It has inherited the look and feel and also full menu functionality.

Here is a review of the advantages of Web templates, as we have shown in this chapter:

- Easy to use.

- Full designer support.

- Code-behind and .aspx files are separate so that visual designers can work on the detail pages without changing code.

These advantages are great and make template usage easy, but the Web template does have a major disadvantage (although it's the only disadvantage we've found): it isn't built using OOP's inheritance features. If you want to change the look and feel of your whole Web application, you will have to change the HTML in all files that were copied from the template file. Changes to the HTML in the template.aspx file won't be automatically inherited from all the file's copies. This is a tremendous disadvantage and we have been searching for ways to circumvent the problem. Later in this chapter, you'll find that much better visual inheritance features exist within Windows Forms. With Windows Forms, true inheritance between a template base form and its inherited children is available. The solution to the inheritance challenge isn't easy, and Microsoft was fully aware of this because they created ASP.NET without giving us true template page inheritance out of the box.

Web Page Templates: The Other Option

A possible solution to the page template challenge is to insert a custom page template between ASP.NET's page class and its code-behind file. Figure 10-8 shows a visual representation.

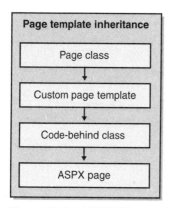

Figure 10-8   ASP.NET page class structure with custom template class

You'll find the sample files in the ASPXInheritance directory of the Web-Template project. To create the custom page template shown in Figure 10-8, we created the PageTemplate.vb file and gave it the *ASPXInheritance* namespace. The main class named *PageTemplate* inherits its behavior from the ASP.NET *Page* class that resides in the *System.Web.UI* namespace. (This is what you see when you create a new .aspx page.) Since this is a class file only, you can't use any HTML designer for the code that lays out the page. Instead, each HTML region of the template page must be created programmatically. This can be done with the help of the *PlaceHolder* object. These *PlaceHolder* objects hold the HTML or user controls necessary to build our template page. Here is the first part of the PageTemplate.vb file:

```
Imports System
Imports System.Web.UI
Imports System.Web.UI.WebControls
Imports System.Web.UI.HtmlControls
Namespace ASPXInheritance          'Namespace for us to use
    Public Class PageTemplate : Inherits Page
        'Inherits from the Web Page Base
        Private mainForm As HtmlForm    'Acts as <form runat='server'> tag
        'Define the page region placeholders.
        Private privateTitle As PlaceHolder
        Private privateHeader As PlaceHolder
        Private privateNavBar As NavBar
        Private privateBody As PlaceHolder
        Private privateWidth As Integer = 700 'Default width of our screen
        Public Sub New()
            mainForm = New HtmlForm() 'Initializes the Form
            'Defines regions on Page
            privateTitle = New PlaceHolder()
            privateHeader = New PlaceHolder()
            privateNavBar = New NavBar()
            privateBody = New PlaceHolder()
        End Sub
         Public Property Width() As Integer'Width Property
            Get
                Return privateWidth
            End Get
            Set(ByVal Value As Integer)
                privateWidth = Value
            End Set
        End Property
        Public Property Title() As String'Allows title to be added
            Get
                Return ""
            End Get
            Set(ByVal Value As String)
                privateTitle.Controls.Clear()
                privateTitle.Controls.Add(New LiteralControl(Value))
            End Set
        End Property
        Public Property Header() As PlaceHolder 'Adds Header
            Get
                Return privateHeader
            End Get
            Set(ByVal Value As PlaceHolder)
                privateHeader = Value
            End Set
        End Property
```

(continued)

```
        Public Property LeftNav() As NavBar'Adds Navigation Bar
            Get
                Return privateNavBar
            End Get
            Set(ByVal Value As NavBar)
                privateNavBar = Value
            End Set
        End Property
        Public Property Body() As PlaceHolder 'Adds Body of text
            Get
                Return privateBody
            End Get
            Set(ByVal Value As PlaceHolder)
                privateBody = Value
            End Set
        End Property
            ⋮
    'The NavBar is an inherited PlaceHolder with some extras.
    Public Class NavBar : Inherits PlaceHolder
        Private navWidth As Integer = 125
        Public Property Width() As Integer
            Get
                Return navWidth
            End Get
                Set(ByVal Value As Integer)
                navWidth = Value
            End Set
        End Property
    End Class
End Class
```

The interesting parts of the preceding code are the *PlaceHolder* definitions: *Title*, *Header*, *NavBar*, and *Body*. You are free to create as many of these as you wish. The *NavBar* is a special subclass of the *PlaceHolder* class, adding specific width information. The initialized variable *mainForm* is defined as an *HtmlForm*, therefore getting the properties, methods, and events of a <form runat='server'> tag. The rest of the properties allow you to set the internal *PlaceHolder* variables.

The next section of code gets a bit more involved. Important to note is the sequence of controls when a Web page is created programmatically. First we override the *OnInit* subroutine for the page. In this part of the code, we add *LiteralControl* objects to the page that contains the main HTML tags such as <HTML>, <Title>, and <Body>. The *Page_Load* method runs and adds more literal controls to the *mainForm* control. It contains the template code within a table and also user controls. First let's look at the code in the *OnInit* method:

```
Protected Overrides Sub OnInit(ByVal e As EventArgs)  'Creates HTML Layout
    AddHandler Me.Load, AddressOf Page_Load
    Dim localStyle As String
```

```
    localStyle = "<style>... BODY { FONT-WEIGHT: normal; FONT-SIZE:
10pt; MARGIN: 0px; WORD-SPACING: normal; TEXT-TRANSFORM:
none; FONT-FAMILY: Tahoma, Arial, Helvetica, Sans-Serif;
LETTER-SPACING: normal; BACKGROUND-COLOR: #aec1eb }</style>"
    'Add the base header essentials.
    AddHTML(("<html>" + ControlChars.Lf + "<head>" + ControlChars.Lf _
        + "<title>"))
    Controls.Add(privateTitle)
    AddHTML(("</title>" + ControlChars.Lf + localStyle + "</head>" _
        + ControlChars.Lf + "<body>" + ControlChars.Lf))
    'Add the Web Form to the page.
    Controls.Add(mainForm)
    'Add the base footer essentials.
    AddHTML(("</body>" + ControlChars.Lf + "</html>"))
End Sub
    ⋮
Private Sub AddHTML(ByVal output As String)
    Controls.Add(New LiteralControl(output))
End Sub
```

The original *OnInit* subroutine is overridden. Next we make sure that the *Load* event is added and that we are in the address space of *Page_Load*. Then we define a string with the style values we want. The rest of the code adds controls as *LiteralControls* to the page. The *LiteralControls* send HTML to the Web page. We created an *AddHTML* subroutine that takes static text and turns it into a new *LiteralControl*. The most important control in the *OnInit* method is *mainForm*. Within it is the total layout of our template page.

Next we look at the code for the *Page_Load* event:

```
Private Sub Page_Load(ByVal sender As [Object], ByVal e As EventArgs)
    Dim colSpan As Integer = 1
    Dim bodyWidth As Integer = Width
    'Determine how many columns that the header as well as the width
    'for the body section of the template.
    If LeftNav.Controls.Count > 0 Then
        colSpan += 1
        bodyWidth -= LeftNav.Width
    End If
    'Construct the Web Form and add the page region PlaceHolder and
    NavSection objects - begin with main template layout.
    mainForm.Controls.Add(New LiteralControl("<table border=""1"" _" _
        + "cellspacing=""0"" cellpadding=""0"" width=""" + _
        Width.ToString() + """>" + ControlChars.Lf))
    mainForm.Controls.Add(New LiteralControl(ControlChars.Tab + "<tr>" + _
        ControlChars.Lf + ControlChars.Tab + ControlChars.Tab + _
        "<td  colspan=""" + colSpan.ToString() + """ valign=""top"">" + _
        ControlChars.Lf))
    'Add a default header if one was not specified.
```

(continued)

```vb
    If 0 = Header.Controls.Count Then
        mainForm.Controls.Add(LoadControl("ucHeader.ascx"))
    End If
    mainForm.Controls.Add(Header)
    mainForm.Controls.Add(New LiteralControl(ControlChars.Lf + _
        ControlChars.Tab + ControlChars.Tab + "</td>" + ControlChars.Lf + _
        ControlChars.Tab + "</tr>" + ControlChars.Lf))
    mainForm.Controls.Add(New LiteralControl(ControlChars.Tab + "<tr>" + _
        ControlChars.Lf))
    'Add the left navBar if it was specified by the page.
        If LeftNav.Controls.Count > 0 Then
            mainForm.Controls.Add(New LiteralControl(ControlChars.Tab + _
            ControlChars.Tab + "<td valign=""top"" width=""" + _
                LeftNav.Width.ToString() + """>" + ControlChars.Lf))
            mainForm.Controls.Add(LeftNav)
            mainForm.Controls.Add(New LiteralControl(ControlChars.Lf + _
                ControlChars.Tab + ControlChars.Tab + "</td>" + _
                ControlChars.Lf))
        End If
    'Add the body; otherwise throw an exception.
    If Body.Controls.Count > 0 Then
        mainForm.Controls.Add(New LiteralControl(ControlChars.Tab + _
            ControlChars.Tab + "<td valign=""top"">" + ControlChars.Lf + _
            ControlChars.Tab + ControlChars.Tab + ControlChars.Tab + _
            "<table border=""0"" cellspacing=""0"" cellpadding=""4"" " _
            + "width=""" + bodyWidth.ToString() + """>" + ControlChars.Lf _
            + ControlChars.Tab + ControlChars.Tab + ControlChars.Tab + _
            ControlChars.Tab + "<tr>" + ControlChars.Lf + _
            ControlChars.Tab + ControlChars.Tab + ControlChars.Tab + _
            ControlChars.Tab + ControlChars.Tab + "<td>" + _
            ControlChars.Lf))
        mainForm.Controls.Add(Body)
        mainForm.Controls.Add(New LiteralControl(ControlChars.Lf + _
            ControlChars.Tab + ControlChars.Tab + ControlChars.Tab + _
            ControlChars.Tab + ControlChars.Tab + "</td>" + _
            ControlChars.Lf + ControlChars.Tab + ControlChars.Tab + _
            ControlChars.Tab + ControlChars.Tab + "</tr>" + _
            ControlChars.Lf + ControlChars.Tab + ControlChars.Tab + _
            ControlChars.Tab + "</table>" + ControlChars.Lf + _
            ControlChars.Tab + ControlChars.Tab + "</td>" + _
            ControlChars.Lf))
    Else
        Throw New Exception("A Body must be present in the " & _
            PageTemplate class.")
    End If
    mainForm.Controls.Add(New LiteralControl(ControlChars.Tab + "</tr>" _
        + ControlChars.Lf))
    End Sub
```

The first couple of lines of this code set up some defaults. Remember, we have to create the HTML and place the user controls programmatically. The sample code in which we add the first control to *mainForm* shows us how this is done. The first two *LiteralControl*s added are a table and a row. *Controls-Char.Lf* creates a linefeed that makes looking at the HTML source code created more bearable. Next we determine whether a specific header was added. If not, ucHeader.ascx is added. Then we close out the row with another *LiteralControl*. Next comes the main body. If none was specified, we throw an exception. Every form must have a body, and we want to make sure it gets added.

Now that we have the *PageTemplate* class completed, we want to see how it's being used. After a new Web page is created, we need to clear out all HTML content. Why do we do this, you might ask? Well, we cannot mix Web page content that gets created with our template class with the HTML of the calling Web page. All additional content to the HTML that is created within the *Page-Template* class must be in user controls. In the HTML portion of the Web pages, there needs to be only one line of code. Here it is for our InheritanceTest.aspx example:

```
<%@ Page Language="vb" AutoEventWireup="false"
    Codebehind="InheritanceTest.aspx.vb"
    Inherits="WebTemplate.InheritanceTest"%>
```

In the code-behind page, we call, or wire-up, the content:

```
⋮
Imports WebTemplate.ASPXInheritance   'Need reference to the page template
Public Class InheritanceTest : Inherits PageTemplate
    'Inherits from our PageTemplate Class that inherits from Page Class
    Private Sub Page_Load(ByVal sender As System.Object,
        ByVal e As System.EventArgs) Handles MyBase.Load
        'Put user code to initialize the page here.
        MyBase.LeftNav.Width = 200
        MyBase.LeftNav.Controls.Add(LoadControl("ucLeftNav.ascx"))
        MyBase.Body.Controls.Add(LoadControl("ucBody.ascx"))
    End Sub
⋮
```

In the *Page_Load* event handler of the Web page, we are calling the *MyBase* class (PageTemplate.vb), setting some of the properties we defined, and adding user controls. In this case we add a left navigation bar in the ucLeft-Nav.ascx user control and the whole body in the ucBody.ascx user control. The ucBody.ascx user control contains the main Web page detail content. Give this example a try but make some modifications so that you can see how they affect the outcome.

Like any solution, using the Web Page template has distinctive advantages and disadvantages. It has the one advantage we found in our previous template approach: it is fully object-oriented. When you change the page template, it changes all pages in the Web application because the pages inherit directly from the template. There are, however, a list of disadvantages to consider:

- There is no HTML designer for the template. The whole content of the template page needs to be translated into hand-written code, as we saw in the PageTemplate.vb file.

- There is no standard way of building the actual Web pages. Code-behind files can interact only with properties and add controls.

- All Web content must be in user controls. The calling page cannot interact with the user controls. They need to live in their own world.

- Building controls through several levels of iteration can cause performance losses.

When you compare both positives and negatives for either creating ASP.NET Web page–based templates or programmatically inherited pages, you'll have to take a close look at what potential difficulties you could run into and what your requirements are. Will you change your whole Web application's look and feel often? If so, using programmatically created templates might be the answer. If you don't plan those kinds of changes and the template will be modified only a little or not at all, you might want to consider the copy-template format. Because we looked for simplicity, wanted an opportunity for our Web designers to be creative up front and on individual pages, and didn't want to make major changes to the template in the near future, we chose to continue HRnet with a template.aspx page that we copy for each additional Web page.

Additional Functionality

We've discussed the requirement for additional functionality that we wanted to add to the logo area. In this area, we want to hook into security, handle session timeout checks, and provide a logoff feature. In Chapter 11, we'll build the information pages, which include the hook into security and session timeout checks. At this point, however, we want to add the logoff feature. This is done in the ucLogo.ascx file. We add a Logout LinkButton to ucLogo.ascx and place it within its own table row and cell to make formatting easier. We use the Link-Button control vs. a Hyperlink control so that we can handle some server-side processing before we re-direct to the logout.aspx page. Here is the code:

```
Private Sub LinkBtnLogout_Click(ByVal sender As System.Object, _
    ByVal e As System.EventArgs) Handles LinkBtnLogout.Click
    Session.Clear()
    Session.Abandon()
    Response.Redirect("/HRnet/Logout.aspx")
End Sub
```

Between *Session.Clear* and *Session.Abandon*, all objects stored in the *Session* object are released and destroyed as soon as this page's code has executed. Since the redirect to the Logout page is next, this will happen right away.

Creating the HRnet Windows Forms Template

Windows Forms has an inheritance feature that allows us to go far beyond templating: visual inheritance. In the same way an inherited object gets all of its parent's properties, methods, and events, an inherited Windows Form gets all of its parent's behavior and also its look and feel. This visual inheritance lets us go beyond the copy-and-paste requirements of our Web template and allows us to treat an inherited Windows form just like its original parent form with full drag-and-drop capability.

Let's take a step back and look at the main reason for inheritance: efficient code reuse. Inheritance is a lot easier than you might think or have heard from speakers, authors, and programmers. Yes, it requires planning and a bit more preparation, but if used correctly, it can be very powerful. We'll prove this in the following paragraphs. In the same way that data access is a functionality we use in most applications, we use some visual and functional elements in most of our user interfaces. The challenge of code-reuse for data access was addressed by creating the data access layer component in Chapter 4. Now we'll do the same for visual and functional elements in Windows Forms. The inheritance features of .NET (and therefore Visual Basic .NET's inheritance features) support inheritance through several levels of layers, called *multilevel inheritance*. Don't confuse this with multiple class inheritance. Multiple class inheritance is when a class derives from two different classes. Multilevel inheritance is supported in .NET, but muliple class inheritance is not. Multilevel inheritance allows us to create a very functional framework.

In the following examples, we'll create several forms that inherit from base forms. In the bottom layer of our inherited forms, we start with very generic functionality. This might include form size, generic data handling, and generic menu handling. The next layer of inherited forms is the first subclass for our particular application. Here we add more application-specific features such as general colors and data handling. Next we either inherit directly the Windows

Forms we use or add more specific functionality when a requirement in a Windows form repeats itself for many other forms. Figure 10-9 shows the base and subclassed (or derived) forms we are using in HRnet. The above approach, going from more generic to more specific tasks in layers, is one of the best ways we've found to use inheritance. In our examples, this is done visually. In general business classes, the same should be done with business rules.

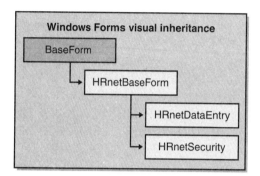

Figure 10-9   Windows Forms class inheritance structure

The examples we use are in the HRnetForms directory that resides in the CH10\WindowsForms subdirectories. Open HRnetForms.sln to view the entire project. The MainMenu.vb form is a menu that calls each one of the base and inherited forms we've created. Let's get started.

BaseForm.vb is the first level (base class form) in our mini framework. The reason for creating the abstraction is to allow us to buffer Visual Studio .NET's implementation of a form. If we don't like something, we can change it, or if we have something very generic, we can add it. All changes and added controls are carried forward. (Remember to recompile the project when you make changes to a base class. This is the only way the changes will be brought to the subclasses.) In the case of BaseForm.vb, we made only some slight changes. First, we don't want this form to be instantiated directly. To help prevent this, we gave it a yellow background color (not to offend anyone that likes to use yellow in their backgrounds) and limited the maximum, minimum, and startup size of the Windows form.

The Base Forms

HRnetBaseForm.vb is our application's most basic form. Its colors are adjusted, and it gets our logo and the common menu structure. Since the menu will be the same for all users who have access rights to the HRnet Windows Forms, we hard-code the menu structure by hand. If you want to do this programmatically, refer to Chapter 7.

So far, we have neither added functionality nor shown you how to create visually inherited Windows Forms. We'll do that now by creating the HRnet-DataEntry Windows form. Right-click the project (in our example that would be HRnetForms), and on the shortcut menu point to Add and then click Add Inherited Form. Give this form a name—we call it HRnetDataEntry. This will bring up the Inheritance Picker dialog box. In it you can choose which form you want to inherit from. We want to inherit from the HRnetBaseForm. The resulting page is shown and is exactly like the form we inherited from. When you investigate this new form more closely, you'll find a little arrow in the upper left corner of the logo. This arrow indicates that this item was inherited and is locked, and that its properties, methods, and events can't be changed.

Note that if you want to allow future inherited forms to change or override functions you've added, you must declare them as public. In this example, you could select the picture box and set the modifiers property to public. Then inherited forms could change the properties of this picture box.

This is also the case for the menu structure. If you want to make changes, you have to either unlock the item as just discussed or make the changes in the parent form that controls access. The resulting new form will be used when data access takes place. We want to include a few basic items of functionality for data access: Save, Add, Cancel, and Exit buttons, with their respective functionality. Instead of calling our middle tier in this example, we'll just show a descriptive message box. We add the four buttons, placing them in a similar fashion to our example, HRnetDataEntry.vb. We also name the buttons and anchor them to allow them to stay in position when the screen is resized. Additionally, the Save and Cancel buttons are invisible at screen startup time. Their visibility is controlled in code. Let's take a look at the functionality added to the form and buttons. We start with the added methods:

```
'BaseDataEntry has a Save Method.
Public Overridable Sub Save()
    MessageBox.Show("Data Base Form Save clicked")
    Me.Close()
End Sub
'BaseDataEntry has a Cancel Method.
Public Overridable Sub Cancel()
    MessageBox.Show("Data Base Form Cancel clicked")
    Me.Close()
End Sub
'BaseDataEntry has an Add Method.
Public Overridable Sub Add()
    EditMode(True)
End Sub
```

(continued)

```
'BaseDataEntry EditMode Method
Public Overridable Sub EditMode(ByVal setEditMode As Boolean)
    If setEditMode = True Then
        btnSave.Visible = True
        btnCancel.Visible = True
    Else
        btnSave.Visible = False
        btnCancel.Visible = False
    End If
End Sub
```

Now let's look at the button's event code:

```
Private Sub btnExit_Click(ByVal sender As System.Object, _
    ByVal e As System.EventArgs) Handles btnExit.Click
    Me.Close()
End Sub
Private Sub btnAdd_Click(ByVal sender As System.Object, _
    ByVal e As System.EventArgs) Handles btnAdd.Click
    Me.Add()
End Sub
Private Sub btnSave_Click(ByVal sender As System.Object, _
    ByVal e As System.EventArgs) Handles btnSave.Click
    Me.Save()
End Sub
Private Sub btnCancel_Click(ByVal sender As System.Object, _
    ByVal e As System.EventArgs) Handles btnCancel.Click
    Me.Cancel()
End Sub
```

Looking at this code, you might ask why we separated the methods from the button *Click* event handlers. Couldn't we just put the code in the subroutines directly into these handlers? Yes, we could do this, however it would not allow us the flexibility we want. Since we might not only want to use this Windows form directly and subclass it once more, we want the ability to use inheritance features fully. We want to use the functionality just as it is in the base form, totally override the base form's functionality, or combine the base functionality with additional code. These three choices are the major choices of inheritance and we should always write code that allows us to implement all three. By creating the *Save, Cancel*, and *Add* methods separately and calling them with *Me.Save, Me.Cancel*, and *Me.Add* with the option overridable on the subroutines, we allow the behavior of using, replacing, or using and adding functionality when we inherit from this Windows form. Run the HRnetDataEntry base form, clicking the buttons to see how our base data entry form behaves. Now, let's go one step further.

The Final Data Entry Form

Although we like the basic functionality and behavior that the data entry base form provides, we want to implement a couple of changes to the HRnetData-Entry base form. First, although we like the features of the Cancel button, which, when clicked, stops all processing and exits the form, we don't like the same behavior when the Save button is clicked. We want it to stay in the current form and replace the base class's *Save* method. Let's subclass HRnetDataEntry one more time.

First we create the HRnetDataEntryNew Web form, inheriting from HRnet-DataEntry. Here are the changes for its code page:

```
'We want to overwrite the Save function totally.
Public Overrides Sub Save()
    MessageBox.Show("ApplicationBaseDataEntry Subclass Save Clicked")
    MyBase.EditMode(False)
End Sub
```

This code overrides the base form's *Save* method totally, first calling a new *Save* method (that's the message box that will need to be replaced with a middle-tier call) and then exiting the edit mode of the page. When you create data entry forms for the HRnet Windows Forms part of the application, you just need to inherit from one of these two data forms and add the actual calls to the business logic.

These short examples have shown how simple but powerful inheritance can be. Don't believe the nay sayers and miss the opportunities offered by Visual Basic .NET, which now supports all .NET OOP features.

Calling Code from Web Pages and Windows Forms

ASP.NET and Visual Basic .NET make it very easy to add additional code in their respective code-behind or code pages. It's extremely tempting to put business logic in these places, but remember the lessons you learned in Chapter 2, in which we talked about proper architecture, and also remember the painful lessons of the past, when you wrote applications that violated that important rule of separating and encapsulating code. We urge you not to put business logic and data access code within these pages. The only exception to this rule should be the handling of client-side validation, or in the case of Web pages, the handling of client-side or server-side validation. In Chapter 11, in which we create the information pages, we have many examples of this.

Conclusion

We started this chapter looking for the best possible way to allow code reuse both with Web Forms and Windows Forms. We found that Windows Forms allows us to use visual inheritance, which is very flexible and efficient for code reuse. We also found that the same functionality is not readily available in Web Forms technology. Either we have to settle for templates that use copy-and-paste functionality to create new Web form pages or we have to create a non-visual template that creates a templated Web form programmatically. Both of these approaches have advantages and disadvantages. The decision to use a certain approach depends on the requirements of your Web application and what you feel comfortable using. It's clear that Microsoft and the creators of ASP.NET have some work left to do to make full visual inheritance come true within the Web environment.

Now that we have the basic building blocks for the HRnet application, we'll create the information pages that make HRnet come alive. We're going to design a user interface and information-page strategy. With this strategy in place, we'll build custom controls that help us encapsulate a lot of the desired behavior. We'll use the controls and components we built in previous chapters, giving us several options for presenting and working with data-driven Web pages.

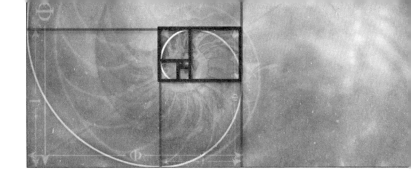

11

Building Information Pages

Information pages are to applications what wheels are to cars: they keep the system moving. Without information pages in which actual data is presented, added, changed, or deleted, there is no application. In this chapter, we create templates of information pages that represent HRnet's data structure. We'll discuss user interface strategies for data access and establish a standards-based approach to viewing and manipulating data. Then we'll create the custom server and user controls that bring these strategies to life. As with the solutions presented in other chapters, you'll be able to reuse these components immediately and also know how to manipulate them to suit your particular needs.

Even though information pages aren't limited to data presentation pages, we're going to cover only data-related information. General Web design, including the process of determining whether to use graphics and which graphics to use, isn't part of this discussion. We generally employ Web design specialists who bring us ideas and graphics that create the look and feel of our Web applications. Other than providing color schemes and recommending how to fit data pages into the general Web application concept, these designers don't touch data-related information pages.

When talking about user interface strategies, we need to remember that the way we present and accept data has as much influence on the success of our Web applications as does correct business logic and attractive design. Even though we constantly hear that we shouldn't judge a book by its cover, it's human nature to judge things by appearance first. (Incidentally, we like the new covers Microsoft is presenting with this generation of books!) When you create an application that has complex and cluttered data representation pages, customers don't want to use it. If your customers are casual Internet users, you'll lose them to the competition. If they are internal customers such as employees or business-to-business intranet partners, you'll have an uphill battle getting the application accepted; even worse, productivity could suffer. Well-designed data presentation pages that are simple to look at and simple to use, and whose functionality is consistent and easy to master, will be winners every time. Let's discuss this a bit more.

A Bit of User Interface Strategy

Have you ever worked with the data pages of an application or a Web application that drove you crazy? Was too much data on one screen? Was it difficult to add data? Was it hard to navigate to a specific record? Was it intuitive? Was there enough validation? Did the pages interact with you? Did the pages have simple instructions when needed? Do you remember the applications you didn't have a positive experience with? Do you remember their names or URLs if they were Internet applications? To address these kinds of negative experiences, you need to ask yourself several questions as you design the layout of data pages: How do we get people to use our applications? What can we do to help them want to come back? How do we set ourselves apart from other applications? Here is a list of data-presentation user interface design goals that begin to answer these questions.

- **Easy to read**   Don't overload the screen with too many fields and options. Decide what data needs to be presented and leave out unnecessary data. (If possible, show conditional data fields only.) Follow the natural flow of data entry fields, for example, left to right, with related data grouped together.

- **Simple to use**   Allow for easy navigation. Avoid deep menu structures. Don't offer too many choices at once.

- **Consistent**   Be consistent in the way you present data. Use the same way of adding, deleting, editing, and saving data.

- **Visually easy to follow**   Lead the eye. Examples of visual clues that help guide the reader are automatic highlighting the current field, highlighting errors, and providing automatic help pop-ups when validation rules apply.

- **Straightforward**   Offer a simple menu structure. Provide well-placed find and sort fields.

- **Helpful**   Allow for an automatic help system. Offer in-place help where possible.

We also standardized data presentation using the list/detail approach, as shown in Figure 11-1.

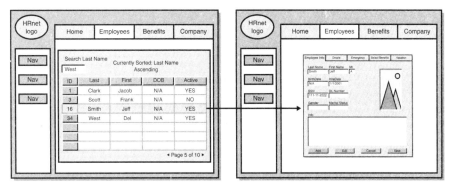

Figure 11-1   List/detail data presentation with two forms

When presenting data, we start with a data list first and then show the detailed page of data when it's requested, or when adding or editing. Additional options for finding data, sorting data, and paging are available in our list-based screens. A list-based screen allows the user to find specific data quickly and navigate to a more complete presentation of the data. When the data to present has a small number of fields, we combine the data list and detail information on one form, as shown in Figure 11-2. We'll cover this combination approach in more detail shortly.

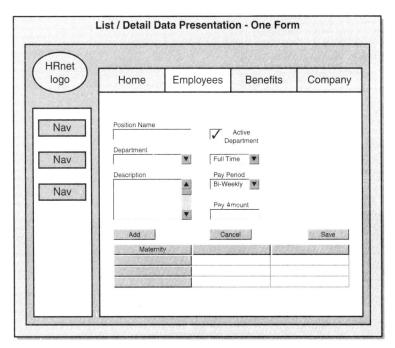

Figure 11-2   List/detail data presentation with one form

Web-Based vs. Windows-Based Data Presentation Forms

When talking to fellow developers, we often find that they adopt either Web-based applications or Windows-based applications, but not both. During the last year, many developers seemed to be following the Web-based application trend, even those creating smaller applications that will be used internally. We think you should keep an open mind. Each approach has distinct advantages and disadvantages, and knowing what they are will allow you to make better choices. It will also allow you to create more functional applications. You should also consider that Windows Forms can easily be integrated into Web applications when you control the environment or write smaller intranet applications. The base requirement for Windows Forms pages in Web applications is the presence of the Microsoft .NET Framework on the client systems. Table 11-1 compares Web Forms and Windows Forms.

Table 11-1   Web Forms vs. Windows Forms

Technology	Advantages	Disadvantages
Web Forms	No client install necessary	State management
	Great dynamic control over user interface	Can cause slow response times
	Changes on server automatically reflect on clients	Disconnected nature (Difficult to allow server to pass event notification to Web Forms)
	Forces disconnected data approach, which inherently improves scalability	
Windows Forms	Fast	Requires .NET Framework on the client
	Easier to create than Web Forms	Dynamic user interface is more limited and harder to create
	Constant connectivity to the server (Easy event notification to client; real-time processing possible)	

Many of the data presentation principles discussed in this chapter will fit both Web Forms and Windows Forms applications. This chapter is dedicated to the creation of information pages in Web Forms. In Chapter 14, we'll show some of the same features in Windows Forms.

Data Presentation Forms

We mentioned previously that we adopted the list/detail–based data presentation approach. It's aligned with the way the brain processes information: from general information to details. For example, when looking at a telephone book, we tend to look for the last name of the person we're looking for. We do this iteratively. When we look for the name *Eberhard*, we start with the first occurrence of *E*, move to *b*, *e*, and so on until we find the name. Then we can find the rest of the information associated with the name. How do we best represent this process in data presentation forms? The answer is the DataGrid. In Web Forms applications, we use ASP.NET's DataGrid control (a highly customized version that we're going to develop shortly), and in Windows Forms, its equivalent. ASP.NET has two other choices for list-based data presentation: the Repeater control and the DataList control. Even though both controls can present data in a list, we chose the DataGrid control. It has more built-in functionality and the flexibility we need to create the list portion of our data presentation forms. Figure 11-3 compares the data bound list controls in ASP.NET.

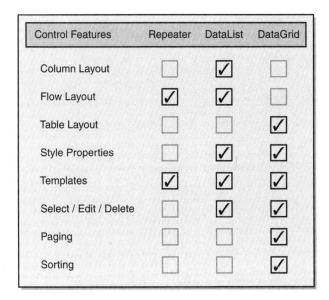

Control Features	Repeater	DataList	DataGrid
Column Layout		✓	
Flow Layout	✓	✓	
Table Layout			✓
Style Properties		✓	✓
Templates	✓	✓	✓
Select / Edit / Delete		✓	✓
Paging			✓
Sorting			✓

Figure 11-3   Comparison of ASP.NET list controls

ASP.NET DataGrid Control for List Forms

The ASP.NET DataGrid control is a very powerful list presentation tool. It has many properties and methods. It also allows for additional customization so that we can add the features we want. Here is our wish list for our enhanced DataGrid:

- Ability to drag and drop the custom DataGrid control we'll create from the Microsoft Visual Studio .NET Toolbox
- Consistent custom view
- Declarative and programmatic column creation
- Customized edit, add, and delete functions
- Normal and custom paging
- Custom sorting with easy visual clues
- Filter/search options

We also want to easily turn the custom properties on and off. Figure 11-4 shows you a design layout of the DataGrid we want to create.

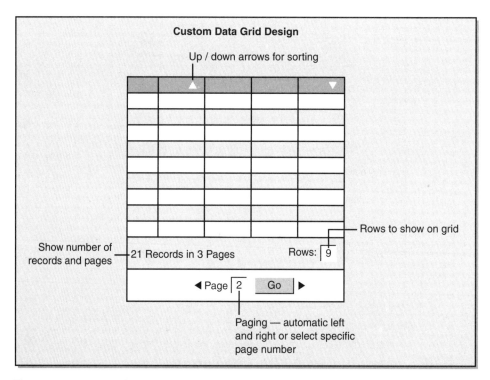

Figure 11-4 HRnet Custom DataGrid server control design

To allow this kind of flexibility and power, we're going to create a custom ASP.NET DataGrid server control. In Chapter 6 we created some basic custom server controls. We're going to take the principles covered there to the next level as we create our HRGrid custom server controls. We'll do this in a step-by-step approach, adding one major feature at a time. This approach will enable you to understand each addition thoroughly so that you can customize the control. We'll start with the ASP.NET default DataGrid control.

We won't cover the details of the ASP.NET DataGrid control's features. Instead, we'll quickly move through an overview of the control and then start adding the features we need. The files are in the InformationPages sample files that accompany this book. The project has references to the business layer created in Chapter 8, the data access layer created in Chapter 4, and the security layer from Chapter 5. The Menu.aspx Web Forms page will allow you to run all samples. Let's take a look at DefaultGrid.aspx. We used drag-and-drop functionality to create an instance of the ASP.NET DataGrid control. Here is the result in HTML:

```
<asp:DataGrid id="DataGrid1" runat="server"></asp:DataGrid>
```

These are the default settings of ASP.NET. Besides the ID of the DataGrid control, no other properties, events, and methods are set here. Now let's move to the code-behind page:

```
Imports Ch8BusinessLayerObjects.BusinessLayer
Public Class DefaultGrid
    Inherits System.Web.UI.Page
    Protected WithEvents DataGrid1 As System.Web.UI.WebControls.DataGrid


#Region " Web Form Designer Generated Code " #End Region


    Private Sub Page_Load(ByVal sender As System.Object, _
        ByVal e As System.EventArgs) Handles MyBase.Load
        'Put user code to initialize the page here
        If Not IsPostBack Then
            'Create the dataset to be bound to the datagrid.
            Dim localAllEmployees As New DataSet()
            'Call the business layer.
            Dim localCompany As New Company("default", "password")
            localAllEmployees = localCompany.GetCompanyEmployees(1)
            DataGrid1.DataSource =
                    localAllEmployees.Tables("Employees").DefaultView
            Page.DataBind()
        End If
    End Sub


End Class
```

To populate the datagrid, we use a dataset. It or any of its tables can be bound directly to a DataGrid control.

> **Note**   Data binding in Visual Studio .NET is very different from data binding in earlier versions of Microsoft Visual Basic. When you bound data directly to a grid or text box, you bound it to a connected database. This is *not* the case with data binding in ASP.NET and Microsoft Visual Basic .NET using Microsoft ADO.NET! The DataSet is an in-memory object on the server, and data binding just hooks it to the specific ASP.NET control—in this case, the DataGrid control. You're no longer connected to the database and any updates, deletions, or additions have to be taken care of separately (including potential conflict resolutions).

> **Note**   To allow the functionality of many default features in the DataGrid control such as paging and sorting, we need to pass it a dataset. A DataGrid control can also bind the results of a DataReader control, disallowing the use of these special features. A lot of developers might have heard that the DataReader is much faster than the DataSet. This is correct; however, there are a number of disadvantages when using the DataReader that limit its use significantly. One of these is the DataReader's requirement of an open connection until the last row of data is read. This can cause connections to stay open for relatively long periods of time. Forgetting to close these connections can be detrimental to Web servers and their resources. Also, passing data through *n*-tier layers is almost impossible with the DataReader. The DataSet is the best choice to use for passing data in Visual Studio .NET unless very large databases are accessed. We'll talk about this at the end of this chapter.

In the first line of the previous code, notice we import our *BusinessLayer* object. It handles security, data connection, the calling of stored procedures, and so on. All we need to worry about in the user interface is the receipt of correct data. During the creation of the Web Forms application, we call the business layer and populate the DataGrid. Let's look at the code that makes this happen:

```
'Create the dataset to be bound to the datagrid.
Dim localAllEmployees As New DataSet()
'Call the business layer.
Dim localCompany As New Company("default", "password")
localAllEmployees = localCompany.GetCompanyEmployees(1)
DataGrid1.DataSource =
      localAllEmployees.Tables("Employees").DefaultView
Page.DataBind()
```

After we declare a local dataset named *localAllEmployees*, we declare a new instance of the *Company* class, named *localCompany*, that resides in the business layer. Notice that we pass our security credentials to the business component. We can do this either as shown by passing name and password or by passing a security object. We hard-coded the security credentials in these examples for simplicity. Now we can access one of the methods in the *Company* class. It's name is *GetCompanyEmployees*. Given a company ID, again hard-coded here for simplicity, the method returns all employees of that company, both active and inactive. We could bind the resulting DataSet directly to the grid as follows:

```
DataGrid1.DataSource = localAllEmployees
```

The DataGrid will find the only DataTable inside the DataSet automatically and call this DataTable's default view. We much prefer to call the table directly, especially because some business layer methods might return more than one table in a DataSet. Here is our preferred code:

```
DataGrid1.DataSource = localAllEmployees.Tables("Employees").DefaultView
```

That's all there is to it. Take the time to run this example.

You can see that, by default, the DataGrid control returns all rows and all fields in the table. The result isn't very pretty, nor is the presentation of the data formatted. Notice that Boolean results are shown as True and False, the column headers are the data field's description, and the format is rather bland. This presentation, however, can be changed by adding and modifying a couple of properties.

Customizing the Default ASP.NET DataGrid Control

Let's take a look at the second example, CustomizedGrid.aspx. It represents two datagrids. The first one is named CustomGrid1. We used the DataGrid control's property builder to change attributes and properties, even though you can enter them directly in HTML. The code-behind page has virtually no changes, only an additional line of code that binds the returning dataset to the second grid. Let's take a look at the HTML code for CustomGrid1:

```
<asp:datagrid id="CustomGrid1" runat="server" BorderColor="Navy"
    BorderWidth="2px" AutoGenerateColumns="False">
<AlternatingItemStyle BackColor="AliceBlue"></AlternatingItemStyle>
<HeaderStyle Font-Size="Small" Font-Names="Verdana" Font-Bold="True"
    BackColor="#3399CC"></HeaderStyle>
<Columns>
    <asp:BoundColumn DataField="EmployeeID"
        HeaderText="ID"></asp:BoundColumn>
    <asp:BoundColumn DataField="LastName"
        HeaderText="Last Name"></asp:BoundColumn>
    <asp:BoundColumn DataField="FirstName"
        HeaderText="First Name"></asp:BoundColumn>
    <asp:BoundColumn DataField="MI" HeaderText="MI"></asp:BoundColumn>
</Columns>
</asp:datagrid>
```

All the changes we made are done declaratively. As we call the DataGrid control, we set *BorderColor* and *Width*. One of the more important settings is *AutoGenerateColumns="False"*. This setting means that the DataGrid control won't create its own columns; we have to do the work ourselves. Next comes the definition of *AlternatingItemStyle*. Since we set the value of *BackColor* to alternate colors, we'll get the checkerboard effect of alternating background colors in the grid. Next, we define the style for the header. See Table 11-2 for a list of graphical items available in the DataGrid control. Each item represents a row in the DataGrid control.

Table 11-2 Graphical Items in the DataGrid Control

Name	Data Bound?	Style Property	Description
Header	No	*HeaderStyle*	First row in datagrid
Footer	No	*FooterStyle*	Last row in datagrid
Item	Yes	*ItemStyle*	Normal row
AlternatingItem	Yes	*AlternatingItemStyle*	Odd numbered rows
SelectedItem	Yes	*SelectedItemStyle*	Currently selected item or items
EditItem	Yes	*EditItemStyle*	Item in edit mode
Separator	No		Separates rows
Pager	No	*PagerStyle*	Bar at bottom of datagrid

After setting the general and visual options of the DataGrid control, we add one of the DataGrid's most useful items: custom data bound columns. You can see that we define both the header text and the data field for each data bound column. There are a total of five column types you can choose from to create custom data bound columns. See Table 11-3 for an alphabetical listing of column types.

Table 11-3   Column Types for the DataGrid Control

Column Type	Description
BoundColumn	Plain text of a bound data field.
ButtonColumn	Command button for each item in column. Its name is common to the column. Its text property can be data bound. If its name is *Select*, its row can be clicked to be selected.
EditCommandColumn	Creates a button column with Edit command. When clicked, datagrid is redrawn with default or custom templates for editing.
HyperLinkColumn	Hyperlink for each item in column. Its text and target URL can be data bound. (Supports target frame.)
TemplateColumn	A template replaces the plaintext field of the BoundColumn.

The second datagrid on the sample Web Forms page is CustomGrid2. We created its look and feel by using the DataGrid control's AutoFormat feature. We chose the Colorful4 selection. You can see that the settings in HTML are similar to the ones we have chosen previously, with a couple of additions. Figure 11-5 shows the customized DataGrid control. You can see how easy it is to create a good-looking DataGrid. Now let's see how easy it is to add functionality.

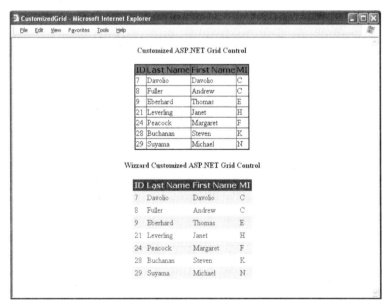

Figure 11-5   Customized ASP.NET DataGrid control

Adding Functionality to a Custom DataGrid Control

We're now ready to create a custom DataGrid server control and encapsulate the behavior we've seen and liked. Then we'll add the desired features.

In the InformationPages solution, provided in the sample files for this book, we added the HRGrids Web Control Library. We renamed the default file WebCustomControl1.vb to DefaultHRGrid.vb and changed the control's code as follows:

```
Imports System.ComponentModel
Imports System.Web.UI
Imports System.Web.UI.WebControls
Imports System.Drawing

Namespace CustomDataGrids

    <DefaultProperty("Text"), ToolboxData( _
    "<{0}:DefaultHRGrid runat=server></{0}:DefaultHRGrid>")> _
    Public Class DefaultHRGrid
        Inherits System.Web.UI.WebControls.DataGrid

#Region "Grid Constructors" #End Region

    End Class
End Namespace
```

If you need to refresh your memory about how to create custom server controls, refer to Chapter 6. Besides renaming the control in the preceding code, we added two additional, important namespaces: the *System.Web.UI.Controls*, in which all default ASP.NET controls reside; and *System.Drawing* for color processing. We named this DataGrid control DefaultHRGrid *(name of the class)* and included it in the *CustomDataGrids* namespace.

Now we want to add default properties and attributes to the DefaultHRGrid. We need to set this information in the constructor of this class. If we set it anywhere else, we can no longer access this control's properties in its properties toolbox or its HTML tags. Here are the settings in the Grid Constructor region:

```
#Region "Grid Constructors"
Public Sub New()
    'Set DataGrid Paging
    PagerStyle.Mode = PagerMode.NextPrev
    PagerStyle.ForeColor = Color.FromArgb(74, 60, 140)
    PagerStyle.BackColor = Color.FromArgb(231, 231, 255)
```

```
    PagerStyle.PageButtonCount = 10
    PagerStyle.HorizontalAlign = HorizontalAlign.Right
    AllowPaging = True
    PageSize = 4
    'Visual Settings
    GridLines = GridLines.None
    CellSpacing = 0
    CellPadding = 3
    BorderColor = Color.FromArgb(231, 231, 255)
    BorderStyle = BorderStyle.Solid
    BorderWidth = Unit.Pixel(1)
    ForeColor = Color.Black
    Font.Size = FontUnit.XSmall
    Font.Name = "Verdana"
    'Settings for Normal Rows
    ItemStyle.ForeColor = Color.FromArgb(74, 60, 140)
    ItemStyle.BackColor = Color.FromArgb(231, 231, 255)
    'Settings for Alternating Rows
    AlternatingItemStyle.BackColor = Color.FromArgb(247, 247, 247)
    'Settings for Selected Rows
    SelectedItemStyle.ForeColor = Color.FromArgb(247, 247, 247)
    SelectedItemStyle.BackColor = Color.FromArgb(115, 138, 156)
    'Settings for Heading
    HeaderStyle.Font.Name = "Veranda"
    HeaderStyle.Font.Bold = True
    HeaderStyle.ForeColor = Color.FromArgb(247, 247, 247)
    HeaderStyle.BackColor = Color.FromArgb(74, 60, 140)
    HeaderStyle.HorizontalAlign = HorizontalAlign.Center
    'Settings for Footer
    FooterStyle.ForeColor = Color.FromArgb(74, 60, 140)
    FooterStyle.BackColor = Color.FromArgb(181, 199, 222)
End Sub
#End Region
```

Notice that we have basically taken the settings of our previous example's DataGrid control, which was created with *AutoStyle*, and filled the properties programmatically. In the DefaultHRGrid.aspx sample Web Forms page, we implemented the new custom server control twice—once with the standard settings for page navigation (previous and next buttons), and once with the page navigation's *PagerStyle* mode set to *numeric*. After we register the *HRGrid* namespace and assembly, we're ready to use our custom DataGrid server control. Here's the registration in the DefaultHRGrid.aspx Web Forms HTML:

```
<%@ Register TagPrefix="cc1" Namespace="HRGrids.CustomDataGrids"
    Assembly="HRGrids" %>
```

And now the code for the first DefaultHRGrid control:

```
<ccl:DefaultHRGrid id="DefaultHRGrid1" onpageindexchanged="DefaultHRGrid1Page"
runat="server">
  <Columns>
    <asp:BoundColumn DataField="EmployeeID"
      HeaderText="ID"></asp:BoundColumn>
    <asp:BoundColumn DataField="Last Name"
      HeaderText="LastName"></asp:BoundColumn>
    <asp:BoundColumn DataField="FirstName"
      HeaderText="First Name"></asp:BoundColumn>
    <asp:BoundColumn DataField="Active"
      HeaderText="Active"></asp:BoundColumn>
  </Columns>
</ccl:DefaultHRGrid>
```

You can see that we called only the custom DataGrid server control. Besides the bound columns for the data fields and the action to be taken when the page is changed (the *OnPageIndexChanged* method raises the *PageIndexChanged* event, which we direct to the *DefaultHRGrid1Page* method in the code-behind page), no other properties are set. Yet we inherit the look and feel we defined in the DefaultHRGrid control. When you run the sample file, notice that the second grid uses numbers for pagination instead of the previous and next arrows. The only line of HTML that needs to be added is this:

```
<PagerStyle Mode="NumericPages"></PagerStyle>
```

Both pagination and sorting of the DataGrid come at some expense: you need to write code to implement them. In our example we added this code line to the sample's code-behind page. We did so not just to show you how it's done but because it's the stepping stone to implementing the same functionality within a custom DataGrid server control. Let's take a look at the code-behind page. We created a subroutine named *UpdateDataView* that collects the data through the business layer and stores it in a session variable the first time it is accessed. Thereafter it pulls the information from the session variable to avoid further round trips to the data server. Once the data is present, it is bound to both custom DataGrid server controls.

We mentioned the *OnPageIndexChanged* method that raises the *PageIndexChanged* event. You saw that we assigned *DefaultHRGrid1Page*, which resides in the code-behind page, to handle the event as shown here:

```
Protected Sub DefaultHRGrid1Page(ByVal sender As Object, _
    ByVal e As DataGridPageChangedEventArgs)
    DefaultHRGrid1.CurrentPageIndex = e.NewPageIndex
    UpdateDataView()
End Sub
```

> **Note**   We are fully aware of the disputes that might arise between developers when using session variables, and even more so from storing a DataSet in them. We'll cover the advantages and disadvantages of this approach later in this chapter and present you with different options to persist or not persist data this way. We'll also discuss the delicate balance between performance and scalability that each approach achieves and give you some options for creating this balance. For now, let's continue to use DataSets and session variables.

Notice right away that we declared this method protected and not private, even though you typically see private methods in code-behind pages. The *Private* keyword restricts access to elements defined in the code-behind page only, which won't help us here since the method that needs to access the *DefaultHRGrid1Page* subroutine lies within the default DataGrid control. The *Protected* keyword will allow other members of this class access and allows the permission needed.

Next we need to set the DataGrid's *CurrentPageIndex* to the new page index returned from the *OnPageIndexChanged* event. You might at first think this setting would be automatic. However, making it automatic would make it impossible to control pagination programmatically when we implement custom solutions.

After this setting change, we need to re-bind the data to both datagrids. This is important to note. The DataGrid control does *not* maintain its *DataSource* in *ViewState*. It caches only its setting and attributes in the page's *ViewState*. If it cached its *DataSource*, the *ViewState* could be enormously big with the return of large datasets, and pages would load very slowly, wasting valuable bandwidth of the Internet or local networks.

Take the time to run this example and use the pagination features of both grids. Even though the results are pretty impressive as is, we'd like to encapsulate the paging functionality inside the custom DataGrid server control. Ultimately, it would be great to just bind the *DataSet* to the control and let the control handle everything else. This is exactly what we'll accomplish next.

First let's take a look at how we pulled the previous example's code-behind page for pagination into the DefaultHRPageGrid custom server control. Since we need to process the *PageIndexChanged* event internally, we need to add an event handler for it. This is done as part of the custom server control's constructor and is actually the only line of code we need to add to the constructor of our previous control. Here it is:

```
AddHandler PageIndexChanged, AddressOf OnPageIndexChanged
```

The event *PageIndexChanged* is delegated to the *OnPageIndexChanged* method. Let's take a look at what we have to do with the *OnPageIndex-Changed* method. Here's the code for it:

```
Public Shadows Sub OnPageIndexChanged( _
    ByVal sender As Object, ByVal e As DataGridPageChangedEventArgs)
    CurrentPageIndex = e.NewPageIndex
    DataBind()
End Sub 'OnPageIndexChanged
```

We declared the *OnPageIndexChanged* method as *Public* and with the *Shadows* keyword. We made it public so that we could invoke it directly from the calling page if needed. We shadow this method so that we can use the same name and arguments of the base class without using the actual base class itself, as you would with inheritance. The rest of the code is similar to what we had in the code-behind page. Our example that uses this custom server control is DefaultHRPageGrid.aspx. We used the same implementation of the subroutine named *UpdateDataView* to access data. In this example's code-behind page, there is only a slight change. Remember we mentioned that datagrids do not persist data themselves. This is why we need to bind data to the custom Data-Grid server control on every postback. When you run this example, you can see it behaving exactly as our previous example.

We've shown you how easy it is to pull functionality into the *DataGrid* class. Next we want to enhance its functionality. We want to add the following features:

■ Change the right and left angle brackets to more sophisticated graphics.

■ Add a footer that shows the number of records returned and the number of pages in the datagrid.

■ Add TextBox and Button controls to allow jumping to a specific page and to show the current page.

■ Add ToolTip information for the items in this list.

Adding Better Graphics

The custom DataGrid server control's name that shows the enhanced pager bar is called DefaultHRPageGridPlus. First, we're going to change the left and right angle brackets to arrows. We find that when we use the Webdings font, number 3 represents a left arrow and number 4 a right arrow. Fortunately, the default DataGrid control allows us to assign custom text to the previous and next page items. We added the following lines of code within the Set DataGrid Paging area of the constructor:

```
Dim leftArrow As String = _
    "<span style='font-family:webdings;font-size:medium;'>3</span>"
Dim rightArrow As String = _
    "<span style='font-family:webdings;font-size:medium;'>4</span>"
PagerStyle.PrevPageText = leftArrow
PagerStyle.NextPageText = rightArrow
```

Changing the Footer

Next we're going to add the footer that displays all current records returned as well as the number of pages in the DataGrid. This will take a bit more effort. In the constructor, we set the *ShowFooter* property to *true* so that it will be displayed:

```
ShowFooter = True
```

Now we need to change the standard footer to our custom footer. To understand the process required, we first need to look at what the datagrid is and how it is created. The datagrid is a table with rows and columns. In Table 11-2, we presented a list of graphical items available in the DataGrid control. Each one of these represents a specific kind of row in the datagrid. ASP.NET builds these items one piece at the time by adding controls that represent the columns and Web controls inside the columns of each item row. The result is a table with headers, items, alternating items, a footer, and so on. The DataGrid control's footer is just another row with columns. The default behavior of the footer is to present a column for each data item. You can look at this like a reverse header. This, however, isn't what we want in our custom footer. We want only one column (Table Cell) and one label within this cell that represents the data we want to present: the number of data rows and the number of pages in our datagrid. Fortunately, the designers of ASP.NET realized that someone might want to customize the individual items of the datagrid. Every time a datagrid item is created, the *ItemCreated* event is raised. The *OnItemCreated* method is then available to us, so we can check for a specific item that was created and change its column and Web control objects as needed. We'll now show you how this is done. We recommend that you study this process thoroughly as the same process is used for many of the other changes we'll make. Understanding this process will also help you to integrate future changes.

In the same way we previously added an internal event handler for the *PageIndexChanged* event, we'll add a handler for the *ItemCreated* event and point it to the *OnItemCreated* method. Here's the code within the control's constructor:

```
    ⋮
    AddHandler ItemCreated, AddressOf OnItemCreated
    AddHandler PageIndexChanged, AddressOf OnPageIndexChanged
End Sub
```

With the handler added, we can shadow the *OnItemCreated* method and add our own implementation. Here's the code in its entirety:

```
Public Shadows Sub OnItemCreated(ByVal sender As Object, _
    ByVal e As DataGridItemEventArgs)
    Dim itemType As ListItemType = e.Item.ItemType

    If itemType = ListItemType.Footer Then
        Dim footerRow As TableCellCollection = e.Item.Cells
        Dim footerCellCount As Integer = footerRow.Count

        Dim i As Integer
        For i = footerCellCount - 1 To 0 Step -1
            e.Item.Cells.RemoveAt(i)
        Next

        Dim newCell As New TableCell()
        newCell.ColumnSpan = footerCellCount
        newCell.HorizontalAlign = HorizontalAlign.Left

        Dim labelReturnRows As New Label()
        Dim totalRows As Integer
        Try
            labelReturnRows.Text = "This is Page " + _
                CType(CurrentPageIndex + 1, String) + " of " + _
                CType(PageCount, String) + " Pages."
        Catch
        End Try

        newCell.Controls.Add(labelReturnRows)
        e.Item.Cells.Add(newCell)
    End If

    If itemType = ListItemType.Pager Then
        Dim cellPager As TableCell = e.Item.Cells(0)
        Dim cellControls As ControlCollection = cellPager.Controls
        Dim leftArrow As WebControl = CType(cellControls(0), WebControl)
        leftArrow.ToolTip = "Previous Record"
        Dim rightArrow As WebControl = CType(cellControls(2), WebControl)
        rightArrow.ToolTip = "Next Record"
```

```
            cellPager.HorizontalAlign = HorizontalAlign.Center
    End If
End Sub
```

Let's take a closer look at each part of this code. When *ItemCreated* is raised and our *OnItemCreated* method called, the event passed is of the *DataGridItemEventArgs* type. This means it carries the name of its *ListItemType*. The one we're looking for is the footer. Here's the code for this:

```
Public Shadows Sub OnItemCreated(ByVal sender As Object, _
    ByVal e As DataGridItemEventArgs)
    Dim itemType As ListItemType = e.Item.ItemType

    If itemType = ListItemType.Footer Then
    ⋮
```

When the footer item is found, we want to get access to its control collections. Since the footer is a table row, its immediate collection contains its table cells. Remember that by default there are as many footer cells as there are columns. For this reason, we need to erase them all and create only one. Before we can do this, we need to know the number of cells in the footer and then we need to remove them. We accomplish this task by declaring the *footerRow* variable as a *TableCellCollection* and assigning it the current row's cells. Once this is done, *footerRow* can return its cell count as follows:

```
Dim footerRow As TableCellCollection = e.Item.Cells
Dim footerCellCount As Integer = footerRow.Count
```

Now we can count down the cells one by one and erase them. In order to avoid a false reference, we start removing the highest cell control first and counting down until none are left (remember that these collections are zero-based):

```
Dim i As Integer
For i = footerCellCount - 1 To 0 Step -1
    e.Item.Cells.RemoveAt(i)
Next
```

We're left with an empty footer row and need to add a new table cell. We also need to make sure that it will have a column span of the full original cell count, so it will use the full width of the DataGrid control. In addition, we give the footer alignment instructions:

```
Dim newCell As New TableCell()
newCell.ColumnSpan = footerCellCount
newCell.HorizontalAlign = HorizontalAlign.Left
```

Now that we have a new cell, we're ready to add a Label control and assign the current page index as well as the page count to it. The code for this is straightforward and should be familiar to us:

```
Dim labelReturnRows As New Label()
Dim totalRows As Integer
Try
    labelReturnRows.Text = "This is Page " + _
        CType(CurrentPageIndex + 1, String) + " of " + _
        CType(PageCount, String) + " Pages."
Catch
End Try
```

We added exception handling because without it, we experienced some irregular behavior when instantiating the DataGrid control. We assume that the first time the *OnItemCreated* method runs, no values for the *CurrentPage-Index* and *PageCount* are assigned, causing these errors. After trapping the exception, we had no more problems. All we have left to do is add the *label-ReturnRows* Label control to the new cell and then the cell to the footer row control, as follows:

```
newCell.Controls.Add(labelReturnRows)
e.Item.Cells.Add(newCell)
```

We now have a footer that represents the total number of records and pages shown in the custom DataGrid server control.

The additional code in the *OnItemCreated* method deals with adding ToolTips to the left and right pager controls. In the same way we added code when *OnItemCreated* was raised after the footer was created, we add code for the datagrid's pager item. We know that the pager item contains only one table cell, which contains the controls for the left and right navigation. For this reason, we need to create only a control collection for the controls inside this one table cell. Here is the code:

```
If itemType = ListItemType.Pager Then
    Dim cellPager As TableCell = e.Item.Cells(0)
    Dim cellControls As ControlCollection = cellPager.Controls
```

Once we have the *cellControls* collection, we need to find the two controls that contain the left and right arrows. By trial and error, we found out that the left navigation is handled in the first control (remember that is 0) and the right navigation is handled in the third control (that is, 2 in the zero-based collection). But how do we get to the control's *ToolTip* property? It's easy. We know that these reuse controls are derived from the Web control. Therefore we can cast their type as that of Web control, which gives us access to the *ToolTip* property. Here's how we accomplished this:

```
Dim cellPager As TableCell = e.Item.Cells(0)
Dim cellControls As ControlCollection = cellPager.Controls
Dim leftArrow As WebControl = CType(cellControls(0), WebControl)
leftArrow.ToolTip = "Previous Record"
Dim rightArrow As WebControl = CType(cellControls(2), WebControl)
rightArrow.ToolTip = "Next Record"
```

Let's test the changes we made in DefaultHRPageGridPlus.aspx. Figure 11-6 shows the results as well as the ToolTip for the next record.

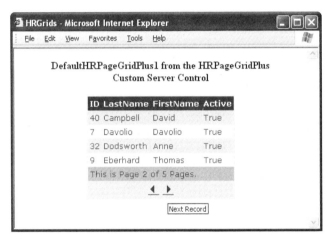

Figure 11-6   Customized ASP.NET DataGrid control with custom paging and footer

Adding the *GoTo* Function

In our next example, we're going to add TextBox and Button controls. We want to be able to enter a page number, validate it, and on the Button control's *Click* event, navigate directly to that page. You probably already guessed that we'll add these items in the *OnItemCreated* method. Before we do that, we need to take care of another challenge. When we add controls such as TextBox controls to the DataGrid, the DataGrid won't automatically maintain the controls' states on post-backs. We could use an elaborate way of finding the unique IDs for the DataGrid and its controls and then create a ViewState for them that we could use later on, but this would mean lot of unnecessary code. We've found a great workaround that will come in very handy when we add sorting and filtering to the DataGrid: adding a *DataGrid* property that allows the *DataSource* property to be handled internally. Even though we still have to set the *DataSource* property on every postback, changes are handled internally before a postback is called. This way, before the postback is processed, we have access to the control's properties in any methods we create internally that manipulate data processing. This workaround sounds more complicated than it actually is. Let's step through the process of adding the required items. The DefaultHRPageGridPlusMore custom DataGrid server control contains all the code for this and we use the Default-HRPagePlusMore.aspx Web Forms page to test the new functions.

First we add the Private Variable And Objects region to the server control, declaring the *DataSet*, *DataView*, *TableName*, and *TextBox* variables we'll use inside the DataGrid server control:

```
#Region "Private Variables and Objects"
    Dim internalDataSet As DataSet
    Dim internalDataView As DataView
    Dim internalTableName As String
    Protected WithEvents textPage As New TextBox()
    Protected WithEvents labelError as New Label()
#End Region
```

Next we add the Public Properties region, which defines the properties that allow the passing of the *DataSet* and an optional *TableName* property:

```
#Region "Public Grid Properties"
    Public Property GridDataSet() As DataSet
        Get
            Return internalDataSet
        End Get
        Set(ByVal Value As DataSet)
            internalDataSet = Value
        End Set
    End Property

    Public Property GridTable() As String
        Get
            Return internalTableName
        End Get
        Set(ByVal Value As String)
            internalTableName = Value
        End Set
    End Property

    Public ReadOnly Property ErrorMessage() as String
        Get
            Return Attributes("ErrorMessage")
        End Get
    End Property
#End Region
```

> **Tip**   We discussed earlier that Web controls persist their attributes in *ViewState*. Instead of using complicated *ViewState* management when we need to store string information, we can add *Attributes* to the control to automatically take care of state management.

Now we're going to add the *Update* method. It will pull the *internalData-View* from the DataSet passed to the *GridDataSet* property after checking whether a *TableName* was passed. We're putting this function call within an exception handling block in case no *DataSet* is passed. Here is the code:

```
#Region "Update() - Internal Data Update"
    Public Sub Update()
        Try
            If internalTableName = Nothing Then
                internalDataView = internalDataSet.Tables(0).DefaultView
            Else
                internalDataView = _
                    internalDataSet.Tables(internalTableName).DefaultView
            End If
            DataSource = internalDataView
            DataBind()
        Catch
            DataBind()   'Calling DataBind will avoid an error
                         'and return an empty grid.
        End Try
    End Sub
#End Region
```

We're ready to add more controls to the pager area of the *OnItemCreated* method. Here's the code that's inserted:

```
If itemType = ListItemType.Pager Then
    ⋮
    textPage.ID = "textPageID"
    textPage.Width = Unit.Pixel(30)
    textPage.Text = CType((CurrentPageIndex + 1), String)
    textPage.ToolTip = "Shows Current Page & allows setting of page number"

    Dim buttonGoto As New Button()
    buttonGoto.Text = "Go"
    buttonGoto.ID = "buttonGoto"
    AddHandler buttonGoto.Click, AddressOf GotoPage_Click
    buttonGoto.ToolTip = "Click to goto selected Page"
```

(continued)

```
        labelError.ID = "labelError"
        labelError.ForeColor = Color.Red
        labelError.Text = Attributes("ErrorMessage")

        cellPager.Controls.AddAt(2, textPage)
        cellPager.Controls.AddAt(3, New LiteralControl(" "))
        cellPager.Controls.AddAt(4, buttonGoto)
        cellPager.Controls.AddAt(7, labelError)

        cellPager.HorizontalAlign = HorizontalAlign.Center
End If
```

Both the *textPage* and the *labelError* controls were already declared previously. We're setting their properties at this time. Notice that the width of the *textPage* control is set with the *Unit.Pixel* delimiter. We also recommend you make it a habit to set the IDs of any control you add. If you forget to do so, you'll get the following error message: "Multiple controls with the same ID_ctl0 were found. FindControl requires that controls have unique IDs." You can see that we set the *textPage.Text* property to the current page. When you look at the *buttonGoto* Button control, you'll see that we included the *buttonGoto.Click* event handler, sending the event to our *GotoPage_Click* method. We could have added the declaration of this button with the declaration of *textPage* and defined the *GotoPage_Click* method with a handler. However, we wanted to show you how to add a control dynamically, even its event handling requirement. The rest of the code just adds our new controls to the page cell. It does this in the correct sequence by using *Controls.AddAt*.

All we have left to do is write the code and validation for the *GotoPage_Click* method:

```
#Region "OnGotoPage Event Handler"
    Private Sub GotoPage_Click(ByVal sender As Object, _
        ByVal e As System.EventArgs)
        Dim newPage As Integer
        newPage = CInt(textPage.Text) - 1
        If newPage >= 0 And newPage <= PageCount - 1 Then
            CurrentPageIndex = newPage
            Attributes("ErrorMessage") = ""
            Update()
        Else
            Attributes("ErrorMessage") = "  Incorrect Page Entry"
            Update()
        End If
    End Sub
#End Region
```

After we get the new page, we compare it with correct values (greater than 0 and less than the page count—watch out for the zero-based indexing). We either set the new *CurrentPageIndex* to the validated number or return an error through the *Attributes* property.

We're ready to test the DefaultHRPageGridPlusMore.aspx Web Forms application. To change data binding in its code-behind page, we had to make just a few simple changes. Here's the code:

```
Private Sub Page_Load(ByVal sender As System.Object, _
    ByVal e As System.EventArgs) Handles MyBase.Load
    If Not IsPostBack Then
        GetDataToSession()
        DefaultHRPageGridPlusMore1.GridDataSet = _
            CType(Session("Allemployees"), DataSet)
        DefaultHRPageGridPlusMore1.GridTable = "Employees"
        DefaultHRPageGridPlusMore1.Update()
    Else
        DefaultHRPageGridPlusMore1.GridDataSet = _
            CType(Session("AllEmployees"), DataSet)
        DefaultHRPageGridPlusMore1.GridTable = "Employees"
    End If
End Sub
```

The *GetDataSession* method assures that the *AllEmployer* dataset is in a session variable. Then we set custom DataGrid server controls: GridDataSet and Grid-Table. Afterward, we call the control's update method. This basically replaces the datagrid's *DataSource* property and *DataBind* method.

Figure 11-7 shows the result with the error invoked after trying to point to a wrong page number. We can also see the ToolTip for the Go button.

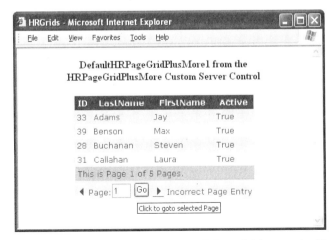

Figure 11-7 Customized ASP.NET DataGrid control with enhanced custom paging and footer

Adding Sorting Capabilities

Sorting has always been on the DataGrid control's "most wanted" list. You usually have to write lots of custom code, even though the ASP.NET DataGrid control has some built-in functionality to help with sorting. Our custom control also has a fair amount of custom code; however, we have to write it only once. We'll totally encapsulate sorting in the DataGrid custom control. Then, all you have to do to have automatic ascending and descending sorting capabilities, is declare which of the bound columns are to be sorted. We'll also enhance the visual presentation of the sorted columns.

Before we delve into the code that enables sorting, we need to be aware of the fact that some data must be persisted across pagebacks. We need the sort expression and sort direction. Both allow us to build a sort expression that can be passed to the *DataView* of the control, automatically rearranging the in-memory DataSet control. Here's how this could be done to sort by *LastName* in ascending order:

```
Dim sortString as String = "lastname asc"
internalDataView.Sort = sortString
```

Not only will we be able to build the sort expression from both variables, we'll also be able to determine the sort direction, which allows us to change an up arrow and a down arrow graphic in the chosen column header. As with other string data, we'll persist these two variables with *Attributes*. The sample custom DataGrid server control is named DefaultHRSortedGrid.vb and can be found in the sample files for this chapter. It includes all the code we've already written for custom pagination and the custom footer. Our first step is to add the attributes we mentioned to the existing properties region. (The read-only setting is recommended so that the attributes cannot accidentally be overwritten.)

```
⋮
Public ReadOnly Property SortExpression() As String
    Get
        Return Attributes("SortExpression")
    End Get
End Property

Public ReadOnly Property SortDirection() As String
    Get
        Return Attributes("SortDirection")
    End Get
End Property
⋮
```

Next, we must change some settings in the control's constructor. We need to tell the control that sorting is allowed. We assign default values to our two attributes:

```
'Set DataGrid Sorting
AllowSorting = True
Attributes("SortExpression") = ""
Attributes("SortDirection") = "ASC"
```

Since we're adding code to the custom server control's constructor, we need to add one more line of code. By default, when *AllowSorting* in the DataGrid control is set to *True* and any sortable column header is clicked, the *SortCommand* event is raised. In the same way we created event handlers for the *ItemCreated* and *PageIndexChanged* events, we'll add an event handler for the *SortCommand* event and direct it to the *OnSortCommand* method:

```
AddHandler SortCommand, AddressOf OnSortCommand
```

The main purpose of the *OnSortCommand* method is to check for the existing status of both the *SortExpression* and *SortDirection* attributes and set their new values. The *OnSortCommand* method returns the *SortExpression* as *e.SortExpression* of the selected column.

```
#Region "Custom Grid Event Handlers - SortCommand"
    Public Shadows Sub OnSortCommand(ByVal sender As Object, _
        ByVal e As DataGridSortCommandEventArgs)
```

First, we need to save the existing *SortExpression* state information from the *SortExpression* attribute and the existing *SortOrder* from its attribute. Next, we can set the *SortExpression* attribute to its new value, which was returned from the event arguments:

```
Dim sortExpression As String = Attributes("SortExpression")
Dim sortOrder As String = Attributes("SortDirection")

Attributes("SortExpression") = e.SortExpression
```

We now have the original state of the sort expression as well as the current state. If they are equal, the same column has been clicked again, requesting a change of sort direction. In this case, we simply reverse the sort direction as follows:

```
If e.SortExpression = sortExpression Then
    If Attributes("SortDirection") = "ASC" Then
        Attributes("SortDirection") = "DESC"
    Else
        Attributes("SortDirection") = "ASC"
    End If
Else
    Attributes("SortDirection") = "ASC"
End If
```

If the *SortExpression* values differ, a new sort column has been chosen. The else statement includes the line of code that will set sort order to its default—ascending. There is little left to do but update the data source. We've also opted to reset the page to the first page when a new sort order is called. This helps to alleviate confusion after a sort command has been issued:

```
        CurrentPageIndex = 0
        Update()


    End Sub
#End Region
```

Before moving on to take care of the additional visual effect we want, let's stay with the sorting logic for another moment. In the preceding lines of code, notice that we call the *Update* method. You might remember that this is the place for us to handle the update of the data source within the DataGrid control. We need to add lines of code that take care of sorting. Here's the entire code for this method, with the changes highlighted:

```
#Region "Update() - Internal Data Update"
    Public Sub Update()
        Try
            If internalTableName = Nothing Then
                internalDataView = internalDataSet.Tables(0).DefaultView
            Else
                internalDataView = _
                    internalDataSet.Tables(internalTableName).DefaultView
            End If
            Dim sortString As String = SortExpression
            If sortString <> "" Then
                If SortDirection = "ASC" Then
                    sortString += " ASC"
                    internalDataView.Sort = sortString
                Else
                    sortString += " DESC"
                    internalDataView.Sort = sortString
                End If
            End If

            DataSource = internalDataView
            DataBind()
        Catch
            DataBind()
        End Try
    End Sub
#End Region
```

If a *SortExpression* exists, we check for the *SortDirection* and combine a sort expression that then gets assigned to the DataView. The DataSet that exists in memory will then sort accordingly. This sorting is done blindingly fast and without any interaction with the data server or business layer.

Last but not least, we need to create the visual effect we want. You guessed correctly that we do this within the *OnItemCreated* method. This time we're looking for the DataGrid control's header:

```
If itemType = ListItemType.Header Then
Dim instanceSortExpression As String = Attributes("SortExpression")
Dim instanceDirection As String = Attributes("SortDirection")
```

For our up and down arrows, we use Webdings, which will match the left and right arrows we used for pagination nicely. Depending on the sort direction, we assign 5 for the up arrow and 6 for the down arrow:

```
Dim webDingItem As String
If instanceDirection = "ASC" Then        'Set the correct WebDing
    webDingItem = " 5"                   '5 = Up Arrow
Else                                     
    webDingItem = " 6"                   '6 = Down Arrow
End If
```

Now we need to find which column in the header corresponds to the current *SortExpression*. We iterate through all columns to find each column's specific *SortExpression*. (This is set as an attribute in the HTML bound columns control.) For each column that has a *SortExpression*, we add the expression as a ToolTip. When both *SortExpressions* match, we've found the correct column. All we need to do is assign the Webding font we defined earlier to a label control and add it to the cell.

```
Dim i As Integer
For i = 0 To Columns.Count - 1
    Dim cell As TableCell = e.Item.Cells(i)
    If Columns(i).SortExpression <> "" Then
        cell.ToolTip = "Sort by: " + Columns(i).SortExpression
            If instanceSortExpression = Columns(i).SortExpression Then
                Dim lblSorted As New Label()
                lblSorted.Font.Name = "webdings"
                lblSorted.Font.Size = FontUnit.XSmall
                lblSorted.Text = webDingItem
                cell.Controls.Add(lblSorted)
            End If
    End If
Next i
```

We're aware that the steps we just described include a lot of code. However, you'll find that the effort was well worth it. Figure 11-8 shows the result of this example: DefaultHRSortedGrid.aspx, which is included with the samples files for this book. We clicked on *LastName*, and you can see that it ordered the contents by last name in ascending order (arrow pointing up). The cursor stayed on *LastName* and called up the ToolTip also.

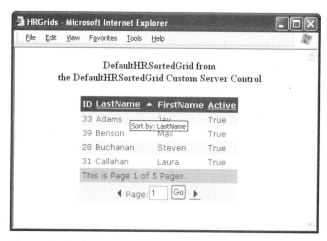

Figure 11-8   Customized ASP.NET DataGrid control with custom sorting and paging

Adding Final Enhancements

Even though we're pleased with the current look and feel as well as the functions of our DataGrid server control, we'd like to make a few more changes. When you run the last example, DefaultHRSortedGrid.aspx, you find that some information is repetitive. If you move from page to page, the footer repeats the statement "This is page 2 of 4 Pages" at the same time the TextBox control shows the current page number. We want to change this to display a record and a page count so that it would state "14 records in 4 Pages." At the same time, we find it restrictive that many grids don't allow us to change the number of rows shown. Therefore, we want to include a TextBox control that allows us to set the row count.

The majority of the changes are within the *OnItemCreated* method. (You should be used to changing this one by now!) Here's the code for the footer area in its entirety. We highlighted the changes to our previous example.

```
If itemType = ListItemType.Footer Then
    Dim footerRow As TableCellCollection = e.Item.Cells
    Dim footerCellCount As Integer = footerRow.Count
```

```
Dim i As Integer
For i = footerCellCount - 1 To 0 Step -1
    e.Item.Cells.RemoveAt(i)
Next

Dim newCell As New TableCell()
newCell.ColumnSpan = footerCellCount
newCell.HorizontalAlign = HorizontalAlign.Center
Dim font, size As String
font = MyBase.Font.Name
size = MyBase.Font.Size.ToString
Dim usedStyle As String = _
    "Style='Font-Size: " + size + "; Font-Family: " + font
newCell.Controls.Add(New LiteralControl( _
    "<Table width='100%' " & usedStyle & "'><TR><TD>"))

Dim labelReturnRows As New Label()
Dim totalRows As Integer
Try
    labelReturnRows.Text = CType(internalDataView.Count, String) + _
        " records in " + CType(PageCount, String) + " Pages."
Catch
End Try

newCell.Controls.Add(labelReturnRows)
newCell.Controls.Add(New LiteralControl("</TD><TD align='right'>"))

newCell.Controls.Add(New LiteralControl(" Rows:"))
newCell.Controls.Add(New LiteralControl("</TD><TD>"))

textRows.ID = "textRows"
textRows.AutoPostBack = True
textRows.Width = Unit.Pixel(20)
textRows.Text = CType(PageSize, String)
textRows.ToolTip = "Input the number of rows to show in Grid"
newCell.Controls.Add(textRows)

newCell.Controls.Add(New LiteralControl("</TD></TR></TABLE>"))
    e.Item.Cells.Add(newCell)
End If
```

We need to keep in mind a couple of issues when we implement these changes. The footer row is only one cell (remember that we had to take out all the cells so that we could use the whole width of the footer). Now we're adding several functions to it. To allow for proper alignment, we need to break the row into cells again—but not the cells dictated by the DataGrid columns. For this reason we'll add a Table control with its own rows and cells into the single footer cell. The one gotcha we encounter by adding a table is that we lose the font and size styles from the DataGrid. In the preceding lines of code, you can see that we formed the style statement, getting the information required from the DataGrid's base properties, and then started a new table using ASP.NET's *LiteralControl* (which instantiates faster than a label control). Here's the code for this:

```
Dim font, size As String
font = MyBase.Font.Name
size = MyBase.Font.Size.ToString
Dim usedStyle As String = _
    "Style='Font-Size: " + size + "; Font-Family: " + font
newCell.Controls.Add(New LiteralControl( _
    "<Table width='100%' " & usedStyle & "'><TR><TD>"))
```

Notice that we changed the *labelReturnRows.Text* information to include a full count of table rows in the *internalDataView*. The other important added control is the *textRows* TextBox control. It allows us to set the number of rows to display. It's important to mention that we must make this TextBox control *AutoPostBack* to allow the newly entered row number to take effect.

Let's not forget that we need to declare the *textRows* TextBox control beforehand so that we can access its events:

```
Protected WithEvents textRows As New TextBox()
```

Next, we need to create the method that gets called when the *Text-Changed* event is raised:

```
#Region "Changed Rows"
    Private Sub txtRows_TextChanged(ByVal sender As Object, _
        ByVal e As System.EventArgs) Handles textRows.TextChanged
        Dim newPageSize As Integer
        newPageSize = CType(textRows.Text, Integer)
        If newPageSize > 0 Then
            CurrentPageIndex = 0
            PageSize = newPageSize
            Attributes("ErrorMessage") = ""
            Update()
        Else
            Attributes("ErrorMessage") = " Incorrect Number of rows set"
            Update()
        End If
    End Sub
#End Region
```

When the number of rows is changed, we validate the entry and reset the DataGrid to its first page (we want to avoid any nasty errors that might be caused when we're at the last page of a DataGrid that shows only a couple of rows.) Then we set the new number of rows.

Figure 11-9 shows the result of this example. The general functionality of our custom DataGrid server control is complete. Best of all, it's easy to use and encapsulates a lot of the functionality we've been looking for.

Figure 11-9   Customized ASP.NET DataGrid control with additional features

The latest version of our DataGrid custom server control is complete and flexible; however, you might want to include other features. Following is a list of features you might think about:

- **Better formatting**   When you want to apply specific formatting such as giving a *Boolean* field more than the simple true and false text values, you can apply templates for different data types. You could even include a default template within the DataGrid control that looks at the data type and selects the correct template automatically. A word of caution though. If you use templates, you must add code for data binding yourself.

- **Combining fields**   Sometimes you might want to combine fields such as last name and first name from two columns into one column. Again a custom template can be used. You'll have to change the way sorting behaves also.

- **Multicolumn sorting** You could create custom sort expressions and write a specific sorting method that takes your custom expressions and combines them into a sort expression specifically designed for the DataView.

- **Filter options** You can add another TextBox control that allows entering of a filter expression.

- **Find feature** Just like the filter option, a TextBox control could be used to find specific information. You could write the logic to allow searching on all fields if none are selected or when a sort field is chosen, to concentrate the search on that field only.

- **In-place editing** Although it's against our user interface design strategies to allow in-place editing within DataGrid controls, you have that option and can use several built-in features to handle it.

Many of these features and more ideas for DataGrid controls are expertly presented by Dino Esposito in his book, *Building Web Solutions with ASP.NET and ADO.NET* (Microsoft Press, 2002).

Showing Detail Information

The number and length of fields that you can show in a DataGrid control are very restricted. This is one of the reasons we don't edit data in a DataGrid control. We use it as a tool for showing a data list overview and for quickly navigating to a specific record to look at its details. We adopted two standards for implementing the list/detail user interface design: the grid and details appear in one page or in separate pages.

The first standard we adopted was to make the grid and details appear in one page. This approach works particularly well when the data to be shown in the detail area consists of few fields that take up little room. Good candidates for this approach are the support information screens. In the HRnet application, these would be the screens that handle data for departments, available benefits, hiring sources, news, and so on. The graphics layout leaves some flexibility. You can have the DataGrid control on the left side with detail information on the right. You can also have the DataGrid either on the top or the bottom of the page with the detail information on the opposite side.

The second standard we adopted is to make the grid and details appear in separate pages. When the data to be shown in the detail page includes many fields, graphics, or larger text areas, we show the details on one or more separate pages. You can see this approach in HRnet when information for the employee or the company needs to be managed.

In the following pages, we'll show you a simple example for both stan-dards. Later, we'll add features, such as passing state information to the detail page, that will allow you to view, edit, add, or delete records.

A One-Page Grid and Detail Form

Following our UI standards, when we combine the DataGrid control and detail information on one page, we mostly continue working with the same DataSet we already requested for the DataGrid *DataSource*. Since there isn't much infor-mation to present, the memory footprint of the DataSet shouldn't be too large. If it is, we'll work with two sets of data: the first set with limited data returned for the DataGrid control, and the second set of data called on a per-selection basis. The latter approach is also used in separate grid and detail pages.

Let's take a look at the GridandDetail1.aspx example, which you can find with the sample files for this chapter. When opening this Web Forms applica-tion in design mode, you'll notice that we're using our custom DataGrid server control named HRGridEdit (this one is a bit enhanced from the previous ver-sion—we'll take a look at that in a minute), and we call a custom user control named DepartmentsBasic1.ascx. One of the changes you'll see right away is a *ButtonColumn* with a graphic. We use this to select a specific row, which in return calls up the detail information in the custom user control. Here's the line of code that defines the *ButtonColumn* in HTML:

```
<ASP:BUTTONCOLUMN Text="<img border=0 alt='Select'
  align=absmiddle src=edit.gif>" CommandName="select"></ASP:BUTTONCOLUMN>
```

The ButtonColumn contains a user-defined button for the whole column. It raises the *ItemCommand* event. By passing a specific *CommandName*, when the *ItemCommand* event is raised, we can create a custom handler that searches for that *CommandName* and executes it. For row selection purposes, *CommandName* must be set to *select*, as you can see in the preceding line of code. When clicked, the specific row automatically is selected, even when no additional code is written. We could use custom code that handles the *Data-GridCommandEventArgs* directly when the *ItemCommand* event is raised by clicking one of the buttons. However, we chose to use the *SelectedIndex-Changed* event to call up detail information, which is called every time a differ-ent row is selected. This also allows us to select a specific row programmatically and still call up the detail information. When we allow selection of a specific line in the DataGrid control, we also need to implement a deselect function. We did this by enhancing the DataGrid server control. We created the *PublicUnse-lect* method in HRGridEdit.vb. It simply sets the *SelectedIndex* to −1, which causes the DataGrid to clear the selected row. We also included calling the

Update method in *Unselect* and replaced all direct calls from other methods within this control to call *Unselect* instead. This way, when you select another page or re-sort the grid, the selection disappears. Here's the code:

```
#Region "Select and Unselect"
    Public Sub Unselect()
        SelectedIndex = -1
        Update()
    End Sub
#End Region
```

By declaring the *Unselect* method as public, we can also call it from outside—that is, from the code-behind page of the Web Forms application that implements our custom DataGrid server control. This takes care of enhancing the DataGrid control.

Next, we need to implement filling in the detail information when we select a specific row. As we discussed earlier, we do this by using the *SelectedIndexChanged* event. Since this code is specific to each Web Forms page that the DataGrid control is used in, we create its code in the Web Forms code-behind file. First we point the event handler to a specific method in the HTML of the DataGrid (highlighted):

```
<ccl:hrgridedit id="HRGridEdit1" runat="server" AutoGenerateColumns="False"
  OnSelectedIndexChanged="SelectedIndexChanged"
  DataKeyField="DepartmentID">
```

Now, we need to create the code for the *SelectedIndexChanged* method:

```
Public Sub SelectedIndexChanged(ByVal sender As Object, _
    ByVal e As EventArgs)
    btnUnselect.Enabled = True
    SelectRecordID(CInt(HRGridEdit1.DataKeys(HRGridEdit1.SelectedIndex)))
End Sub
```

We included an Unselect button on the Web Forms application to demonstrate calling the DataGrid control's *Unselect* method. We enable the button only when a row has been selected. Then we call the specific method that finds the selected row in the DataSet and populates our custom user control. Notice that we need to pass it the unique ID of the record represented by the row selected. We get the unique ID by calling the DataGrid control's data key from its selected Index. We defined the *DataKeyField* previously as an attribute of the DataGrid control:

```
<ccl:hrgridedit id="HRGridEdit1" runat="server" AutoGenerateColumns="False"
  OnSelectedIndexChanged="SelectedIndexChanged"
  DataKeyField="DepartmentID">
```

The code that gets the unique ID is this:

```
HRGridEdit1.DataKeys(HRGridEdit.SelectedIndex)
```

Now that we have the unique ID, we can select it from the DataSet and populate the user control's fields. Here's the code:

```
Private Sub SelectRecordID(ByVal DepartmentID As Integer)
    Try
        Dim selectDataSet As DataSet = _
            CType(Session("Departments"), DataSet)
        Dim selectTable As DataTable = selectDataSet.Tables("Departments")
        Dim selectRow() As DataRow = selectTable.Select("DepartmentID=" + _
            DepartmentID.ToString)
        With DepartmentsBasic1
            .DepartmentID = CInt(selectRow(0)("DepartmentID"))
            If Not IsDBNull(selectRow(0)("Name")) Then _
                .DepartmentName = CStr(selectRow(0)("Name"))
            If Not IsDBNull(selectRow(0)("Description")) Then _
                .DepartmentDescription = CStr(selectRow(0)("Description"))
            If Not IsDBNull(selectRow(0)("Active")) Then _
                .DepartmentActive = CBool(selectRow(0)("Active"))
            If Not IsDBNull(selectRow(0)("DateCreated")) And _
                Not IsDBNull(selectRow(0)("Createdby")) Then _
                .Entered = CStr(selectRow(0)("DateCreated")) + " by " + _
                CType(selectRow(0)("Createdby"), String) Else _
                .Entered = "N/A"
            If Not IsDBNull(selectRow(0)("DateModified")) And _
                Not IsDBNull(selectRow(0)("Modifiedby")) Then _
                .Modified = CStr(selectRow(0)("DateModified")) + " by " + _
                CType(selectRow(0)("Modifiedby"), String) Else _
                .Modified = "N/A"
            lblMessage.Text = ""
        End With
    Catch selectException As Exception
        DepartmentsBasic1.ClearEntries()
        lblMessage.Text = "<B>Error searching for records</B> " + _
            selectException.Message
    End Try
End Sub
```

After finding the selected row, we populate the properties of the *DepartmentsBasic1* custom user control that in return populates the Label and TextBox controls. We enclosed this process into a *Try...Catch* block for exception handling.

In the DepartmentsBasic1 custom user control, we defined the properties needed to populate the Label, CheckBox, and TextBox controls. We also included a public function that allows the clearing of these controls. When you take a closer look at this custom user control, you'll find that we used an enhanced version of the custom TextBox Server control introduced in Chapter 6. Figures 11-10, 11-11, and 11-12 show the GridandDetail1.aspx example in design mode, running without a selection, and then when a selection took place. The example is included with the sample files for this chapter.

Note When accessing fields in the database, null values can be returned. We need to take care of this eventuality. The best way to do this is by implementing the *IsDBNull* function. Here's an example:

```
If Not IsDBNull(selectRow(0)("Name")) Then
    .DepartmentName = CStr(selectRow(0)("Name"))
```

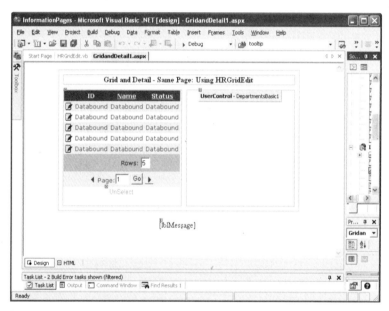

Figure 11-10   Customized ASP.NET DataGrid and detail area in design mode

You can see that we are easily able to add a detail area to our custom Data-Grid server control. Almost all the additional code involved has to do with accessing the DataSet, getting specific information about the selected record, and passing that information to the detail area. In our case, we use a custom user control. We could just as easily have used Label and Text controls on the same Web form that contains the DataGrid control. What we have not yet implemented is a way to add, save, and cancel functions. We'll do this shortly after looking at a list/detail form in which we call a separate Web Forms application for the detail area.

Figure 11-11   Customized ASP.NET DataGrid and detail area without selection

Figure 11-12   Customized ASP.NET DataGrid and detail area with selected record

Grid and Detail Forms Separated

Often, we find it necessary to create a separate Web Forms page for the detail information, simply because there is too much information to show on the same page as the DataGrid control. Our next example will show the list/detail information in separate pages. Following our user interface standards, the list part is a DataGrid named GridEmployees1.aspx. Its detail page is EmployeeDetail1.aspx.

With a lot of detailed information, a fully loaded dataset could get rather large. For this reason, we call the full set of data required for the detail Web Forms page only when we supply it with a specific ID—in our case the *EmployeeID*. In a production application, a specific method would return a list of all employees through the business layer with only a small subset of information needed in the DataGrid control. Another method of the business layer would return all information on a specific employee by using *EmployeeID*. The only major difference from the previous example, in which we show both the DataGrid and the detailed information on one Web Forms page, is in the *SelectRecordID* method:

```
Private Sub SelectRecordID(ByVal EmployeeID As Integer)
    Dim localQueryString As String = "EmployeeID=" + EmployeeID.ToString
    Dim urlEmployeeDetail As String = "EmployeeDetail1.aspx"
    HRGridEdit1.Unselect()
    Response.Redirect(urlEmployeeDetail + "?" + localQueryString)
End Sub
```

All we need to do in this method is to build a URL with the query string information that contains the *EmployeeID*. As with the previous example, we get the *EmployeeID* from the *DataKeys* function, which returns the specific data key of the selected row, as follows:

```
Public Sub SelectedIndexChanged(ByVal sender As Object, _
    ByVal e As EventArgs)
    SelectRecordID(CInt(HrGridEdit1.DataKeys(HrGridEdit1.SelectedIndex)))
End Sub
```

With the *Response.Redirect* and the URL we built previously, we arrive at the EmployeeDetail1.aspx Web Forms page. Our first task is to retrieve the specific data for the *EmployeeID* that is passed in the query string. Here's the code for this step:

```
Private Sub GetDataToSession()
    Dim localEmployeebyID As DataSet
    Dim localCompany As New Employee("default", "password")
    localEmployeebyID = _
        localCompany.GetEmployeeDetail( _
        CInt(Request.QueryString("EmployeeID")), 1)
    Session("EmployeebyID") = localEmployeebyID
    localCompany = Nothing
```

```
End Sub
```

Some readers might wonder why we populate a dataset in session state if we could have called a local dataset and populated the fields of the Web Forms directly. The main reason for this is that we might want to give our clients the chance to revert changes when editing the fields.

After data is present, we call a *LoadFields* method, which we created to populate this Web Forms control. Here's an excerpt from the code:

```
Private Sub LoadFields()
    Try
        Dim singleEmployee As DataTable = _
            CType(Session("EmployeebyID"), DataSet).Tables(0)
        Dim selectRow As DataRow = _
            CType(Session("EmployeebyID"), DataSet).Tables(0).Rows(0)
        If Not IsDBNull(selectRow("LastName")) Then
            txtLastName.Text = CStr(selectRow("LastName"))
        Else
            txtLastName.Text = ""
        End If
        If Not IsDBNull(selectRow("FirstName")) Then
            txtFirstName.Text = CStr(selectRow("FirstNAme"))
        Else
            txtFirstName.Text = ""
        End If
        If Not IsDBNull(selectRow("NickName")) Then
            txtNickName.Text = CStr(selectRow("NickName"))
        Else
            txtNickName.Text = ""
            ⋮
            lblMessage.Text = ""
        End If
    Catch selectException As Exception
        ClearEntries()
        lblMessage.Text = "<B>Error showing this Employee Record</B>" _
            + selectException.Message
    End Try
End Sub
```

We extract the only row in the only table of the DataSet control, that is, the specific employee's information returned by its *EmployeeID*. We then check for *NULL* fields and populate the controls. That's all there is to it. Figures 11-13 and 11-14 show, respectively, the GridEmployees1.aspx example representing the DataGrid control with the list of employees, and EmployeeDetail1.aspx as the specific detail page.

Figure 11-13   Customized ASP.NET DataGrid control for the employee list

Figure 11-14   Detail form for one employee

Enhancing the Page Grid and Detail Form

Having covered the basics of DataGrid and detail Web Forms pages, we're now going to add features. Two of the most important features we can add are permission and state information. Here are the permission levels we would like to manage:

1. View DataGrid only

2. View detail information

3. View/edit detail information

4. View/edit and add detail information

5. View/edit, add, and delete detail information

State information accompanies each of these permission levels and will create the correct settings by enabling or disabling buttons and controls on the detail page. Let's take a look at how this is done.

We created the GridandDetailState.aspx example, which you can find with the sample files for this chapter, to allow you to select each of our five permission levels. When selected, the same information is passed as a state to the custom user control which in return processes its controls accordingly. The custom user control we use for this example is named DepartmentsBasic-Enhanced.ascx.

Creating Columns Programmatically

To allow for the different functions required by our five permission levels, we need to be able to dynamically add columns to the DataGrid. Before we show you the code for this, we need to remind you that programmatically created columns do *not* persist themselves on postbacks, unlike those columns defined at design time. For this reason, you'll have to call the methods that create the correct columns for every postback event. We named the method you need to call as *PermissionSettings*. Here is the *Page_Load* code for our sample file:

```
Private Sub Page_Load(ByVal sender As System.Object, _
    ByVal e As System.EventArgs) Handles MyBase.Load
    If Not IsPostBack Then
        GetDataToSession()
        HRGridEditEnhanced1.GridDataSet = _
            CType(Session("Departments"), DataSet)
        PermissionSettings()
```

(continued)

```
    Else
        HRGridEditEnhanced1.GridDataSet = _
            CType(Session("Departments"), DataSet)
        PermissionSettings()
    End If
End Sub
```

Notice that we call the *PermissionSettings* method on initial page entry, after we populate the *Session* with the DataSet, and then again on every postback.

Now let's look at how the *PermissionSettings* method handles the five desired permission levels. We'll show you the entire code and then explain the important parts:

```
Private Sub PermissionSettings()
    Dim intPermission As Integer = rbPermissions.SelectedIndex + 1
    If intPermission = 1 Then
        DepartmentsBasicEnhanced1.Status = 1'View grid only
    End If
    If intPermission = 2 Then          'View detail
        viewButton()
        DepartmentsBasicEnhanced1.Status = 2
    End If
    If intPermission = 3 Then          'View/edit detail
        editButton()
        DepartmentsBasicEnhanced1.Status = 3
    End If
    If intPermission = 4 Then          'View/edit and add detail
        editButton()
        DepartmentsBasicEnhanced1.Status = 4
    End If
    If intPermission = 5 Then          'View/edit, add and delete
        editButton()
        deleteButton()
        DepartmentsBasicEnhanced1.Status = 5
    End If
    HRGridEditEnhanced1.Update()
End Sub
```

To make testing of this code easier, we use the RadioButtonList control named *rbPermissions*. With it we can choose all the permission and states we allow. Normally you would get the correct permission information from the business or security layer. Each permission level sets the status property of the DepartmentsBasicEnhanced1 custom user control (*DepartmentsBasic-Enhanced1.Status*). Besides passing the status, all but the first permission level calls for the creation of DataGrid columns. Table 11-4 provides a list of the columns required for each permission level.

Table 11-4 **Permission Levels and Required Columns**

Permission	Columns
1—View grid only	N/A
2—View grid and detail	View button
3—View grid and detail and edit	Edit button
4—View grid and detail with edit and add	Edit button (Add button is added by control's state but can be added to the DataGrid control)
5—View grid and detail with edit, add, and delete	Edit button (Add button is added by control's state but can be added to the DataGrid control)
	Delete button

Based on the information in Table 11-4, we need to be able to dynamically add a combination of three ButtonColumns to the DataGrid control. In the preceding code, we named the methods that we defined *viewButton, editButton*, and *deleteButton*.

Within these methods we create the additional ButtonColumns and add them to the DataGrid. Let's look at the code for the *viewButton* and *editButton* methods since they are both select buttons and therefore need no additional code when the *SelectedIndexChanged* event is raised. (We already took care of this code in previous examples.)

```
Private Sub viewButton()
    Dim viewButton As New ButtonColumn()
    viewButton.CommandName = "select"
    viewButton.Text = _
        "<img border=0 alt='View Only' align=absmiddle src=View.gif>"
    HRGridEditEnhanced1.Columns.AddAt(0, viewButton)
End Sub

Private Sub editButton()
    Dim editButton As New ButtonColumn()
    editButton.CommandName = "select"
    editButton.Text = _
        "<img border=0 alt='View/Edit' align=absmiddle src=edit.gif>"
    HRGridEditEnhanced1.Columns.AddAt(0, editButton)
End Sub
```

Creating a new column for DataGrid controls isn't magical. We declare a new ButtonColumn, give it the name *select* (to get the automatic behavior of selecting the clicked row), and add some text. Hold on for a minute! The text seems to be rather strange. Since any text is allowed, we opted to make it an

HTML image control pointing to either the View.gif (an icon of an eye) or the Edit.gif (an icon of a paper with a pencil) and gave it some alternative text. This works beautifully and makes the DataGrid look much more professional. Notice that we use the DataGrid control's *Columns.AddAt* method. This allows us to position the added column as the first one displayed in the DataGrid.

Adding Custom Event Handling to a ButtonColumn

The delete button is causing us a bit more work. Not only do we have to define it in a similar way as the previous two buttons, but we also need to assign it a different event handler. Here's the definition of this button's column:

```
Private Sub deleteButton()
    Dim deleteButton As New ButtonColumn()
    deleteButton.CommandName = "Delete"
    deleteButton.Text = _
        "<img border=0 alt='Delete' align=absmiddle src=Delete.gif>"
    HRGridEditEnhanced1.Columns.Add(deleteButton)
End Sub
```

We need to make only a few changes. First, we add a different picture, Delete.gif, which is an icon representing a red X. We also give this ButtonColumn a different *CommandName*. We need this command name to handle the event it raises when clicked. Another slight change is that we used the *Columns.Add* method instead of the *Columns.AddAt* method. This adds this column as the last one in the DataGrid control.

Second, we need to take care of the event for this button. To make this work, we need to add the *OnItemCommand* property to the DataGrid definition in HTML (highlighted):

```
<ccl:hrgrideditenhanced id="HRGridEditEnhanced1" EditMode="true"
    runat="server" AutoGenerateColumns="False"
    OnItemCommand="HandleButtonColumns"
    OnSelectedIndexChanged="SelectedIndexChanged"
    DataKeyField="DepartmentID">
```

Then we add the method that will handle the DataGrid's *ItemCommand* event and give it the same name we declared for the earlier DataGrid control. We do this in the code-behind page:

```
Public Sub HandleButtonColumns(ByVal sender As Object, _
    ByVal e As DataGridCommandEventArgs) _
    Handles HRGridEditEnhanced1.ItemCommand
    If e.CommandName = "Delete" Then
        Dim intDepartmentID As Integer = _
            CType(HRGridEditEnhanced1.DataKeys(e.Item.ItemIndex), Integer)
        lblMessage.Text = "You wanted to delete the record with ID =" + _
            CStr(intDepartmentID)
```

```
     End If
     HRGridEditEnhanced1.Update()
End Sub
```

The event carries several items we need. First, it carries the command's name. This will allows us to filter for one specific *Button* event. Remember that we called the *CommandName* for the delete button *Delete*. This feature allows us to add as many ButtonColumns as we want and separates their *Click* events to run different code for each one. In this case, we look for *e.CommandName = "Delete"*. The next item the event passes us is the *e.Item.Index*. With it we can extract the data key for the record to be deleted. For testing purposes, we simply set a message label and report which record ID would be deleted.

For demonstration purposes, we didn't attach working code to any of the add, edit, and delete events in this example. We'll instead do this in Chapter 14, where we build the rest of the HRnet application. In this example, instead of calling the business layer for these functions, we send messages to Label controls on the screen.

State Handling in the Detail Custom Server Control

All the code in the Web Forms page of the DataGrid control is complete. But how are we going to handle the permission level state information that is passed to the detail custom server control? Let's take a look at the Departments-BasicEnhanced.ascx code-behind file. We added a new public property (write-only) and declared a variable that carries the state information for the methods in this code-behind page:

```
Dim internalStatus as Integer

Public WriteOnly Property Status() As Integer
    Set(ByVal Value As Integer)
        internalStatus = Value
    End Set
End Property
```

In the *Page_Load* event of the code-behind page, we call for the *SetSecurity* function on every postback. We pass this function the permission state, which causes it to handle all controls on this page for each permission state. Here's the *Page_Load* event code for this custom user control:

```
Private Sub Page_Load(ByVal sender As System.Object, _
    ByVal e As System.EventArgs) Handles MyBase.Load
    SetSecurity(internalStatus)
End Sub
```

In the *SetSecurty* function, we have to take care of three major features:

- Displaying and enabling buttons, or hiding and disabling them
- Hiding all input controls or showing them
- Enabling or disabling input controls (edit or view-only)

Here's a portion of the code that creates these features:

```
Private Sub SetSecurity(ByVal securitySetting As Integer)
    Select Case securitySetting
    Case 1
        HideDataEntryControls()
        btnSave.Visible = False
        btnSave.Enabled = False
        btnCancel.Visible = False
        btnCancel.Enabled = False
        btnAdd.Visible = False
        btnAdd.Enabled = False
    Case 2
        ShowDataEntryControls()
        DisableDataEntryControls()
        btnSave.Visible = False
        btnSave.Enabled = False
        btnCancel.Visible = False
        btnCancel.Enabled = False
        btnAdd.Visible = False
        btnAdd.Enabled = False
    Case 3
        ShowDataEntryControls()
        EnableDataEntryControls()
        btnSave.Visible = True
        btnSave.Enabled = True
        btnCancel.Visible = True
        btnCancel.Enabled = True
        btnAdd.Visible = False
        btnAdd.Enabled = True
        ⋮
    End Select
End Sub
```

You can see that we call different methods for each permission state. Each one of these determines whether the controls are hidden, visible, or disabled (view-only). The method names are *HideDataEntryControls*, *ShowDataEntryControls*, and *DisableDataEntryControls*. They simply set the controls' properties for visibility and for being enabled or disabled. Following is one example—the *HideDataEntryControls* method:

```
Private Sub HideDataEntryControls()
    txtName.Visible = False
    txtDescription.Visible = False
    chkActive.Visible = False
    lblID.Visible = False
    lblEntered.Visible = False
    lblModified.Visible = False
End Sub
```

After calling the correct hide and show methods for the page's controls, we control the Save, Cancel, and Add buttons. You probably noticed that we used both their *Visible* and *Enabled* properties and set them both to either *True* or *False*. We did this because we find that older browsers, especially Netscape, misinterpret a *visible = false* setting and still tend to show the buttons. With our strategy, they are at least disabled.

We're now ready to test this example. Make sure you try all combinations of permissions including selecting the TextBox controls and using the visible buttons. Figure 11-15 shows the Grid/Detail form by default—with no permissions except to view the DataGrid. (We could have made the custom user control invisible also.)

Figure 11-15   Grid/Detail form with View Grid Only permissions only

Figure 11-16 shows the Grid/Detail form in View Details mode. It allows the viewing of detail information, but as you can see, editing is not allowed, nor are the add and delete functions.

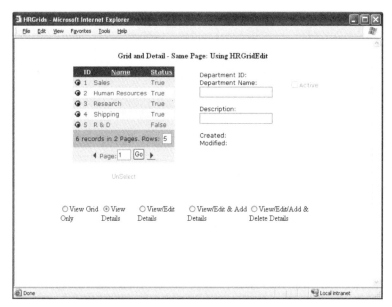

Figure 11-16   Grid/Detail form with View Details permissions

Figure 11-17 shows the Grid/Detail form in the All Permission mode. Notice how the icons have changed in the DataGrid control. You can also see that we clicked the Save button to try deleting the fourth record, Shipping.

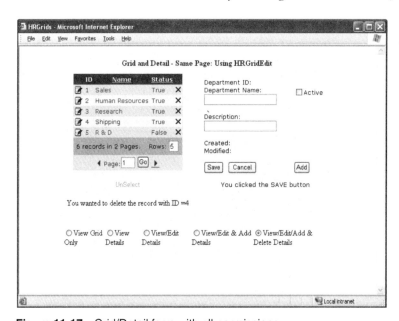

Figure 11-17   Grid/Detail form with all permissions

We didn't include an example for grid and detail in separate forms. The process is the same with the exception of passing the permission state information in a query string to the detail form.

Scalability and Performance

Earlier we touched on the topic of scalability and performance with the promise to cover it in more detail and explain why we use session variables, even with DataSets. The time for this discussion has now arrived. Let's look at two possible extreme positions concerning scalability and performance.

The first extreme position has to do with how to get a Web application to perform faster. The answer is simple: by using the session state and datasets in the session state. Session state is in the memory of the Web server. Memory is always accessed a lot faster than data on a SQL server over a network. Using this strategy also limits the round trips to the SQL server. But what is the major downfall? It is not, and we repeat, *not* the session state problem we experienced in former versions of ASP. Session state works well in ASP.NET, even allowing us to let it run as a separate thread from Microsoft Internet Information Services (IIS). The major downfall was the limitation of memory on the server, which limited scalability.

The second extreme position is to not use session state or to use it very little while using the DataReader and making lots of round trips to the SQL server. This will surely alleviate the scalability problems we experienced in the first solution—or will it? Somewhat but not totally. With increased traffic on the network, multiple open connections for the DataReader, and accessing the SQL server with multiple components simultaneously, we'll also hit a scalability ceiling, but worse, we'll do this at the expense of performance, which would be lacking even when the application doesn't have thousands of simultaneous users.

So what is the best solution for this problem? We'll recommend a step-by-step approach that has and is working well for us. You move through these steps as the requirements of scalability increase. We do recommend that you use the DataSet. It passes well through layers, has inherent XML capabilities, works great with Web services, and so on. We also recommend that you use the session state, even with DataSets. Here are our recommendations, one stage or step at a time:

1. **Create a limit for returned records in the business layer**   Nobody will want to look at thousands of records in a paged DataGrid with hundreds of pages. Learn to return a reasonable amount of records and limit the return. There is nothing wrong with having the business layer return the request for a better filter.

2. **Use small DataSets in sessions** If you learn to return small DataSets, you'll see that their memory footprint is rather small. When you move away from the DataGrid that used the DataSet from session state, simply remove the DataSet from it.

3. **Serialize larger DataSets to XML files that you store on a per-session basis on the Web servers' hard drive** Should you run into the need to return a larger DataSet, why not serialize it to a local XML file (you will have a lot more hard drive space on your servers than memory) and on postback retrieve it from the hard drive? We'll show you an example of this in a bit.

4. **Increase memory on the Web server and Web server farm** Memory is cheap now. See whether you can increase it as you watch the memory requirements on your Web servers increase. (Don't wait too long though; you don't want upset customers when things don't work right.)

5. **Use a separate SQL Server for the Web server and Web server farm** Although this decreases performance, having a SQL server for the Web server or Web server farm will allow you to scale your application to almost infinite numbers of simultaneous users.

These suggestions should give you a great balance between a fast-performing Web application and the required level of scalability.

Persisting Data Through Local XML Files

We recommended earlier to serialize larger DataSets to XML files that you store on a per-session basis on the Web servers' hard drive. Even though this will perform slower than a DataSet in a *Session* object, it will conserve a lot of server memory and use the much more abundant and cheaper hard drive space of a Web server. Better yet, as long as the Web server has ample free memory, this process will be cached and give you the same re-read performance you could expect from the DataSet in the *Session* object. Because ADO.NET's DataSets have the capability to serialize themselves and read/write XML directly, serializing larger DataSets to XML files is a rather simple process.

The name of our example is XMLSerial.aspx, and it is included in the sample files for this book. When we enter this Web Forms page the first time, we receive the DataSet through the business layer and write it to disk by serializing it into an XML file. In subsequent postbacks, we read the local file, deserialize it back to a DataSet, and populate the DataGrid. Here is the XMLSerial.aspx code-behind page for the *Page_Load* event:

```
Private Sub Page_Load(ByVal sender As System.Object, _
    ByVal e As System.EventArgs) Handles MyBase.Load
    If Not IsPostBack Then
        Dim EmployeeDataSet As DataSet = GetDataToXML()
        DefaultHRGridPlus1.GridDataSet = EmployeeDataSet
        DefaultHRGridPlus1.GridTable = "Employees"
        DefaultHRGridPlus1.Update()
        Dim dirInfo As New DirectoryInfo(Server.MapPath(Nothing) + _
            "/SessionXML/")
        Dim aFiles As FileInfo() = dirInfo.GetFiles("*.xml")
        DataGrid1.DataSource = aFiles
        DataGrid1.DataBind()
    Else
        Dim EmployeeDataSet As DataSet = GetDataFromXML()
        DefaultHRGridPlus1.GridDataSet = employeedataset
        DefaultHRGridPlus1.GridTable = "Employees"
    End If
End Sub
```

The boldface code shows you the major changes needed to populate the Data-Grid. The first time the Web Forms page is executed, we call the *GetDataToXML* function, and in subsequent postbacks, we call the *GetDataFromXML* function.

Serializing the DataSet

Let's look at the *GetDataToXML* function next:

```
Private Function GetDataToXML() As DataSet
    Dim localAllEmployees As DataSet
    Dim localCompany As New Company("default", "password")
    localAllEmployees = localCompany.GetCompanyEmployees(1)
    localCompany = Nothing
    Dim strDir As String = Server.MapPath(Nothing) + "/SessionXML/"
    Dim dirInfo As New DirectoryInfo(strDir)
    dirInfo.Create()
    lblMessage.Text = strDir + Session.SessionID + ".xml"
    Dim localPath As String = strDir + Session.SessionID + ".xml"
    Dim xmlWriter As New XmlTextWriter(localPath, Nothing)
    localAllEmployees.WriteXml(xmlWriter)
    xmlWriter.Close()
    Return localAllEmployees
End Function
```

You should be familiar with the first four lines of code in which we return a DataSet from the business layer. The next three lines of code make sure that a local directory named SessionXML exists within the current Web applications directory. Then we create a new instance of *XMLTextWriter* with the specific path and filename that we previously created using the unique identifier of the current session ID:

```
Dim localPath As String = strDir + Session.SessionID + ".xml"
Dim xmlWriter As New XmlTextWriter(localPath, Nothing)
```

You can see how we combined the path and the session ID to create the *localPath* string. The *XMLWriter* uses this information to create the file. The second parameter defines the XML encoding method used to write this file. When you select Nothing, as we have in the preceding example, the *XMLWriter* creates a UTF-8-compatible XML string and adds the correct attributes. With the *XMLTextWriter* ready, we can use the DataSet's *WriteXML* method:

```
localAllEmployees.WriteXml(xmlWriter)
```

The DataSet saves all its information, which includes the data, data structure, and state information, in the XML file. The process is called *serialization*. After closing out the *XMLTextWriter*, we simply return the DataSet that will be bound to the DataGrid.

We also added a little test DataGrid. It shows you all the XML files currently in the directory.

Deserializing the DataSet

We're ready to take a look at how we retrieve, or deserialize, the DataSet in the *GetDataFromXML* function:

```
Private Function GetDataFromXML() As DataSet
    Dim strDir As String = Server.MapPath(Nothing) + "/SessionXML/"
     Dim localPath As String = strDir + Session.SessionID + ".xml"
    Dim xmlReader As New XmlTextReader(localPath)
    Dim returnDataSet As New DataSet()
    returnDataSet.ReadXml(xmlReader)
    xmlReader.Close()
    Return returnDataSet
End Function
```

The code for this function is just as simple as the code for the *GetData-ToXML* function. You can look at it as a set-by-step reversal. First, we define the path to the XML file. This is the same code as before. Then we create a new instance of the *XMLTextReader* and pass it the location and filename. Again, the DataSet does most of the work. We call its *ReadXML* method with the specific *XMLTextReader*, and voila! The DataSet is back, including all records, structure, and state information. All we have left to do is close the reader (release resources) and return the DataSet. Figure 11-18 shows this example and the additional DataGrid that returns all the existing session files. It also shows the current DataSet XML file. Take the time to sort and page through the DataGrid.

You'll notice that the performance is as instantaneous as DataSets in session objects. The only slowdown you might experience is when a large DataSet is saved to the local file.

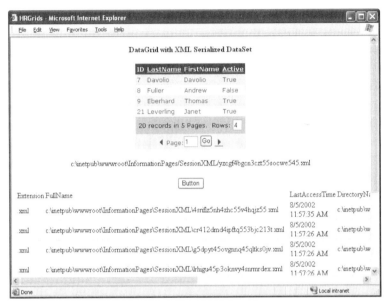

Figure 11-18   Grid/Detail form persisting data with serialized DataSet XML files

So what are the drawbacks of using XML serialized DataSets? We can think of only two:

- The slowdown when the DataSet is serialized to a local directory

- The cleanup you have to do after using the DataSet

If you don't erase the specific XML session file you created, you'll soon run out of hard drive space on your Web server. This is obviously not good. In our example, we included some code that can delete the specific session XML file. When you click the button associated with this code, the file is deleted and an error occurs during postback since no more data is available. Obviously we need to add exception handling to the code. We deliberately left this out so that you can see the process. Here's the code that deletes the current session's XML file:

```
Private Sub Button1_Click(ByVal sender As System.Object, _
    ByVal e As System.EventArgs) Handles Button1.Click
    Dim strDir As String = Server.MapPath(Nothing) + "/SessionXML/" + _
        Session.SessionID + ".xml"
```

(continued)

```
        Dim deleteFile As New FileInfo(strDir)
        deleteFile.Delete()
End Sub
```

The *FileInfo* method has a lot of built-in file handling capabilities, including the ability to delete a specific file, as we showed earlier. The question is, where do you put this code? There are several choices, one of which is to delete this file as soon as you leave the current Web Forms page and just before a *Response.Redirect* or *Server.Transfer*. Another place to delete the session-specific XML file is in a method that is called by the *SessionStateModule.end* event. Whenever a session is lost or otherwise terminated, this event is raised. Whatever solution we implement, there's a good chance that XML files will be stuck in the SessionXML directory. In addition to the solutions we've discussed, we created a Windows service that periodically looks at the files in the SessionXML directory and, when they are older than a specified date, deletes them.

Conclusion

We spent a lot of time establishing general guidelines and design methods for data presentation. We recommend you adopt our recommended standard or create your own. Consistency is the key. We created powerful yet simple Data-Grid server controls that follow our user interface strategy and can be used as stand-alone controls or in conjunction with detail forms on the same or different Web pages. We showed how you can use different levels of permissions and state management with these forms. The power and flexibility that these controls give us comes very close or surpasses that of similar functions in former Microsoft Visual Basic forms or existing Windows Forms in .NET. As in previous chapters, we explained the functions in enough detail to either let you use these components directly or modify them to your specific standards and needs. With features like the ones we showed you in this chapter, data-driven Web sites can be created quickly and efficiently.

In Chapter 14 we'll combine all components and techniques in this book to continue the HRnet Web application. We'll take the List/Detail examples shown here to the next level and integrate them with user security and permission as well as with the business layer to allow adding, editing, and deleting files. We'll also use examples to show you how similar the capabilities of Windows Forms DataGrids are.

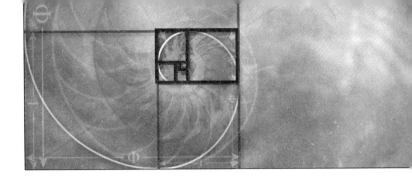

12

Implementing the Business Layer: XML Web Services

Let's pick up the discussion started in Chapter 8 and examine the design and implementation of the second part of the business layer. We'll look at how to consume existing Web services and expose the functionality through the business layer for the HRnet sample application. We'll also create an XML Web service to expose the benefits of an employee given an employee ID and the proper authorization credentials. Then we'll spend the balance of the chapter on an advanced example and learn how easy it is to create and consume SOAP headers. In the process, we'll create the business object portion of the business layer.

In many ways, the resource sharing that Web services allow across the Web seems like magic. The majority of industry analysts and players acknowledge that although just in its infancy, Web services brings us closer to realizing full interoperability.

This chapter is not a beginning tutorial on XML Web services and related concepts. Many books provide that level of information, including *Microsoft .NET XML Web Services Step by Step* by Adam Freeman and Allen Jones. (If you aren't familiar with XML Web services, refer to the MSDN Web Services Developer Center at *http://msdn.microsoft.com/webservices/*.) The purpose of this chapter is to examine XML Web services as they pertain to an object framework implementation.

Implementing XML Web Services

For the HRnet application, we needed a few XML Web services to implement the needed functionality. Let's start with the basic XML Web service, which will return a list of benefits for a given employee, to illustrate how the data layer inside the XML Web service is used to retrieve the requested information. Keep in mind that this first example is unsecured—we'll discover how to add the security functionality through the use of SOAP headers later in the chapter. Here's the entire function:

```
<WebMethod()> Public Function GetEmployeeBenefits( _
    ByVal EmployeeId As Integer) As DataSet
    Dim localDSOutput As DataSet
    Dim ParamsStoredProcedure As String = "usp_getEmployeeBenefits"

    Try
        'if authenticated then pass in employeeid and retrieve benefits
        Dim localOutPutServer As New SQLServer(PrivateConnectionString)

        localOutPutServer.AddParameter( "@EmployeeId", EmployeeId, _
            SQLServer.SQLDataType.SQLInteger, , _
            ParameterDirection.Input)

        localDSOutput =  _
            localOutPutServer.runSPDataSet(ParamsStoredProcedure)

            Return localDSOutput

    Catch
        'Throw the exception.
        Dim se = New SoapException("Invalid Login", _
            SoapException.ClientFaultCode)
        Throw se
        Exit Function

    Finally
    End Try
End Function
```

One of the first aspects of the code that should jump out at you is its adherence to the pattern used throughout the application. The use of the lower utility layers for all data access is by design. We're passing in the employee ID, calling the appropriate stored procedure, and returning the information to the calling procedure as a dataset. Any application that can consume XML Web services would then have access to the information, including both server applications (such as Microsoft SQL Server and Microsoft BizTalk Server), and clients (such as browsers, Pocket PCs, Windows Forms applications, and Microsoft Office XP).

Let's now take a look at the XML Web service output and examine how the dataset we're returning is exposed by the XML Web service.

```xml
<?xml version="1.0" encoding="utf-8" ?>
  <DataSet xmlns="http://businesslayer.hrnet.net">
  <xs:schema id="NewDataSet" xmlns=""
    xmlns:xs="http://www.w3.org/2001/XMLSchema"
    xmlns:msdata="urn:schemas-microsoft-com:xml-msdata">
  <xs:element name="NewDataSet" msdata:IsDataSet="true">
  <xs:complexType>
  <xs:choice maxOccurs="unbounded">
  <xs:element name="Table">
  <xs:complexType>
  <xs:sequence>
  <xs:element name="EmployeeBenefitsID" type="xs:int" minOccurs="0" />
  <xs:element name="EmployeeID" type="xs:int" minOccurs="0" />
  <xs:element name="BenefitID" type="xs:int" minOccurs="0" />
  <xs:element name="Active" type="xs:boolean" minOccurs="0" />
  <xs:element name="EffectiveDate" type="xs:dateTime" minOccurs="0" />
  <xs:element name="EligibilityDate" type="xs:dateTime" minOccurs="0" />
  <xs:element name="DateCreated" type="xs:dateTime" minOccurs="0" />
  <xs:element name="CreatedBy" type="xs:int" minOccurs="0" />
  <xs:element name="DateModified" type="xs:dateTime" minOccurs="0" />
  <xs:element name="ModifiedBy" type="xs:int" minOccurs="0" />
  </xs:sequence>
  </xs:complexType>
  </xs:element>
  </xs:choice>
  </xs:complexType>
  </xs:element>
  </xs:schema>
  <diffgr:diffgram xmlns:msdata="urn:schemas-microsoft-com:xml-msdata"
    xmlns:diffgr="urn:schemas-microsoft-com:xml-diffgram-v1">
  <NewDataSet xmlns="">
  <Table diffgr:id="Table1" msdata:rowOrder="0">
  <EmployeeBenefitsID>3</EmployeeBenefitsID>
  <EmployeeID>7</EmployeeID>
  <BenefitID>1</BenefitID>
  <Active>true</Active>
  <EffectiveDate>2002-07-26T00:00:00.0000000-05:00</EffectiveDate>
  <EligibilityDate>2001-07-24T00:00:00.0000000-05:00</EligibilityDate>
  <DateModified>2002-06-23T18:20:03.5400000-05:00</DateModified>
  <ModifiedBy>7</ModifiedBy>
  </Table>
```

When an XML Web service sends or retrieves a DataSet as part of the stream, the DataSet is formatted as a DiffGram. A *DiffGram* is an XML representation that is used to compare the original version with the changed version of a data element. The primary purpose of a DiffGram in the Microsoft .NET Framework is to transport the DataSet over HTTP to another XML-enabled application or platform. Another point that you should be aware of in the preceding code is that the schema information is present. Within datagrams, this is entirely optional. You can include data, the schema, or both within DataSets. The advantage of including both is that the schema gives context to the corresponding data, making the combination extremely powerful.

Although DiffGrams are primarily used to transport DataSets within the .NET Framework, they also can be used to change data within Microsoft SQL Server 2000 tables and to communicate between different platforms and the .NET Framework.

You can see the query results in the Table1 section in the previous code. We've broken that section out here.

```
<Table diffgr:id="Table1" msdata:rowOrder="0">
<EmployeeBenefitsID>3</EmployeeBenefitsID>
<EmployeeID>7</EmployeeID>
<BenefitID>1</BenefitID>
<Active>true</Active>
<EffectiveDate>2002-07-26T00:00:00.0000000-05:00</EffectiveDate>
<EligibilityDate>2001-07-24T00:00:00.0000000-05:00</EligibilityDate>
<DateModified>2002-06-23T18:20:03.5400000-05:00</DateModified>
<ModifiedBy>7</ModifiedBy>
</Table>
```

We can pass a lot of information via standards-based protocols and formats, which is great. Let's continue to the next step: consuming.

Consuming XML Web Services

After we build the XML Web service, our next step is to use it. So far, we've just tested the XML Web service using the browser. The URL for our sample XML Web service is *http://localhost/HRNetWS/HRNetWebService.asmx/GetEmployee-Benefits?EmployeeId=7*. When you view this page in your browser, you'll get a standard test user interface, provided by .NET.

Since we're invoking a method in the calls to the XML Web service, we use HTTP *GET* from the browser. This is accomplished by first appending */GetEmployeeBenefits* to the XML Web service URL, where *GetEmployeeBenefits* is the method to invoke. Then the query string parameters are appended for each parameter (if any) to the method. The first query string parameter is introduced by a question mark, with subsequent query string parameters being preceded by an ampersand.

We've demonstrated how to access an XML Web service using the browser, so now let's do it programmatically. We'll examine a Web page that uses a proxy class, provided by the sample XML Web service, to retrieve the desired information.

If you've developed or consumed COM components in Microsoft Visual Basic 6, you've almost certainly written applications to test their functionality. Typically, you'd begin by writing a simple test harness application, then adding to the project a reference to the component's type library, and finally writing code to call the methods of the component. In similar fashion, you can test your XML Web services using Microsoft Visual Studio .NET. You can write a simple Microsoft ASP.NET Web Forms application to serve as your test user interface (UI), adding a Web reference to the test application to expose the proxy classes that the client will use.

If you expand the Web References folder in Solution Explorer, you'll see a subfolder for the host on which the Web service resides. Within this folder are WSDL files for each Web service referenced. Here's what the Web References section looks like from within the integrated development environment (IDE), as shown in Figure 12-1.

Figure 12-1   Web References section

Now that we've referenced the XML Web service, we can create a new instance of the proxy class.

```
Dim wsProxy As localhost.HRNetWebServices = _
    New localhost.HRNetWebServices()
```

Next, we call the method on the XML Web service proxy class that communicates with the HRnet XML Web service's *GetEmployeeBenefits* method.

```
ds = wsProxy.GetEmployeeBenefits(7)
```

Finally, for testing purposes, we'll display the results of the method in the DataGrid.

```
DataGrid1.DataSource = ds
```

In the preceding test code, we referenced the XML Web service as .localhost.HRNetWebServices. The first component of this name is the subfolder name under the Web references folder that contains the XML Web service's reference. When the reference is added, the default folder name is that of the Web server that hosts the XML Web service. Rename this folder to use more meaningful names in Web references if you'd like. The final component of the reference is the actual XML Web service name. Our example XML Web service is named HRNetWebServices.

To simplify the process, we could import the namespace, as shown here:

```
Imports HRNetWS.localhost
```

We could then change an instantiation statement to read as follows:

```
Dim objWebService As New HRNetWebServices
```

Under the Proxy's Hood

Let's examine what goes on behind the scenes when using Web references within our projects. The proxy class generated by the XML Web service hides the communication details of the client application and the XML Web service. When you make method calls to an XML Web service using a Web reference, the code for the proxy class is generated automatically when the Web reference is added. The IDE actually calls the wsdl.exe command line utility to generate the proxy class source code. You can run this utility directly from the command line outside of the IDE. It accepts the WSDL document's URL for an XML Web service and can currently produce resulting proxy classes in either C#, Visual Basic .NET, or Java Script .NET.

Using Publicly Available Services

As you'll see, our XML Web service is accessed in the same way the earlier example, which was created on the local machine in .NET, was accessed. For this example, we'll consume as a test service a publicly available Web service that is provided by Unisys.

The functional specification for the HRnet application includes a weather information section for the company intranet based on the company's headquarters location. After a diligent search, we located the Web service for this example by going to *http://www.xmethods.com*. One of the services listed gives the weather information for any United States zip code. After testing the Web service and reviewing the output to ensure that it met the stated requirements, the design and implementation began. Here we create a Web reference within the project and then instantiate the appropriate objects:

```
Dim WeatherServices _
    As New net.k2unisys.vs.hosting001.WeatherServices()
Dim WeatherForecast _
    As New net.k2unisys.vs.hosting001.WeatherForecast()
```

You might notice something different about this code. There are two objects instead of only one. The first line is the proxy object that is used to communicate with the service. The second line is the object that is exposed by the service that will return results.

Next, we look at the WSDL exposed by the service to determine how to use the object within the project. I've excerpted the following code section pertaining to the exposed class.

```
<s:complexType name="WeatherForecast">
<s:sequence>
  <s:element minOccurs="0" maxOccurs="1" name="ZipCode" type="s:string" />
  <s:element minOccurs="0" maxOccurs="1" name="CityShortName"
    type="s:string" />
  <s:element minOccurs="0" maxOccurs="1" name="Time" type="s:string" />
  <s:element minOccurs="0" maxOccurs="1" name="Sunrise" type="s:string" />
  <s:element minOccurs="0" maxOccurs="1" name="Sunset" type="s:string" />
  <s:element minOccurs="0" maxOccurs="1" name="CurrentTemp" type="s:string"
    />
  <s:element minOccurs="0" maxOccurs="1" name="DayForecast"
    type="s0:ArrayOfDailyForecast" />
</s:sequence>
</s:complexType>
<s:complexType name="ArrayOfDailyForecast">
<s:sequence>
  <s:element minOccurs="0" maxOccurs="unbounded" name="DailyForecast"
    nillable="true" type="s0:DailyForecast" />
</s:sequence>
</s:complexType>
<s:complexType name="DailyForecast">
<s:sequence>
  <s:element minOccurs="0" maxOccurs="1" name="Day" type="s:string" />
  <s:element minOccurs="0" maxOccurs="1" name="Forecast" type="s:string" />
```

(continued)

```
<s:element minOccurs="0" maxOccurs="1" name="Abbrev" type="s:string" />
<s:element minOccurs="0" maxOccurs="1" name="HighTemp" type="s:string" />
<s:element minOccurs="0" maxOccurs="1" name="LowTemp" type="s:string" />
</s:sequence>
</s:complexType>
```

This section tells us quite a bit about the data being returned: the data hierarchy, the number of occurrences for each data element, the name of the data element, and the datatype. The first six elements (ZipCode, CityShortName, Time, Sunrise, Sunset, CurrentTemp) are pretty straightforward. We can tell the following about them:

- They are returned in the sequence in which they are defined.

- They can occur zero times or one time.

- They are string data types.

The next element is a bit more challenging; it's an array consisting of another class:

```
<s:element minOccurs="0" maxOccurs="1" name="DayForecast"
  type="s0:ArrayOfDailyForecast" />
<s:complexType name="DailyForecast">
<s:sequence>
  <s:element minOccurs="0" maxOccurs="1" name="Day" type="s:string" />
  <s:element minOccurs="0" maxOccurs="1" name="Forecast" type="s:string" />
  <s:element minOccurs="0" maxOccurs="1" name="Abbrev" type="s:string" />
  <s:element minOccurs="0" maxOccurs="1" name="HighTemp" type="s:string" />
  <s:element minOccurs="0" maxOccurs="1" name="LowTemp" type="s:string" />
</s:sequence>
</s:complexType>
```

Crikey! What should we do? After a bit of thought, we chose the following solution. We created a structure that mirrors the main class returned by the WeatherService Web service:

```
Public Structure WeatherInformation
    Dim City As String
    Dim Time As String
    Dim DayForecast As DailyForecastInfo()
    Dim Sunrise As String
    Dim Sunset As String
    Dim Status As String
    Dim ZipCode As String
End Structure
```

Next we created a structure that mirrors the array class returned by the Weather-Service Web service:

```
'Struct for weather
Public Structure DailyForecastInfo
    Dim Abbrev As String
    Dim Day As String
    Dim Forecast As String
End Structure
```

Once we defined the data, we instantiated an array object based on the array class exposed by the Web service we referenced:

```
Dim DailyForecast(2) As net.k2unisys.vs.hosting001.DailyForecast
```

The next task was to create a function that used the old, reliable data layer to retrieve the company's zip code based on the company ID. We passed this to the XML Web service to get our weather information:

```
Private Function GetCompanyPostalCode(ByVal CompanyId As Integer) _
    As String
    PrivateStatusInfo = "All Access to the requested information"
    Dim localDSOutput As ArrayList

    Dim ParamsStoredProcedure As String = "usp_GetCompanyPostalCode"

    Try
        Dim localOutPutServer As New  _
            SQLServer(PrivateConnectionString)
        localOutPutServer.AddParameter( _
            "@Companyid", CompanyId, _
            SQLServer.SQLDataType.SQLInteger, _
            ParameterDirection.Input)
        localOutPutServer.AddParameter( _
            "@PostalCode", , SQLServer.SQLDataType.SQLString, 15, _
            ParameterDirection.Output)

        localDSOutput = _
            localOutPutServer.runSPOutput(ParamsStoredProcedure)

        Return CInt(localDSOutput.Item(0))

    Catch ExceptionObject As Exception
        LogException(ExceptionObject)

    Finally
    End Try
End Function
```

Now that we have the zip code, it's time to create a method to expose the weather information through the business layer. We do this based on the company ID.

```
Public Function GetCompanyWeatherForecast( _
    ByVal CompanyId As Integer) As WeatherInformation
    Dim i As Integer
    Try

        Dim strPostalCode As String = GetCompanyPostalCode(CompanyId)

        WeatherForecast = WeatherServices.GetWeather(strPostalCode)

        With GetCompanyWeatherForecast
          .City = WeatherForecast.CityShortName
          .Sunrise = WeatherForecast.Sunrise
          .Sunset = WeatherForecast.Sunset
          'redim array for forecast
          Dim intWeather As Integer = _
              WeatherForecast.DayForecast.GetUpperBound(0)
          ReDim .DayForecast(intWeather)

          For i = 0 To intWeather
            .DayForecast(i).Day = _
                WeatherForecast.DayForecast(i).Day
            .DayForecast(i).Forecast = -
                WeatherForecast.DayForecast(i).Forecast
            .DayForecast(i).Abbrev = _
                WeatherForecast.DayForecast(i).Abbrev
          Next

          .Time = WeatherForecast.Time

          .Status = "Normal"
        End With

    Catch ExceptionObject As Exception
        GetCompanyWeatherForecast.Status = "Forecast Unavailable"
        LogException(ExceptionObject)

    Finally
    End Try
End Function
```

First we call *GetCompanyPostalCode* function and retrieve the zip code through the data layer:

```
Dim strPostalCode As String = GetCompanyPostalCode(CompanyId)
```

Next we get the weather for the company headquarters based on the zip code just retrieved:

```
WeatherForecast = WeatherServices.GetWeather(strPostalCode)
```

Now we can transfer the weather data obtained from the XML Web service to our structure that is to be returned to the calling procedure:

```
With GetCompanyWeatherForecast
    .City = WeatherForecast.CityShortName
    .Sunrise = WeatherForecast.Sunrise
    .Sunset = WeatherForecast.Sunset
```

We also need to take into account that the dimension of our array for the daily forecast needs to be changed to the upper bound of the array object returned by the XML Web service:

```
Dim intWeather As Integer = WeatherForecast.DayForecast.GetUpperBound(0)
ReDim .DayForecast(intWeather)
```

The next step is to grab the forecast information from the XML Web service and put it in the structure created earlier:

```
For i = 0 To intWeather
    .DayForecast(i).Day = _
        WeatherForecast.DayForecast(i).Day
    .DayForecast(i).Forecast = _
        WeatherForecast.DayForecast(i).Forecast
    .DayForecast(i).Abbrev = _
        WeatherForecast.DayForecast(i).Abbrev
Next
```

The last item we need to think about is how we want to indicate that the XML Web service is unavailable. If the XML Web service is down, we still want to send a message and then log it appropriately. In this case, we added an element to the structure, named Status, which we populate as follows:

```
        .Status = "Normal"
    End With
Catch ExceptionObject As Exception
    GetCompanyWeatherForecast.Status = "Forecast Unavailable"
    LogException(ExceptionObject)
```

The WeatherInfo Web Control

We need a convenient way to pass the weather information to the presentation layer. In this case, we decided to encapsulate the functionality into a Web control. You learned about the benefits of Web controls in Chapter 6. Let's see how the Web control is implemented in the Web page. We place the control functionality in the page's *Load* event. Notice that after instantiating our business layer object (*BLUtility*) and variables, we simply call the *GetCompanyWeather-Forecast* method with the corresponding company ID. It's a snap to then load the data into an *ArrayList* and bind the *ArrayList* to a list box. Easy as pie.

```
Private Sub Page_Load(ByVal sender As System.Object, _
    ByVal e As System.EventArgs) Handles MyBase.Load
    'Put user code to initialize the page here
    Dim x As New BlUtility("nDavolio", "nDavolio")
    Dim al As New ArrayList()
    Dim i As Integer = 7
    Dim weatherforecast As BlUtility.WeatherInformation

    weatherforecast = x.GetCompanyWeatherForecast(1)
    With weatherforecast 'weatherinfo
        If .Status = "Normal" Then
            al.Add("Current Weather for:")
            al.Add(.City.ToString)
            al.Add(" ")
            ' using the array's getupperbound method with
            ' 0 will give us the upper boundary
            Dim intWeather As Integer = _
                weatherforecast.DayForecast.GetUpperBound(0)

            For i = 0 To (intWeather)
                al.Add(.DayForecast(i).Day)
                al.Add(.DayForecast(i).Forecast)
                al.Add(.DayForecast(i).Abbrev)
                al.Add(" ")
            Next
            al.Add(.Time.ToString)
        Else
            al.Add(.Status.ToString)
        End If

    End With
    ListBox1.DataSource = al
    ListBox1.DataBind()
End Sub
```

Once the control is created, we can add it to a Web page. Here's the register directive that we add to the Web page so that we can use the control, as we learned in Chapter 6:

```
<%@ Register TagPrefix="uc1" TagName="Weather"
    Src="Weather.ascx" %>
```

Figure 12-2 illustrates what the finished Web control looks like with output.

I hope you can see that consuming and publishing XML Web services allows for some pretty remarkable things. Now let's take a brief look at beefing up the EmployeeBenefits XML Web service that we examined in the first part of this chapter and pass the username and password to the service's SOAP header information.

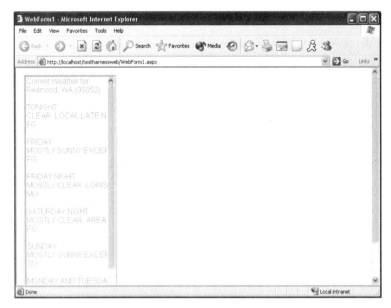

Figure 12-2   WeatherInfo Web control output

SOAP: Your XML Web Service's New Best Friend

SOAP is a vendor-independent standard for sending data between a client and a server and is implemented as a simple, lightweight XML-based protocol. SOAP is the standard protocol designed to implement the remote procedure call functionality for XML Web services. Using XML, SOAP handles the structured data encoding and decoding that is sent to and received from an XML Web service and its clients.

Currently Supported Protocols

SOAP is the protocol of choice for XML Web services access. Designed for remote procedure call–like functionality, SOAP messages are the most feature-rich access approach. Independent of transport protocols, SOAP messages can travel on HTTP, SMTP, or raw sockets (known as Direct Internet Message Encapsulation, or DIME). XML Web services can also be accessed by HTTP *GET* and *POST* messages. When you use .NET to create an XML Web service, your service will support SOAP, HTTP *GET*, and HTTP *POST* automatically.

SOAP Document Structure

The World Wide Web Consortium at *http://www.W3c.org* defines standard schemas for SOAP messages, and these are referred to by SOAP documents using standard XML namespaces. Therefore, a SOAP document is actually an XML document that uses a SOAP namespace.

The elements of a SOAP message are the Envelope, the Header, and the Body. Let's briefly review each in preparation for manipulating the header.

Envelope

Similar to a postal envelope, the main purpose of this required root element is to contain the message.

Header

The Header element contains information related to the message, such as routing. This element is SOAP's extensibility mechanism—the developer, not the SOAP standard (as we'll see in the example), defines the information sent inside the header. The SOAP Header element is optional. However, if present, it must be the first child element of the Envelope. The Header element is a container for header blocks. All child elements of the Header element are actually header blocks that specify information pertaining to the entire message.

Body

Every SOAP message contains a Body element, which is the second child element of the Envelope and appears after the Header (if present). If no Header is present, the Body element is the Envelope's first child. The Body element, like the Header element, serves as a container for its corresponding blocks.

Body blocks contain the content portion of the message. For example, in an XML Web service method call, the body block contains the method name along with any of its input parameters values. Both the data structure and type sent within a body block are extensible and not defined by the SOAP standard. However, the data encoding methods are specified. The only exception to the structure and type of data sent is the SOAP Fault.

A SOAP Fault is a SOAP standard body block used to communicate error information. A Fault element includes an error number (faultcode), an error description (faultstring), and the error source (faultactor). A SOAP message can contain only one Fault element. As we'll discover in the following example, we can utilize this functionality through the *SOAPFault* class exposed by the .NET framework.

Now that we've reviewed a little about SOAP, let's see how easily we can add information to the SOAP Header using the classes within the .NET Framework.

Given the sensitivity of employee data, we should add some security functionality to the EmployeeBenefits Web service. As promised earlier, we're going to examine how to use the SOAP header to pass security credentials back to the server for authentication. First we have to create a class that will be used as our custom header. This header will store the information we want to pass. It inherits the functionality of the SOAP Header class.

```
Public Class HRNHeader : Inherits SoapHeader
    Public Username As String
    Public Password As String
End Class
```

In this case, the information we are passing to the XML Web service client is the username and password for validation.

Now we'll instantiate an object based on the header class just created:

```
Public SecureHeader As HRNHeader
```

Then we want to add the *SoapHeader* attribute to the *Webmethod* tag to give access to the custom header object and its information:

```
<WebMethod(), SoapHeader("SecureHeader", _
    Direction:=SoapHeaderDirection.InOut, _
    Required:=True)> Public Function GetEmployeeBenefits( _
    ByVal EmployeeId As Integer) As DataSet
```

After instantiating the necessary variables and objects, we call the *Login* method, which is exposed by the security layer, and pass in the username and password we sent in the custom header class:

```
If SecurCheck.Login(SecureHeader.Username, SecureHeader.Password) _
    = True Then
```

If successful, we use the data layer to return benefit information for a given employee:

```
localOutPutServer.AddParameter( _
    "@EmployeeId", EmployeeId, _
    SQLServer.SQLDataType.SQLInteger, , _
    ParameterDirection.Input)

localDSOutput = _
    localOutPutServer.runSPDataSet(ParamsStoredProcedure)
Return localDSOutput
```

If the login is unsuccessful, we generate a SOAP Fault by creating an XML document, adding the necessary details as nodes, and tying it to the SOAP exception. We then throw the SOAP exception as we would any other:

```
Dim SoapExceptionDoc As New System.Xml.XmlDocument()
Dim SoapExceptionNode As System.Xml.XmlNode = _
    SoapExceptionDoc.CreateNode(XmlNodeType.Element, _
    SoapException.DetailElementName.Name, _
    SoapException.DetailElementName.Namespace)

Dim SoapExceptionDetails1 As System.Xml.XmlNode = _
    SoapExceptionDoc.CreateNode(XmlNodeType.Element, _
    "SoapExceptionInfo1", "http://businesslayer.hrnet.net")

Dim SoapExceptionDetails2 As System.Xml.XmlNode = _
    SoapExceptionDoc.CreateNode(XmlNodeType.Element, _
    "SoapExceptionInfo2", "http://businesslayer.hrnet.net")
Dim SoapExceptionAttribute As XmlAttribute = _
    SoapExceptionDoc.CreateAttribute("t", _
    "attrName", "http://businesslayer.hrnet.net")
SoapExceptionAttribute.Value = "attrValue"
SoapExceptionDetails2.Attributes.Append(SoapExceptionAttribute)

SoapExceptionNode.AppendChild(SoapExceptionDetails1)
SoapExceptionNode.AppendChild(SoapExceptionDetails2)

se = New SoapException("Invalid Login", _
    SoapException.ClientFaultCode, _
    Context.Request.Url.AbsoluteUri, SoapExceptionNode)
Throw se
```

Now let's assemble the entire function and pull all the pieces together:

```
'The SoapHeader Attribute specifies the header info
'with our header object
<WebMethod(), SoapHeader("SecureHeader", _
    Direction:=SoapHeaderDirection.InOut, _
    Required:=True)> Public Function GetEmployeeBenefits(_
    ByVal EmployeeId As Integer) As DataSet
    Dim localDSOutput As DataSet
    Dim ParamsStoredProcedure As String = "usp_getEmployeeBenefits"

    Try
        'validate with the security layer passing in info from the header
        If SecurCheck.Login(SecureHeader.Username, SecureHeader.Password) _
            = True Then
            'if authenticated then pass in employeeid and retrieve benefits
            Dim localOutPutServer As New SQLServer(PrivateConnectionString)
            localOutPutServer.AddParameter( _
                "@EmployeeId", EmployeeId, _
                SQLServer.SQLDataType.SQLInteger, , _
                ParameterDirection.Input)
```

```
                localDSOutput = _
                    localOutPutServer.runSPDataSet(ParamsStoredProcedure)
                Return localDSOutput
            Else
                Dim SoapExceptionDoc As New System.Xml.XmlDocument()
                Dim SoapExceptionNode As System.Xml.XmlNode = _
                    SoapExceptionDoc.CreateNode(XmlNodeType.Element, _
                    SoapException.DetailElementName.Name, _
                    SoapException.DetailElementName.Namespace)

                Dim SoapExceptionDetails1 As System.Xml.XmlNode = _
                    SoapExceptionDoc.CreateNode(XmlNodeType.Element, _
                    "SoapExceptionInfo1", "http://businesslayer.hrnet.net")

                Dim SoapExceptionDetails2 As System.Xml.XmlNode = _
                    SoapExceptionDoc.CreateNode(XmlNodeType.Element, _
                    "SoapExceptionInfo2", "http://businesslayer.hrnet.net")
                Dim SoapExceptionAttribute As XmlAttribute = _
                    SoapExceptionDoc.CreateAttribute("t", _
                    "attrName", "http://businesslayer.hrnet.net")
                SoapExceptionAttribute.Value = "attrValue"
                SoapExceptionDetails2.Attributes.Append(SoapExceptionAttribute)

                SoapExceptionNode.AppendChild(SoapExceptionDetails1)
                SoapExceptionNode.AppendChild(SoapExceptionDetails2)

                se = New SoapException("Invalid Login", _
                    SoapException.ClientFaultCode, _
                    Context.Request.Url.AbsoluteUri, SoapExceptionNode)
                Throw se
                Exit Function

            End If
        Finally
        End Try
End Function
```

Calling from the Client

Let's switch over to the client side and discover how to use the new function-ality from the client (in this case, a Windows Forms smart client), step by step. The initial tasks, after adding the Web reference, are to both instantiate and populate our header so that it passes back to the XML Web service:

```
Dim HRNetSoapHeader As localhost.HRNHeader = _
    New localhost.HRNHeader()

HRnetSoapHeader.Username = "nDavolio"
HRnetSoapHeader.Password = "nDavolio"
```

Next we'll create a new instance of the proxy class and add the MyHeader SOAP header to the SOAP request:

```
Dim wsProxy As localhost.HRNetWebServices = _
    New localhost.HRNetWebServices()

wsProxy.HRNHeaderValue = HRNetSoapHeader
```

Then we simply call the method on the XML Web services proxy class that communicates with the HRnet XML Web service's *GetEmployeeBenefits* method:

```
ds = wsProxy.GetEmployeeBenefits(7)
```

After that, we display the results of the method in the DataGrid:

```
DataGrid1.DataSource = ds
```

Finally, because we're using an XML Web service and passing information in the header, we need to check for a SOAP exception and display the appropriate information:

```
Catch ExceptionObject As SoapException
    MsgBox(ExceptionObject.Message)
End Try
```

Now the client can pass the information to the XML Web service in the header. Of course, while this process is more secure than HTTP, we would obviously want to encrypt such sensitive information in a production application.

Conclusion

In this chapter, we discussed how XML Web services relate to and can be used by component-based applications as another portion of the business layer. We examined using the data layer to provide functionality for both our published and consumed XML Web services. We discovered how to consume publicly available XML Web services while taking into account the special data requirements of those XML Web services, and then we exposed them through the business layer. Finally, we reviewed SOAP and learned how to pass information between an XML Web service and its clients via SOAP header information. In the next chapter, we'll continue the journey by pondering the mysteries of .NET remoting.

13

Using Remoting for Communication

Now that we've walked through the basics of our objects and application, let's take a look at how to use the business objects and security object from a Microsoft Windows client using Microsoft .NET remoting. Remoting is a powerful set of technologies for remote communication. It's also complex and requires some forethought before you jump in with both feet and use it to wire applications together. In this chapter, we'll go over some basics of remoting and then discuss how to make remoting work.

.NET remoting is a technology for communicating between applications. You can think of remoting as DCOM all grown up. DCOM was easy to use but didn't offer you many communication mechanisms, or *channels*. Remoting is a different animal, providing you with several. These options make using remoting in our application, in which Windows clients communicate directly with the business objects on a server, easy. The flexibility in remoting also allows changes to options after the application is up and running without any help from the developer. For more information about .NET remoting, see *Microsoft .NET Remoting* by Scott McLean, James Naftel, and Kim Williams (Microsoft Press, 2003).

Starting Out

We like to kick the tires of any application or technology before we use it so that we can test it in a simple fashion and make sure it works. Testing the technology also gives us baselines that we can refer to when problems occur, especially as we use more complex features. To start using remoting, we created a simple test environment in which we used a basic sample provided in the MSDN documentation, Remoting Hello.

To tackle the first part of the remoting puzzle, you need to create the server objects that you'll use. The HelloService sample is a good choice because it's quite short. The full source for this *HelloService* class is shown here:

```
Imports System
Namespace Hello
    Public Class HelloService
        Inherits MarshalByRefObject
        Public Function ReturnGreeting(ByVal name As String _
            As [String]
            Dim message As String = _
                "Hi there " + name + ", _
                you are using .NET Remoting"
            Console.WriteLine(message)
            Return message
        End Function 'ReturnGreeting
    End Class 'HelloService
End Namespace 'Hello
```

There's nothing really special about the *HelloService* class except that the *Inherits MarshalByRefObject* is part of the class statement. (*Inherits* derives this class from *MarshalByRefObject* to allow the class to be marshaled by reference and not by value. We'll come back to this discussion a bit later.) To build the class, create a new Class Library project named Hello, add the *HelloService* class to the project, and then build the assembly. You should end up with a Hello.dll file that contains the *HelloService* class. By the way, you can delete the namespace in this code if you name your project Hello since the project name becomes the default root namespace.

Now, let's take a look at the client. As we all know, a client application must have a reference to a class before it can use it. Remoting is no different and requires a reference to the interface for the remote class or a reference to the class itself. For instance, in Figure 13-1, the client application needs a reference to the remote *HelloService* that is located on the server.

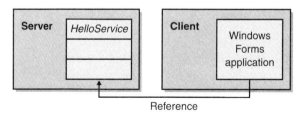

Figure 13-1   The client application must have a reference to a class to call the class remotely.

We decided to implement the reference by building an assembly with the interfaces and using the assembly with the client. This enables the client to compile, and we can avoid deploying all the business objects to the client. So, before we go too far, let's look at one way to generate these interfaces. We like automation, so we were intrigued to find the Soapsuds tool that comes with the Microsoft .NET Framework.

Soapsuds is an executable file that can be used to generate interfaces for a remote object (among other things). This tool appears to be simple to use, but it does have some anomalies that we'll discuss in a moment. Before we can use Soapsuds to build our client assembly, we need to set up the remoting server and then start it. Then Soapsuds file pulls the interface information from the server for us.

Creating the Server

Most of the samples that deal with .NET Framework are written in C#. So, the first thing we did was convert the samples to Microsoft Visual Basic .NET and test them. We created the server by building a new Microsoft Windows Forms application and naming it HelloHostServer. In the form's *Load* event for Form1, we placed the following subroutine call:

```
ConfigureRemoting()
```

Next, we added a module named *RemotingRoutines* to the application and entered the following *Imports* statement:

```
Imports System.Runtime.Remoting
```

Next, enter the following code in the module:

```
Dim localConfigFileName As String = _
    "HelloHostServer.exe.config"
Sub ConfigureRemoting()
    RemotingConfiguration.Configure( _
        localConfigFileName)
End Sub
```

The magic of this module is the call to the *Configure* method. This loads the HelloHostServer.exe.config file, which is specified via the variable *local-ConfigFileName*. The file should be placed in the same folder as the server's executable (the bin folder by default). The *Configure* method loads the remoting configuration data from the file, so the data doesn't have to be set programatically. The configuration for the sample looks like this:

```
<configuration>
  <system.runtime.remoting>
    <application name="RemotingHello">
      <service>
        <wellknown mode="SingleCall"
          type="Hello.HelloService,
          Hello" objectUri="HelloService.soap" />
      </service>

      <channels>
        <channel ref="http" port="8000" />
      </channels>
    </application>
  </system.runtime.remoting>
</configuration>
```

Let's walk through the key options, one by one. The first important option is the application name:

```
<application name="RemotingHello">
```

This option sets the name that clients will use to access the server. It's important that you carefully enter all items in the configuration files; if you make a mistake, you'll generate errors when you load your server or when a client tries to access the application.

The <*service*> entries are next. This option allows you to define the items that will be remoted by the server. Our sample has only one entry for this option, but you can add any number of objects to remote. The *wellknown* tag defines objects that are known to both the server and the client. Setting the mode to *SingleCall* causes a new instance of the object to be created for each client instantiation. You can also set the mode to *Singleton* to cause only one object to be created on the server, regardless of the number of client requests.

The *type* attribute is set to the full namespace for the class. In this case, the *Hello* namespace is defined as the name of the project, and *HelloService* is the class name. The option that follows the full namespace is the assembly name, which is Hello (as in Hello.dll).

Finally, the *objectUri* option defines two things. First, it defines how the client will connect to the server. The *objectUri* is combined with the server name, port number, and application name to make the URL the client uses to connect. Second, *objectUri* defines the formatting with its file extension (either .soap or .rem).

The final entry in the config file is the channel definition. This sample file uses the port number to define an HTTP channel on port 8000:

```
<channel ref="http" port="8000" />
```

The config file should be named appname.exe.config, where *appname* is the name of your application. You should also place the config file in the bin folder of the application or wherever you place the executable file. Later we'll show you an example of moving the config file to another location.

Before you're ready to move on to the next step, you must add Hello.dll to the host application. You can do this by simply copying Hello.dll to the bin folder (HelloHostServer\Bin) of the host application. Double-click HelloHost-Server.exe to start the host.

Building Your First Remoting Client

Here's the fun part of the process. As mentioned earlier, the client must have a reference to the interface of the remote object or to the object itself. We like to keep the client simple and thin for deployment. One of the ways to do this is to use Soapsuds to generate a DLL file that is essentially an assembly that contains the interface for our application. We've never been great fans of creating separate interfaces and using implementations because of the extra work. It's nice to have a tool like Soapsuds do it for us.

To use Soapsuds, start the Visual Studio .NET command prompt, and then navigate to the directory in which you want to place the assembly with the interfaces (the metadata). Then execute the command like this:

```
soapsuds -url:http://localhost:8000/helloservice.soap?wsdl
 -oa:Hello.dll -nowp
```

This command specifies that Soapsuds connects to the HelloService we defined earlier and then extracts the Web Services Description Language (WSDL) for the class. The *–oa* option specifies the output file name (and the assembly name). The *–nowp* option specifies that we don't want a wrapper generated.

Both the server and the client assembly names must be the same. Use the assembly name as the name of the output file when you generate metadata with the *–oa* option since that name is used to set the assembly name. For instance, the next command generates Hello.dll correctly:

```
soapsuds -url:http://localhost:8000/helloservice.soap?wsdl
 -oa:Hello.dll -nowp
```

The next command generates another output file but with a different assembly name.

```
soapsuds -url:http://localhost:8000/helloservice.soap?wsdl
 -oa:hellosfdsfdf.dll -nowp
```

This generates the assembly name hellosfdsfdf.dll. You can see this in Figure 13-2. The output in this figure was generated by opening the assemblies manifest using the MSIL Disassembler (ILDASM).

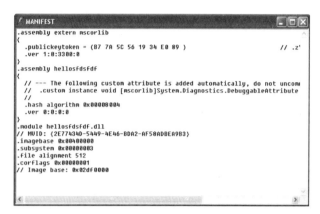

Figure 13-2 Part of the manifest for the incorrectly generated assembly

To fully understand what's going on, let's take a quick look at the metadata that was generated. Using ILDASM again, we opened both the server assembly and client metadata assembly. Then we looked at the Microsoft intermediate language (MSIL) generated for the *ReturnGreeting* function. The top of Figure 13-3 shows the IL for the client metadata representation, and the bottom of the figure shows the server object implementation.

You can see how the top part of the figure shows the interface for the *ReturnGreeting* method as well as the reference to the .NET remoting SOAP protocol. You can also see references to the code in the actual implementation in the bottom part of the figure.

Now that you have your Hello.dll, what do you do with it? Add a new Windows Forms project to the solution for your server, and name it ClientRemotingTester. Rename Form1 to *frmMain*, and set its *Text* property to *Remoting Hello Tester*. Open *frmMain*, and add a button named *cmdReturn* with the *Text* property set to *Return Greeting*. Then add a text box named *txtOutput* and the following property settings:

Property	Value	
Size	464, 216	
Location	24, 72	
Multiline	*True*	

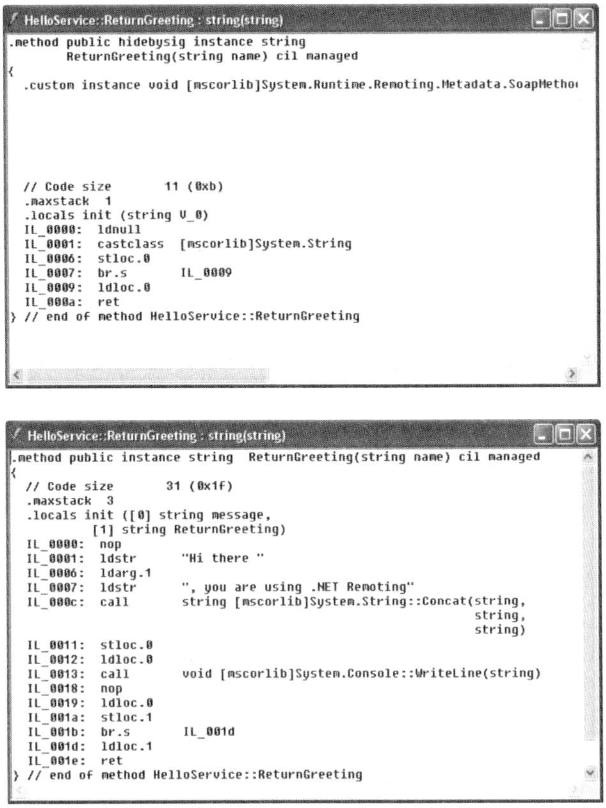

```
HelloService::ReturnGreeting : string(string)
.method public hidebysig instance string
        ReturnGreeting(string name) cil managed
{
  .custom instance void [mscorlib]System.Runtime.Remoting.Metadata.SoapMetho

  // Code size       11 (0xb)
  .maxstack  1
  .locals init (string V_0)
  IL_0000:  ldnull
  IL_0001:  castclass  [mscorlib]System.String
  IL_0006:  stloc.0
  IL_0007:  br.s       IL_0009
  IL_0009:  ldloc.0
  IL_000a:  ret
} // end of method HelloService::ReturnGreeting
```

```
HelloService::ReturnGreeting : string(string)
.method public instance string  ReturnGreeting(string name) cil managed
{
  // Code size       31 (0x1f)
  .maxstack  3
  .locals init ([0] string message,
           [1] string ReturnGreeting)
  IL_0000:  nop
  IL_0001:  ldstr      "Hi there "
  IL_0006:  ldarg.1
  IL_0007:  ldstr      ", you are using .NET Remoting"
  IL_000c:  call       string [mscorlib]System.String::Concat(string,
                                                              string,
                                                              string)
  IL_0011:  stloc.0
  IL_0012:  ldloc.0
  IL_0013:  call       void [mscorlib]System.Console::WriteLine(string)
  IL_0018:  nop
  IL_0019:  ldloc.0
  IL_001a:  stloc.1
  IL_001b:  br.s       IL_001d
  IL_001d:  ldloc.1
  IL_001e:  ret
} // end of method HelloService::ReturnGreeting
```

Figure 13-3 This figure demonstrates the IL for both the server (bottom) and the client (top) metadata assemblies.

Double-click the form to open the code window. Add this line just before the form's *Load* event:

```
Dim sApplicationName As String = Application.ProductName
```

Add the following code to the form's *Load* event:

```
Me.Text = sApplicationName

If InitializeRemoting() Then
    txtOutput.Text &= _
        "Obtaining Proxy for HelloService, using new" _
        & vbCrLf
    InitializeHello()

Else
    txtOutput.Text = _
        "An error occurred while initializing remoting"
End If
```

This code calls two functions that we'll put into a module in the application. *InitializeRemoting* will set up the client's remoting features. The *InitializeHello* function will initialize the remote object. Putting these functions into a module allows us to isolate the routines, and when we get into a production application, we can simply drop them in a module and change them as needed. It also allows us to potentially change the way the remote object is instantiated later in the application's cycle.

Add a module named *RemotingClientRoutines* to the project and add the following *Imports* statements to the module:

```
Imports System.Runtime.Remoting
Imports System.Runtime.Remoting.Channels
Imports System.Runtime.Remoting.Channels.Http
```

Add the following definitions to the module:

```
Friend channelRemote As HttpChannel
Friend typeHello As type = GetType(Hello.HelloService)
Friend urlHello As String = _
    "http://localhost:8000/RemotingHello/HelloService.soap"
Friend helloService As Hello.HelloService
```

Create the *InitializeRemoting* function, and add the *privateSuccess* variable:

```
Function InitializeRemoting() As Boolean
    Dim privateSuccess As Boolean
```

Add the following lines to create a new HTTP channel, and then register it:

```
Try
    channelRemote = New HttpChannel()
    ChannelServices.RegisterChannel(channelRemote)
```

Now, add the next line to register the *hello* class:

```
RemotingConfiguration.RegisterWellKnownClientType( _
    typeHello, urlHello)
```

You can finish the subroutine's code by adding the following code to finish the *Try...Catch* statement and set the return value:

```
        privateSuccess = True
    Catch exc As Exception
        privateSuccess = False
    End Try
    Return privateSuccess
End Function
```

Next create the *InitializeHello* procedure. This procedure simply instantiates the remote object.

```
Sub InitializeHello()
    helloService = New Hello.HelloService()
End Sub
```

The *InitializeHello* procedure is quite simple but important. We'll enhance it later in the real client application.

Now create a *Click* event for the *cmdReturn* button and enter this code:

```
Dim name As String = "Bill"

txtOutput.Text &= "Calling HelloService.ReturnGreeting(0)" _
    & vbCrLf

Application.DoEvents()

Dim greeting As [String] = helloService.ReturnGreeting(name)

txtOutput.Text &= "  returned: " & greeting & vbCrLf
```

Before you run the application, open the Configuration Manager from the Build menu. Clear the Build check box for HelloHostServer. This prevents HelloHostServer from being built when you run the client. Since you're running HelloHostServer, the output files (DLL and .pdb) are locked and won't be updated when you press F5. That's because when you press F5, all projects are built unless you change the configuration.

Now you can run the client application. You should see output that looks like Figure 13-4.

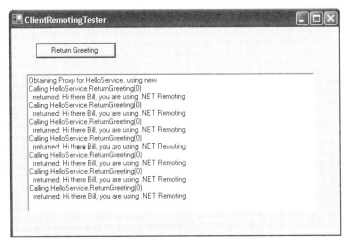

Figure 13-4   Simple client application using remote *Hello* object

You can apply the same concepts you learned when interacting with the remote object to implement remoting in our HRnet application. You'll see that the process gets more complicated as we select the features we need.

Building the Remote Host

Before we remote the business objects, we must take care of one more task. Before an object can be remoted, there must be a host application for it. This host application provides the channel between the client and the business object so that the client can communicate with the business object. Let's create the host for them. We're going to create two different hosts: one for testing and one for production. The testing host will be a Windows application that is similar to the host we used in the first example. The main difference will be the use of a custom configuration file that is stored in a common folder. The production host will be a Windows service that uses the same configuration file we used earlier. The Windows service is nice because it can be set to start automatically when the server boots, making it easy to use and resilient because it will always be running, ready to host the objects for any clients.

Windows Hoster

We created a new solution named Ch13RemotingHosters that will host both of the hosting projects. To create the Windows hoster, add a new Windows application to this solution.

Rename Form1 to *frmMain*, and set the *Text* property of the form to *BizObject Hosting Server*. Next add a Textbox to the form and set its properties as follows:

Property	Value
Name	*txtOutput*
Size	464, 248
Multiline	*True*
Location	24, 24

Create a *Load* event handler for the form, and add the following code:

```
Try
    ConfigureRemoting()
Catch exc As Exception
    txtOutput.Text = exc.Message
End Try
```

Add a module to the project, and name it *RemotingRoutines*. Then add the following *Imports* statement:

```
Imports System.Runtime.Remoting
```

Finally, add this code to the module:

```
Dim localConfigFileName As String = _
    "C:\BuildOOP\Ch13\BizObjectConfigurationFiles\HRApp.exe.config"
Sub ConfigureRemoting()
    RemotingConfiguration.Configure(_
        localConfigFileName)
End Sub
```

That's it. This is our remoting hoster, and we can now use it to test our hosting objects. This host is easy to use because you can stop and start it quickly as well as debug it easily.

Windows Service Hoster

The Windows service will use almost exactly the same code as the Windows version of the hoster. The main difference is that the service has no interface, and thus we write entries to the event log when an event occurs. The event log allows the system administrator to see what's going on in the service.

To create the service, add a new Windows service project to the solution and name the project HRBizObjServerWinService. Rename *Service1* to *service-Hoster*.

Since we're going to use code that is nearly identical to the code used in the Windows hoster, we can use the module we created earlier. Use the drag-and-drop feature to copy the RemotingRoutines.vb file from the Windows hoster project to the service project.

Switch back to the designer for the service. Drag an event log component from the Toolbox, and drop it on the designer. Set the name of the event log object to *eventlogHosterService*, and set the properties as shown here:

Property	Value
Log	*HRApp*
Machinename	Using the period sets the machine name to the local system.
Source	*HostingService*

Press F7 to switch to code view. Add code to the existing events as shown here:

```
Protected Overrides Sub OnStart(ByVal args() As String)
    eventlogHosterService.WriteEntry("Service Started")
    Try
        ConfigureRemoting()
        eventlogHosterService.WriteEntry( _
            "Remoting Configured")
    Catch exc As Exception
        eventlogHosterService.WriteEntry( _
            "Error occurred on configure remoting" _
            & " -- " & exc.Message)
    End Try
End Sub


Protected Overrides Sub OnStop()
    eventlogHosterService.WriteEntry("Service Started")
End Sub
```

Now you can use your hosting service, but let's make it a little easier to install. We can do this by adding an installer to the project that can be used to install items such as a Windows service or a custom event log. Switch back to design view for the service. Right-click the design surface, and click Add Installer on the shortcut menu. This will add a *ProjectInstaller* class to the project. Open the *ProjectInstaller* class, and select the *ServiceProcessInstaller* object on the design surface. Set the *Account* property to *LocalSystem*.

Next, select the *HRHosterServiceInstaller* object in the designer and set the properties:

Property	Value
DisplayName	*HR Hosting Application* (Windows Service)
StartType	*Automatic*
ServiceName	*serviceHoster*

Let's do the same thing for the event log. Switch back to design view for the service. Select the event log object, right-click it, and then click Add Installer on the shortcut menu. This will add an entry to the installer to create the custom event log during installation if a log doesn't already exist.

Now you can install your service using the InstallUtil program that is installed with the .NET Framework. This utility calls the routines in the installer to install the service and the event log. The easiest way to use this utility is to start the Visual Studio .NET command prompt, and then run InstallUtil and pass it the name of the service assembly file (DLL). You can also use the */u* switch to uninstall a service.

Controlling the Service

You can, of course, use the Computer Management utility to control your service. This utility makes the service easy to use, but you must dig for the utility each time you need to use it. You can also create your own custom controller. For instance, you can create a new Windows project and then use the *Service-Controller* class to create the management utility. Let's walk through a simple example for the service we just created.

Create a new Windows application named HRBizObjectServerController. Rename Form to *frmController*, and set its *Text* property to *HR Application Service Controller*. Add a check box control with the following properties to the form:

Property	Value
Name	*chkStatusCheck*
Text	*Check Status?*
CheckedState	*Checked*

Add two buttons with the following properties to the form:

Property	Value
Name	*cmdStart*
Text	*Start*
Name	*cmdStop*
Text	*Stop*

Add a StatusBar to the form and leave its default properties.

Next, we need a menu, so add a ContextMenu to the form and create the following menus:

Property	Value
mnuOpen	*Open*
mnuStart	*Start*
mnuStop	*Stop*
mnuClose	*Close*

Add a Timer control to the form, and set its *Interval* property to 10000 and its *Enabled* property to *True*. Finally, add a Notify icon to the form and set its properties as follows:

Property	Value
Icon	Pick an icon from the Visual Studio .NET icons
Text	*HR Application Hoster Service*
ContextMenu	*ContextService*

Add a *Click* event handler for each button and each menu item. Then add a *CheckedChanged* event handler to the check box. Finally, add a *Tick* event to the timer.

Add the following procedures to the form's code:

```
#Region "Private Functions"
    Sub StartService()
        Try
            myController.Start()
        Catch exp As Exception
            MsgBox("Could not start service")
        End Try
    End Sub
    Sub StopService()
        If myController.CanStop Then
            myController.Stop()
        Else
            MsgBox("Service cannot be stopped")
        End If
    End Sub
    Sub CheckStatus()
        myController.Refresh()
        ServiceStatus.Text = myController.Status.ToString
        NotifyIcon1.Text = "HR App Hoster Service" _
            & " (" & ServiceStatus.Text & ")"
    End Sub
#End Region
```

Enter this code for the form's *Load* event:

```
myController = New ServiceController("serviceHoster")
CheckStatus()
```

Add this code for the *Timer1_Tick* event:

```
If chkStatusCheck.Checked Then
    CheckStatus()
End If
```

Add the following code to the *Click* events for the Start menu and Start button:

```
StartService()
CheckStatus()
```

Add the following code to the *Click* events for the Stop menu and Stop button:

```
StopService()
CheckStatus()
```

Add this code to the *Click* event for the Open menu:

```
Me.WindowState = FormWindowState.Normal
Me.Show()
Me.Visible = True
```

Enter this code for the Close menu:

```
End
```

Finally, add the following code to the *CheckChanged* event of the check box:

```
If chkStatusCheck.Checked Then
    Timer1.Enabled = True
Else
    Timer1.Enabled = False
End If
```

Now you can run this application. When the application runs, it won't show the form, but you will see it displayed in the status notification area of the taskbar (the system tray). You can hover the mouse cursor over the icon to see whether the service is running. You can right-click the icon and use the context menu to manipulate the service or show the form and use it to control the service. This simple controller provides you with a complete service controller for your remoting host. You could even extend this controller and your service to allow for changing parts of it, such as the config file, on the fly.

Remoting the Business Objects

Now for the fun. It's time to consider remoting our business objects. Remoting them will allow us to build a Windows client that communicates with the business objects. Now that we have the hosts for the remote objects as well as the remote objects built, we're ready to remote them, right? Not so fast! As we mentioned earlier, .NET remoting is extremely powerful and flexible and thus is complex, so you need to consider a number of rules and issues when dealing with remoting objects. Let's discuss some of these issues in the context of remoting our HRnet application in a client/server scenario.

The first issue we came across was the need to call the remote objects on the server, so we want to remote them by reference and not by serializing the object down to the client. Remoting by reference is really doing marshaling by reference. This process requires that the remote objects (such as our business layer) inherit from *MarshalByRefObject*. It's simple enough but brings up some interesting considerations.

We can simply put the following *Inherits* clause in the base class of the business objects like so:

```
Inherits MarshalByRefObject
```

Now that we've changed the base class, all the other objects will inherit it from here. This strategy works fine unless you're using the Component Designer in your classes, in which case changing the inheritance breaks the designer because you can't do multiple inheritance with the .NET Framework.

Security Layer

Let's try remoting our security layer first because we'll need logon services for our client. It turns out that the security layer is easy to remote. Why? In this case, we needed only one method from the security layer, the *Login* method. Instead of changing the security layer, we created a facade layer named *Security-Facade*. The face class is named *LoginService*. We created this as a separate Class Library project. Then we set a reference to the security layer. Next we added an *Inherits* clause to the *LoginService* class:

```
Public Class LoginService
    Inherits MarshalByRefObject
```

Then we added a *Login* function that calls the *Login* method of the security layer:

```
Function Login( _
    ByVal UserName As String, _
    ByVal Password As String) _
    As Boolean

    Dim privateSuccess As Boolean
    Dim oUser As New SecurIt.UserSecurity()

    Try
        privateSuccess = oUser.Login(UserName, Password)
    Catch exc As Exception
        Throw New Exception( _
            "An error occurred accessing the " _
            & "Securit component -- " & exc.Message)
    End Try

    Return privateSuccess

End Function

End Class
```

That's it. No rocket science or other difficult tasks—just a simple facade layer that implements the marshaling for us.

Business Layer

We'll save you from experiencing all our trials and tribulations and instead offer what we discovered when we remoted the business objects.

We started out thinking we would just remote the objects as they are. That's when we came across this error message in some testing:

```
>? exc.message
"Can not run a non-default constructor when connecting to well-known objects."
```

This message means that you can't have a custom constructor in a remotable object. After much trial and error, we decided on the following approach. We used client-activated objects instead of server-activated objects, which allowed us to instantiate an object on the server, work with that object, and then let the object die at some point. If we had used server-activated objects, we would have had to pass the security credentials on each method call, thus changing every public method in the business objects and changing all the code that uses them, among other consequences.

In using the simpler client activation approach, we had to make minor changes to the business objects. Let's look at the base class first. We added the following *Imports* statements to the base class:

```
Imports System.Runtime.Remoting.Lifetime
Imports System.Windows.Forms
```

Then we added the *Inherits* clause for the marshaling:

```
Inherits MarshalByRefObject
```

Now for the hard part. We moved the initialization code from the constructors to a procedure named *InitializeObject*. The code for this overloaded procedure is shown here:

```
Friend Sub InitializeObject( _
    ByVal sUserName As String, ByVal spassword As String)
    privateModuleName = Me.GetType.ToString
    'Given the sensitive nature of HR data we
    'must verify proper access
    VerifyAccess(sUserName, spassword)
End Sub
Friend Sub InitializeObject( _
    ByVal objSecurit As SecurIt.UserSecurity)
    Try
        privateModuleName = Me.GetType.ToString
```

(continued)

```
        VerifyAccess(objSecurit)
    Catch ExceptionObject As Exception
        LogException(ExceptionObject)

    Finally
    End Try
End Sub
```

The two constructors were changed to call *InitializeObject*. Then a new constructor, which is the default constructor with no parameters, was added:

```
Public Sub New()
    'The msgbox can be uncommented to show when the
    'class is instantiated.
    'MsgBox("Constructed -- now default constructor")
    privateLoginRequired = True
End Sub
```

This is the constructor that will be called when the class is called using remoting.
    We added the following method to the Public Methods region:

```
Region "LoginUser"
Public Sub LoginUser( _
    ByVal sUserName As String, ByVal sPassword As String)

    InitializeObject(sUserName, sPassword)

    privateLoginRequired = False
End Sub
#End Region
```

This method allows the client to instantiate the remote object and then call *LoginUser* to perform the tasks that the constructors normally accomplished.
    We added the *InitializeLifetimeService* procedure to the base class. *InitializeLifetimeService* is called by the remoting system when the object is instantiated. It initializes the lifetime of the object to 20 seconds while also setting sponsor and renewal times, allowing you to control how long the object will run on the server.

```
#Region "InitializeLifetimeService"
Public Overrides Function InitializeLifetimeService() _
    As Object
    Dim lease As ILease = _
        CType(MyBase.InitializeLifetimeService(), _
        ILease)
    If lease.CurrentState = LeaseState.Initial Then
        lease.InitialLeaseTime = TimeSpan.FromSeconds(20)
        lease.SponsorshipTimeout = TimeSpan.FromMinutes(1)
        lease.RenewOnCallTime = TimeSpan.FromSeconds(18)
```

```
          'MsgBox("Initialize lifetime called")
      End If
      Return lease
  End Function 'InitializeLifetimeService
  #End Region
```

The only changes we made to the business object classes were to add the new default constructor. Now the business objects are ready to deploy.

For an interesting aside, consider this. When we added the *InitializeLifetimeService* function, we already had the business objects working with remoting. So we changed the base class, built the project, and then deployed the project. Magic. The new lifetime features were picked up when we recalled the object. That's the advantage of object-oriented programming.

Remoting Deployment

Now let's deploy these objects. The following XML defines the configuration file we used. This file is named HRApp.exe.config and is located in the c:\Build-OOP\Ch13\BizObjectConfigurationFiles folder.

```
<configuration>
  <system.runtime.remoting>
    <application name="HRHost">
      <service>
        <wellknown mode="SingleCall"
          type="SecurityFacade.LoginService,
          SecurityFacade"
          objectUri="LoginService.soap" />
        <wellknown mode="SingleCall"
          type="BusinessLayer.Company, BizCompany"
          objectUri="Company.soap" />
        <wellknown mode="SingleCall"
          type="BusinessLayer.Employee,
          BizEmployee" objectUri="Employee.soap" />
      </service>
      <channels>
        <channel ref="http" port="8000" />
      </channels>
    </application>
  </system.runtime.remoting>
</configuration>
```

You'll need to stop the remote host before replacing a DLL. Once you have the configuration file in place, copy all the DLLs used (such as the business objects, the base layer, the data access layer, and the security layer) to the bin directory of the hoster. Then start the hoster application.

Here are a couple of points to consider when dealing with hoster applications. If you try to start a second host application that is listening on the same protocol/network address/port as the first host application—for instance, they use the same URL and port number—you get the message shown in Figure 13-5.

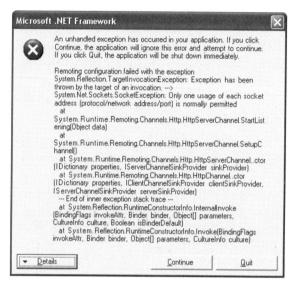

Figure 13-5   Error message when two hosters try to use the same channel

When you deploy the remoting application into production, make sure you assign the business objects strong names and put them in the global assembly cache (GAC). Then it's easy for the Web and remoting applications to use them.

Creating the Client

Let's create the Windows application that will use our remote objects. The sample client project is named Ch13HRWinClient. This is not a complete application but instead a simple application that allows us to test the remote classes. Start out by creating the project, and then add a module named *modGeneral*. Add the following code to this module:

```
Imports System.Windows.Forms
Imports System.Drawing
Module modGeneral
Friend UserName As String
Friend UserPassword As String
```

```vb
Sub SetStandardFromSize(ByVal frmName As Form)
    Dim oSize As New Size()
    Dim oPoint As New Point()

    oPoint.X = 600
    oPoint.Y = 400
    oSize.Height = oPoint.Y
    oSize.Width = oPoint.X
    frmName.Size = oSize
    oSize = Nothing
    oPoint = Nothing
End Sub
Function Login(_
    ByVal sUserName As String, _
    ByVal spassword As String) As Boolean
    Dim sRole As String
    Dim privateValidUser As Boolean

    'Login and authenticate based on passed credentials
    Try
        privateValidUser = loginService.Login( _
            sUserName, spassword)
        If privateValidUser Then
            'Save credentials
            UserName = sUserName
            UserPassword = spassword
        Else
            LogOut()
        End If
    Catch exc As Exception
        Throw New Exception( _
            "Error occurred trying to login user" _
            & " - " & exc.Message)
    End Try
    'Return login status
    Return privateValidUser
End Function

Function LogOut() As Boolean
    UserName = ""
    UserPassword = ""
End Function
```

Add a module named *modRemotingRoutines*, and add the following code
to it. This code implements the client-side remoting functions we need and also
provides procedures to instantiate the remote objects.

```vb
Imports System.Runtime.Remoting
Imports System.Runtime.Remoting.Channels
Imports System.Runtime.Remoting.Channels.Http
Imports BusinessLayer
Imports System.Timers.Timer
Module modRemotingClientRoutines
Friend channelRemote As HttpChannel

'Define types
Friend loginType As Type = _
    GetType(SecurityFacade.LoginService)
Friend companyType As Type = GetType(Company)
Friend employeeType As Type = GetType(Employee)
'Define urls to server objects
Friend urlLogin As [String] = _
    "http://localhost:8000/HRHost/LoginService.soap"
Friend urlCompany As [String] = _
    "http://localhost:8000/HRHost/Company.soap"
Friend urlEmployee As [String] = _
    "http://localhost:8000/HRHost/Employee.soap"

'Define ref variables for server objects
Friend loginService As SecurityFacade.LoginService
Friend localCompany As Company
Friend localEmployee As Employee

#Region "Initialization Functions and events"
Public Function InitializeRemoting() As Boolean
    Dim privateSuccess As Boolean

    Try
        channelRemote = New HttpChannel()
        ChannelServices.RegisterChannel(channelRemote)

        'Initialize remote objects
        InitializeCompany()
        InitializeEmployee()
        InitializeSecurity()

        privateSuccess = True

    Catch exc As Exception
        privateSuccess = False
    End Try
    Return privateSuccess
End Function

Sub InitializeCompany()
```

```vb
        RemotingConfiguration.RegisterWellKnownClientType( _
            companyType, urlCompany)
    End Sub

    Sub InitializeEmployee()
        RemotingConfiguration.RegisterWellKnownClientType( _
            employeeType, urlEmployee)
    End Sub
#End Region

#Region "Company"
    Sub InstantiateCompany()
        Try
            If localCompany Is Nothing Then
                localCompany = New Company()
            'Login in the user
            localCompany.LoginUser( _
                UserName, UserPassword)

            End If
        Catch exc As Exception
            Throw New Exception( _
                "msg" & " - " & exc.Message)
        End Try
    End Sub
    Sub DestroyCompany()
        localCompany = Nothing
    End Sub
#End Region

#Region "Employee"
    Sub InstantiateEmployee()
        Try
            If localEmployee Is Nothing Then
                localEmployee = New Employee()
                'Login in the user
                localEmployee.LoginUser( _
                    UserName, UserPassword)
            End If
        Catch exc As Exception
            Throw New Exception("msg" & " - " & v _
                exc.Message)
        End Try
    End Sub
    Sub DestroyEmployee()
        localEmployee = Nothing
    End Sub
#End Region
```

(continued)

```
#Region "Security"
Sub InitializeSecurity()

End Sub
Sub InstantiateSecurity()
    loginService = _
        CType(Activator.GetObject( _
        loginType, urlLogin), _
        SecurityFacade.LoginService)
End Sub

Sub DestroySecurity()
    loginService = Nothing
End Sub
#End Region
End Module
```

This module has procedures to handle all the object instantiation and destruction routines. Isolating these functions in this way gives us the option of changing the way we instantiate the remote objects later in the application's lifetime without otherwise altering the application. Isolating the instantiation process will make it easy to change from one method of instantiation to another.

The application's main form is *frmMain*. This form contains a menu and a status bar. The interface just after the application starts and before the user logs on is shown in Figure 13-6.

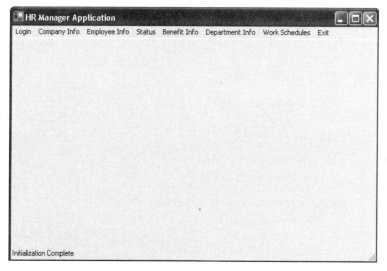

Figure 13-6   Interface for *frmMain* from the remoting client test application

The code from the form's *Load* event looks like this:

```
SetStandardFromSize(Me)
localFromText = Me.Text

StatusBarforForm.Text = "Obtaining Proxy " & _
    "for Remote Services" & vbCrLf
If InitializeRemoting() Then
    StatusBarforForm.Text = _
        "Initialization Complete"
Else
    StatusBarforForm.Text = _
        "An error occurred while " & _
        "initializing remoting"
End If
```

This code initializes the remoting system and the form.

The login menu code looks like this:

```
Dim frm As New frmLogin()
If frm.ShowDialog() = DialogResult.OK Then
    Me.Text = localFromText & " -- Logged In " & _
        UserName
Else
    Me.Text = localFromText & " -- Logged Out"
End If
frm = Nothing
```

This code illustrates the use of the dialog box in which the user logs on and the dialog box returns the status of the logon.

Let's look at the code for the *frmLogin cmdLogin* event, which calls the security facade layer and checks the user's credentials:

```
InstantiateSecurity()
If txtUserName.Text.Length > 0 _
    And txtPassword.Text.Length > 0 Then
    If Login(txtUserName.Text, txtPassword.Text) Then
        Me.DialogResult = DialogResult.OK
    Else
        Me.DialogResult = DialogResult.Abort
    End If
End If
DestroySecurity()
```

This code is no different from a local application except that we use the two procedures *InstantiateSecurity* and *DestroySecurity* to create and destroy the objects, respectively.

One more form, *frmCompanies*, is also quite straightforward since the remoting routines are all buried in a module. The form simply creates the object, and then calls the appropriate method and loads the *DataGrid*.

```
Dim ds As DataSet
Try
    InstantiateCompany()
    ds = localCompany.GetCompanyDepartments

    DataGrid1.DataSource = ds.Tables(0)
    DestroyCompany()
Catch exc As Exception
    Throw New Exception("Failed to load data")
End Try
```

The call to *DestroyCompany* can be removed. When it is, the lifetime settings from the server object will take care of managing the life of the remote objects.

Conclusion

As you can see from this chapter, .NET remoting is quite powerful. You have many options that allow you tremendous flexibility. You also have the ability to use configuration files to control how remoting is implemented so that you can make changes administratively. In HRnet, we use configuration files on the server but not on the client because our client is going to be auto downloadable and thus won't have access to the configuration files.

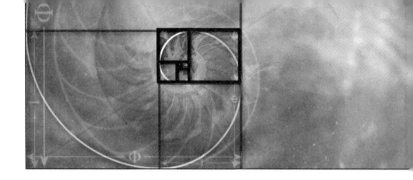

14

Wiring the Application Together

One of the most exciting times we experience in the application life cycle is what we call the "wiring together" phase. During this phase, we take the base components and framework classes we have created and turn them into a real application. We're going to do that in this chapter. You'll be astounded at how quickly and efficiently an application can be put together when its building blocks are well designed. We chose the phrase *wiring together* to describe this phase because that's exactly what we do. We take the components, template pages, menu structures, information pages with client controls, and security objects, and connect them with one another while adding certain parts of the business layer that enable the actual functionality required. Don't confuse this process with rapid application development, or RAD. In RAD, interface and functional items are brought together in a drag-and-drop fashion, which allows an application to be built very quickly. Just as quickly as these types of applications get created, however, they tend to fall apart. The major reasons for this are the lack of application planning and design that typically accompany the RAD approach as well as poorly designed business objects. Most of these types of applications lack any or all the features required to build flexible, stable, scalable, high-performing applications. What we are talking about when we say "wiring applications together" is rapid application building. This approach requires the application to be well designed up front, meaning an analysis of business rules has been conducted, workflow requirements are outlined, and a database is in place. (See Chapter 2 for more information.) Although some components are more universally usable (security components, client-side custom controls, menu handlers, templates, and the data access component), other components or framework classes must be created according to the application's design (that is, the business layer, process flow, and Web services). We create these items before we wire the application together.

Steps for Wiring the Application

Once all the components and code we've created in the preceding chapters are available, we progress through five steps that constitute the application wiring process. Table 14-1 shows us these steps.

Table 14-1 Application Wiring Steps

Step	Description
Step 1	Menu structure and templates
Step 2	Security
Step 3	Home page
Step 4	Information and data pages
Step 5	Microsoft Windows Forms

Of course, you're not locked into the steps in Table 14-1. For example, you might not need security or Windows Forms. However, you'll find that the sequence we suggested will make the application wiring process smoother.

Once we have the generic steps, we create a more detailed list of tasks for each step. Table 14-2 shows the specific steps we'll implement for HRnet.

As we implement the application one step at a time, we often find ourselves needing to fine-tune components or add features to them. We need to be very careful when doing this because we don't want to add the wrong types of features. We want to keep universally usable components small and efficient, so we don't add application-specific features to them—only universally usable features are added. For example, consider the custom TextBox server control we created in Chapter 6. After we added the capability to include a label, place it on the top or on the left side of the control, and include custom validation controls, we found a great way to allow highlighting when focus is set to the text box. We didn't originally include this feature but thought it universally usable, so we added the custom highlighting options to our universal custom TextBox server control. However, if we wanted our application to always show labels on the left and use a highlight color of yellow, we wouldn't include these features in the universal server control. Instead, we'd create a new control that derives from this universal custom server control and make the changes therein. This new control would be application-specific.

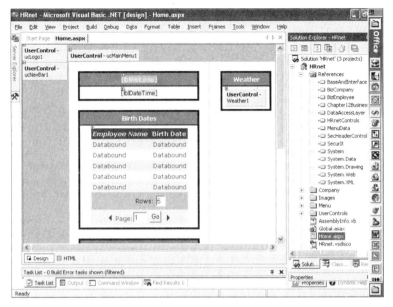

Figure 14-2   HRnet home page with referenced components

The other two references you can see In Figure 14-2, *HRnetControls* and *SecHeaderControl*, are project references to the HRnetControls project and the SecHeaderControl project, respectively, which are directly linked to the HRnet solution.

Step 2: Security

After adding the reference to the SecurIt.dll file, we're ready to use the custom security component built in Chapter 5. By implementing the secure header custom server control in every page of the application, each Web Forms page that is accessed is checked against security credentials and allows or disallows access to each page.

The Login.aspx Web Forms Page

Whenever security credentials are not available, processing will be redirected to a Login.aspx Web Forms page. We need to create this form first. Figure 14-3 shows the Login.aspx Web Forms page in design view, and Figure 14-4 shows it in run-time view with validation controls in use and the HRText custom server control with automatic highlight on focus.

Both TextBox controls are created with our custom HRText server control. We copied the original control created in Chapter 6 into the HRnetControls project and added the automatic highlight on focus functionality.

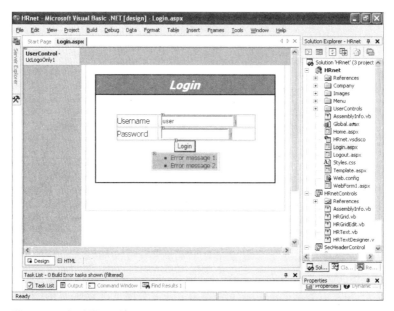

Figure 14-3   HRnet Login.aspx Web form in design view

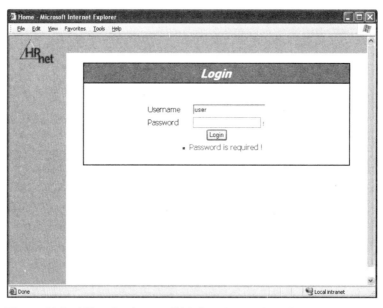

Figure 14-4   HRnet Login.aspx Web form in run-time view

The interesting part of the code for this Web Forms page is executed when the Login button is clicked:

```
Private Sub btnLogin_Click(ByVal sender As System.Object, _
    ByVal e As System.EventArgs) Handles btnLogin.Click
    Dim isValid As String
    oUser = New SecurIt.UserSecurity()
    isValid = CStr(oUser.Login(txtUsername.Text, txtPassword.Text))
    oUser.Dispose()
    oUser = Nothing
    If isValid = "True" Then
        btnLogin.Text = "Login"
        btnLogin.ForeColor = Color.Black
        Response.Redirect("Home.aspx")
    Else
        btnLogin.Text = "Invalid Login - Try Again"
        btnLogin.ForeColor = Color.Red
    End If
End Sub
```

After instantiating the *oUser* object as a *UserSecurity* object of the SecurIt component, we pass *oUser* both the username and password. The *oUser* object returns a string variable that is either set to *true* or *false*, depending on whether the user is authorized. Only when the logon succeeds do we redirect the user to the home page. (To see the details of the SecurIt component, refer to Chapter 5.) Once a user is authorized, the user's information (his name and roles) are held in session variables that are accessed through the *HttpContext* object. Every time a page is accessed, we check the information in *HttpContext* through the SecurIt component and re-evaluate the user's security settings. Adding the security header control to every existing and future page will make this possible.

The Security Header Control

The SecHeader server control was created to be a header in each Web Forms page. It checks security credentials on every Web Forms page entry and, if it doesn't find them, it redirects processing to the Login.aspx Web Forms page. Fortunately, we created a custom user control named ucLogo.ascx that is automatically included in all our Web Forms applications. (See Chapter 6 for more information on custom user controls and Chapter 10 for the specific ucLogo.ascx user control we are talking about.) This custom user control requires that we add the SecHeader only one time and inherit it in all Web Forms applications that use our template. The ucLogo.ascx user control includes the SecHeader server control. Here is the HTML code for it:

```
<%@ Control Language="vb" AutoEventWireup="false" Codebehind="ucLogo.ascx.vb"
    Inherits="HRnet.ucLogo"
    TargetSchema="http://schemas.microsoft.com/intellisense/ie5" %>
<%@ Register TagPrefix="cc1" Namespace="SecHeaderControl"
  Assembly="SecHeaderControl" %>
```

(continued)

```
<table id="idLogoTable" cellpadding="0" cellspacing="0"
  border="0" width="100">
  <tr>
    <td width="100"> 
      <cc1:SecHeader id="SecHeader1" text=""
        imagepath="/HRnet/Images/HRnet.jpg" runat="server"
        Width="80px" Height="50px"></cc1:SecHeader>
    </td>
  </tr>
  <tr>
    <td align="middle">
      <P>
        <asp:Label id="lblUser" runat="server" Font-Size="XX-Small"
          ForeColor="Gray"></asp:Label>
        <asp:LinkButton id="LinkBtnLogout" runat="server"
          ToolTip="Click Here to Log Off" ForeColor="CornflowerBlue"
          Font-Size="Medium" Font-Bold="True"
          Font-Names="Arial">Logout</asp:LinkButton>
        <IMG height="1" src="/HRnet/Images/spacer.gif" width="90">
      </P>
    </td>
  </tr>
</table>
```

In the preceding code, we highlighted in boldface the areas of interest. First is the registration of the *SecHeaderControl* assembly with a *TagPrefix* of *cc1*. Second, we actually use the control on the page with the name set to nothing and the *imagepath* pointing to the HRnet logo file. You might remember that the SecHeader control includes the picture, and if desired, we could include header text in addition to the code that authenticates the user. The other two Microsoft ASP.NET controls on this Web Forms page are a Label control (to show the user and his role) and a LinkButton control (to allow logging out). Before we take a look at the modified SecHeader control, here's the code-behind page for the ucLogin.ascx custom user control:

```
Private Sub Page_Load(ByVal sender As System.Object, _
    ByVal e As System.EventArgs) Handles MyBase.Load
    If Not IsPostBack Then
        Dim oUser As New SecurIt.UserSecurity()
        lblUser.Text = oUser.UserName + " > " + _
            CStr(oUser.Roles.GetValue(0))
    End If
End Sub


Private Sub LinkBtnLogout_Click(ByVal sender As System.Object, _
    ByVal e As System.EventArgs) Handles LinkBtnLogout.Click
```

```
Dim oUser As New SecurIt.UserSecurity
oUser.Logout("Normal")
oUser.Dispose()
oUser = Nothing

Session.Clear()
Session.Abandon()
Response.Redirect("/HRnet/Logout.aspx")
End Sub
```

The actual code that checks the user's credentials on every Web Forms page is encapsulated in the SecHeader control. Therefore, the ucLogin.aspx form's code-behind page deals with only two functions: extracting and displaying the username and initial role, and logging out via a button. Let's look at these functions in a little more detail. Regarding the first function, when the page is accessed, we instantiate an *oUser* object and extract the user's name and the user's first role, which we display in the logo control. We included this for your convenience so that you can check which username you used for logging on and which role the user has. You might want to delete this function from the control in your final application. For the second function, the Logout button, we first use the *oUser* Security object to call the *Logout* method, and then we destroy any session variables left and abandon the current session, forcing Microsoft Internet Information Services (IIS) to assign a new session ID. You might consider this overkill; however, we think that the more safely we can log out, the tighter our application's security becomes.

We mentioned that the SecHeader server control needs a little change. We need to modify the layout of the logo we're using. The HTML this control needs to create is different from our examples in Chapter 5. The only code that needs to change is within the *render* method, as follows:

```
Protected Overrides Sub Render(ByVal output As
    System.Web.UI.HtmlTextWriter)
    output.Write("<TABLE id=""TableHeader"" cellSpacing=""1""" & _
        cellPadding=""1"" width=""100%"" border=""0"">")
    output.Write("<tr>")
    output.Write("<TD><IMG style=""WIDTH: 92px"" src=""" & _
        ResolveUrl(ImagePath) & """></TD>")
    output.Write("<TD>")
    output.Write("<H1 align=""center""><FONT color=""red"">" & _
        [Text] & "</FONT></H1>")
    output.Write("</TD>")
    output.Write("</TR>")
    output.Write("</TABLE>")
End Sub
```

The lines in boldface in the preceding code show that we gave the image control a specific width that fits our application.

Once we've made the modifications we've been discussing, user security will be available for us in every single Web Forms page of the application. Authentication simply can't get any easier than this.

Security Permissions

Now that authentication is implemented, we need to decide what kind of permissions we'll give different groups of users. We wanted to keep this aspect simple, so we implemented four levels of permissions for demonstration purposes. Table 14-3 shows these four permission levels and the menu items that they can access. We also included record-specific data access permissions.

Table 14-3   Four Permission Levels of HRnet

Group	Permissions
Executive	All available menu options
	All available view, details, save, change, add functions
HRManager	Menu options and data access permissions
	Home page tab
	Employee tab
	Employee List: full view
	Details: full view, edit, save, cancel
	Address: full view, edit, save, cancel
	Emergency Info: full view, edit, save, cancel
	Company tab
	News Items: view only
	Departments: full view only
	Positions: full view only
	Job Titles: full view only
Employee	Menu options and data access permissions
	Home page tab
	Employee tab
	Employee List: list view only
Other	Menu options and data access permissions
	Home page tab

In a moment we'll show you how we limit available menu options for users. Data access permissions are specific to information pages; we'll show you these in the section "Step 4: Information and Data Pages."

Secure Menu Structure

Thanks to *MenuDataClass* (see details in Chapter 5), adding dynamic menu structures to support the four levels of permissions is very easy. The MenuData-Class.vb file is in the HRnet\Menu directory. For each permission level, we have to create a unique MenuData dataset, which is defined within *MenuData-Class*. Our first modification to *MenuDataClass* adds an instance of the *SecurIt* object and retrieves the current user's primary role. The second modification is achieved by adding a *Select Case* statement that dynamically creates the menu tabs and navigation bar items for the user's primary role. Here's the complete code for *MenuDataClass*:

```
Public Class MenuDataClass
    Public Function getMenuDataSet() As DataSet
        Dim oUser As New SecurIt.UserSecurity()
        Dim localUser As String = UCase(CStr(oUser.Roles.GetValue(0)))
        Dim localMenuTables As New MenuDataServer()

        Select Case localUser
            Case "EMPLOYEE"
                localMenuTables.AddMainMenuParameter(1, "Home", _
                    "/HRnet/Home.aspx", False, "HRnet Home Page")
                localMenuTables.AddMainMenuParameter(2, "Employees", _
                    "/HRnet/Template.aspx", True, "Employee Information")
                localMenuTables.AddNavBarParameter(2, 1, "Employee List", _
                    "EmployeeList.aspx", False, "List all Employees")


            Case "HRMANAGER"
                localMenuTables.AddMainMenuParameter(1, "Home", _
                    "/HRnet/Home.aspx", False, "HRnet Home Page")
                localMenuTables.AddMainMenuParameter(2, "Employees", _
                    "/HRnet/EmplolyeesMain.aspx", True,
                    "Employee Information")
                localMenuTables.AddMainMenuParameter(3, "Company", _
                    "/HRnet/CompanyMain.aspx", True, "Company Information")
                localMenuTables.AddNavBarParameter(2, 1, "Employee List", _
                    "EmployeeList.aspx", False, "List all Employees")
                localMenuTables.AddNavBarParameter(2, 2, "Details", _
                    "EmployeeDetails.aspx", False, "Specific Employee's " _
                    & "Information")
                localMenuTables.AddNavBarParameter(2, 3, "Address", _
                    "Template.aspx", False, "Specific Employee's Address")
                localMenuTables.AddNavBarParameter(2, 4, "Emergency Info", _
```

(continued)

```vb
            "Template.aspx", False, "Specific Employee's " & _
            "Emergency Info")

        localMenuTables.AddNavBarParameter(3, 1, "News Items", _
            "NewsDetail.aspx", False, "Current and Archived News")
        localMenuTables.AddNavBarParameter(3, 2, "Departments", _
            "Template.aspx", False, "Our Company's Departments")
        localMenuTables.AddNavBarParameter(3, 3, "Positions", _
            "Template.aspx", False, "Our Company's Positions")
        localMenuTables.AddNavBarParameter(3, 4, "Job Titles", _
            "Template.aspx", False, "Our Company's Job Titles")

    Case "EXECUTIVE"
        localMenuTables.AddMainMenuParameter(1, "Home", _
            "/HRnet/Home.aspx", False, "HRnet Home Page")
        localMenuTables.AddMainMenuParameter(2, "Employees", _
            "/HRnet/EmployeesMain.aspx", True, _
            "Employee Information")
        localMenuTables.AddMainMenuParameter(3, "Benefits", _
            "/HRnet/Template.aspx", True, "Available Benefits")
        localMenuTables.AddMainMenuParameter(4, "Company", _
            "/HRnet/CompanyMain.aspx", True, "Company Information")

        'Add info to the NavBar Table
        localMenuTables.AddNavBarParameter(2, 1, "Employee List", _
            "EmployeeList.aspx", False, "List all Employees")
        localMenuTables.AddNavBarParameter(2, 2, "Details", _
            "EmployeeDetails.aspx", False, "Specific " & _
            "Employee's Information")
        localMenuTables.AddNavBarParameter(2, 3, "Address", _
            "Template.aspx", False, "Specific Employee's Address")
        localMenuTables.AddNavBarParameter(2, 4, "Emergency Info", _
            "Template.aspx", False, "Specific Employee's " & _
            "Emergency Info")
        localMenuTables.AddNavBarParameter(2, 5, "Benefits", _
            "Template.aspx", False, "Specific " & _
            "Employee's Choosen Benefits")
        localMenuTables.AddNavBarParameter(2, 6, "Work Schedule", _
            "Template.aspx", False, "Specific " & _
            "Employee's Work Schedule")
        localMenuTables.AddNavBarParameter(2, 7, "My Info", _
            "Template.aspx", False, "Specific " & _
            "Employee's Work Schedule")
        localMenuTables.AddNavBarParameter(3, 1, "Health", _
            "Template.aspx", False, "List Health Benefits")
        localMenuTables.AddNavBarParameter(3, 2, "Disability", _
```

```
        "Template.aspx", False, "List Disability Benefits")
    localMenuTables.AddNavBarParameter(3, 3, "401K", _
        "Template.aspx", False, "List Retirement Benefits")
    localMenuTables.AddNavBarParameter(3, 4, "Education", _
        "Template.aspx", False, "List Education Benefits")
    localMenuTables.AddNavBarParameter(3, 5, "Other", _
        "Template.aspx", False, "List Education Benefits")
    localMenuTables.AddNavBarParameter(3, 6, "Add", _
        "Template.aspx", False, "List Education Benefits")
    localMenuTables.AddNavBarParameter(4, 1, "News Items", _
        "NewsDetail.aspx", False, "Current and Archived News")
    localMenuTables.AddNavBarParameter(4, 2, "Departments", _
        "Template.aspx", False, "Our Company's Departments")
    localMenuTables.AddNavBarParameter(4, 3, "Positions", _
        "Template.aspx", False, "Our Company's Positions")
    localMenuTables.AddNavBarParameter(4, 4, "Job Titles", _
        "Template.aspx", False, "Our Company's Job Titles")

Case Else
    localMenuTables.AddMainMenuParameter(1, "Home", _
        "/HRnet/Home.aspx", False, "HRnet Home Page")
End Select
Return localMenuTables.GetMenuDataSet
localMenuTables.Dispose()
localMenuTables = Nothing
    End Function
End Class
```

The code in boldface in the preceding listing creates the security object; extracts the user's main role; and in the *Select Case* statement, chooses the correct menu structure. This menu structure has three main levels of permissions. The fourth level of permission was added to support any users who are authenticated but have not received their roles. We want to grant them access to HRnet but not further than the home page. Unauthorized users won't be able to log on at all.

Step 3: The Home Page

The design of HRnet's home page (see Chapter 10) calls for general information for HRnet's employees. Besides a custom greeting, we show a list of employees with birthdays in this month, a list of active news items, and the weather in the geographic area in which the company resides. Figure 14-5 shows the design of HRnet's home page. In the next few sections, we discuss how we add each design feature of HRnet's home page.

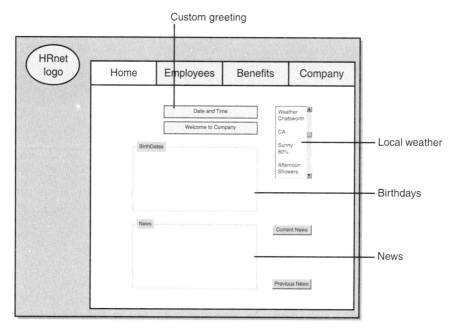

Figure 14-5 HRnet's home page design

Custom Greeting

The custom greeting welcomes the user with the time of day (morning, afternoon, or evening) and the user's name. It also shows today's date and time. We added two Label controls for the custom greeting. The first is named *lblWelcome* and is placed in a table header. The second is named *lblDateTime* and is placed directly under the greeting header. In the Home.aspx code-behind page, we dynamically set both Label controls. Here are only the lines of code that create the results for these labels:

```
Private Sub Page_Load(ByVal sender As System.Object, _
    ByVal e As System.EventArgs) Handles MyBase.Load
    lblDateTime.Text = "The current date and time is: " & Now()
    lblWelcome.Text = getTimeFrame() + getUserName()
    GetNewsAndBirthData()

    If Not IsPostBack Then
        ⋮
End Sub
```

```
Private Function getTimeFrame() As String
    Dim nowHour As Integer
    nowHour = Now().Hour
    Select Case nowHour
        Case Is < 12
            Return "Good Morning "
        Case 12 To 18
            Return "Good Afternoon "
        Case Is > 18
            Return "Good Evening "
    End Select
End Function

Private Function getUserName() As String
    Try
        Return proper(CStr(Session("UserName")))
    Catch
    End Try
End Function

Private Function proper(ByVal text As String) As String
    Dim convertText As String = text
    Dim lengthText As Integer = convertText.Length
    convertText = LCase(convertText)
    Dim firstLetter As String = Left(convertText, 1)
    firstLetter = UCase(firstLetter)
    Return firstLetter + Right(convertText, lengthText - 1)
End Function
```

Since both labels contain time-sensitive information, we want to make sure they get updated every time the page loads. The *lblDateTime* Label control is simply set to the current time:

```
lblDateTime.Text = "The current date and time is: " & Now()
```

The *lblWelcome* label control, on the other hand, needs a bit more work. We need the greeting first and then the username. We decided to create two functions that return both:

```
lblWelcome.Text = getTimeFrame() + getUserName()
```

The *getTimeFrame* functions checks the hour of the day (in a 24-hour format) and returns "Good Morning" when the time is before noon, "Good Afternoon" from noon until 6:00 P.M., and "Good Evening" after 6 P.M. The *getUserName* function returns the *UserName Session* variable. The SecurIt component creates this session variable upon logon. Notice that the *getUserName* function calls another support function we created, *proper*, that simply capitalizes the first letter of any text.

Birthdays and News

To show the current birthdays and news information, we're going to use the custom DataGrid server control we created in Chapter 11. We copied the original custom DataGrid server control into the HRnetControls project and renamed it HRGrid. Figure 14-2 showed the design view layout of the HRnet Home.aspx page with the DataGrid for birthdays. Directly beneath the datagrid you can see the header for the news area that contains the datagrid for news items. One of the first steps the code for the home page does is register the assembly and namespace of the controls used. The following code shows the HTML for Home.aspx page's directive and registrations. The registration for HRnetcontrols is in boldface:

```
<%@ Page Language="vb" SmartNavigation="true" Trace="true"
  AutoEventWireup="false" Codebehind=Home.aspx.vb
  Inherits="HRnet.Home" %>
<%@ Register TagPrefix="cc2" Namespace="HRnetControls"
  Assembly="HRnetControls" %>
<%@ Register TagPrefix="uc1" TagName="weather"
  Src="UserControls/weather.ascx" %>
<%@ Register TagPrefix="cc1" Namespace="SecHeaderControl"
  Assembly="SecHeaderControl" %>
<%@ Register TagPrefix="uc1" TagName="ucFooter"
  Src="UserControls/ucFooter.ascx" %>
<%@ Register TagPrefix="uc1" TagName="ucLogo"
  Src="UserControls/ucLogo.ascx" %>
<%@ Register TagPrefix="uc1" TagName="ucNavBar" Src="Menu/ucNavBar.ascx" %>
<%@ Register TagPrefix="uc1" TagName="ucMainMenu"
  Src="Menu/ucMainMenu.ascx" %>
```

Next, we're going to show the HTML code for both datagrids in the Home.aspx Web Forms page. When you compare these lines of code with previous datagrid examples, you'll notice that we use a TemplateColumn. Here is the code for the *gridBirthDates* DataGrid control. (The TemplateColumn code is in boldface.)

```
<cc2:hrgrid id="gridBirthDates" runat="server">
  <Columns>
    <asp:TemplateColumn SortExpression="LastName"
      HeaderText="Employee Name">
      <ItemTemplate>
        <asp:Label Runat="server" Text='<%# "<b>" +
          DataBinder.Eval(Container.DataItem, "lastname") + "</b>, " +
          DataBinder.Eval(Container.DataItem, "firstname") %>'/>
      </ItemTemplate>
    </asp:TemplateColumn>
    <asp:BoundColumn DataField="birthdate" HeaderText="Birth Date"
```

```
      DataFormatString="{0:MMMM dd}">
      <ItemStyle HorizontalAlign="Right"></ItemStyle>
   </asp:BoundColumn>
  </Columns>
</cc2:hrgrid>
```

And here is the code for the *gridNews* DataGrid control. Again, the Tem-plateColumn code is in boldface.

```
<cc2:hrgrid id="gridNews" runat="server">
  <Columns>
    <asp:TemplateColumn SortExpression="newssubject"
      HeaderText="Subject">
      <ItemTemplate>
        <asp:Label Runat="server" Text='<%# "<b>" +
          DataBinder.Eval(Container.DataItem, "newssubject") +
          "</b>" %>' ID="Label2"/>
      </ItemTemplate>
    </asp:TemplateColumn>
    <asp:BoundColumn DataField="newsinfo"
      HeaderText="News"></asp:BoundColumn>
    <asp:BoundColumn DataField="newsdate" HeaderText="Date"
      SortExpression="newsdate"
      DataFormatString="{0:MM/dd/yy}"></asp:BoundColumn>
  </Columns>
</cc2:hrgrid>
```

This is the first time we use a TemplateColumn in a datagrid. The DataGrid control examples in Chapter 11 included BoundColumns and ButtonColumns. BoundColumns can show information only in plaintext fields. When we need to combine several data fields in one column (such as last name and first name), or apply special formatting not available for text boxes, we need to use TemplateColumns. In these columns, we can use any combination of ASP.NET controls to show and format data. Being able to do this does come at a cost—TemplateColumns don't allow automatic databinding. All code that shows data needs to be manually coded. At first, we were a bit upset with this limitation, however, we quickly came to agree that this limitation makes sense. How else would you bind two or more data fields to a single column? To bind a specific data field to any of the ASP.NET controls in an ItemTemplate (the ItemTemplate resides within a TemplateColumn), we use the *DataBinder.Eval* function. It allows us to call a specific data field's contents by using the *Container.DataItem* command. For example, if we want to return the last name of the current record, we use the *DataBinder* function as follows:

```
DataBinder.Eval(Container.DataItem, "lastname")
```

The rest is easy. We build the *DataBinder* function into a ASP.NET control such as a Label control. For the preceding example of the *gridBirthDate* DataGrid control, the code that brings the employee's last name and first name into one column is shown here:

```
<asp:Label Runat="server" Text='<%# "<b>" +
  DataBinder.Eval(Container.DataItem, "lastname") + "</b>, " +
  DataBinder.Eval(Container.DataItem, "firstname") %>'/>
```

Now that we defined the DataGrid controls for birthdays and news, we need to fill their data sources. Here's the code in the Home.aspx Web Forms page's code-behind module:

```
Private Sub Page_Load(ByVal sender As System.Object, _
    ByVal e As System.EventArgs) Handles MyBase.Load
    ⋮
  GetNewsAndBirthData()

  If Not IsPostBack Then
      gridNews.PageSize = 2
      gridNews.GridDataSet = CType(Session("News"), DataSet)
      gridNews.Update()
      gridBirthDates.AllowPaging = False
      gridBirthDates.ShowFooter = False
      gridBirthDates.GridDataSet = CType(Session("Births"), DataSet)
      gridBirthDates.Update()
  Else
      gridNews.GridDataSet = CType(Session("News"), DataSet)
      gridBirthDates.GridDataSet = CType(Session("Births"), DataSet)
  End If
End Sub


Private Sub GetNewsAndBirthData()
  If Session("Births") Is Nothing Or Session("News") Is Nothing Then
      Dim localActiveNews As DataSet
      Dim localBirthdays As DataSet
      Dim localCompany As New Company()
      localActiveNews = localCompany.GetCompanyActiveNews(1)
      localBirthdays = localCompany.GetEmployeeBirthdays(1)
      Session("Births") = localBirthdays
      Session("News") = localActiveNews
  End If
End Sub
```

Every time the page is loaded, we want to check whether the datasets for both DataGrid controls are still available or need to be loaded through the middle-tier business objects. We created the *GetNewsAndBirthData* method, which checks the availability of both datasets and if necessary loads them into *Session* variables. The first time the Home.aspx Web Forms page is loaded, we not only set the DataGrids' *GridDataSet* properties but also set some run-time properties of the HRGrid custom server control. In the preceding code, you can see that we limited the *gridNews* DataGrid control to a *PageSize* of 2. Also notice that we set the *gridBirthDates* DataGrid control's properties to hide its footer and pager bars. These settings are necessary only on the first load of the home page since the DataGrid controls will hold their values in their own state information. On postbacks, we need to refresh only the DataGrids' data source—the *Grid-DataSet* property. That's all there is to it. Only one more item of the home page is left to incorporate: the local weather. Let's take care of this next.

Local Weather

Thanks to the business components and the work we did in Chapter 12, it will take a only a couple of lines of code to show the current weather and weather forecast for the selected company's location. We included the weather information in the weather.ascx user control that resides in the HRnet\UserControls directory. We also made slight modifications to the examples in Chapter 12. The most important cosmetic change is the use of the HRGrid custom server control instead of the DataList control. The reason for this change is to create a consistent look and feel for the HRnet application. Modifications in the code-behind page are a bit more detailed. We decided to build a DataSet that contains the weather information programmatically instead of using an ArrayList as we did in the original user control. Here is the code in the code-behind page of weather.ascx:

```
Sub GetData()
    If Session("Weather") Is Nothing Then
        Dim oUser As New SecurIt.UserSecurity()
        Dim x As New BlUtility(oUser)
        Dim i As Integer

        Dim loadDataSet As New DataSet()
        Dim table As New DataTable("WeatherItems")
        Dim rowDataRow As DataRow
        table.Columns.Add("Weather", System.Type.GetType("System.String"))

        Dim weatherforecast As BlUtility.WeatherInformation

        weatherforecast = x.GetCompanyWeatherForecast(1)
        With weatherforecast
            If .Status = "Normal" Then
                rowDataRow = table.NewRow
                rowDataRow("Weather") = "<B>Current Weather for: " + _
                    .City.ToString + "</B>"
```

(continued)

```
                    table.Rows.Add(rowDataRow)
                    Dim intWeather As Integer = _
                        weatherforecast.DayForecast.GetUpperBound(0)
                    For i = 0 To intWeather
                        rowDataRow = table.NewRow
                        rowDataRow("Weather") = "<b>" + .DayForecast(i).Day + _
                            ":</b> <br>" + .DayForecast(i).Forecast + "<br>" + _
                            .DayForecast(i).Abbrev + " "
                        table.Rows.Add(rowDataRow)
                    Next
                    rowDataRow = table.NewRow
                    rowDataRow("Weather") = .Time.ToString
                    table.Rows.Add(rowDataRow)
                Else
                    rowDataRow = table.NewRow
                    rowDataRow("Weather") = .Status.ToString
                    table.Rows.Add(rowDataRow)
                End If
            End With

            loadDataSet.Tables.Add(table)
            Session("Weather") = loadDataSet
            weatherforecast = Nothing
            x = Nothing
        End If
End Sub
```

After initializing a business layer object (*BlUtility*), we create a *DataTable* object to which we add the weather Web service's (*GetCompanyWeatherForecast* method of the business layer object) return information, one record at a time. The resulting table is added to a DataSet that persists itself as a *Session* variable.

We now have a finished Home.aspx Web page and are ready to give it a try. Right-click Home.aspx in Solution Explorer and select Build And Browse. Instead of being greeted with the Home.aspx Web Forms page, you'll see the Login.aspx page. Why? Because you haven't yet passed user authorization through the *SecurIt* business object and are redirected to log on instead. Once you have entered the username and password (see Table 14-2 for several username and password options), you are presented with the home page and its contents, as shown in Figure 14-6.

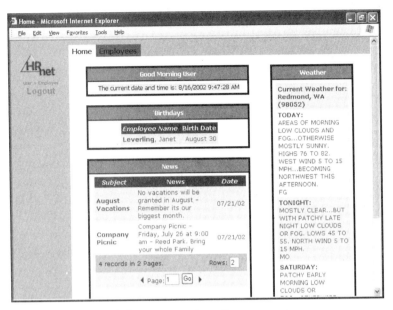

Figure 14-6   HRnet's home page at run time

Step 4: Information and Data Pages

Information pages, especially data-driven Web Forms pages, have always been an exciting challenge in the past. ASP.NET has made creating well-designed and functioning information pages a lot easier. We covered the basics in Chapter 11 and are going to use that information in the HRnet application as we examine two examples. The first example adds one Web Forms page that manages the company's news items. This will be a Web Forms page with a datagrid and detail information on one page. The second example adds two Web Forms pages that manage parts of the employee information—the first employee Web Forms page contains only the DataGrid control, and the second employee Web Forms page includes the detail information. Let's get started.

News Items: DataGrid and Detail Information in One Web Forms Page

The company news items are managed in one Web Forms page. Figure 14-7 shows this form in detail view mode (HRManagers).

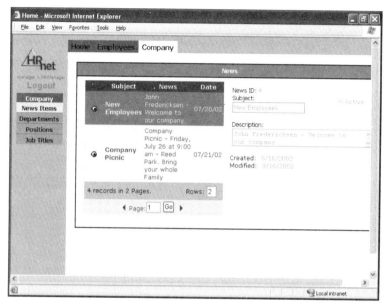

Figure 14-7 HRnet's News Management page (detail view mode only)

Figure 14-8 shows the same form with full access mode (logon permissions for vice presidents). All other permission levels do not have access to the news Web Forms page.

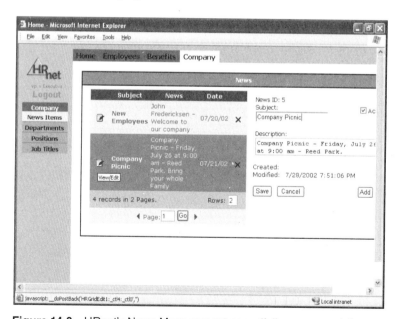

Figure 14-8 HRnet's News Management page (full access mode)

Although large portions of the news Web Forms page are similar to the GridandDetailState.aspx example from Chapter 11, there are some differences and additional features. (You might want to refresh your memory regarding the functions for this example.) Instead of calling the detail information in a custom user control, we included the datagrid and detail information on the same Web Forms page. This allows us to have direct access to the ASP.NET controls for the detail information instead of having to deal with properties and events of a user control. See Figure 14-9 for the Design view of the NewsDetail.aspx Web Forms page in the HRnet application.

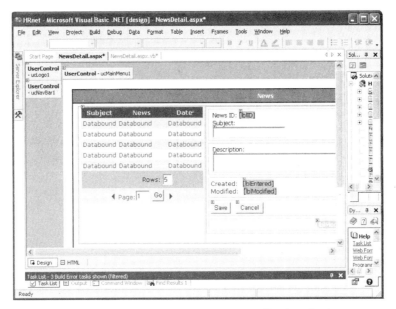

Figure 14-9   HRnet's News Management page (Design view)

Adding a message box   Let's go through the NewsDetails.aspx's code-behind page and look at the changes and additional code we created. First, we added the following lines of code to the *Page_Load* event:

```
Private Sub Page_Load(ByVal sender As System.Object, _
    ByVal e As System.EventArgs) Handles MyBase.Load

    btnSave.Attributes.Add("onclick", "return confirm('OK to Save?');")
    btnCancel.Attributes.Add("onclick", "return confirm('OK to Cancel?');")
    lblMode.Text = ""
    ⋮
End Sub
```

Have you ever wondered how to add an OK/Cancel message box to your Web Forms application? Well, it takes exactly one line of code to accomplish this! All we need to do is add an attribute to each button we want to have a message box. You can see that we added the message box to the *btnSave* and *btnCancel* buttons. Note that we can define the message we want to show when the message box appears. Figure 14-10 shows the message box feature when the *btnCancel* button is clicked.

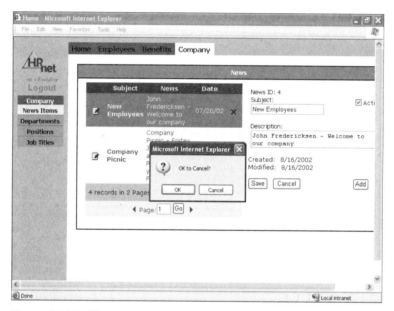

Figure 14-10 The message box in action

Adding permission settings Next, we add the permission settings and state information region to determine the look and feel of the DataGrid control and the controls for the news details.

```
#Region "Permission Settings and State Information"
    Private Sub PermissionSettings()
    Dim oUser As New SecurIt.UserSecurity()
    Dim localPermission As String = UCase(CStr(oUser.Roles.GetValue(0)))

    Select Case localPermission
        Case "HRMANAGER"
            viewButton()
            buttonSave(False)
            buttonCancel(False)
            buttonAdd(False)
            enableControls(False)
```

```
        Case "EXECUTIVE"
            editButton()
            deleteButton()
            buttonSave(True)
            buttonCancel(True)
            buttonAdd(True)
            enableControls(True)
        Case Else
            HRGridEdit1.Visble = False
            buttonSave(False)
            buttonCancel(False)
            buttonAdd(False)
            enableControls(False)
        End Select
    End Sub

    Private Sub viewButton()
        Dim viewButton As New ButtonColumn()
        viewButton.CommandName = "select"
        viewButton.Text = "<img border=0 alt='View Only' " & _
            "align=absmiddle src=images/View.gif>"
        HRGridEdit1.Columns.AddAt(0, viewButton)
    End Sub

        ⋮

    Private Sub buttonSave(ByVal enabled As Boolean)
        btnSave.Enabled = enabled
        btnSave.Visible = enabled
    End Sub

        ⋮

    Private Sub enableControls(ByVal enabled As Boolean)
        lblID.Enabled = enabled
        chkActive.Enabled = enabled
        txtSubject.Enabled = enabled
        txtInfo.Enabled = enabled
        lblEntered.Enabled = enabled
        lblModified.Enabled = enabled
    End Sub
#End Region
```

After declaring the *oUser* security object and returning the role, we check for the two main roles that have access to this Web Forms page. The HRManagers role allows us to view details, and the Executive role allows us to view all. We use the *Select Case* statement and set the individual options. We are adding a column dynamically to the DataGrid control to allow for viewing or editing a row. The *viewButton* method that is called in the *Case "HRMANAGER"* statement adds the image of an eye to a ButtonColumn in the first column of the DataGrid control. We explained this code in Chapter 11. After adding the correct dynamic column to the DataGrid control, we determine which, if any, of the Web Forms page's button controls will be displayed. The Web Forms page's detail area will have a maximum of three buttons: *btnSave*, *btnCancel*, and *btnAdd*. We added a method for each one, passing a *Boolean* value that determines whether to show or hide, or enable or disable the button control. Here is the code for the *btnSave* button control:

```
Private Sub buttonSave(ByVal enabled As Boolean)
    btnSave.Enabled = enabled
    btnSave.Visible = enabled
End Sub
```

The last part of the *Select Case* statements either enables or disables the controls in the detail area of NewDetail.aspx.

Showing the detail information   When a specific row is selected in the Data-Grid control, we need to display the detail information. If all the data for the DataGrid control and the detail information is returned in the same dataset, we simply recall the dataset and filter it to the unique ID. In the case of news items, the data returned in the dataset for the DataGrid control is not complete. Therefore we need to call the business layer to get the full detail information for each selected row. Here's the code for the DataGrid control's *SelectedIndexChanged* event:

```
Public Sub SelectedIndexChanged(ByVal sender As Object, _
    ByVal e As EventArgs)
    Dim selectedNewsID As Integer = _
        CInt(HRGridEdit1.DataKeys(HRGridEdit1.SelectedIndex))
    lblMessage.Text = "News ID = " + CStr(selectedNewsID)
    LoadFields(selectedNewsID)
End Sub
```

The *DataKeys* function of the DataGrid control returns the specific key of the selected index, in our case the *NewsID* stored in the *selectedNewsID* variable. We then pass the *selectedNewsID* to another method named *LoadFields* that selects the correct News row and sets the detail control's values. Here is the code for the *LoadFields* method:

```
Private Sub LoadFields(ByVal newsID As Integer)
    Dim localCompany As New Company()
    Dim singleNewsRow As DataRow = _
```

```
            localCompany.GetCompanyNewsDetail(newsID).Tables(0).Rows(0)
        localCompany = Nothing
        Try
            If Not IsDBNull(singleNewsRow("NewsID")) Then lblID.Text = _
                CStr(singleNewsRow("NewsID")) Else lblID.Text = _
                "News ID unknown"
                ⋮
            lblMessage.Text = ""
        Catch selectException As Exception
            ClearEntries()
            lblMessage.Text = "<B>Error showing this Employee Record</B>" + _
                selectException.Message
        End Try
End Sub
```

The method fills a single DataTable row returned from the *GetCompanyNews-Detail* method of the business layer. (The method needs the *NewsID* key field to pull a specific record.) Then we pass the returned values to the Web Forms page's controls. We enclosed the previous process in an exception handling block so that we can pass a more meaningful message to the Web Forms page in the event of a problem accessing the data.

Saving data   Saving data is a bit more challenging, in part because we're required to determine whether we're saving a new record or updating an existing one. For this reason we added a ViewState field named NewsAddEdit to the NewsDetail.aspx Web Forms page. This field is set to *true* when the *btnAdd* button is clicked. Here is the code for the *btnAdd* button's *Click* event:

```
Private Sub btnAdd_Click(ByVal sender As System.Object, _
    ByVal e As System.EventArgs) Handles btnAdd.Click
    lblMessage.Text = "You clicked the ADD button"
    lblMode.Text = "Adding new Record"
    ClearEntries()
    btnAdd.Enabled = False
    ViewState("NewsAddEdit") = True
    SetFocus(txtSubject)
End Sub
```

The *btnAdd Click* event does a lot more than set the NewsAddEdit View-State field. It shows a message in two label controls, clears any entries, and calls a method that sets focus to the first control in the detail area. We'll show you shortly how to set focus to a specific control on a Web Forms page.

With the NewsAddEdit ViewState field set to either *true* for adding a record or to nothing, we can now create an intelligent *btnSave* click event. Here is the complete code for the *btnSave* event handler:

```
Private Sub btnSave_Click(ByVal sender As System.Object, _
    ByVal e As System.EventArgs) Handles btnSave.Click
    lblMessage.Text = "You clicked the SAVE button"
    btnAdd.Enabled = True
    If CBool(ViewState("NewsAddEdit")) = True Then
        'New Add
        lblMessage.Text += " --> WE are adding a new record"
        Dim addNews As New Company()
        Try
            addNews.AddNews(1, chkActive.Checked, Now(), txtSubject.Text, _
                txtInfo.Text, 1)
            lblMessage.Text += " - ADDING SUCCESSFUL"
            Session("AllNews") = Nothing
            Response.Redirect("newsdetail.aspx")
        Catch addException As Exception
            lblMessage.Text += " - ERROR ADDING NEW RECORD"
        Finally
            AddNews = Nothing
            ViewState("NewsAddEdit") = False
        End Try
    Else
        'Update
        lblMessage.Text += " --> WE are saving an edited record"
        Dim saveNews As New Company()
        Try
            saveNews.SaveNews(CInt(lblID.Text), 1, txtSubject.Text, _
                txtInfo.Text, 1)
            lblMessage.Text += " - SAVING SUCCESSFUL"
            Session("AllNews") = Nothing
            Response.Redirect("newsdetail.aspx")
        Catch saveException As Exception
            lblMessage.Text += saveNews.StatusInfo()
            lblMessage.Text += " - ERROR UPDATING RECORD"
        Finally
            saveNews = Nothing
        End Try
    End If
End Sub
```

The business layer has an *AddNews* method and a *SaveNews* method. After determining that we are actually adding a new record, we invoke the AddNews method, pass it the correct parameters, reset the session variable containing the dataset for the DataGrid control, and redirect the page to itself. Why do we clear the *DataSet* session variable and redirect the page to itself? First, we clear the session variable so that the page is forced to call the data from the business layer again. We added a new record and want to show it in the DataGrid control. Second, we want to clear all other state-related information. The easiest way to do this is to start the page from scratch. That's why we redirect the page to itself.

Saving edited information is almost identical to the process of adding a new record. The difference is the requirement to use the *SaveNews* method of the business layer.

Deleting data   Deleting a specific record is an easy process. The business layer has a *DeleteNews* method that needs a specific *NewsID*. We call this method when the Delete button is clicked. Here is the code:

```
Public Sub HandleButtonColumns(ByVal sender As Object, _
    ByVal e As DataGridCommandEventArgs) Handles HRGridEdit1.ItemCommand
    If e.CommandName = "Delete" Then
        Dim intNewsID As Integer = _
            CType(HRGridEdit1.DataKeys(e.Item.ItemIndex), Integer)
        lblMessage.Text = "You wanted to delete the record with ID =" + _
            CStr(intNewsID)
        Dim deleteNews As New Company()
        Try
            deleteNews.DeleteNEws(intNewsID)
            lblMessage.Text += " - RECORD DELETED"
            Session("AllNews") = Nothing
            Response.Redirect("newsdetail.aspx")
        Catch deleteException As Exception
            lblMessage.Text += " - ERROR IN DELETE"
        Finally
            DeleteNews = Nothing
        End Try
    End If
End Sub
```

Setting focus to a control   We really wish the developers at Microsoft had included a *setFocus* function for ASP.NET controls. Unfortunately, they didn't. Thanks to some good old Java Script code, we can accomplish this task ourselves. Here is the code in the *SetFocus* method:

```
Public Shared Sub SetFocus(ByVal ctrl As Control)
    Dim stringJava As New StringBuilder()
    stringJava.Append("<SCRIPT LANGUAGE='JavaScript'>")
    stringJava.Append("function SetInitialFocus()")
    stringJava.Append("{")
    stringJava.Append("    document.")
```

(continued)

```
          Dim passedControl As Control = ctrl.Parent
          While Not TypeOf passedControl Is System.Web.UI.HtmlControls.HtmlForm
              passedControl = passedControl.Parent
          End While

          stringJava.Append(passedControl.ClientID)
          stringJava.Append("['")
          stringJava.Append(ctrl.UniqueID)
          stringJava.Append(":textBox1")
          stringJava.Append("'].focus();")
          stringJava.Append("}")
          stringJava.Append("window.onload = SetInitialFocus;")
          stringJava.Append("</SCRIPT>")
          ctrl.Page.RegisterClientScriptBlock("InitialFocus", _
              stringJava.ToString())  'Block is registered
End Sub
```

This code looks a lot more complicated than it really is. All we want to do is add some Java Script that will set focus to a specific control on the form and get executed only when the *btnAdd* button is clicked. The page class has a method named *RegisterClientScriptBlock* that allows dynamic registration of Java Script to the beginning of an HTML form. In our case, we want to add this script only on the postback caused by the click event of *btnAdd*. On every other postback, the Java Script won't be added.

So what JavaScript do we want to add to allow focus of a control? We want to set the *window.onload* event to call a script block. Here is the script block we want to create when we want to set focus to the txtSubject:textBox1 control:

```
<SCRIPT LANGUAGE='JavaScript'>
  function SetInitialFocus(){
    document.Form1['txtSubject:textBox1'].focus();
  }
  window.onload = SetInitialFocus;
</SCRIPT>
```

The solution is to build this script block dynamically, which is what we did in the *SetFocus* method. We use the *StringBuilder* object to accomplish this task. We have only one challenge: how do we get the specific information we need to call the correct control? On the postback of the form, we need to generate the Java Script code block shown in the preceding code. First, we must know the name of the form. This we can get from the control's parent information, as follows:

```
Dim passedControl As Control = ctrl.Parent
While Not TypeOf passedControl Is System.Web.UI.HtmlControls.HtmlForm
    passedControl = passedControl.Parent
End While
```

```
stringJava.Append(passedControl.ClientID)
```

Once we find the control of type HtmlForm, we can get its *ClientID* and add it to the *StringBuilder*. The next hurdle is the specific control's name. That one is easy—it's in the *ctrl.UniqueID* parameter. What's not apparent is that we aren't using a TextBox control directly but rather our composite custom server control. Within this custom server control, we included several ASP.NET controls such as a Label control, a TextBox control, and validation controls. We know the name of the specific TextBox control within our server control. It is *textBox1*. With this, we can build the correct control name in the *StringBuilder*:

```
stringJava.Append(ctrl.UniqueID)
stringJava.Append(":textBox1")
```

That's all there is to it. We can quickly adjust the *SetFocus* method to allow us to programmatically set focus to any area of a Web Forms page.

The NewDetail.aspx Web Forms page's features are now complete and allow a straightforward and simple way to manage data presentation, edit data, add data, and set permissions. You can quickly duplicate this process for other pages in which the DataGrid control and detail information fit on one Web Forms page. The other forms in our HRnet application that can be created this way are the Departments Web Forms page, the Positions Web Forms page, and the Job Titles Web Forms page. Adding these forms to HRnet will give you great practice applying the principles of this chapter.

Employees: DataGrid and Detail Web Forms Pages Separated

We're now going to show you how to wire up the DataGrid and detail pages in separate Web Forms. You might also have a situation in which a single DataGrid control has more than one detail page. Many of the techniques used in the preceding examples in which you have a DataGrid control and detail information on one form apply for separate Web Forms pages also. We'll therefore concentrate on the differences. Figure14-11 shows the Employee DataGrid control with the permission settings for standard users.

Figure 14-12 shows the Employee DataGrid control with permission settings for managers. Notice that managers can select a specific record. Additional navigation options available let managers choose details, addresses, and emergency information.

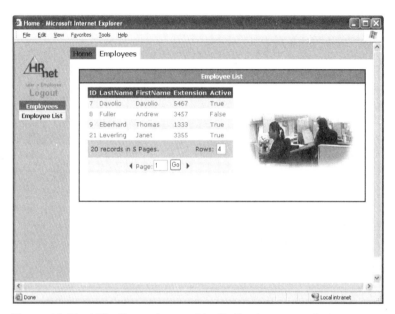

Figure 14-11 HRnet's employee grid with Employee permissions

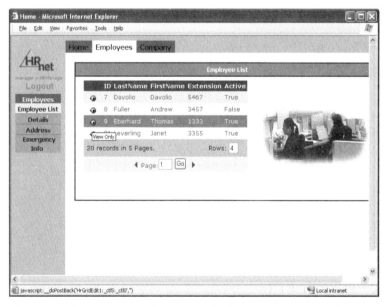

Figure 14-12 HRnet's employee grid with HRManager permissions

Figure 14-13 shows the Employee DataGrid control with permission settings for executives. This time, permissions are granted not only for viewing but for editing and deleting records also. In addition, the Work Schedule and My Info navigation bars are added.

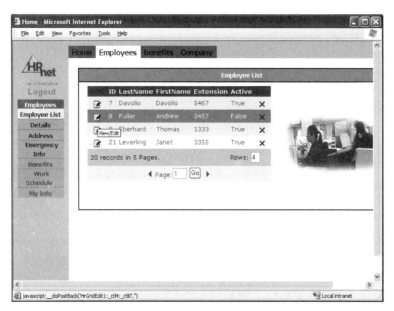

Figure 14-13   HRnet's employee grid with Executive permissions

The List form and its state   When the detail area is in a separate form, our major consideration is the requirement to pass certain state information about the current selection of the DataGrid and permission settings for the specific detail page. In the selected detail page, this information is in turn processed to pull up a certain record and/or apply the permission settings. In the EmployeeList.aspx and EmployeeDetails.aspx examples, we pass this information in three session variables. The first one is *EmployeeIDStatus*, which contains the standard permission settings we use. The second one is *EmployeeID*, which contains the currently selected unique index to the Employee table. The third session variable is named *GridState* and contains the page and index information of the Data-Grid control so that we don't lose the position of the row selected when we navigate to the DataGrid after processing information in the detail Web Forms page. Let's take a look at how this is done, starting with the EmployeeList.aspx's code-behind page and its *Page_Load* event. The lines of code that differ from previous examples are in boldface:

```
Private Sub Page_Load(ByVal sender As System.Object, _
    ByVal e As System.EventArgs) Handles MyBase.Load
    If Not IsPostBack Then
        GetDataToSession()
        HrGridEdit1.GridDataSet = CType(Session("Allemployees"), DataSet)
        HrGridEdit1.GridTable = "Employees"
        HrGridEdit1.PageSize = 4
        PermissionSettings()
        If Session("EmployeeID") Is Nothing Or Session("GridState") _
            Is Nothing Then
            HrGridEdit1.SelectedIndex = 0
            HrGridEdit1.Update()
            Session("EmployeeID") = _
                CInt(HrGridEdit1.DataKeys(HrGridEdit1.SelectedIndex))
            If Session("EmployeeIDStatus") Is "VIEW" Then
                HrGridEdit1.SelectedIndex = -1
            End If
        Else
            If Not Session("GridState") Is Nothing Then
                SelectGrid()
                HrGridEdit1.Update()
            End If
        End If
        HrGridEdit1.Update()
    Else
        GetDataToSession()
        HrGridEdit1.GridDataSet = CType(Session("AllEmployees"), DataSet)
        HrGridEdit1.GridTable = "Employees"
        PermissionSettings()
        HrGridEdit1.Update()
    End If
End Sub
```

The first time we load the EmployeeList.aspx Web Forms page, we need to check whether the state information in *EmployeeID* and *GridState* is available. If not, we set the DataGrid control to highlight the very first record, along with the specific *EmployeeID*. If state information is available, we know that the EmployeeList.aspx Web Forms page was visited and a specific record was selected. We simply grab the *GridState* information and set the correct page and row. How do we set the correct page and row, and even more important, how do we get that information in the first place? The place to set the DataGrid's page and row information is in the *SelectedIndexChanged* method. In addition to setting the correct *EmployeeID* to pass to the detail pages, we create the GridState session variable. Here is the code:

```
Public Sub SelectedIndexChanged(ByVal sender As Object, _
    ByVal e As EventArgs)
    Session("EmployeeID") = _
        CInt(HrGridEdit1.DataKeys(HrGridEdit1.SelectedIndex))
    Dim gridState As New ArrayList()
    gridState.Add(HrGridEdit1.CurrentPageIndex)
    gridState.Add(HrGridEdit1.SelectedIndex)
    Session("GridState") = gridState
    gridState = Nothing
    HrGridEdit1.Update()
End Sub
```

Now that we added the code to create the DataGrid's page and row state information, we also need a way to set the DataGrid back to a specific state. This is done in the *SelectGrid* method, as follows:

```
Private Sub SelectGrid()
    If Session("GridState") Is Nothing Then
        HrGridEdit1.CurrentPageIndex = 0
        HrGridEdit1.SelectedIndex = 0
    Else
        Dim gridState As ArrayList = CType(Session("GridState"), ArrayList)
        HrGridEdit1.CurrentPageIndex = CInt(gridState(0))
        HrGridEdit1.SelectedIndex = CInt(gridState(1))
    End If
End Sub
```

The last information we need to pass to the detail page is the permission setting in the *EmployeeIDStatus* session variable. This is done in the *Permission-Settings* method:

```
Private Sub PermissionSettings()
    Dim oUser As New SecurIt.UserSecurity()
    Dim localPermission As String = _
        UCase(CStr(oUser.Roles.GetValue(0)))
    Select Case localPermission
      Case "EMPLOYEE"
          Session("EmployeeIDStatus") = "VIEW"
          HrGridEdit1.SelectedIndex = -1
      Case "HRMANAGER"
          viewButton()
          Session("EmployeeIDStatus") = "VIEW DETAIL"
      Case "EXECUTIVE"
          editButton()
          deleteButton()
```

(continued)

```
            Session("EmployeeIDStatus") = "ALL"
        Case Else
            Session("EmployeeIDStatus") = "NONE"
    End Select
End Sub
```

With the correct information available, we're able to add the Employee-Details.aspx Web Forms page, linked to the state information of Employee-List.aspx.

The Detail form   When accessing the Detail Web Forms page, we must take the state information that was set by the previous List Web Forms page. This means setting permissions and calling up the correct record (unless we are adding a new one). Figure 14-14 shows the Detail Web Forms page with the permission settings for managers. Only the Exit button is visible; all controls are disabled.

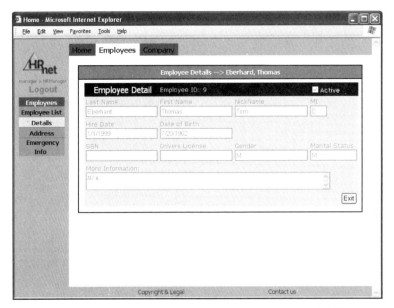

Figure 14-14   HRnet's employee detail information with HRManager permissions

Figure 14-15 shows the Detail Web Forms page with the permission settings for executives. Notice that all data controls are enabled and the action buttons are visible also.

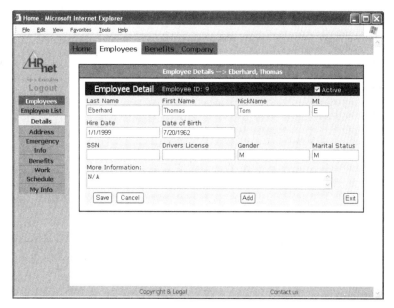

Figure 14-15   HRnet's employee detail information with Executive permissions

Let's take a look at the code that takes the state settings and populates the EmployeeDetails.aspx Web Forms page. We start with the *Page_Load* event:

```
Private Sub Page_Load(ByVal sender As System.Object, _
    ByVal e As System.EventArgs) Handles MyBase.Load
    btnSave.Attributes.Add("onclick", "return confirm('OK to Save?');")
    btnCancel.Attributes.Add("onclick", "return confirm('OK to Cancel?');")
    lblMode.Text = ""
    SetPermissions()
    If Not IsPostBack Then
        privateEmployeeID = CInt(Session("EmployeeID"))
        lblHeader.Text = "Employee ID: " + CStr(privateEmployeeID)
        GetDataToSession()
        LoadFields()
    End If
End Sub
```

When the page is loaded, we set a private variable within the page that holds the specific *EmployeeID* from its session variable. Then we need to obtain the correct data in the *GetDataToSession* method, after which we populate the fields in the *LoadFields* method.

In the *GetDataToSession* method, we fill the *EmployeebyID* session variable with the *DataSet* of the specific record returned to us by the *GetEmployee-Detail* function in the business layer logic:

```
Private Sub GetDataToSession()
    Dim localEmployeebyID As DataSet
    Dim localCompany As New Employee()
    localEmployeebyID = _
        localCompany.GetEmployeeDetail(CInt(Session("EmployeeID")), 1)
    Session("EmployeebyID") = localEmployeebyID
    localCompany = Nothing
End Sub
```

The *LoadFields* and *PermissionSettings* methods are the same as in previous examples. The rest of the EmployeeDetail.aspx Web Forms page's functionality is identical to the NewsDetail example we showed earlier.

We hope these two examples showed how effortlessly you can wire an application together when all its pieces are available. You can easily take the principles shown thus far in this and preceding chapters and apply them to your applications. Many of the components we've discussed are ready to use or easy to modify. We still want to show you one Windows Forms example and discuss the deployment of applications and versioning.

An HRnet Windows Form: Titles

We're going to add a Windows Forms example to the HRnet application. One of the most exciting results of this example is the realization that the process, and even much of the code, is almost the same for Windows Forms applications as it is for Web Forms applications. A layered approach with business objects, data access objects, and security objects allows nearly identical lines of code to be used for both types of applications.

Titles: DataGrid and Detail in One Windows Form

The example solution for the HRnet Windows Forms application resides in the C:\BuildOOP\CH14\HRnetWindows directory. It's named HRnetWindows and consists of two forms, the HRnetMenu Windows form and the Titles Windows form. HRnetMenu was created with the same principles we covered in Chapter 7. A menu is automatically built using the *MenuTest* class. Figure 14-16 shows the menu form with the Titles option in the Company menu tab. Clicking it will bring up the Title Windows form.

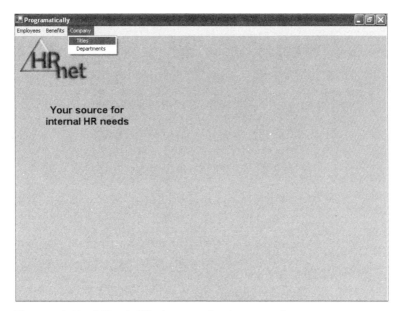

Figure 14-16   HRnet's Windows application menu form

Figure 14-17 shows us the Title Windows form in action. Just like its New-Detail.aspx counterpart in the HRnet Web applications, it is a combination of a DataGrid control and detail information on one page.

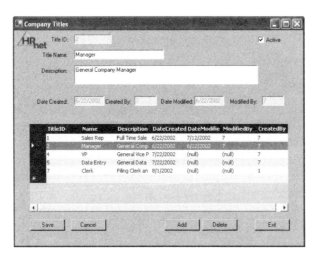

Figure 14-17   HRnet's Title Management Windows form

To keep this example simple, we didn't create a logon screen and security. Just like Web Forms applications, Windows Forms applications have a

Form_Load event. We're going to use this to get data from the business layer and set the DataGrid's *DataSource* property. The good news for data persistence in Windows Forms is that we don't have to use session variables. Here is the *Form_Load* event code:

```
Dim localTitleData As DataSet
Dim localAddState As Boolean = False

#Region "Form Load and Data Gathering"
    Private Sub Form_Load(ByVal sender As System.Object, _
        ByVal e As System.EventArgs) Handles MyBase.Load
        GetDataLocal()
        SetGrid()
    End Sub

    Private Sub GetDataLocal()
        If localTitleData Is Nothing Then
            Dim localCompany As New Company()
            localTitleData = localCompany.GetCompanyTitles(1)
            localCompany = Nothing
        End If
    End Sub

    Private Sub SetGrid()
        With HRTitleGrid
            .AllowSorting = True
            .DataSource = localTitleData
            .DataMember = "Titles"
        End With
    End Sub
#End Region
```

The code is straightforward and should look very familiar to you. When the form loads, we call two methods, the first of which is the *GetDataLocal* method. It uses the business layer to return all titles found. Notice that we can assign the results to the local variable *localTitleData* and don't have to worry about its persistence as long as the Windows form is alive. The second method we call, *SetGrid*, sets the DataGrid's *DataSource* and *DataMember*.

Selecting a specific row works a bit differently when we use the DataGrid control in a Windows form. Here is the code:

```
Private Sub HRTitleGrid_Click(ByVal sender As System.Object, _
    ByVal e As System.EventArgs) Handles HRTitleGrid.Click
    lblMessage.Text = CStr(HRTitleGrid.CurrentRowIndex)
    Dim currentRow As Integer = HRTitleGrid.CurrentRowIndex
    Dim titleKey As Integer = CInt(HRTitleGrid.Item(currentRow, 0))
    LoadFields(titleKey)
End Sub
```

Since the DataGrid control in a Windows form does not bind a specific data key to a selected row, we have to get to the unique *TitleID* by using the information from the current row's first column. The first column is the *TitleID*. You can see that the DataGrid control gives us the *CurrentRowIndex*, which we use to get the DataGrid's *item*, which is the first column in the row—the required *TitleID*.

We included the code for the *LoadFields* method. It's exactly the same as the code for our HRnet Web Forms application counterparts:

```
Private Sub LoadFields(ByVal titleID As Integer)
    'Import Data Into Fields
    Dim localTitle As New Company()
    Dim singleTitle As DataRow
    singleTitle = _
        localTitle.GetCompanyTitleDetail(titleID).Tables(0).Rows(0)
    localTitle = Nothing
    Try
        If Not IsDBNull(singleTitle("TitleID")) _
            Then txtTitleID.Text = CStr(singleTitle("TitleID")) _
            Else txtTitleID.Text = "Unknown ID"
        If Not IsDBNull(singleTitle("Name")) _
            Then txtTitle.Text = CStr(singleTitle("Name")) _
            Else txtTitle.Text = ""
            ⋮
        lblMessage.Text = ""
    Catch selectException As Exception
        ClearEntries()
        lblMessage.Text = "Error showing this Employee Record: " + _
            selectException.Message
    Finally
        singleTitle = Nothing
    End Try
End Sub
```

The next code we present takes care of adding, deleting, saving, canceling, and exiting. We included it so that you can see the similarities to our HRnet Web Forms application. Here it is:

```
Private Sub btnSave_Click(ByVal sender As System.Object, _
    ByVal e As System.EventArgs) Handles btnSave.Click
    If MsgBox("Do you really want to save this record?", _
        MsgBoxStyle.YesNo, "Save Button") = MsgBoxResult.Yes Then
        If localAddState = True Then
            lblMessage.Text = "You are saving an ADDED record"
            localAddState = False
            Dim addTitle As New Company()
```

(continued)

```
                Try
                    addTitle.AddTitle(True, txtTitle.Text, _
                        txtDescription.Text, 1)
                Catch addException As Exception
                    ClearEntries()
                    lblMessage.Text = "Error adding a record: " + _
                        addException.Message
                Finally
                    addTitle = Nothing
                End Try
            Else
                lblMessage.Text = "You are saving an EDITED record"
            End If
            localTitleData = Nothing
            GetDataLocal()
            SetGrid()
        End If
    End Sub

    Private Sub btnCancel_Click(ByVal sender As System.Object, _
        ByVal e As System.EventArgs) Handles btnCancel.Click
        If MsgBox("Do you really want to cancel?", _
            MsgBoxStyle.YesNo, "Cancel Button") = MsgBoxResult.Yes Then
            localAddState = False
            ClearEntries()
        End If
    End Sub

    Private Sub btnAdd_Click(ByVal sender As System.Object, _
        ByVal e As System.EventArgs) Handles btnAdd.Click
        localAddState = True
        ClearEntries()
        txtTitle.Focus()
    End Sub

    Private Sub btnDelete_Click(ByVal sender As System.Object, _
        ByVal e As System.EventArgs) Handles btnDelete.Click
        If MsgBox("Do you really want to delete this record?", _
            MsgBoxStyle.YesNo, "Delete Button") = MsgBoxResult.Yes Then
            localAddState = False
            Dim currentRow As Integer = HRTitleGrid.CurrentRowIndex
            Dim titleKey As Integer = CInt(HRTitleGrid.Item(currentRow, 0))
            Dim deleteTitle As New Company()
            Try
                deleteTitle.DeleteTitle(titleKey)
            Catch deleteException As Exception
                ClearEntries()
                lblMessage.Text = "Error deleting Record: " + _
                    deleteException.Message
```

```
        Finally
            deleteTitle = Nothing
        End Try
        localTitleData = Nothing
        GetDataLocal()
        SetGrid()
    End If
End Sub

Private Sub btnExit_Click(ByVal sender As System.Object, _
    ByVal e As System.EventArgs) Handles btnExit.Click
    MyBase.Dispose()
End Sub
```

We'll explain only the lines of code in boldface. You might wonder why we clear the *localTitleData* variable. Well, when saving the data from adds, edits, and deletes, the underlying data changes. Since the data for the DataGrid control is cached in the *localTitleData* variable, we simply eliminate it, recall it through the business layer, and bind it back to the DataGrid.

Take the time to test the functionality of this Windows form. Its functional similarities to our previous Web Forms application examples are astounding. By the way, when you want to select a row, you need to do this in the empty space left of the first column. You can also try sorting. The DataGrid in Windows Forms applications is much more powerful and has many more built-in features than the DataGrid in Web Forms applications. For this reason, we didn't create a custom server control.

Deploying an Application

Have you ever had the nightmare of deploying an application that you wrote with pre-.NET technology and one of the supporting DLLs conflicted with one that someone else installed? How about the old "copy it and it will work" deployment we experienced in the MS DOS days? Well, XCOPY deployment is back again—almost. Deploying Visual Basic .NET and ASP.NET applications is practically a copy-and-paste process as long as the Microsoft .NET Framework is installed on the system. If you installed one or more of the sample applications included in this book and followed the readme instructions, you will have found this to be true.

Gone is the need to register components in the system's registry, and gone is the need to stop and restart the Web server or operating system. Gone is the problem with multiple versions of the same DLL. Gone is the problem of DLL hell (as long as you don't need legacy stuff on your system or interoperability with pre-.NET components).

You can deploy an application in three different ways. The first is the XCOPY approach, the second is to manage global deployments, and the third is to create a Windows Installer package. Let's take a look at all three.

Deploy with XCOPY

We really don't like to call this process *XCOPY* deployment. XCOPY brings up old memories of the clunky MS DOS days. Using the term XCOPY might even imply that you *have* to use the XCOPY command to deploy a .NET application. You don't. You can use any means of copying a .NET application, as long as your approach copies all the required files, including subdirectories, into the proper directory on the proper system. You can use the copy-and-paste feature of Microsoft Windows Explorer, FTP commands, or—yes—the XCOPY command. In the case of an ASP.NET application, you need to create a new Web site or a virtual Web directory, as we have shown in the readme files for the examples that accompany this book. That's about all there is to it. We can get on with life after we consider some other issues and discuss other ways of deploying applications or part of them.

Updating an XCOPY-Deployed Application

After we perform an XCOPY deployment and take care of the required IIS settings, we might need to update or add features to our application. Most of this is handled automatically by the common language runtime, or CLR.

When you update Web.config files, Global.asax files, code-behind files, or custom server controls, the CLR causes our IIS application to restart automatically. This might cause some delays for users since these files get re-compiled.

When the HTML portion of a Web page or of custom user controls changes, the next request after the change will get the new version. Users don't usually see any delays when this happens.

Deploy Global Files

Let's say you've written some assemblies that you want to use for more than one application. You can globally deploy these into the global assembly cache (GAC). Good examples of these assemblies are some of the components we've written such as the data access component, the security component, and the custom server controls component. Unfortunately, copying and pasting these assemblies into the GAC, which generally resides in the C:\windows\assembly or C:\winnt\assembly directory, is not sufficient for deployment. To register a specific assembly with the GAC, you have to use .NET's command-line utility named GacUtil.exe. GacUtil is installed by default in the C:\Program

Files\Microsoft Visual Studio .NET\FrameworkSDK\Bin directory. Before applying the GacUtil to an assembly, there is one more requirement: the assembly to be included in the GAC must have a strong name, which is a secure name that identifies the assembly by name, version number, and a public key. In the next few sections, we'll outline the process that prepares and registers an assembly in the GAC.

Step 1: Add the *AssemblyVersion* Attribute

The *AssemblyVersion* attribute contains the version number for the specific assembly to be included in the GAC. It needs to be added to the AssemblyInfo.vb files, which reside in the root of the application. Here is the unchanged default AssemblyInfo.vb file in the HRnet application:

```
Imports System.Reflection
Imports System.Runtime.InteropServices


' General Information about an assembly is controlled through the following
' set of attributes. Change these attribute values to modify the
' information associated with an assembly.
' Review the values of the assembly attributes

<Assembly: AssemblyTitle("")>
<Assembly: AssemblyDescription("")>
<Assembly: AssemblyCompany("")>
<Assembly: AssemblyProduct("")>
<Assembly: AssemblyCopyright("")>
<Assembly: AssemblyTrademark("")>
<Assembly: CLSCompliant(True)>


'The following GUID is for the ID of the typelib if this project is exposed to
COM
<Assembly: Guid("EB6F25B0-2B0F-48B3-A9AE-8069FAE1EE98")>


' Version information for an assembly consists of the following four values:
'
'       Major Version
'       Minor Version
'       Build Number
'       Revision
'
' You can specify all the values or you can default the
' Build and Revision Numbers by using the '*' as shown below:

<Assembly: AssemblyVersion("1.0.*")>
```

If you wanted to add the version number 1.0.2.499 to this assembly, you would include the following line of code as the last line of AssemblyInfo.vb:

```
<Assembly: AssemblyVersionAttribute("1.0.2.499")>
```

Step 2: Generate a Strong Name

The strong name required before registering an assembly in the GAC is created by sn.exe. This utility creates an output file that contains a public and private key as well as a digital signature. It needs to be stored in the virtual root directory of the application. Here is the command-line command that creates the MyAssemblyStrongName.snk file in the MyAppDirectory directory:

```
sn -k MyAppDirectory\MyAssemblyStrongName.snk
```

Next, we add a reference to this file in the AssemblyInfo.vb file from Step 1:

```
<Assembly:
  AssemblyKeyFileAttribute("MyAppDirectory\MyAssemblyStrongName.snk")>
```

Step 3: Add the Assembly to the GAC

Now we're ready to add the assembly to the GAC. Here is the command-line command for the gacutil.exe:

```
gacutil /i MyAssemblyDLLPath\MyAssemblyDLL.dll
```

You probably guessed that the MyAssemblyDLLPath points to the directory in which the MyAssemblyDLL.dll (the file to register) resides.

GacUtil's common switches are */i* for installing, */u* for uninstalling, and */l* for listing all assemblies in the GAC.

Step 4: Register a GAC Assembly in the Application

If assemblies in the GAC are going to be used within our applications, we must register them in the machine.config file. Here is the section in which you need to add them:

```
<configuration><system.web><compilation><assemblies>
```

We need to find out the public key token that we named *xxxxxx*. (Run the GacUtil command with */l* to get this number.) Here's what this would look like for our example:

```
<add assembly=" MyAssemblyDLL.dll, Version=1.0.2.499,
  Culture=nutral, PublicKeyToken=xxxxxx" />
```

Congratulations, you just learned how to do a global deployment. If you're a tools developer, you'll probably want to write a script that will do all this automatically.

Deploy by Creating a Windows Installer Package

What if you need to deploy a .NET application on a machine without the .NET Framework and you need to hide complicated interaction from users? This is when the Windows Installer comes to the rescue. The basic process of creating a Windows Installer package is relatively simple. Don't be fooled by this tool's apparent simplicity. Many of its options allow maximum flexibility but they take a while to learn. Although we won't cover this part of the installation process in detail, we would like to show you the principles of using the Windows Installer by adding an Installer package to HRnet.

To create a Windows Installer package, we need to add a setup template project to our application. Figure 14-18 shows you the dialog box for adding an empty Installer project to the HRnet solution.

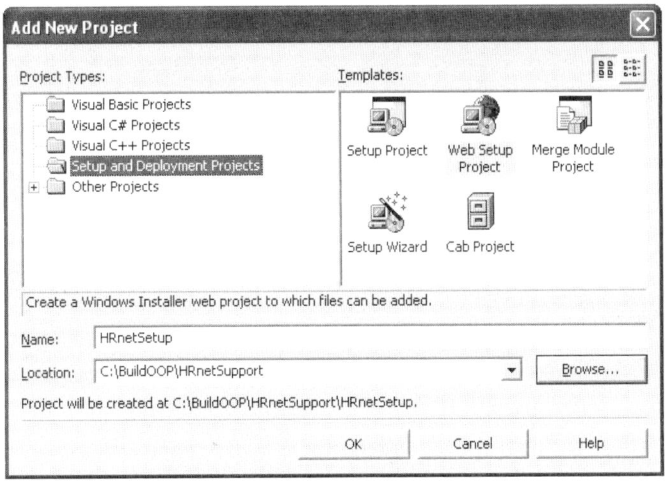

Figure 14-18 Add a Web Setup project

Next we need to add the project to be deployed. You do this by right-clicking the Web Application folder, pointing to Add, and then clicking Project Output on the shortcut menu. The Add Project Output Group dialog box opens. We chose the Primary Output and Content Files options for the HRnet Project, as shown in Figure 14-19.

With the Web Application folder selected, in the Properties window, you can change some options such as the default document and virtual directory. See Figure 14-20 for the settings we chose.

We left the rest of the properties at their default settings. After building the HRnetSetup project, you can see the result files in the HRnetSetup directory we defined in C:\BuildOOP\HRnetSupport. The setup files we created are in Figure 14-21.

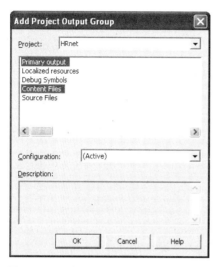

Figure 14-19   Add a project output to the Web Setup project

Figure 14-20   Properties of the Web Application Folder option

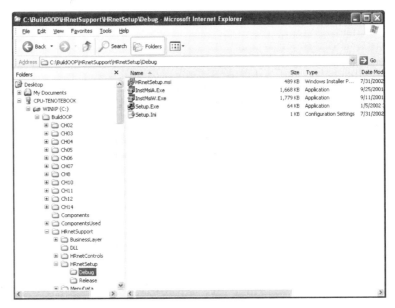

Figure 14-21   Setup files created by the Windows Installer

Deployment and installation hasn't been this easy since the MS DOS days. The three options covered here will give you enough flexibility to cover almost any deployment requirement.

Assemblies and Versioning

This chapter would not be complete without a few words about assemblies and versioning. .NET allows us to avoid DLL hell; however, we have to version assemblies correctly or we risk conflicts.

Assemblies typically consist of a single DLL (although one DLL could be made up of several files). A closer look at assemblies reveals that they consist of Portable Executable (PE) files that are either DLLs or EXEs. Assemblies are self-describing through the use of metadata that fully describes the classes, methods, and types. Assemblies also include manifests that describe in detail anything that is contained within them. These details contain data that identifies the assembly (name, version, etc.) and references by the assembly.

You are no longer required to register assemblies. When you place them into a Web application's \bin directory, they are automatically registered with that Web application. The CLR fulfills two important functions for us that make working with assemblies very easy. First, instead of locking the original DLL, the CLR creates a shadow copy of it in memory. This leaves the original file unlocked. We can replace it at any time. Second, the CLR monitors the \bin directory constantly. When a new version of a DLL is copied to the directory, the CLR will use it for the next request referencing it. Once the old version goes out of scope, it is released from memory. What a slick solution to the old world of locked DLLs and DLL hell!

When we include application-specific assemblies in the \bin directory, versioning is limited to the files residing in this directory. Public assemblies, however, can have as many versions as you wish. The application links itself automatically to the correct version it was developed with.

One little challenge we've found is using assemblies that rely on other assemblies that used different versions of each other. OK, this sounds complicated. Let's look at an example. In all our examples starting with those in Chapter 4, we used the DataAccessLayer.dll file—our Data Access component. Let's say that another component, MenuData.dll, also uses DataAccessLayer.dll. Suppose MenuData.dll needed to make a change to the DataAccess component using the modified version of the component instead of the original. Everything works fine until we try to register the DataAccessLayer.dll and the MenuData.dll in the same project. Now there is a conflict. Remember that local files don't use versioning. The error message you might get can be similar to this one:

```
Warning: The dependency 'DataAccessLayer, Version=1.0.939.31943, Culture=
neutral' in project 'HRnet' cannot be copied to the run directory because
it would overwrite the reference 'DataAccessLayer, Version=1.0.942.37660,
Culture=neutral'.
```

We've had some sleepless nights over this problem and came up with a good solution. We created a DLL directory for all assemblies that will be in the final project. The one for HRnet is in C:\BuildOOP\HRnetSupport DLL. For each project that creates an assembly (a DLL file), we take out any existing references and recreate the required references so that they point to the DLL directory. Then we copy the resulting assembly into the DLL directory that will be used by other referenced projects.

Another, better solution is to copy the general assemblies into the GAC, using the GacUtil utility as explained previously. However, we didn't want to take that approach until the components were thoroughly debugged and a reasonably finished version could be installed into the GAC. Yes, we know that you can have different versions installed in the GAC, but how many is too many to keep track of? The solution that uses a specific directory for DLLs works well during development.

Conclusion

We've come to the end of this chapter and this book. I hope the journey of discovering .NET's features and powerful options has been as exciting to you as it has been for us. In the past, we always tried to develop our applications with multiple tiers, as much object orientation as possible, components and inheritance, and so on. Only since the availability of the .NET platform has the implementation of these objectives become as easy and straightforward as you've seen in the examples we've provided, especially for scalable Web applications. It was our goal to explain the new and improved features of Visual Basic .NET, the common language runtime, and ASP.NET in a way that would allow you to leverage this information—and the components we created in the process—to rapidly build large, well-performing applications. We wish you a happy and successful future in the exciting world of application development.

Index

OLE DB provider example, 118
running, without parameters, 111–12
stored procedures
business layers and, 244, 245, 248–55
Command objects and, 89–90
data access component, 96
data access with, 37–39, 45–49, 97
DataSet object and, 93–94
get-related, 249–51, 255–56
insert-related, 257–59
methods with. *See* stored procedure methods
naming conventions, 245
queries based on business rules, 248–55
security and, 132–33, 145
transactions, data concurrency, and, 119
update-related, 259–61
String class, 8, 11
string handling, 10–12
StringBuilder class, 12, 446–47
strings. *See* connection strings; SQL strings; string handling
strong names, 410, 461, 462
strongly typed data, 85
structured exception handling, 59–81
concept of, 61–62
creating application exception class hierarchies, 80–81
data access component, 96, 103–4, 109
error handling vs., 12–13
errors vs. exceptions, 60. *See also* errors; exceptions
exception-handling objects. *See* exception-handling objects
history, 59
logging, 61, 75–77, 96, 103–4, 401
.NET Framework and, 60–61
object-oriented, 62–63
syntax of Try statement, 63–66
structures, 19–20
style
DataGrid AutoFormat feature, 327
menu style sheets, 221–22, 236
Web template and, 298–99, 304
Windows Forms template visual inheritance, 311–12
subclassed forms, 312
subroutines. *See* methods

summary page, HRnet, 290–91
SuppressFinalize method, 106
system analysis, 54–55
System.Data namespace, 118
System.Diagnostics namespace, 75
System.Drawing namespace, 190, 328
SystemException class, 67
System.Runtime.Remoting namespace, 393
System.Web.UI namespace, 304
System.Web.UI.Controls namespace, 328
System.Web.UI.Design namespace, 199
System.Web.UI.HtmlControls namespace, 176
System.Web.UI.Page, 3–4
System.Web.UI.WebControls namespace, 181, 195
System.Windows.Forms namespace, 206, 207

T

tab controls, menu, 218–19
Table controls, 347–48
TableDirect option, 89
tables
menu data, 217, 223–29
user credential, 128–29
Web template, 298–99
Tables collection, 93, 94
Tabular Data Stream (TDS), 84, 119
TagName, 165–66, 180
TagPrefix, 165–66, 180, 181–82
TagPrefixAttribute attribute, 181–82
taskbar, Windows service and, 405
TemplateColumns, DataGrid control, 433–34
templates
DataGrid control formatting, 349
full custom server control, 179
HRnet, 216, 419–21
menu, 222, 224, 236
user interface. *See* user interface templates
Web. *See* Web templates
Windows Forms, 311–15
wiring together, 419–21
testing
data access component, 108–10, 116–17
menu and navigation component, 236
menu component, 227–29
performance, 83
remoting, 391–93

Ken Spencer

Ken, who works at 32X Tech Corporation, has authored and coauthored numerous technical textbooks, including *Windows 2000 Server: Management and Control* (Prentice Hall, 2000) and *Programming Visual InterDev* (Microsoft Press, 1999). He also writes for several popular magazines: the "Advanced Basics" column for *MSDN Magazine* and articles for *Windows 2000 Magazine* and *SQL Server Magazine*.

Tom Eberhard

Tom is CIO of InfoLink Screening Services, Inc., a pre-employment background screening company, and president of CPU, Inc., a business Internet consulting firm. Tom has been programming in different languages since he was 14. He is a frequent speaker at industry events, such as VS Connections and VB Connections conferences. He has designed and written several large-scale enterprise solutions, including an early adopter .NET Web application for the background screening industry. His consulting firm was one of the first to help businesses use the Internet as a tool to reach more customers, service them better, and grow their businesses.

John Alexander

John is a recognized Microsoft Certified Trainer (MCT) and Microsoft Certified Solution Developer (MCSD) and has served as an MSDN regional director for the last five years. As a consultant, he is experienced in the delivery of scalable, stable, and open enterprise-level .NET applications, and he has taught all over the globe. In addition, John has written Microsoft Official Curriculum and speaks at industry conferences such as VBITS, VB Connections, and Developer Days. This is John's second .NET book published in eight months, and he is eagerly anticipating the movie adaptation of this title.

Digital Micrometer

A *digital micrometer* is like a caliper but measures much smaller distances—down to one ten-thousandth of an inch. Micrometers are used to accurately gauge the thickness of paper, plastic film, paperboard, and fine-tolerance metal parts. The principle of a micrometer is based on the turning accuracy of a fine screw thread. The object to be measured is placed in the opening of the micrometer frame. Another part, called the thimble, is rotated until the object is held in place. Readings are taken on the thimble and barrel scales to determine the correct measurement. A digital micrometer is as easy to read as the odometer on your car, with a clear digital display that indicates thicknesses in small increments.

At Microsoft Press, we use tools to illustrate our books for software developers and IT professionals. Tools very simply and powerfully symbolize human inventiveness. They're a metaphor for people extending their capabilities, precision, and reach. From simple calipers and pliers to digital micrometers and lasers, these stylized illustrations give each book a visual identity, and a personality to the series. With tools and knowledge, there's no limit to creativity and innovation. Our tagline says it all: *the tools you need to put technology to work*.

The manuscript for this book was prepared and galleyed using Microsoft Word. Pages were composed by Microsoft Press using Adobe FrameMaker+SGML for Windows, with text in Garamond and display type in Helvetica Condensed. Composed pages were delivered to the printer as electronic prepress files.

Cover Designer:	Methodologie, Inc.
Interior Graphic Designer:	James D. Kramer
Principal Compositor:	Dan Latimer
Interior Artist:	Michael Kloepfer
Copy Editor:	Victoria Thulman
Proofreader:	nSight, Inc.
Indexer:	Shane-Armstrong Information Services

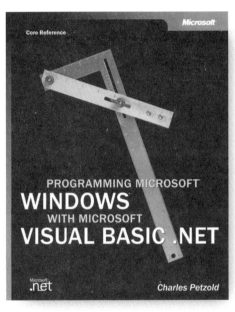

Create
killer applications
using best practices for
Visual Basic .NET!

**Practical Standards for
Microsoft® Visual Basic® .NET**
U.S.A. $49.99
Canada $72.99
ISBN: 0-7356-1356-7

The same attributes that make Visual Basic .NET exceptionally productive and easy to use can also lead to unexpected problems, especially when you upgrade. Using standardized programming techniques can help you solve those problems so you can exploit all the power of rapid development—without creating hidden land mines in performance and maintainability. This book shows you proven practices to help you eliminate "voodoo variables," create interfaces that make users more productive, write self-documenting code, simplify code modifications, and more. Each chapter illustrates common pitfalls and practical solutions with code samples—many from real-world projects. Whether you're writing just a few lines of code or working with a team to build an enterprise application, you'll learn how to use practical standards to develop better, more reliable code for every process.

Microsoft®
microsoft.com/mspress

Get a **Free**
e-mail newsletter, updates,
special offers, links to related books,
and more when you

register on line!

Register your Microsoft Press® title on our Web site and you'll get
a FREE subscription to our e-mail newsletter, *Microsoft Press Book
Connections.* You'll find out about newly released and upcoming books
and learning tools, online events, software downloads, special offers
and coupons for Microsoft Press customers, and information about
major Microsoft® product releases. You can also read useful additional
information about all the titles we publish, such as detailed book
descriptions, tables of contents and indexes, sample chapters, links to
related books and book series, author biographies, and reviews by other
customers.

Registration is easy. Just visit this Web page and fill in your information:

http://www.microsoft.com/mspress/register

Microsoft

Proof of Purchase

Use this page as proof of purchase if participating in a promotion or rebate offer on
this title. Proof of purchase must be used in conjunction with other proof(s) of
payment such as your dated sales receipt—see offer details.

OOP: Building Reusable Components with Microsoft® Visual Basic® .NET

0-7356-1379-6

CUSTOMER NAME

Microsoft Press, PO Box 97017, Redmond, WA 98073-9830